BETWEEN THE

SWASTIKA AND THE

CROSS OF LORRAINE

BETWEEN THE
SWASTIKA AND THE
CROSS OF LORRAINE

SAMUEL HUSTON GOODFELLOW

FASCISMS
IN INTERWAR
ALSACE

NORTHERN ILLINOIS UNIVERSITY PRESS • DEKALB • 1999

Library of Congress
Cataloging-in-Publication Data
Goodfellow, Samuel Huston.
Between the swastika and the cross of
Lorraine : fascisms in interwar Alsace /
Samuel Huston Goodfellow.
    P.   cm.
Includes bibliographical references and index.
ISBN 0-87580-238-9
1. Fascism—France—Alsace. 2. Alsace
(France)—Politics and government.
3. France—Politics and government—
1914–1940.
I. Title
DC650.5.G66 1998
335.6'0944'383—dc21
98-8822
CIP

Chapter 4 contains portions of the author's
article, "From Communism to Nazism: The
Transformation of Alsatian Communists,"
Journal of Contemporary History 27 (1992):
231–58. Used with permission of the publisher.

Chapters 1 and 6 contain portions of the author's article, "From Germany to France? Interwar Alsatian National Identity," *French
History* 7, 4 (1993): 450–71. Used with permission of the publisher.

CONTENTS

Preface vii

Abbreviations ix

Introduction 3

PART 1. THE FIRST GENERATION OF FASCISM: THE 1920S

1   The Alsatian Malaise and the Autonomist Movement   13

2   Legitimizing Nazism   *Concervatives and Fascists in the
     Union Populaire Républicaine*   28

3   The First Generation of French Fascism
     The Action Francaise, the Légion, and the Faisceau   42

PART 2. THE SECOND GENERATION OF FASCISM: THE 1930S

4   Beefsteak Nazis?   *The Alsatian Communist Autonomists*   69

5   Regional Fascism   *The Bauernbund*   86

6   The Alsatian Nazis   103

7   The New French Fascists, 1934–1939   119

8   Mass Fascism   *The Parti Social Francais*   135

9   The War and Beyond   149

Notes   163

Bibliography   201

Index   225

PREFACE

The problem of fascism in the post–Cold War world seems as vexing as ever. Despite prognostications that the dialectic of history has run its course, suspicion remains that reports of the death of fascism have been premature. Although the topic of fascism has once again become chic, in many ways it remains as subjective as ever.

This book looks at interwar fascism not as an isolated and possibly aberrant phenomenon but as a complex set of interactions over time between different fascisms, within the geographical constraint of Alsace. Existing research has generally delved into fascism in different nations (especially Germany and Italy), the history of specific parties, and the typology of international fascisms. The study of Alsace, however, almost necessarily focuses on different problems, because it was a place where French, German, and Alsatian political cultures clashed and vastly different fascist organizations and ideological variants developed simultaneously. A detailed examination of fascisms in Alsace reveals not only an astonishing variety of fascisms but also a tremendous fluidity between apparently incompatible fascisms. Local issues skewed the agendas of national fascist groups. Mainstream parties sometimes harbored fascists, sometimes emulated fascist style, and sometimes condemned the movement. From a sociological point of view, support for fascism came from a range of social groups causing a corresponding range of ideological interpretations. Fascists' perceptions of themselves were in many ways inconsistent over time. Fascists alternately fought each other and forged alliances such as the Volksfront. In this context, the idea of a monolithic fascism—or even of fascism as divorced from its regional, national, or international contexts—seems untenable.

My gratitude for the support, advice, and encouragement that I have received is far greater than I can acknowledge here. I owe special thanks to James Diehl, William B. Cohen, and Alfred Diamant for teaching me how to conduct research. Bob Asch, Vicki Caron, Stephen Harp, Sylvia Neely, and Robert Soucy have provided invaluable feedback and personal encouragement at critical times during the research and writing. Without the intangible support of family and friends, I would have never been able to finish this book. During the early stages of writing, Robin Bisha, Bill Bishel,

Mauricio Borrero, Georg'anne Cattelona, Phyllis Conn, Jeanne Kerl, and Andy Stein forced me to confront my more egregious errors and inconsistencies in argumentation. Jim Brophy, George Makowsky, and Tom Prasch put a great deal of additional thought and effort into critiquing drafts.

Numerous institutions have also facilitated my research. The librarians and archivists at the Bibliothèque Nationale et Universitaire de Strasbourg, the Archives Départementales in Strasbourg and Colmar, and the Archives Nationales in Paris all provided advice and assistance despite the sensitivity of the topic. Financial assistance from Indiana University's History and Western European Studies departments, and the Institut Français de Washington made research and writing possible. Support from a host of colleagues at Loyola University, Chicago, the University of California, San Diego, and Westminster College, in Fulton, Missouri, has kept me going.

Finally, I owe special thanks to my wife, Judy, who has patiently endured this process from the beginning.

ABBREVIATIONS

AF	Action Française
AN	Archives Nationales (Paris)
APNA	Action Populaire Nationale d'Alsace
BB	Bauernbund
BR	Bas-Rhin
EABP	Elsäßische Arbeiter- und Bauernpartei
EBB	*Elsäßisches Bauernblatt*
ELBB	*Elsaß-Lothringisches Bauernblatt*
ELP	Elsaß-Lothringische Partei
ELZ	*Elsaß-Lothringische Zeitung*
HR	Haut-Rhin
IVKO	Internationale Vereinigung Kommunistische Opposition
JP	Jeunesses Patriotes
KPDO	Kommunistische Partei Deutschland Opposition
KPO	Kommunistische Partei-Opposition
Nasos	Parti National-Socialiste Français (sometimes called Parti Socialiste-National Français)
NSDAP	Nationale Sozialistische Deutsche Arbeiter Partei
PCF	Parti Communiste Français
PPF	Parti Populaire Français
PRF	Parti Réaliste Français
PSF	Parti Social Français
SA	Sturmabteilung
SFIO	Section Française de l'Internationale Ouvrière
SPD	Sozialistische Partei Deutschlands
SS	Schutzstaffeln
UPR	Union Populaire Républicaine
VAF	Völkständische Arbeiterfront

BETWEEN THE

SWASTIKA AND THE

CROSS OF LORRAINE

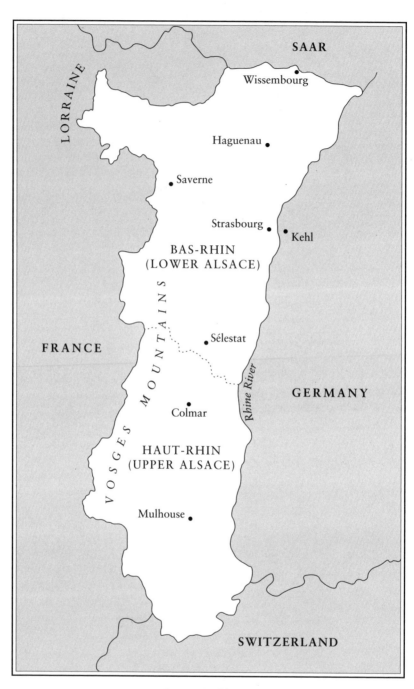

Interwar Alsace

On February 7, 1940, a French firing squad executed the Alsatian autonomist leader Karl Roos within earshot of about fourteen of his comrades in the Nancy prison. Roos's execution was the symbolic climax of two decades of autonomist and fascist activity in Alsace. From 1918 to 1940, Alsace struggled with its transition from Germany to France and was a hotbed of conflicting national identities, which were most vigorously expounded by German, French, and Alsatian fascists. The pro-Nazi autonomists were merely the most dramatic part of the picture; the various French fascist movements challenged, and at times even outnumbered, the pro-Nazis. Roos and his cohort are emblematic of the extent to which fascism permeated Alsace, legitimized political violence and extremism, and politicized national identity.

Alsace is a particularly useful region for the study of fascism because it is one of the few areas where different nationalist strands—French, German, and regional—met. Situated on the Rhine, Alsace truly lay on the crossroads between western and central Europe, north and south, and Germany and France. Never fully assimilated into a larger entity, over the centuries Alsatians cultivated their own regional dialect and identity. Alsace constitutes an empirical case study that allows us to examine how fascist leaders interacted with each other, how movements competed, and how their social constituencies were formed. Despite a flood of literature on universal fascism and the broader phenomenon of fascism, almost no one has actually made the effort to do a case study that examines the interactions between national fascisms. International fascism can actually be studied in Alsace without the distorting lens of World War II and the Quislings, Vichys, and Nazi imperialism that followed in its wake.

The German annexation of Alsace-Lorraine in 1870 had inaugurated a new nationalist era for Alsatians. Not content merely to ignore Alsace's cultural orientation, the incoming Germans set about integrating the region into the cultural, economic, and political life of the Second Reich while the humiliated French worked just as assiduously to create a French Alsace and the myth of revanche. Following World War I and the return of Alsace to France, its significance for both countries did not diminish; on the contrary, tension over identity and affiliation increased. In this context, the national fascist movements—the German Nazis on one side and the various French fascist groups on the other—articulated the most basic and extreme versions of Alsatian identity. Middle ground was not permitted as ideologues posed the stark choice of being either French or German to a populace that was somewhat bewildered from the frequent change of rule. In addition regional fascists posed a third choice for Alsatians. Thus, by the 1930s, Alsace contained multiple and conflicting fascist movements.

Alsace's role as a border region subject to intensified debate over national (and regional) identity from both within and without made the issue of cultural identity more central here than elsewhere. Rather than making Alsace aberrant, however, this means it was representative of the European-wide tenacity of border conflicts. Fiume, Tyrol, Danzig, Schleswig-Holstein, Sudetenland, and even Austria are just a few parallel regions where national identity was contested. As flashpoints for more radical political activity, these regions often served to educate the main national constituencies about ideology, serving also as places where fascists could test their mettle. In the broader European context, Alsace assumes considerable centrality as an example of a site where fascisms were on the edge.

The study of fascisms in Alsace also involves considerable discussion of French fascism, which was in some ways more illustrative of the problems of interwar European fascism than those of Italy or Germany. The French demonstrated considerable fascination and engagement with fascism and struggled with the question of how to apply it to the singularities of the French context. As a result, French fascism never became the monolith the Nationale Sozialistische Deutsche Arbeiter Partei (NSDAP) was. Instead, France mirrored the conflicts and varieties of interwar fascisms across Europe, from Spain to Poland and from Finland to Italy. Alsace's ambivalent relationship to France makes it peculiar among French regions, and caution should be used when generalizing about French fascist movements from the Alsatian example. Nevertheless, the French fascist movements were relatively successful in Alsace. Outside of Paris, Alsace was consistently one of the most fruitful regions for French fascist recruitment. Only Lorraine was subject to similar nationalistic pressures.[1] Alsace may have been unique in France, but it was still part of it.

Although many scholars concede the existence of a pathbreaking French fascist movement before 1914, the interwar years remain problematic and many historians persist in belittling the fascist groups of the 1920s and 1930s. The civil rift between collaborators, resisters, and *attentistes* during Vichy and beyond has encouraged many French to minimize the fascist experience in the interest of social harmony.[2] The association of fascism with Nazism has contributed to the confusion on the subject. The sheer diversity of fascism in Alsace alone should dispel the myth that French fascism was virtually nonexistent.

Not only were there a plurality of fascisms in Alsace, the number and influence of fascists in the region were far from negligible. The fascist movement in Alsace was much more than the sum of its parts. By 1938 the overall fascist movement consisted of around forty thousand activists. The Alsatian Nazi movement, although fragmented, totaled roughly fifteen thousand between 1936 and 1938. The Croix de Feu/Parti Social Français (PSF) added another twenty or thirty thousand militants on the French side of the ledger. This figure does not include the passive support for these organizations, and it errs on the conservative side by including only activists. To put this in perspective, in 1938 there were only 14,426 card-carrying members of the Catholic Union Populaire Républicaine (UPR), the region's dominant party.[3] Thus, fascism dwarfed the most successful political party in Alsace, although it lacked the unity to translate the numbers into absolute power. Fascism failed to make the sort of electoral dent that the UPR made in the 1.15 million Alsatian public (only men had the franchise, so only half this number could vote), since it did not consistently manifest itself in elections. Nevertheless, fascism exercised an influence beyond quantification by attracting the energies of the most politically active and by shaping the political discourse.

For a working definition, I argue that the groups under discussion were fascist insofar as they all shared a basic political ideology that sought cultural homogeneity through the subordination of the individual to a community (be it French, German, or Alsatian) enforced by the party-state. Each believed in the ideal of an integrated, hierarchical, corporatively represented, and orderly state, unmarred by either the decadence of liberal individualism or the conflict of class warfare. Although this definition cannot be the final word on the subject, consider it a tool that will expedite the exploration of what these groups had in common.

. . .

This study can be divided roughly into two chronological groups: the 1920s and the 1930s. The first three chapters encompass the fascisms of the 1920s. Chapter 1 lays out the fractured nature of Alsatian society, resulting from long-standing indigenous divisions across geographic, class, religious, and linguistic lines. In the absence of a clear-cut national identity, Alsace became a cultural battleground. To be French, German, or Alsatian became the subject of a bitter debate. Fascists prospered in this debate because they advocated the most simple and accessible answers. Most Alsatians, moreover, were profoundly dissatisfied with the treatment they had received from the French government, which provided a wellspring for antiparliamentarian movements. The "Alsatian malaise"—the term for the pervasive discomfort with French rule and externally imposed national identity—formed an important backdrop to the formation and success of fascism. It did this most obviously through the creation of the autonomist movement, which brought the multi-partisan critics of French rule together in a loose coalition of opposition. Many of these autonomists became Nazis in the 1930s.

Chapter 2 deals with another factor contributing to the rise of fascism and Nazism in Alsace, namely, the role played by the clerical autonomists and the Catholic UPR, the region's dominant political party, in the dissemination of German cultural nationalism and fascist ideology. Although not fascist itself, the UPR legitimized Nazi ideology by mimicking its paramilitary style, by advancing hypernationalist ideologies, both French and German, and by advocating corporatism. The UPR had the additional distinction in the 1920s of including both French fascists and Alsatian autonomists, which points to the sloppiness of the interaction between national fascisms.

The election of the leftist coalition, the Cartel des Gauches, in 1924 triggered widespread Alsatian discontent with the French government, which the Action Française (AF) and the Faisceau tried to channel into pro-French fascist activity. Chapter 3 examines the first generation of French fascism, which united the style and ideology of Mussolini's fascism with French nationalism. At the heart of this unsuccessful synthesis was the struggle between the AF, the first proponent of integral nationalism, and the impatient Faisceau, which broke with the AF in its attempt to radicalize the nationalist movement. Despite their differences, the French fascists of the 1920s drew from the same constituency, consisting almost solely of the upper-middle and professional classes, and the same ideology, differing primarily on the issue of action. Limited by their internecine quarreling and unable to persuade the working and lower-middle classes to support them, the first generation of French fascists failed to produce a fascist revolution. By 1928 the AF operated under a papal ban and the Faisceau had dissolved.

Between 1928 and 1932 the fascist movements, both German and French, languished. The depression, Poincaré's authoritarian leadership, and governmental moderation toward Alsace-Lorraine contributed to fascism's ineffectiveness. This was less a period of inactivity, however, than a turning inward in preparation for more propitious times. Abandoning the populist strategy, the fascists evolved out of necessity into avant-garde parties consisting of tightly knit bands of like-minded and deeply committed ideologues who could take advantage of circumstances to become the nucleus of a mass party. It was at this time that the autonomists struggled with the precipitous decline in public enthusiasm for autonomism and moved toward Nazism.

Hitler's seizure of power in 1933 and the Parisian riots of February 1934 reanimated the fascist movement. Unlike the 1920s movements that had organized largely in response to a perceived leftist threat, the fascists of the 1930s embraced a philosophy that appeared to have captured the new Zeitgeist. Whereas the 1920s fascisms stressed national identity, the 1930s versions emphasized political ideology. Individual mobility between national fascisms attests to the change in fascist ideology. Consequently, the character of the new fascist movements became more dogmatic, direct, violent, confident, fragmented, and socially diverse. Social groups that had hitherto been deaf to fascist blandishments began to experiment with fascist ideology.

Although no self-respecting fascist doubted that fascism would reign in Alsace (and France), no one knew exactly what fascism meant or what path it would take en route to a French *Machtergreifung*. Similarly there was no unanimity on how to make fascism most persuasive to the Alsatians. As a result, the fascisms of the 1930s were characterized by a great deal of fluidity between groups. Most of the new French fascist movements were short-lived, and enthusiasts leapt nimbly from one sinking ship to the next. Adherents of the AF and the Jeunesses Patriotes (JP) extended their support to the Staatsreform movement. Francistes and Nationales-Social-istes (Nasos), however much they quibbled, often attended each other's meetings and even switched parties. Collaboration between pro-French and pro-German fascists also occurred, most notably among the separatist, pro-Nazi Landespartei members who converted to Francisme. These experiments in fascism may not have been successful on their own, but considered together they demonstrate the new fluidity and radicalness of the 1930s fascisms.

The radicalization of the 1930s can be seen in the evolution of the communist autonomists to Nazism, the subject of Chapter 4. As the only group to arrive at fascism from the left, the members of the Kommunistischen Partei-Opposition (KPO) proved that the fascistization of the left did happen. Charles Hueber, in fact, brought a uniquely leftist revolutionary style to the Alsatian Nazi movement. This was not the result of an inherent similarity between Marxism and fascism, but of a series of ideological transformations that fundamentally changed Hueber and his followers into Nazis. Dogged adherence to autonomism acted as a bridge from left to right. Further undermining the widespread belief in the similarity of Marxism and fascism is the evidence that, at each step of his transformation into a Nazi, Hueber lost more of his following.

Another component of 1930s fascism that illustrates the flexibility of fascist ideology was the Bauernbund (see Chapter 5). Initially an offshoot of the autonomist movement and a representative of peasant interests, the Bauernbund became, under the leadership of Joseph Bilger, a movement that focused on the creation of an integral Alsatian society based on peasant values. Unlike all the other fascist movements in Alsace, the Bauernbund did not rely solely on either French or German nationalism to define its cultural and "national" community. Drawing on Nazi ideology (especially its antisemitism) while remaining linked with French fascist movements, Bilger created a hybrid form of regional fascism based on the Alsatian peasantry. Bilger joined forces with French fascists such as Henri Dorgères, yet he integrated his organization into the Nazi system after 1940. The Bauernbund was the most powerful fascist movement in Alsace until 1938, attracting a sizable portion of the Catholic peasantry with its antisemitism and rural corporatism.

Perhaps most typical of the direction of the 1930s fascist movements was the proliferation of Alsatian Nazi organizations (see Chapter 6). As autonomism lost force, and frustrated by the French government's conciliatory attitude after 1929, autonomist leaders moved decisively toward Nazism. Because of its commitment to German culture, the autonomist Landespartei believed that Nazism offered the best protection of Alsatian cultural interests. Alsatian Nazism was no more uniform than the fascist movement in general or, for that matter, the German Nazi Party. Reasons for espousing the Nazi cause varied widely, as did the level of commitment. Least tied to Hitler were the clerical autonomists in the UPR who followed Joseph Rossé and Marcel Stürmel. Although they favored union with Nazi Germany and admired much of what Hitler had done, the clerical autonomists did not actually affiliate themselves with any Nazi Party until World War II. Commitment to Catholicism and to Alsatian interests mitigated their enthusiasm for the secularizing and centralizing aspects of Nazism. The autonomist Landespartei had closer ties to Nazism. In fact, its leaders had no qualms about Nazism's secular agenda and directly affiliated themselves with elements in the German Nazi Party. Nevertheless, the Landespartei's Nazism naively expected some degree of decentralization. The most extreme of the Alsatian Nazis were the Jungmannschaft activists led by Hermann Bickler. Whereas the Landespartei and the clerical autonomists turned to Nazism as the only viable guarantor of Alsatian culture, the circle around Bickler fully accepted that Alsace would be subsumed into a secular, centralized Nazi Germany. During the occupation, the differences between the Alsatian Nazis continued to be apparent when Landespartei leaders joined the party and held numerous political positions, while their Jungmannschaft colleagues joined the Schutzstaffeln (SS).

At the same time that Alsatian Nazism was on the rise, the French fascist movement underwent a transformation. Like the Nazis, the new French fascists (see Chapter 7) were more extreme and more violent than their predecessors. The Francistes, the Parti Populaire Français (PPF), the Nationale-Socialistes, and several ephemeral antisemitic movements all sought a new synthesis of fascism. These groups imitated communist organization and articulated more revolutionary versions of corporatism that favored lower-middle-class interests. Yet the same notables who had directed the 1920s fascisms continued to exercise influence over the new movements.

The fascist movement in Alsace culminated in the Croix de Feu/PSF (see Chapter 8) as part of a general reaction against the formation of the Popular Front in 1936. Steadily increasing its membership from the early 1930s until 1939, the Croix de Feu/PSF became a mass party that linked the various strands of fascism together into a single amorphous movement. At least organizationally, the party more closely resembled its Italian fascist and German Nazi counterparts. One of the party's chief advantages lay in its growing influence in France and the expectation that it could succeed in changing French government where all the other fascist movements had failed.

. . .

It is all too easy to leave the reader with the uneasy suspicion that a fascist was hiding behind every bush and under every bed. Such was not the case in Alsace; the vast majority of its inhabitants avoided fascism and just went about their daily lives. Nevertheless, fascism affected Alsace far more than most analysts have admitted. It penetrated deeply into the region's political life, affecting the political discourse of mainstream parties and manipulating the pressing question of national identity. Fascism also attracted a sizable following in its own right, which rivaled and even surpassed its socialist, liberal, and conservative competitors.

The ability of fascist ideology to strike roots within every social class in Alsace, with the exception of the industrial working class, contributed to both its success and its ultimate failure. On the one hand, fascist ideology enjoyed widespread credibility. Fascist ideas and sentiments began creeping into the programs of a wide variety of parties. On the other hand, different nationalities and social interests found themselves pitted against each other. This created serious barriers to the emergence of any group as the single fascist party capable of achieving the perfect fascist synthesis of nation, party, and state—which makes the achievement of the PSF all the more impressive.

Interwar Alsace was a microcosm of Europe. Throughout the continent Europeans seized upon the idea of fascism as the wave of the future and tried to apply it to their own social, national, local, and personal situations. Universal fascism never fully materialized, even though most fascists clearly perceived a great deal of commonality, because fascism meant different things to different fascists. Precisely because Alsatians were metaphorically caught between the swastika and the cross of Lorraine (an important symbol for French fascists), the region is an excellent place to study the development of multiple fascisms.

THE FIRST GENERATION OF FASCISM

PART ONE

The 1920s

THE ALSATIAN MALAISE AND THE
AUTONOMIST MOVEMENT

Hans in Schnokeloch has all that he wants. And what he has he doesn't want, and what he wants he doesn't have. Hans in Schnockeloch has all that he wants! —*Alsatian folk song*

Hans in Schnokeloch, the quintessential Alsatian, is an apt symbol for Alsatian society and politics during the interwar era.[1] Malcontent under Wilhelm II, Alsace remained dissatisfied under France's Third Republic. In response to overbearing pressure to assimilate into the respective national polities, Alsace began to look inward for its identity. Alsatian resistance to assimilation and centralization peaked between 1924 and 1929 during the "Alsatian malaise," when local anger at the systematically stifling and insensitive French policy erupted in the form of mass protests and the political organization of the Alsatian autonomist movement.

Autonomism loomed over the Alsatian fascist movement, not simply because many autonomist leaders ultimately collaborated with the Nazis, but because autonomism radicalized the question of national identity in Alsace. Loosely defined as an ideology that demanded freedom from French administration in favor of self-determination and self-administration, autonomism became the crucible for all the issues affecting Alsatians during the mid-1920s.

In Alsatian politics and society, important distinctions apply between the concepts of regionalism, autonomism, and separatism;

although related, they are not completely interchangeable concepts. Regionalism encompasses both autonomism and separatism and draws on the individual's natural sense of place to create a political sensibility concerned with the preservation of local identity and rights within the context of a larger whole. Paradoxically, regionalism in Alsace came to mean assimilationism, since the so-called regionalists' major concern was the reintegration of Alsace into France. Pro-French groups such as the Action Française (AF), for example, repeatedly stressed the importance of regionalism in direct contrast to autonomism.

Autonomism aggressively channels regional sensibilities into a political movement that advocates the devolution of responsibility away from the center to the political periphery. In mid-1920s Alsace, autonomists dominated the political discourse because they took the initiative in the debate and effectively harnessed the Alsatians' sense of place and outrage at the central government's rejection of demands for administrative autonomy. Drawing on historical, cultural, administrative, religious, and linguistic differences between Alsace and France, the autonomists argued that Alsace should be a federated state within France, analogous to the relationship between Bavaria and the German Second Reich.

Many autonomists were in fact separatists, whose real objectives were the severing of all ties with France in favor of return to Germany. In this, Alsatian separatists differed from other separatists in France. Breton separatists, for example, simply advocated separation from France in favor of a new Breton state.[2] More extreme than the autonomists, Alsatian separatists argued that Alsace was not simply different from France; it was culturally, linguistically, racially, and philosophically German. "We are Germanophile!" screamed one headline in the *Elsaß-Lothringer Zeitung (ELZ)*, the principal autonomist paper, "because we ourselves are part of the German *Volk*."[3] Very few Alsatians heeded calls from the other side of the Rhine for the establishment of an independent Rhenish state, because those who believed in the separation of Alsace from France wanted to become part of Germany, not part of a reincarnated medieval duchy.[4] As it was treason to publicly espouse Anschluß (annexation) with Germany, many separatists felt constrained to limit their rhetoric to the constant reiteration of autonomist demands. Hence, in practice it is often difficult to distinguish between an autonomist's expression of Alsatian uniqueness and a separatist's implicit argument for the return of Alsace to Germany.

Understanding the peculiar fragmentation of Alsace along linguistic, religious, economic, and cultural lines is crucial for comprehending the development of fascism in Alsace. From 1870 onward, Alsace's uncertain status and its own internal divisions left the region vulnerable to a bitter debate over national and cultural identity, which fueled fascist growth. The second half of this chapter examines the formation of the post-1918 autonomist movement, showing how the local problems began to manifest themselves specifically. Since one of the major characteristics of fascism is hypernationalism, the preeminence of an extremely bitter debate over regional identity contributed to the viability of both German and French fascist movements. Under such conditions, the most extreme formulations of national affiliation dominated more moderate and nuanced evaluations of the Alsatian identity. The escalating violence of the cultural debate and the widespread criticism of the Third Republic—and, by implication, the value of liberal democracy—contributed directly to a legitimization of fascist ideology and organization.

THE DEVELOPMENT OF ALSATIAN IDENTITY: BACKGROUND TO THE RISE OF AUTONOMISM

The catalyst of the Alsatian malaise, the French term for autonomism, was the election of the Cartel des Gauches in 1924. Edouard Herriot, the Cartel's selection for prime minister, triggered Alsatian discontent when he declared, "The government is persuaded that it will faithfully interpret the wishes of the cherished population which has finally returned to France in hastening the coming of the day when the final legislative differences between the recovered provinces and the rest of the territory of the Republic will be erased." Toward this end, Herriot announced his intention "to introduce into Alsace and Lorraine the republican legislation in its entirety."[5] For most Alsatians, this promise to impose French anticlerical laws in a region that had remained faithful to the traditional connection between church and state meant an escalation of the cultural repression that had been going on since 1918. Herriot's importune remarks in 1924 mobilized latent Alsatian resentment by giving it a visible target, the French government.

Although 1924 marked the crystallization of Alsatian resentment toward France, one must turn to the unusual circumstances of Alsatian history during the late nineteenth century to understand fully the context. Indeed, the idea of a distinct Alsatian identity first emerged after 1870 in response to the pervasiveness throughout Europe of nationalism as an ideology. Bombarded simultaneously by German nationalist propaganda and French revanchist sentiment, Alsatians came under intense external pressure to accept a definitive national identity. The very notion of a region called Alsace-Lorraine was the product of the Franco-Prussian War, when the region became a pawn in nationalist politics. Caught between two cultural and political powers at a time when nationalism increasingly defined politics, Alsatians could not feign indifference to the question.[6] Reintegration into France in 1918 only increased the stress on the average Alsatian's sense of identity.

Both the French and the Germans came to perceive Alsace in highly unrealistic and ideological terms. Germany, influenced by *völkisch* nationalism, concluded that Alsatians were part of the Germanic race and inevitably desired, therefore, to be part of the German nation. The French, for their part, acted as if all Alsatians were revanchist, and upon regaining the eastern territories in 1918, they believed that the Alsatians wanted to become cultural Frenchmen.[7] In neither case did such national narcissism accurately depict Alsatian reality. The discrepancy between the official treatment of Alsace by both countries and the complex reality of the region posed a major obstacle to any permanent resolution of the national identity question.

Unable or unwilling to decide between France and Germany, many Alsatians resolved their uncertain national identity by imagining Alsace as a unique community. Before 1918, French-nationalist Alsatians such as Abbé Wetterlé and the playwright Gustave Stoskopf, who wrote in Alsatian dialect, were particularly forceful in their formulation of a separate Alsatian identity, largely because "the alternative to Germany was no longer France . . . but Alsace."[8] To choose France meant either emigration or treason. Therefore, in order to remain within the bounds of legal propriety in Germany while creating an alternative identity, Francophile Alsatians founded the Alsatian folk museum and encouraged the study of Alsatian folklore. The Germans countenanced and even fostered this revival of folklore because it corresponded to a revival of the study of the *Heimat* (homeland) and Germanic culture.[9] Indeed, the German Wissenschaftliches Institut der Elsäßer und Lothringer im Reich an der Universität Frankfurt, founded in 1920, continued the study of the German *Volkstum* (national characteristics) in Alsace into the interwar era, with the explicit purpose of proving that Alsace was German.[10] It is ironic that the pro-French fought germanization with intellectual weapons forged in Germany. The idea of a separate Alsatian cultural identity never fully disassociated itself from the choice between France and Germany.

Every knowledgeable observer of Alsace points to the mixture of French and German roots in Alsatian culture. The historian Karl-Heinz Rothenberger argues, for example, that Alsace is culturally German, but politically French. Even the Alsatian writer Frédéric Hoffet, whose sympathies during the 1920s lay with the pro-French right, argued after World War II that Alsace has always been characterized by "duality."[11] In effect, polarization over the question of national identity split the French yin from the German yang, leaving Alsace sociologically, psychologically, and culturally divided. Both sides, at their extremes, sought an artificially organic Alsace based on a willful ignorance of a significant part of Alsatian identity.

The chief characteristic differentiating Alsace from France was linguistic. Paul Lévy, in his study of Alsace's linguistic history, concludes that World War I "interrupted an evolution, which . . . sooner or later would have led to the absolute predominance of the German language." At the height of the Alsatian malaise in 1926, only 192,842 out of a total population of 1,153,396 used French at home or in ordinary conversation, as opposed to 940,944 who spoke either German or Alsatian.[12] Since Alsatian is a German dialect comparable to Bavarian, Swabian, or Saxon, the Alsatians were far more intimately bound to the cultural nation of Goethe than to that of Voltaire. Furthermore, Protestant Alsatians viewed the language of Luther as an integral part of their religious and cultural heritage. A linguistic and cultural gulf separated Alsatians from the French and, in an important sense, from each other. Language became an even more important part of the national question after World War I, under the cultural imperialism of the French.

The Alsatians had an alternative nation, Germany, in which they would be part of the majority. When asked why he became an autonomist, Karl Roos, the head of the separatist Landespartei, responded, "I did not become an autonomist out of dissatisfaction at my well-being. I am an autonomist for cultural reasons."[13] The radical autonomists based their resentment on the injustice of French civilization repressing German *Kultur*. Thus, the Alsatians believed that, although they were a cultural minority in France, inclusion in one of the most important national cultures in Europe would empower them.

Interwar autonomism also had its roots in Alsace's protracted struggle to acquire states' rights within the German federal system in the Wilhelmine era. Despite Germany's well-deserved reputation for authoritarianism, excessive state power, and intolerance regarding ethnic minorities, the creation, in 1871, of a unified Germany from a fragmented group of principalities resulted in a federal system with a surprising amount of autonomy delegated to its constituent parts.[14] Joseph Rossé and his autonomist colleagues emphasized the importance of federalism on the growth of "Alsatian self-awareness," which eventually "found its political expression in the demand for autonomy within an affirmation of membership in the Reich."[15]

Although Alsace-Lorraine was a *Reichsland* (Imperial province) ruled directly by the Kaiser, many Alsatians held out hope that it could become an independent *Land* (province) with the same rights and privileges as Bavaria or Baden.[16] The 1911 constitution—although it failed to turn Alsace-Lorraine into an autonomous German *Land* and was perceived by most Alsatians as completely inadequate—acted as a catalyst for the debate over self-government.[17] Despite considerable legislative leeway in France, the possibilities for self-rule under German control seemed much greater, simply because France was not a federation.[18]

The development of the German Socialist Party (SPD) and the Catholic German Center Party (Center) before the war also affected the political consciousness of Alsace. Both Catholics and socialists built strong political parties in Alsace based largely on opposition to the Reich's treatment of minorities and on a defense of regional interests.[19] Whereas the Catholic Center Party pushed for a more particularist agenda, the socialists sought to place Alsace in a broader international context. The German socialist Karl Liebknecht attacked German nationalism in 1917 by arguing that

Alsace should be freed from Prussia in order to join the less repressive French state.[20] Once Alsace was joined to France, however, both parties discovered that they lacked the national resonance they had enjoyed in Germany. Parliamentary politics in France reflected neither the organization nor the discipline of the German parties.[21] Although both socialists and Catholics split internally over national issues after 1918, many socialists longed to be reunited with the SPD or the German Communist Party and the Catholics missed the shelter of a national party like the Center in Germany. Consequently, the best-organized political parties in Alsace had cultural and political reasons to be critical of their new life in France.

Local antagonisms across class, religion, and space fueled the debate over Alsatian national identity. In many ways, the debate over national identity was merely a vehicle for advancing the ancient divisions that undermined Alsatian society.[22] Although the question of national identity in Alsace was inherently divisive, the issue took on an even greater urgency through its convergence with class differences. Indeed, the reason the debate over national identity struck such a deep chord in Alsace was that the divisions between social groups in many ways mirrored the divisions in national affiliation.

The urban "middle class," according to the French police, was "quite clearly Francophile" and tended as a result to favor assimilation into France.[23] This attachment was the result of a historical pas de deux between France and the local bourgeoisie, which was especially close during the early nineteenth century. Not only did Alsatian urban entrepreneurs and notables find economic and political common cause with the French authorities, they converted to French customs and language to strengthen their economic ties.[24] Even the pro-French police noted that autonomists had their success among "the rural masses," while "the middle-class bourgeoisie" and "the liberal and anticlerical elements" resisted autonomism.[25]

The post-1918 autonomists resented the notables who, in their view, comprised a "caste" of large landowners, city lawyers, and doctors. Clerical autonomists bitterly attacked the notables' right to exercise regional leadership and to occupy the pinnacle of the Alsatian social and political hierarchy, criticizing their materialistic attitude, their values, and their self-interested political instinct. According to autonomists, the main benefit of fifty years as a German *Reichsland* was that it ended the rule of notables "through its emancipation of the common man, its political schooling, and the building up of the democratically organized parties."[26] New political parties such as the Alsatian Center Party and the SPD had, in the meantime, extended political participation to the masses.[27] Peasants and workers were no longer shackled by their use of German, which in the Wilhelmine era became the language of the rulers. Cultural and linguistic barriers to advancement crumbled under German rule. Return to France, according to the autonomists, meant a return to the dominance of the hated notables.

Opposed to the French-speaking bourgeois elite were the peasants and the rapidly growing urban working class who lived, worked, and prayed in German or Alsatian. Their attachment to the region and its language made them especially sensitive to the centralizing and culturally chauvinistic tendencies of the Third Republic. So, too, the disruption caused by the migration to the cities most profoundly affected the lower classes. The additional social and political advantages accruing to the bourgeoisie simply because they spoke French aggravated the German and Alsatian speakers' sense of inferiority. The clerical autonomist faction of the UPR centered around Abbé Haegy and Joseph Rossé, and Joseph Bilger's Bauernbund catered to rural discontent, while the Alsatian communists led by Charles Hueber and Jean-Pierre Mourer mobilized the urban lower class, particularly in Strasbourg.

Religion added another dimension to the conflict between the pro-French bourgeoisie and the pro-German masses. In general, Protestants were more closely associated with the bourgeoisie, and Catholics with the peasant and working classes. Although a minority in the region, Protestants wielded an incommensurate amount of economic and political clout because they tended to be wealthier, better educated, and more urban. Catholics, on the other hand, were far more numerous, constituting 61.9 percent of the population in Bas-Rhin and 83.5 percent in Haut-Rhin in 1900. They had larger families, lived in more rural areas, and operated under a more communal system in which the curé held a great deal of local power.[28]

Such persistent differences in Alsace between confessions were a backdrop to crises within the churches. Alsatian Protestants suffered a severe blow to their communal religious life when many Lutheran pastors elected to remain in Germany after the war.[29] Furthermore, the heavy concentration of Lutherans, especially in Bas-Rhin, was an aberration in France, not merely because France was Catholic but because in the rest of France most Protestants were Calvinist.[30] Alsatian Lutherans consequently found their religious and national identity to be profoundly at odds with France—and hence the high number of pastors remaining in Germany. It is not surprising that Protestants figured prominently in the Nazi groups of the 1930s.[31] The dislocation and disorientation of the day-to-day running of the Lutheran Church after 1918 contrasted unfavorably with the nurturing climate of natural affiliation within the German Lutheran establishment in Wilhelmine Germany. Divisions within the Alsatian Protestant community and its ambivalence about the national question made it susceptible to the blandishments of nationalist extremists.

Catholics also had cause to distrust the French government. When Alsace left France in 1871, church-state relations had not been severed.

Wilhelmine Germany maintained a close constitutional connection between church and state so that Alsace avoided the anticlerical debate that took place in France. As a result, when Alsace was reintegrated into France in 1918, religious Alsatians (especially Catholics) were mistrustful and uncertain of the effects of the secularization of the French state. The delayed debate over the effect of the French anticlerical laws of 1905 on the financial viability of the Church, the justifiability of confessional schools, and the potentially corrosive spiritual and moral effects of secularization added to Alsatian insecurity, since this debate took place simultaneously with the debate over national identity. The religious issue was especially bitter since Alsatians had not participated in the original debate and therefore believed that this was an unfair imposition of secular French values. In fact, the religious issue proved to be *the* flashpoint for regional hostility. Alsatians perceived the attack on the traditional Alsatian religious laws in 1924 to be part of a systematic attempt to dismantle unique Alsatian legal and cultural practices—especially the retention of clerical schools and the state payment of religious officials.

Further complicating the religious picture was the existence of a small but significant Jewish community. Alsace has had a long history of antisemitism, which did not abate after 1918. Since Jews tended to favor inclusion in France, the land of emancipation, pro-German autonomists tended to lump them together with the chauvinist bourgeoisie as their oppressors.[32] Although the Jewish population shrank by over a third from 1870 to 1932, anti-Jewish sentiment grew even more virulent in the 1930s.[33] For example, at that time the Bauernbund made antisemitism a major plank, along with rural corporatism. Nazi influence helped fan the flames of indigenous racism. A small but activist minority of Alsatians supported Nazism in Alsace solely on the basis of antisemitism.

Alsace lacked not only religious, cultural, and class harmony; the idea that its two departments, Haut-Rhin and Bas-Rhin, were essentially the same is a fiction. One Alsatian from Haut-Rhin wrote at the turn of the century:

> The Upper Alsatian (drinker of wine, generally Catholic) is more imaginative, more impulsive, more enthusiastic, more expressive, more capable of impartiality and excitement over an idea; he makes decisions quickly and acts immediately. The Lower Alsatian (beer drinker) is more sluggish, more indifferent, more inscrutable, more matter of fact.[34]

In short, Alsatians from Haut-Rhin were more French. Even the Protestants were more likely to be Calvinist than Lutheran. Alsatians from Bas-Rhin were more likely to favor Germany. Strasbourg, the capital of Bas-Rhin, was a far more German city than Colmar and Mulhouse in Haut-Rhin.

FROM DISCONTENT TO OUTRAGE:
THE IMMEDIATE CAUSES OF THE ALSATIAN MALAISE

Between the time World War I ended and the ink had dried on the Treaty of Versailles, Alsatians had already begun to object to their return to France. Charles Hueber and the Alsatian socialists advocated neutralism, hoping for the right to self-determination according to Wilson's Fourteen Points. Their affinity for German socialism swayed these revolutionary socialists toward Germany, eventually pushing them by the mid-1930s into the Nazi camp. Immediately after the war, a host of short-lived autonomist movements sprang up for the purpose of defending the traditions of Alsace at the critical moment when Alsace returned to France.[35] The Parti Fédéraliste d'Alsace-Lorraine, with about a thousand members, advocated an autonomous Alsatian republic federally connected to France.[36]

The vast majority of Alsatians, however, listened with great hope to the words of General Joffre, who promised in 1918, "Your return is definitive. You are Frenchmen forever. France brings you, along with the liberties which she has always represented, respect for your Alsatian liberties, for your traditions, for your beliefs, and for your customs. I am France. You are Alsace. I bring you the salutation of France."[37] General Joffre's statement reassured Alsatians because it represented an official promise not to interfere with their cultural life. With this in mind, they unreservedly celebrated the entry of the French army into Alsace in a display of enthusiasm that autonomists subsequently found difficult to explain. Even Abbé Haegy, the indefatigable clerical autonomist, admitted in a private conversation in the halls of the Reichstag in October 1918 that a plebiscite would show that the vast majority of Alsace-Lorrainers supported return to France.[38]

This outpouring of enthusiasm for France notwithstanding, full reintegration was fraught with problems. In the aftermath of World War I, much of Alsace's economic infrastructure had been physically destroyed. As in Germany, the economy of Alsace-Lorraine had been devastated and bled dry in an irresponsible all-or-nothing attempt to win the war, which had extensive dislocating effects on the middle classes.[39] That which survived had to make a difficult transition from one national economy to another. New markets had to be found in France to replace the German ones. The natural flow of goods down the Rhine and into Germany was replaced by the more arduous and costly trade across the Vosges. Some industries failed to make the transition. The Alsatian wine industry, for example, languished as a result of Gallic indifference to white wine. Family-owned textile factories, many of which were destroyed by the war, struggled against competition from firms in northeast France. In the short run the local economy prospered because of rebuilding activity and a transition period of five years, during which Alsace had free access to German markets.

After 1925, however, the structural problems asserted themselves.[40]

"Over the course of the last sixty years the lives of the people have changed as never before," lamented the clerical autonomist Joseph Rossé in 1932.[41] The physical expansion of Strasbourg and the other Alsatian cities before World War I attests to the flood of peasants to the city. France's economic growth did not match Germany's; nevertheless Alsatian migration from country to town continued after 1918, creating a potentially explosive sociopolitical situation that manifested itself in the rise of socialist parties and the autonomist movement. In short, the economic transition from the booming economy of fin-de-siècle Germany to the "nation of shopkeepers" was not smooth, and the ensuing economic dislocation provided a background of support for radical right-wing movements, autonomist and otherwise.

Immediately after the war, the French policy of classifying each person differentially according to their degree of Germanness split many families.[42] Indigenous Alsatians were given A-cards, those born of German and Alsatian parents received B-cards, non-German foreigners carried C-cards, and Germans received D-cards. Possessors of different cards were subject to different exchange rates (Marks to francs) and different rights and privileges.[43] Many Alsatian families, however, after forty-eight years of German rule had acquired German relatives through intermarriage.[44] The French designed the policy to force all Germans either to emigrate or to accept second-class citizenship. It also created arbitrary inequities between and within extended and nuclear families, as some families were purely Alsatian and therefore eligible for a better exchange rate, whereas other families found themselves sinking into poverty as relatives emigrated solely because of nationalist, perhaps even racial, prejudice. In the end, most Germans opted for Germany and clogged the bridges over the Rhine in an exodus that, to the late twentieth-century observer, was more reminiscent of the Nazi treatment of the pro-French Alsatians in 1940 than the voluntary departure of the Francophiles in 1871.[45] The distinction between French, German, and Alsatian—somewhat fuzzy before 1871—was now rigorously enforced by the full strength of the state. Such distinctions were offensive to most Alsatians and formed a background to the latent resentment that exploded in 1924.

Another irritant was the sudden imposition of French bureaucracy in 1918, which created two major problems. First, it excluded from government service a large number of German-trained bureaucrats who had spent long arduous years training for responsibility and patiently waiting to move up the professional promotional ladder. Instead, bureaucratic posts went largely to "interior" Frenchmen whose loyalty was assured and whose command of French fit the needs of the government. The result was a large number of unemployed but well-educated and articulate Alsatian bureaucrats whose professional frustration and dissatisfaction were highly visible.[46] The influx of foreign Frenchmen to fill jobs previously held by Alsatians contributed to the local conviction that France was treating Alsace like a colony. One autonomist paper, for example, had a cartoon entitled "Eine schwarze Elsässerin" who is described as "an Alsatian woman, who has become black since 1918 because of the influence of the colonial method."[47] Second, the official language had become French. Therefore all court cases were in French, which was discriminatory to the majority of Alsatians who spoke primarily in dialect. This left Alsatians with the distinct impression of powerlessness before a foreign judicial system.

The linguistic issue extended beyond the realm of bureaucracy to the critical area of education. The French favored the "direct" method, which consisted of immersing Alsatians in French from their first day of school. This was a departure from the German system of education. Although the Wilhelmine government had pursued a policy of germanization, it permitted instruction in French in those Alsatian communities that were predominantly French. Autonomists cited evidence that the refusal to use a German, or even bilingual, educational system left graduating students incapable of communicating effectively in either French or German.[48] This perception of educational ineffectiveness was reinforced in 1926 when the Chambre des Métiers complained, "Most candidates no longer know proper German, do not yet know enough French, and are therefore incapable of expressing themselves except in dialect."[49]

In addition, the exclusive use of French in the classroom disrupted the cultural life of Alsace by denigrating the Alsatian dialect, ignoring German, and detaching the students from their families. Alsatians in general preferred bilingual education because it would ensure competence in French while still protecting the indigenous culture. Obviously, the importance of education as a means of creating or reinforcing good citizenship was a contested issue because of the lack of unanimity between national education policy and local educational needs.[50] Alsatians from less privileged stations also had legitimate cause for feeling that they were excluded from educational opportunity, which contributed to their general sense of being second-class citizens. The Alsatian communists pointed out that the exclusion of German from the schools favored the bourgeoisie, who had the resources to ensure that their children learned French.

The terrible economic conditions in Germany and the fairly conciliatory attitude of Alexandre Millerand, the general commissioner appointed by the Third Republic to administer Alsace-Lorraine, mitigated Alsatian discontent from 1919 until 1924. The economic condition of Germany was dire and certainly did not elicit enthusiasm from Alsatians for a return to Germany.[51] It is significant that the French anticlerical laws were not extended to Alsace during this period. Perhaps the Alsatians were patient enough to wait a few years for the resolution of some of the outstanding problems in Alsace. The reservoir of goodwill toward France, although strained at times, did not evaporate until 1924.

Herriot's threat to the religious continuity of the region, by extending the French anticlerical laws to Alsace, triggered a massive protest. According to Rothenberger, "Alsatiandom and Catholicism went hand in hand" in common protest against the government. Within days, twenty-one out of twenty-two Alsatian deputies signed a letter of protest. This was followed by action at the departmental and then communal levels. Bishop Ruch of Strasbourg encouraged the rank-and-file clergy to mobilize their flocks in opposition to the proposed laicization of Alsace. Fifty thousand faithful turned out in Strasbourg to demonstrate in favor of preserving the religious statutes.[52]

Although forced to back down on the religious issue, Herriot had not yet given up on the repeal of the Falloux Law still in effect in Alsace, which guaranteed the maintenance of confessional schools. Here too he met with determined opposition. Bishop Ruch called for a regionwide school strike in March 1925. Over half the population favored "the integral maintenance of the existing school regime."[53] Popular opinion and vigorous clerical leadership combined to produce an overwhelming turnout, especially in the rural communes.

That this initial protest was directed by such influential segments of society raised the question of what kind of Frenchmen the Alsatians were. The Alsatian deputy Camille Bilger claimed that his constituents were "conditional Frenchmen" *(Bedingungsfranzosen)*, calling into question the very nature of Alsace's affiliation with France. Abbé Haegy, the tsar of the Alsatian Catholic press, wrote, "When one is a Catholic Alsatian, then it requires considerable effort to take pleasure in being French." Such open attacks on the French administration of Alsace by the local notables simultaneously reflected and fueled popular grievances against the French government, extending well beyond issues of church and state.[54]

In 1925, autonomists began to organize outside the existing party structures. The first stirrings came on May 9, 1925, with the premiere of an autonomist weekly entitled *Die Zukunft,* edited by Emile Pinck and the future Nazi Paul Schall. *Die Zukunft* attracted the support and collaboration of all shades of autonomists (save the communists) and marked the beginning of an organized intellectual opposition to France, based on culture rather than on specific grievances against French policies. "Alsace-Lorrainers are, to be sure, part of the French state *(Staatsvolkes),* but not part of the French nation," *Die Zukunft* reasoned. *Die Zukunft* and the autonomist movement were morally supported by refugee Alsatians in Germany and financially supported by private wealthy donors in Germany.[55]

Out of *Die Zukunft*'s cultural critique grew a political movement whose sole goal was autonomism. On June 8, 1926, the manifesto of the Heimatbund was published in the local Catholic press. Signed by 101 "functionaries, pastors, priests, general counsellors, town counsellors, doctors, businessmen, industrialists, etc.," the Heimatbund claimed, "We only want a new organization, not a party, that will impel the existing parties to give up the politics of delay, weakness, and deception and lead the struggle for the provincial rights of the Alsace-Lorrainian people with relentless energy."[56]

Despite vigorous repression by the French government, which fired all government employees who signed the Heimatbund's manifesto and banned *Die Zukunft,* the idea of a political movement animated by autonomism prospered. On September 25, 1927, the Unabhängige Landespartei für Elsaß-Lothringen (Independent Landespartei) held its first meeting. The Landespartei went slightly further than the Heimatbund, its goal being "a free Alsace-Lorraine belonging to the United States of Europe and bridging France and Germany."[57] This was separatism and constituted a serious radicalization of autonomism.

In addition, local politicians scrambled to profit from the indisputable mass appeal of autonomism. The question was not whether but how to be autonomist. The UPR, by far the dominant party in Alsace, was divided between its "nationalist wing," which advocated assimilation, and its "provincial rights *[heimatrechtliche]* wing," which nurtured most of the key autonomists. The Radical-Republican and Radical-Socialist Party split in April 1927, when Georges Wolf formed the Elsäßische Fortschrittspartei (Alsatian Progressive Party). Wolf, a Lutheran pastor, castigated "assimilationist politics" as being "inimical to *Kultur* and immoral" and demanded linguistic and administrative rights for Alsace.[58] Camille Dahlet, another radical, joined Wolf and became one of the most prominent autonomists. Dahlet may have been one of the only autonomists who actually adhered strictly to an autonomist ideology and who was not seduced by the idea of return to Germany. Even the communists split over the issue of autonomism (although not until 1929), despite their initial unanimity that Alsace was the victim of French imperialism. Battle lines between the autonomists on one side and the French government and Alsatian Francophiles on the other became entrenched in the party system.

These battle lines created unusual allies. The French communists called for a rally protesting the central government's repression of autonomism to be held on August 22, 1926. The autonomist wing of the UPR, consisting of clerical and conservative autonomists, was to join with the Parti Communiste Français (PCF) in common cause against the imperialist French government. Orthodox opinion in both parties could only be shocked at the willingness of communists and Catholics to fight "shoulder to shoulder" for Alsace.[59] Francophile fascists, led by the AF, fought back by occupying the Salle des Catherinettes (where the rally was to be held) and tried forcibly to prevent Eugène Ricklin, a clerical autonomist and the keynote speaker, from reaching the meeting hall. Despite injuries to about sixty people, including Dr. Ricklin, the rally proceeded as planned. The importance of the meeting and the public violence gave the date August 22 the sobriquet of "Bloody Sunday."

The French government saw its control over events slipping away. Its reflex was to step up the repression of autonomism. First, it banned *Die Zukunft* along with two other autonomist journals in November 1927, on the obscure grounds that the government had the right to interdict any publication published in France in a foreign language.[60] Indeed, the government persisted in banning subsequent autonomist journals in 1928.

The high point of French repression came in May 1928 during the Colmar trial of twenty-two autonomists for complicity in a German-backed plot to separate Alsace from France.[61] Considerable evidence came to light establishing a connection between Germany and the Alsatian autonomists.[62] The trial, however, failed to establish conclusively that the use of German funds constituted an attempt by the autonomists to separate Alsace from France. Nevertheless, the jurors found four of the defendants—Dr. Eugène von Ricklin, Joseph Rossé, Abbé Fasshauer, and Paul Schall—guilty and sentenced them to one year in prison and five years of exile from Alsace. "A powerful wave of discontentment unfurled" in response to the Colmar trial judgments.[63] Outside the courthouse the crowd sang "O Straßburg, O Straßburg!" instead of the "Marseillaise" and hissed at the prosecution lawyers. Even before the Colmar trial began on May 1, Alsatians had expressed their opinion by electing Ricklin and Rossé to the National Assembly. When the assembly invalidated their mandates, since the two autonomists had been found guilty of plotting against France, the Alsatian public elected two other Colmar defendants, Marcel Stürmel and René Hauss.

Harsh measures had proved woefully inadequate in squelching the Alsatian malaise. The panicked Strasbourg elite, for example, proposed a host of propaganda initiatives to counteract their disadvantage vis-à-vis Abbé Haegy's autonomist press. The central government began to moderate. First, it pardoned the Colmar prisoners in July. When Karl Roos, the exiled head of the Landespartei and defendant in absentia at the Colmar trials, decided to return to France to face trial, the government showed that it had learned its lesson. Roos's trial was held in Besançon in June 1929 and resulted in his acquittal. From the Besançon trial through the 1930s, France steered carefully away from confrontation with the autonomists and to a large extent succeeded in defusing much of the tension.[64]

. . .

The pervasive discontent with French policy provided a context within which the autonomists acted for their own political profit, and they shaped the political discourse in Alsace throughout the 1920s. Each party had to address these problems or risk becoming irrelevant. Consequently, such diverse groups as the communists, the royalists, and the Catholics vigorously attacked the Third Republic for its abuses in the administrative, linguistic, and religious spheres, whereas other parties such as the French socialists and the radicals, although acknowledging French shortcomings, supported the frenchification of Alsace. Even the French fascist movements, normally dedicated to the idea of a centralized state that embodied and enforced cultural and national norms, saw fit to argue for regionalism in Alsace.[65]

The causes of the Alsatian autonomist movement are important to the study of Alsatian fascism. Local grievances cut deeply into the daily experiences of Alsatians. Street signs were changed from German to French. Children learned a different language in school. All interaction with the government, from the most banal bureaucratic transactions to the most gripping court cases, became confrontations between cultures. The specific resentments at French cultural imperialism were not as important, however, as the fact that they gave life to the religious, class, cultural, and economic schisms within Alsace. The issues that brought autonomism to a head constituted the context of Alsatian politics during the 1920s and continued to affect the region into the 1930s. Alsatian autonomism was a far more important problem in Alsace than fascism; it touched more people and articulated a more compelling analysis of the region's problems. Nevertheless, the political discourse engendered by the rise of autonomism was consistent with, and legitimized, fascist ideology.

Without autonomism, the pattern of fascism in Alsace would have been unrecognizably different. Its critique of the colonialism of the Third Republic legitimized and popularized antirepublicanism, lending credibility to the antiliberalism of the fascists. Moreover, there was a symbiotic relationship between autonomism and hypernationalism. It is no coincidence that the first wave of French fascism broke over Alsace at the same time as the autonomist movement reached its peak in 1924–1926. Unlike the rest of France, where fascism and communism were binary opposites (each thriving on the fear produced by the other), Alsace had the additional—and distinct—complication of autonomism. The most radical of the autonomists turned to Nazism in the 1930s, in frustration at their political impotence and because they were attracted to the cultural agenda of Hitler's party. Fascism was the most extreme, determined, and logical expression of national identity, and as such it benefited from the preeminent position of the national identity question in Alsace.

LEGITIMIZING NAZISM

CONSERVATIVES AND FASCISTS IN THE

UNION POPULAIRE RÉPUBLICAINE

Joseph Rossé, one of the leaders of the Catholic Union Populaire Républicaine (UPR), died a broken man in 1951 while serving a sentence of hard labor for his complicity in the Nazi annexation of Alsace.[1] Rossé had held several prominent positions under the Nazis and was one of several token native Alsatian leaders who the Nazis publicized as examples of their regional sensitivity. Unlike most Nazi collaborators, however, Rossé had neither created nor openly joined a fascist party before the war. As an effective and charismatic leader of the UPR, he already had an established political base.

Although Rossé did not typify the political attitude of the UPR, he is a useful example of the complex relationship between the UPR and Nazism. He was, after all, one of the party's most visible leaders during the late 1920s and 1930s and he did embrace Nazism (albeit inconsistently and clandestinely) before the war. The UPR, appreciative of his grassroots constituency, never expelled him and proved incapable of limiting his activity, if in fact it ever seriously wanted to do so. Rossé's populist base was too solid.

The *Freie Presse,* Alsace's socialist daily, spoke for many anti-German Alsatians when it argued that "without Alsatian clericalism, . . . without the UPR, the mistress of the Alsatian clergy, Alsatian autonomism would never supply a solid argument for Hitler's

Germany."[2] The police agreed, reporting that "personalities of note in Alsatian and Lorraine politics, especially in the UPR" (including Rossé), were critical to the success of autonomism with its pro-German bent. And during the 1930s, these same notables flirted with Alsatian Nazism and met with German Nazis.[3] Even if most Catholics were pious and conservative without embracing fascism or Nazism, the leadership of the UPR's autonomist wing nurtured fascist and Nazi ideas. It did this in two key ways: its political philosophy paralleled Nazi ideology; and a faction of the UPR admired, imitated, and accepted money from the German Nazis.

. . .

The UPR exerted a powerful and persistent influence over Alsatian political life. Established immediately after World War I as the successor to the Wilhelmine Alsatian Center Party, the UPR was easily the dominant party in Alsace. From 1919 to 1939, the UPR maintained a steady political majority with nine out of sixteen deputies and between four and six senators in the National Assembly. The party's membership grew steadily from an estimated 10,369 in 1920 to 14,426 in 1938, despite the defection of its assimilationist wing in 1929.[4] This made it the largest party in the region, where it captured the political center between the Marxist and the radical right parties.

From its inception, the UPR organized and defended the interests of Alsatian Catholics. Its aims were twofold: to preserve regional rights, particularly the Alsatian school system and the commingling of church and state; and "to collaborate in the restoration of Christian thought to the life of the French state."[5] Throughout the interwar era, the UPR remained deeply concerned with regional issues and critical of the anticlerical and centralized Third Republic. Two wings, corresponding to the party's two goals, developed within the party: a "left" wing that focused on Alsatian issues as a means of mobilizing a broad spectrum of Alsatian voters; and a "right" wing that consisted of upper-middle-class Francophile notables engaged in defining Alsace's relationship to France. (The terms *right* and *left* in this context have little in common with Marxist usage; they simply refer to the differences between the notables and the masses within the party.)

The UPR epitomized the ambivalent relationship between conservatism and fascism.[6] The two "isms" shared many assumptions such as anticommunism, authoritarianism, and antimaterialism, yet many conservatives balked at the totalitarian style and putative social content of the fascists. Although the UPR played a considerable role in fostering Nazism, the party itself was not fascist. The majority of UPR leaders were Catholic conservatives, who grudgingly accepted the Third Republic's parliamentarianism, defended regional interests, and preserved the status quo. Their emphasis on Christianity as a guide for political action differentiated and often alienated them from Nazi secularism. Even the elements that experimented with Nazi and fascist ideas did not always do so consistently or even deliberately. UPR enthusiasm and commitment to Nazism appears especially lukewarm in comparison with the activity of the hard-core Alsatian Nazis (see Chapter 8).

UPR leaders did not shrink, however, from wholehearted support for fascists during times of crisis.[7] This was particularly true whenever the left gained political credibility or power. In 1924, when Herriot and the Cartel des Gauches threatened to eliminate Alsatian religious privileges, clerics from both wings of the party turned to fascist alternatives to combat the anticlerical, decadent French state. The formation of the Popular Front in 1936 constituted another such crisis.

The UPR's leaders seriously considered fascism a viable alternative to the "atheistic state."[8] Charles Didio, a pro-German cleric who later sat on the directing committee of the UPR, wrote an anti-AF article in 1925 that reveals the political affinity of the UPR to fascism.[9] Declaring himself a "republican of the head and not of the heart [Vernunftsrepublikaner]," Didio confessed to a certain approval for the AF, because it showed "greater understanding and cooperation for our regional character" than any other national party. He objected to the AF on the grounds that it had no chance of grasping power and that therefore the "disappearance of authority and the growing spiritual anarchy" would not be rectified.[10] Concern for order, spiritual constancy, and particularism favorably inclined many well-informed Catholics toward fascist parties.

The UPR also played a key role in shaping autonomism. The party's left wing led the struggle for Alsatian rights in religious, cultural, and administrative spheres, while the right wing turned to French fascist movements such as the AF, the Jeunesses Patriotes (JP), and the Faisceau for help in asserting the preeminence of French nationalism. In 1929, the division became unbridgeable and the right wing of the party seceded from the UPR to form the Action Populaire Nationale d'Alsace (APNA). During the 1930s, the UPR's left wing turned increasingly toward Germany and Nazism as providing the best defense for Alsatian culture. The result was more than just a schism based on national orientation. Abbé Haegy pointed out that the APNA was "heavily supported by the capitalists," whereas his autonomist faction, which had retained control of the UPR, catered to the particularism of the average Alsatian. Meanwhile, the head of the Bas-Rhin chapter of the APNA, Pierre Schmidt-Le-Roi, accused the UPR autonomists of "inciting the worker against his boss."[11]

"The UPR is caught between two fascisms," commented the national liberal paper.[12] This observation summed up the dilemma of the UPR, which was divided between upper-class Francophiles and more plebeian Germanophiles throughout the interwar era. Except for 1929, when differences over the national question forced it to split into two parties, the UPR embraced German and French nationalists simultaneously. This was brought about for many reasons. First, the center of the UPR worked to keep the party together in order to maximize its national and regional power. Second, the pro-French and the pro-German factions had greater clout as part of the UPR (borne out by their ineffectiveness after they split). Third, all members of the UPR, despite national differences, shared a common right-wing social and political agenda. Both left and right wings of the party despised the Third Republic; the autonomists because they resented its cultural repression and the Francophile right because the Third Republic was responsible for undermining the structure of society through anticlericalism, liberalism, and socialism.

Important components of fascist ideology such as corporatism, virulent antiliberalism and anti-Marxism, and a belief in the salutary effects of a unified *Volk* were central concepts for the clerical autonomists. Clerical autonomists differed from the communist autonomists and the Nazi autonomists because they based their regionalism on the defense of Catholicism. Because of this, almost all of the clerical autonomists were in the UPR. Autonomist leaders within the UPR imitated Nazi style through the creation of paramilitary youth groups and by claiming an exclusive monopoly on activism, in contrast to the "materialistic, desiccated" parliamentary parties. The UPR also attacked the "Godless movement" in Russia and Germany, which constituted "a worldwide threat for Christian culture and humanity."[13] In addition to stimulating paranoia about the Bolshevist Revolution, the UPR implied the presence of Jews in this international community.

Antisemitism permeated the UPR, although this remained largely unstated until the 1930s. Inherent in the UPR's defense of an Alsace-Lorraine Christian community was the rejection of non-Christians, be they Freemasons, atheists, or Jews. In 1937, in opposition to Blum's abortive attempt to reform the school system, the left wing of the UPR published an offensive pamphlet entitled "No! Herr Blum, Never! The Response to the Declaration of War on Christian Alsace-Lorraine."[14] This was a merciless attack on Jews, which took advantage of every stereotype and every latent Alsatian prejudice. One cartoon, for example, depicted Jews stoning a nun whose body was protecting a cross. Freemasons and Jews were explicitly linked in an unholy alliance against the Church. Contemporary observers noted the rise of antisemitism during the 1930s.[15] To be sure, antisemitism was not a defining or necessary characteristic of fascism. Nevertheless, the UPR's antisemitism—especially in the 1930s when German and French fascists escalated their antisemitism—served to legitimize racism. The UPR failed to condemn the fascist vision of antisemitism, and its willingness to jump on the antisemitic, anti-Blum bandwagon encouraged even more violent antisemitic activity. The UPR's antisemitism also seriously hampered its ability to oppose or even criticize the Alsatian Nazi movement.

The only significant tenet of fascism that was missing was the preeminence of the state. This omission owed as much to the autonomists' bitter struggle against centralization as to philosophical opposition. The autonomists certainly favored order and authority at every level from the family to the state. In the end, most Catholics in the UPR turned against Nazism, repulsed by Hitler's treatment of their coreligionists. Nevertheless, the combination of fascist ideology and German culture articulated by the UPR went a long way toward creating a receptive milieu for Nazism.

It is ironic that even the anti-German, assimilationist wing of the UPR legitimized Nazism in Alsace. In general, assimilationists emanated from the well-to-do, notable segment of the UPR.[16] Vehemently opposed to any pro-German inclination, leaders such as Joseph Pfleger and Alfred Oberkirch embraced radical right-wing French nationalism and were among the most vigorous opponents of Nazism. Yet their participation in fascist groups such as the AF, the Faisceau, and the JP in the 1920s represented a shared political agenda with the Nazis, including antiliberalism, anticommunism, and the formation of a unified cultural community. Their only major disagreement with the Nazis—and it was profound—concerned the question of national identity (which was at least in part a function of UPR's class, religious, and local identity).

The right wing had close connections with the AF. The antisecular ideology of the AF had supporters in the UPR as early as 1919.[17] Despite paying lip service to the dogma that all parties are evil, the AF conceded that the UPR's 1926 regional program was essentially "a translation of the program of the AF." Such a comment should not be construed to mean that the AF was actually republican. On the contrary, the royalists were complimenting the UPR's antirepublican tone. One UPR deputy, Joseph Pfleger, saw fit to write an editorial in *Le National d'Alsace,* the AF's local paper, on "The Helpers of German Propaganda," in which he attacked the policy of Herriot for contributing to German propaganda against Alsace's reintegration into France. The local AF even deployed its shock troops—the Camelots du Roi—to protect Michel Walter, the political head of the regionalist, pro-German wing of the UPR in Colmar.[18]

Leaders of the UPR's right wing also figured prominently in the other Francophile fascist groups. Pfleger (along with Schmidt-Le-Roi, a leader in the UPR and later in the APNA) was also associated with the Légion, a fascist Francophile veterans' league of the mid-1920s. Born in 1873 and raised in Alsace, Pfleger was an advocate of Alsatian autonomy before 1918 and became an important UPR leader after the war. Intensely pro-French, he opposed the post-1918 autonomist movement and dabbled in several far right nationalist movements.[19] Similarly, Schmidt-Le-Roi and Alfred Oberkirch, a UPR deputy from 1919 to 1940, supported the PSF; the former was vice president of the Strasbourg section.[20]

When Francophile Catholics, frustrated with the success of autonomism and the growing influence of the UPR's rank and file, broke away from the UPR to form the APNA on November 3, 1928, their political agenda shared a great deal with the fascist groups. Democratic procedure through a legislative body was, in their view, inefficient. They wanted instead to strengthen executive power. Their middle- to upper-class constituency and political clout made it only natural that they should support authority. Reform of the state ought to give more power to the corporate organizations. The APNA, like the fascists, bemoaned the importance of the individual inherent in liberalism and Marxism, which had, according to the right, a deleterious effect on the moral cohesiveness of community.

In August 1926 the UPR's right wing applauded the violent actions of the Camelots du Roi, the JP, and other fascist groups against the autonomists.[21] Paramilitary and political violence was commonplace, to be sure, yet the UPR's enthusiasm signaled an acceptance of fascist style that contributed to the erosion of political order. The party's antisocialism often blinded it to the consequences of political violence. Ostensibly against the "suppression of the working classes," the APNA was even more opposed to Marxism. In any event, the APNA conceded that its duty was to "defend the middle classes, artisans, farmers, and vintners, who are the bulwark of the nation." Here were the same social groups that assumed such importance in the success of the Nationale Sozialistische Deutsche Arbeiter Partei (NSDAP).[22]

Espousal of French fascism by the assimilationists during the 1920s legitimized the subsequent pro-Nazi critique of the Third Republic. Both French fascists and Alsatian Nazis attacked parliamentary representation, demanded greater authority for the state, and objected to the jacobinism of the French government. Moreover, recourse to French hypernationalism indirectly stimulated the German alternative by channeling a wide range of social and political resentment into the limited discourse of national identity. Although the different wings of the party could not agree on Alsace's national identity, they did agree on the importance of nation as an expression of community.

The emphasis upon Christianity as the guide for social activism shared by both wings of the party differed from the racial motivations of Nazism. But religiosity does not automatically disqualify anyone as fascist; apart from German Nazism and Nazi-derived groups, most fascists had close connections with either the Catholic Church or Protestantism. Particularly problematic is the common view that Catholics opposed Nazism in Germany and therefore were somehow inoculated against fascism. In Germany, Catholics were a minority and therefore uncomfortable with the Nazi tendency toward homogenization. Even so, at times Catholics could be enthusiastic supporters of Nazism.[23] Proponents of the idea of Austrofascism, a unique form of fascism evolving out of the Catholic and corporatist milieu of Austria, argued that Catholicism was not incompatible with fascism. Mussolini, to take another prominent example, reversed his anticlericalism as early as 1921 in his first appearance in parliament and eventually reached an accommodation with the Vatican in 1929.[24] Likewise, the UPR's apparent stress on regional autonomy contradicted the totalitarianism of Nazism. Nevertheless, the APNA's emphasis on authority, anti-Marxism, and its critique of liberal democracy coincided with the Weltanschauung of the NSDAP. However much the Francophile radical right objected to and even fought against Nazism, its political philosophy contributed to a discourse that was favorable to the Nazis, and this despite the fact that during World War II this wing of the UPR, to a man, opposed the German takeover of Alsace. It is also important to note that they contributed to the general apathy of Alsatians toward Nazism in the 1930s.

Moderate party members also contributed to the legitimization of Nazism through their negative stance toward the Republic. Because the extremist wings of the party set the agenda in the 1920s, the center had to bridge the differences between the nationalist extremes by espousing radical right-wing conservatism. Accordingly, the UPR claimed to represent "the cultural, political, religious, and economic interests of our *Volk*." Along with the quest for "order and freedom" and a defense against "the anticlericalism of the different bourgeois parties concentrated in the lodges and in all shades of socialism from the Bolshevist elements to the government socialists," this formed the backbone of the UPR's program.[25] While the UPR's particularism and clericalism differed from Nazism, its radical right-wing emphasis on combating Freemasons, socialists, and bourgeois liberals constituted a rejection of liberal parliamentary government and encouraged a search for alternatives.

Bishop Ruch, appointed to Strasbourg Cathedral immediately following World War I, led the "moderate" attack on the system that had produced the Cartel des Gauches.[26] Although he later renounced both the AF and the extreme autonomists, Ruch mobilized both in his efforts to maintain church privileges in Alsace. While he called the activists of the AF "his best watchdogs," his defense of religious schools triggered the proclamation of the Heimatbund manifesto, which eventually turned into the organized autonomous movement.[27]

A dedicated Frenchman as well as a loyal Catholic, Ruch eventually called upon Alsatians to refrain from participating in either the AF or the Landespartei, on the grounds that both placed politics ahead of God. That he did this after politically mobilizing Alsatians against the French government reflected the right-wing nature of Alsatian Catholicism's "apolitical" prejudice against parliamentarianism. It was not coincidental that Ruch's condemnation came in 1928, after Poincaré took over the national government, thus easing the apparent threat from the left and reducing the need for radical right-wing organization.

The UPR was a divided and complicated party that embraced a wide range of views. And, as Christian Baechler rightly points out, the UPR democratized Alsatian politics as it extended representation to an unprecedented range of voters. Nevertheless, its political philosophy either inadvertently or consciously legitimized fascism and Nazism. Although corporatism, anticommunism, antimaterialism, and authoritarianism are not necessarily fascist in themselves, the conjunction of these concepts in the UPR made it difficult for the party to distinguish itself clearly from the fascist parties.

. . .

Perhaps even more important for the legitimization of Nazism than the parallels between the ideologies of the UPR and fascism was the development of an actively pro-Nazi faction within the party. The left wing of the party, led by Abbé Haegy, Joseph Rossé, and Marcel Stürmel, built a powerful grassroots constituency by catering to the Alsatian speakers. Ignoring the specificity of Alsatian peasant culture and German pre–World War I discrimination against Alsatian *Wackes* (a German term of derision for Alsatians made famous by the 1913 Zabern Affair), the clerical autonomists in the UPR insisted that Alsace was Germanic.[28] Behind the clerical autonomists' passivity toward Nazism in the 1930s was the omnipresent question of national cultural identity. In addition to stimulating radical right-wing ideology, the UPR's autonomist wing brought the question of German language and culture to the foreground of politics. Although this was an important issue in the party's expansion of its constituency during the interwar years to include middle- and lower-class Alsatians, the UPR's emphasis on German culture also dovetailed with the political agenda of the Nazi Party. Influenced by pseudoscientific arguments that the German *Volk* constituted a separate unity, and deeply convinced of Alsace's Germanness, many autonomists came to accept Nazism during the 1930s as the clearest expression of their pan-Germanism.

UPR leaders such as Abbé Xavier Haegy, Joseph Rossé, and Marcel Stürmel wielded considerable influence as spokesmen for an increasingly politicized rural and lower-middle-class, German-speaking, Catholic constituency. In the mid-1920s, Abbé Haegy came to represent the anti-French cultural aspirations of the majority of Alsatian Catholics.[29] Until his death in 1932, Haegy oversaw a broad range of publications ranging from *Der Elsäßer Kurier* and the *Mülhauser Volksblatt* (two dailies with a circulation of thirty-two thousand each in 1929) to such monthlies as the more intellectual *Die Heimat*. His publishing empire constituted about a third of the regional press.[30] His editorship, along with his increasingly important role within the UPR as a representative of rural Catholic Alsatians, made him one of the most influential opinion shapers in Alsace.[31]

Haegy's success was predicated on his personification of the contradictory and stubbornly complex nature of Alsatian politics and society. "I am above all a priest," Haegy declared, "then an Alsatian, and finally a loyal French citizen, just as I was a loyal German subject."[32] Prior to 1918, he was a deputy in the Reichstag, where he was known as a *Franzosenkopf* (French head) for his defense of Alsace-Lorraine interests against the Second Reich.

Yet, as a witness at the Colmar trials in 1928, Haegy supported the anti-French autonomist movement by linking it to the struggle for regional rights under German rule. Haegy led an important struggle within the Catholic Church against the Francophile, urban, and bourgeois tendencies of Bishop Ruch.[33]

Haegy's consistent espousal of autonomism under both Germany and France and his devout Catholicism suggest that he would have looked upon the Nazis with distaste. Nevertheless, during the 1920s he threw his weight behind an extremely Germanophile opposition, which after his death in 1932 became a spearhead for Nazi activity in Alsace. His political agenda was radical right-wing. "I do not love France," Haegy confided to Senator Scheurer, "it is an atheist land, a Freemason state. I do not love it!"[34] Despite his abiding commitment to the autonomist cause, Haegy retained "a memory of sympathy" for the AF activist Fernand Heitz, who knew and corresponded with him. Haegy detested the liberal, anticlerical Third Republic more than the French nation. He also reviled all forms of Marxism. During his tenure as editor of the Alsatia publishing house, he published an anonymous pamphlet accusing the communist and socialist movements of initiating an international conspiracy to eliminate Christianity. Although he was no Nazi, his critique of liberalism coupled with his belief in the cultural Germanness of Alsace legitimized subsequent Nazi activism.[35]

When Haegy died in 1932, Joseph Rossé inherited his position as head of the Catholic autonomist press and spokesman for Alsatian particularism.[36] Unlike Haegy, Rossé became implicated in German espionage. The socialist paper claimed that he was "more national-socialist than Catholic" and that his notion of the future was "only a question of shirt color." The socialists noted in particular Rossé's unwillingness to challenge the goals of the Croix de Feu and his sympathy for Nazism: "From sympathy for Hitler to sympathy for the Croix de Feu is a short step."[37] His assumption of responsibility took the autonomist wing of the UPR beyond a simple espousal of regional rights to outright active support for reunification with Germany. His actions, however, fell short of the ideological standards set by the Alsatian Nazis in the Landespartei and the Jungmannschaft.

Joseph Rossé began his public career as a teacher in the German educational system before being sent to the Russian front as an officer in the German army during World War I. Following the war, Rossé presided over the Fédération des Fonctionnaires d'Etat et des Instituteurs, one of the most significant white-collar unions in Alsace. Teachers and bureaucrats were especially hard hit by assimilation.[38] The length of training they had already invested, along with the French government's new requirements for advancement, discriminated against German speakers. Pensions were lower under the French, and incoming French officials generally treated their Alsatian colleagues with condescension.[39] These officials constituted an educated cohort of Alsatians who channeled their alienation into a cultural attack on France.

Rossé's role as a martyr for the autonomist cause elevated him from an obscure bureaucrat to a regional symbol. As the union's representative, Rossé signed the Heimatbund manifesto, and his prominence in the autonomist movement eventually cost him his job in 1926 when the government banned him from teaching. Then, on Christmas Eve 1927, the government arrested him and put him on trial in Colmar for conspiracy against France. In response, in the time between his arrest and his trial, the Alsatians elected him to the Chamber of Deputies. In June the court found him guilty and sentenced him to one year in prison and five years banishment. The Chamber of Deputies argued that a convicted traitor should not be allowed to take office and, by an overwhelming vote (194 to 29 with 350 abstentions), refused to seat either Rossé or Eugène Ricklin, the other elected Colmar defendant. New elections were held and returned two acquitted autonomist codefendants, Marcel Stürmel and René Hauss. Released in the summer of 1928 and amnestied, Rossé returned to public office, replacing the late Abbé Haegy as deputy of Colmar in 1932.[40]

Undaunted by either his conviction or his expulsion from the National Assembly, Rossé continued to agitate for autonomism and drew ever closer to Germany, eventually becoming a spy for the Nazis. Emboldened by his release in the summer of 1928, Rossé proclaimed at a Landespartei meeting that "we were not unhappy under the Germans," and "we do not want to assimilate."[41] Rossé was not just talk: a Colmar teacher testified to the police that Rossé acted as an informant for Albert Bongartz, the "right hand of Dr. Ernst," the head of the Deutschen Schutzbund (German Protection League).[42] Stationed in Freiburg, just across the Rhine from Alsace, Bongartz was a key conduit for German funds to Alsatian autonomists. The Bongartz-Rossé connection continued throughout the 1930s. When Swiss authorities arrested Bongartz in 1938 after he had met with Rossé in Basel, they found papers relating to the autonomist movement.[43] Following the outbreak of war in 1939, French authorities arrested Rossé, along with leaders of the overtly Nazi organizations, for pro-German activity.

The invasion of France saved Rossé from possible execution. Rescued from jail along with other autonomist leaders, Rossé signed the declaration of les Trois-Epis on July 18, 1940, which called upon Alsatians to work for integration into Hitler's Germany. He went on to hold several public positions under the Nazis, including *Gauredner* (district speaker) and Colmar municipal councillor. After joining the Nazi Party in 1941, Rossé made a fortune in publishing and banking. Despite his open collaboration, Rossé also maintained a certain distance from the Nazis by publishing anti-Nazi materials, especially after 1942.[44] On balance, however, his actions from the 1930s through the war were tantamount to Nazism, however disenchanted he might have become by 1945.

Although Marcel Stürmel had less influence than either Haegy or Rossé, his career is another example of the manifold connections between the UPR and the Nazis. After serving in both German and French armies (he was called up by the Germans in 1918 and after the armistice served the French until 1921), Stürmel worked in the railroads. He acquired notoriety as a signatory of the Heimatbund manifesto and as one of the defendants at the Colmar trials. As a result, the canton of St. Amarin elected him *conseiller général* (departmental councillor) and then—spectacularly, given his youth (twenty-nine) and lack of credentials—the voters of Altkirch elected him in the 1929 by-election to the National Assembly to replace the disqualified Ricklin.

Throughout his career, Stürmel had close ties to Germany. In his capacity as journalist for the autonomist papers *Die Zukunft, Die Volksstimme,* and *Der Elsäßer Kurier,* and as editor of *Die Heimat,* Stürmel received money from Germany.[45] The UPR forced him to resign his position as editor of *Die Heimat* in June 1939 after he admitted that he had accepted money from the German agent Abbé Scherer.[46] Stürmel's resignation resulted from a series of revelations after the arrest of Scherer, the German agent Bongartz, and the Swiss liaison Wildi in 1938. The ensuing controversy over German influence in Alsatian politics, specifically the UPR, and the approach of war forced the UPR to repudiate its extremists. Shortly thereafter Stürmel was arrested for pro-German activity, along with other leading autonomists. Like Rossé, he signed the declaration of les Trois-Epis after the Germans liberated him in 1940. The Nazis needed a cachet of autonomists such as Stürmel to legitimize their de facto annexation of Alsace. A member of the Nazi Party after 1940, Stürmel became the assistant mayor of Mulhouse and was liberally reimbursed by the German government for his suffering as a "pioneer of Germanism" in Alsace.[47]

Unlike the leaders of the Landespartei, who wholeheartedly embraced Nazism, Rossé and Stürmel retained some vestiges of clericalism. They accepted Nazism, but with reservations about the anti-Catholic and totalitarian aspects of Hitler's regime. Stürmel, for example, protected a number of Alsatian resisters and deportees, most notably Robert Heitz, whose affiliation with the AF led him to support France during the war.[48] After August 25, 1942, when the Germans reneged on their promise not to mobilize Alsatians in the war effort, Rossé and Stürmel drifted away from the party.[49] Whether this was due to self-preservation, ideological alienation, or a combination thereof is not clear.

Rossé and Stürmel represented the Nazi faction of the UPR. They worked within the UPR to carry fascist tendencies to a logical extreme. After the election of the Popular Front in 1936, for example, the UPR attempted to sponsor an Alsatian Front that would unite the opponents of Léon Blum. However, the autonomist wing, led by Rossé and especially Stürmel, rejected the UPR's attempt to create a democratic alternative to the Popular Front. Instead, they argued that the Alsatian Front should combine the forces of autonomism against the Third Republic.[50] This would have entailed the reconstitution of the Volksfront, uniting all autonomist parties from the "communist" Elsäßische Arbeiter- und Bauernpartei (EABP) to the clerical UPR, that had been so successful at the end of the 1920s. By this time, the EABP and the Landespartei had committed themselves to Nazism, making the proposed Alsatian Front an alliance with Nazism. This agenda stressed separation from France and, by implication, unification with Nazi Germany. The center of the party neither endorsed this plan nor rejected the Nazi element.

The clerical autonomists' predilection for Nazi style was most evident in their blatant attempts to imitate Nazi paramilitary organization, and by their ambivalent response to events in Germany. An example of the UPR's complicity was its youth group, the Jeunesses de l'UPR (*Jungvolkspartei* in German). Founded in 1928, the Jeunesses had few adherents and was geographically limited to the area around Colmar until Rossé's tenure.[51] Rossé took over in 1931 and guided the Jeunesses along a Nazi path by organizing and channeling the energies of youth into the UPR. Under Rossé's leadership, the UPR did not perceive the Jeunesses to be about "sport or other typical issues of youth conventions, but rather the demand for activist participation by youth in politics."[52] Railing at the "incomprehensible centralism, the ossified bureaucracy, and the preeminence of financial and economic groups" that marked the French state, the Jeunesses sought radical reform of the political system. The movement rejected "a dictatorship of nationalist groups" and "the dictatorship of one class" in favor of democracy. This is a classic example of the neither-right-nor-left dialectic shared by all fascists. "Such a democracy, which opens the path for the notable free deployment of corporative interests, regionally and locally justified," the Jeunesses argued, "can be founded only on the eternal principles of Christianity and on the directives of the grand encyclicals." Like most fascist groups, the Jeunesses believed that the individual's dignity could only be preserved by "the integration of private activity within the ensemble of the common body of the people [corps populaire] and of humanity." Marching around in gray shirts, they declared "war without mercy" on those who disagreed with them, showing their affinity—at least superficially—with the style of Nazi paramilitary organizations.[53]

The Jeunesses espoused a form of corporatism that lent itself to Nazism. The Catholic paper *Der Elsäßer Bote* wrote, "this group had always invoked Austrian corporative organization and the principles of Italian fascism."[54] Like the French fascist Drieu la Rochelle, the Jeunesses "saw in the corporatist movement the deadly reaction against the doctrine of economic liberalism, which atomized society and rendered the individual weak and unprotected." Likewise, it opposed the "collectivist doctrine" of Marxism. Although it subscribed to the same basic dialectic (neither right nor left) used by all fascist parties, it moderated somewhat its notion of corporatism by rejecting "demagogic phrases devoid of all common sense" and, more important, by declining to work for the "demolition of political parties."[55]

Corporatism was a vague but trendy political concept in the interwar period and the use of the term generally implied a critique of parliamentarianism shared by all groups on the radical right. Significant differences in corporatist theory did exist between Nazis, fascists, and Catholics. Perhaps a few of their respective leaders even understood the differences. The overall effect of the term's ubiquity, however, was to inure the public to a radical critique of liberal democracy and to blur the line between conservatives and fascists.

In spite of such qualifications, the leadership of the Jeunesses de l'UPR openly expressed sympathy and respect for the Nazis. Georges Gromer, a departmental councillor in Hagenau and leader of the autonomist wing of the UPR, extolled the power of youth in bringing about a "movement of renewal" in fascist Italy and Nazi Germany. The Nuremberg extravaganza particularly impressed him. The Germans for their part viewed the Jeunesses as a favorable sign that the "youth of Alsace is turning its back on Paris and wants to have nothing to do with France."[56]

By 1932, the Jeunesses had grown from 5 or 6 groups around Colmar to 38 throughout both departments. In 1934, the gray shirts mustered about 150 people for a demonstration in the relatively hostile community of Wissembourg. The organization continued to grow steadily, reaching 148 groups in 1938.[57] That same year the Jeunesses claimed to have drawn 5,000 people to a meeting at Ste. Odile.[58] Compared to the Francophile fascist youth groups, the Jeunesses was successful. The AF's Camelots du Roi, for example, rarely mobilized more than 50 activists at any given time, its small number being consistent with its elitist university orientation. The Bauernbund's comparable youth organization, the Green Shirts, included around 500 activists.[59] The pro-Nazi Jungmannschaft also paled in comparison, consisting of only a few hundred activists, many of whom scarcely qualified as youths.[60]

As an attempt to mobilize the youth of Alsace, the Jeunesses was far more successful than the more overtly fascist groups. The UPR's use of the Jeunesses reinforced the cult of youth and the emphasis on activism. Whether the UPR imitated Nazism in order to profit from its successful techniques or whether it genuinely subscribed to the assumptions about youth, politics, and society made popular by the Nazis is immaterial. Whatever its motivations, by creating a gray-shirted paramilitary youth cadre, the UPR perpetuated fascist style and fascist ideology.

. . .

The arguments of clerical autonomists, formulated in the mid-1920s in order to justify the preservation of the existing social and political elite against the intrusion of foreign French elites, were taken to extremes by radical autonomists. Certain factors specific to Alsace—in particular the German cultural heritage of the region—contributed to the clerical autonomists' acceptance of Nazism. The passage of time and the imposition of events, most notably the rise of Nazism in Germany, created a qualitative difference between the extreme autonomism of the 1920s and that of the 1930s. The expression of an exaggerated cultural homogeneity that distinguished an organic Alsatian nation from the French nation meshed ideologically with *völkisch* trends in Weimar and Nazi Germany. Many autonomist leaders within the UPR were compromised by their acceptance of financial donations from German governmental and private sources, which further bound them to national socialism. The elevation of Germanic culture by the autonomists, as well as their attachment to the idea of a *Volk*, ultimately pushed some clerical autonomists to support Nazism. The cultural Germanness of the extreme autonomists necessitated that they rejoin Germany, regardless of the cost.

In order to articulate a coherent and powerful critique of French centralization without turning to Marxism, UPR leaders utilized a combination of elements from the recent, and still dynamic, Italian Fascist movement and the cultural nationalism of Germany. This allowed autonomists to attack the weakness of the Third Republic as a pawn of party politics and, at the same time, to bemoan the cultural imperialism of the overly intrusive French state. In short, fascist ideology was convenient for the purposes of the autonomous movement because it provided a ready-made and accessible critique of the status quo, and because it gave the Alsatians the illusion of resonance with wider European trends. In all fairness to the Alsatians, however, the use of fascist ideology was widespread in Europe during the confused interwar era. Almost all of the political parties, for example, saw fit to form some sort of paramilitary youth group in order to demonstrate their respective activism and their capacity to project their movements into the future. Clerical autonomists saw Nazism as the best (or last) defense of Alsatian culture, unlike Alsatian Nazis who saw Alsatian culture as the best vehicle for the dissemination of Nazism.

Fascism resonated in the political discourse of the 1920s and 1930s. Distinctions between imitation and the real article are often difficult to make. The UPR was not fascist, but it supported fascism; it was certainly not Nazi, but it contained Nazi elements and helped legitimize Nazism. Without the inadvertent compliance of the UPR, especially its autonomist wing, Nazism would have been an even more marginal movement than it turned out to be.

THE FIRST GENERATION OF FRENCH FASCISM

THE ACTION FRANÇAISE, THE LÉGION, AND THE FAISCEAU

Herriot's promise to secularize Alsace in 1924 did not just galvanize the autonomist movement; it also goaded the French radical right in Alsace into action. Two issues motivated the right: the protection of France from liberal and socialist encroachments in the area of religion and culture, and combating the Germanophile tendencies of the autonomist movement. In effect, the pro-French right argued that Alsace, which remained outside the legal separation of church and state, symbolized the true, historic, and unified France. To make this argument work, of course, French nationalists had to quash the uncomfortably persistent regional notion that Alsace was distinct from France.

Leading the way was the royalist Action Française, which used the Alsatian malaise to criticize the Third Republic. As the oldest and most prominent French fascist organization, the AF became the first representative for the assimilationist alternative to the autonomist solutions advanced during the Alsatian malaise. Initial success, however, gave way to stasis in 1926 when the pope banned the movement and in 1928 when Poincaré replaced Herriot. Close on the heels of the Action Française came the Légion and the Faisceau, which, inspired by Mussolini's dramatic success in Italy and impatient with the endless rhetorical posturing of the AF, demanded faster and more concrete action against the Third Republic. After several years of indefatigable activity with no appreciable results, activists in the Faisceau (into which the Légion had already merged) gave up and the entire first generation of French fascism collapsed.

Although the first generation of French fascism flashed across the political firmament of Alsace only briefly, it burned brightly. In a quantifiable sense this was true given the crowds that attended the rallies of the AF, Légion, and Faisceau. The three movements also played an important role in shaping the political parameters of Alsatian identity in the mid- to late 1920s. Opposing the separatism of the Landespartei, which sought reunification with Germany, the Francophile fascist parties defined the opposite extreme—complete integration into France. Together, these extremist versions of national identity drowned out the regional middle ground, forcing an awkward and uncomfortable set of choices for most Alsatians and twisting local politics into a more radical and polarized discourse.

THE ACTION FRANÇAISE

The AF began its activity in Alsace only after World War I, since the German administration prohibited any openly anti-German revanchist movement such as the AF. In a sense, however, the AF had already begun to influence Alsace well before 1918 through its appeal to Alsatian expatriots, who returned to Alsace at war's end. In addition, Frenchmen from the "interior"—that ill-defined part of France that constituted the permanent core of French sensibility—triumphantly reentered Alsace in 1918 and occupied important positions in banking and the bureaucracy. Many of these interior Frenchmen were royalist, and it was their activism that enabled the AF, as early as April 1919, to open up a branch in Bas-Rhin and distribute tracts to the "local priests of the communes."[1]

The Alsatian AF grew very slowly until 1924. In December 1920, the Comte Renauld de Chaumont-Guitry, a foreigner in Alsace, invited select Alsatians and Frenchmen to attend a meeting to discuss "the creation of a provisional committee for royalist action in Strasbourg." About twenty attended. The following year, Chaumont-Guitry presided over at least five private meetings, each attended by about forty royalists, most of whom were not native Alsatians.[2]

Interior Frenchmen with a fiercely nationalist and conservative agenda dominated the AF's leadership. Chaumont-Guitry was born in Paris, as was the secretary of the movement, Edouard Cauchois, who had spent a good part of his professional career in Saigon. Marcel Valot, who replaced Chaumont-Guitry as president of the local AF in 1922 after the count's professional responsibilities forced him to resign, came from the Haute Saône region.[3] For these Frenchmen, Alsace represented a unique region where the anticlericalism of the French state could be critically juxtaposed with the traditional religious laws retained by Alsace. As long as the AF was dominated by interior Frenchmen, whose attachment to Alsace was suspect, the movement did not effectively recruit local Alsatians. Such was the situation until after the election of the Cartel des Gauches.

It is ironic that the AF understood earlier than any other French national parties the nature of the Alsatian problem. In 1920 Maurice Pujo, one of the national AF's founding members, published *Problèmes d'Alsace et de Lorraine,* in which he argued for the protection of linguistic rights and addressed the explosive issue of the bureaucracy's ethnic composition.[4] Pujo, however, did not write out of altruistic concern for Alsace but from a theoretical point of view. Basing his opinion on only one visit to Alsace-Lorraine, Pujo's sole concern was to integrate Alsace into France as quickly as possible. The fact that he anticipated the "Alsatian malaise" of 1924 was accidental. His book went largely unnoticed until 1924, when the electoral successes of the left and the growth of the AF's local organization had reached the point where many Alsatians were willing to consider joining the AF, and his predictions concerning the alienation of Alsace appeared to come true.

The party stepped up its national activity in 1923 in response to the murder of Marius Plateau, the head of the Camelots du Roi, and the controversial death of Léon Daudet's son, Philippe. Both events catalyzed the movement because they emphasized the implacable public and governmental opposition to the AF.[5] Although the AF's national militancy may have affected the Alsatian chapter, the victory of the Cartel des Gauches in 1924 proved to be a more immediate stimulus for the Alsatian AF. Suddenly the Alsatians began to fear that the Bolshevist Revolution, abortive in 1918, could recur in Alsace.

Locally, more pressing issues reigned. The left's success also catalyzed the pro-German autonomist movement, centered around the Zukunft. The exaggerated fear of Alsace's Germanness pushed many Francophile Alsatians toward the right, causing membership in the AF to soar and enabling the publication of a regional royalist weekly, *Le National d'Alsace.* Although autonomism, like the AF, attacked the secular Republic and its offensive against traditional Alsatian rights, the AF objected to the Zukunft's attempt to monopolize the future. *"Die Zukunft?* Is this the paper of the past of William II's reign?" the AF asked.[6] Nevertheless, *Die Zukunft* forced local political discourse to address the question of national identity, which made the AF the leading advocate for assimilation into France.

As a result, the AF suddenly blossomed. On February 27, 1925, the AF drew two hundred people to a private meeting, a considerable increase over the twenty who had showed up in 1920. A few months later, the AF claimed that five hundred attended a meeting in Colmar, which generated fifty-three new members. A mass rally on June 27, 1926, probably marked the high point of AF activity in Alsace, when nearly three thousand royalists met in Strasbourg.[7]

Le National d'Alsace, which began publication in December 1924, was an ambitious project, providing a public trumpet for the AF. Ostensibly bilingual, most of the *National*'s articles were written in German in an effort to expand interest in the AF to German-speaking, but potentially pro-French, notables. As *L'Action Française* was written in French, the publication of a bilingual journal that appealed directly to the region and was filled with local news items was critical for the AF's local growth. The local AF printed somewhere between two and three thousand copies of *Le National* weekly between 1924 and 1927.[8]

Comparison of the circulations of *Le National* and *L'Action Française*, the AF's national daily journal, is one way to estimate the strength and influence of the Alsatian royalists relative to the national movement. The AF printed 96,415 copies of *L'Action Française* on April 19, 1925; by March 27, 1928, the number of issues produced had dropped to 70,035.[9] The *National*'s circulation of 3,000 represents 3.2 percent of the AF's 1925 national circulation. Since much of *L'Action Française* was sold in Paris or abroad, this made Alsace one of the most pro-AF regions in France.

Another way to judge the AF's local popularity is to gauge the membership of the Ligue d'Action Française. In May 1925 the League had an estimated 50,000 members nationally, 9,000 or 10,000 of whom were from Paris and the Seine. Some police estimates go as high as 13,500 or 15,000 *ligueurs* in the Seine. The heart of the League lay in the provinces, however, where anywhere from 35,000 to 40,000 League members were active. The police reported that "1,500 *ligueurs* of both sexes" were on the membership rolls at the central office of the Alsatian AF in 1925. The local League continued to grow over the next year to somewhere between 2,000 and 2,500. For a region where the AF organized late and that remained ambivalent about the return to France, the AF in Alsace compared favorably to the rest of provincial France.[10]

Many historians take a strictly statistical view of the AF, and indeed of the entire fascist movement, in order to minimize its impact on French society. Out of a total population in Alsace of 1.7 million (which includes women and children who did not vote), 3,000 activist royalists seem insignificant. A total enrollment of 50,000 *ligueurs* in all of France scarcely qualifies as a major mass movement. Simply looking at the numbers, however, is not enough. The influence of the Alsatian AF, like its national parent, extended well beyond its numerical support. In the first place, the intellectual impact of the AF was pervasive. A Belgian Catholic journal, for example, discovered in 1925 that most of its young readers believed that Charles Maurras, the intellectual and spiritual head of the AF, was the most influential writer of the last twenty-five years.[11] There is no reason to believe this was not also true in Alsace, particularly in light of the way *Le National* articulated an assimilationist regionalism that became a major part of the debate in Alsatian politics. In addition, merely tabulating the number of activists reveals nothing about those people who sympathized with the AF but did not join, out of personal apathy or because of other more pressing commitments. Finally, since many French fascist movements, including the AF, eschewed elections, a numeric estimate of passive support for fascism is next to impossible. Thus, an absolute figure is quixotic, although a look at the social composition of the AF can give an idea of how extensive this passive support may have been.

The social composition of the AF is important given the oceans of ink spilled on the social roots of the European fascist and Nazi movements.[12] Industrialists, bankers, landlords, engineers, doctors, lawyers, shopkeepers, students, state employees, and women constituted the backbone of the Alsatian AF. At a well-attended meeting in Mulhouse, the audience consisted of "industrialists, merchants, people of good society, and employees."[13] The administrative committee set up to fund and direct *Le National* relied heavily on industrialist and middle-class support. Paul Armbruster, the editor of *Le National,* was also on the board. He came from a small wine-growing family and in 1924 had just finished his military service. The AF's emphasis on pre-1789 France, hierarchical social order, and a state based on royalistic paternalism provided a ready-made justification for a privileged, but nervous, bourgeoisie.[14]

This was hardly surprising since the urban bourgeois in Alsace had been conspicuously pro-French since the mid–nineteenth century. The French-speaking bourgeoisie was particularly strong in Haut-Rhin around the industrial centers of Mulhouse and Colmar. Along the same lines, the AF was far stronger in Haut-Rhin than in Bas-Rhin. Only 9 members of the League showed up at a Strasbourg meeting on January 30, 1925, and Strasbourg had only 160 *ligueurs* and 75 student members, which points to the obvious conclusion that the AF was strongest in Haut-Rhin.[15]

Other middle-class professions show up in police reports on the membership. The treasurer of the Strasbourg AF, for example, was a bureaucrat at the post office.[16] The bureaucracy, especially the postal service, was a hotbed of nationalistic antagonism. The banking profession was also well represented. Many bankers came from "interior" or upper-middle-class families, which predisposed them toward a Francophile and socially conservative movement such as the AF. The founder of the Alsatian chapter, for example, Chaumont-Guitry was an inspector at a Société Générale bank. The banks and the bureaucracy had many white-collar workers, including women, whose exact motivations (career advancement, social frustration, fear of the lower classes, economic uncertainty) were unclear but who were attracted to the AF because of their pro-French orientation.[17]

The medical profession also occupied an important place in the AF.[18] Nationally, doctors merited their own corporate journal. In Alsace, doctors held over forty banquets where they gathered to diagnose the ills of society in the congenial professional atmosphere of their peers. As in Nazi Germany, doctors seemed to be attracted to radical right-wing ideology not just out of fear at the prospect of class revolution, but also because they were predisposed to support an ideology that stressed the organic nature of society.[19] Right-wing ideology was a weapon in the physicians' struggle with professionalization and social status.[20] Doctors were susceptible to the idea that they were guardians of the national health. In addition, the medical profession in France tended to be antisemitic, because of the fairly large number of foreign-born Jewish doctors. Since antisemitism was an integral part of Maurras's program, many doctors in Alsace joined in the hopes of somehow limiting the number and influence of their Jewish competitors.

All fascist parties wooed youth and the AF was no exception. Whether as a guarantor of the future, as an easy source of activist support against the old republicans, or out of generational solidarity, European youth was a valued commodity in the interwar radical revolutionary movements.[21] The quest for youth in the form of ubiquitous youth groups spread to all political movements and assumed an organizational and ideological importance of considerable magnitude. The paramilitary tenor of the interwar era, with its uniforms and its rhetorical emphasis on struggle, marked a decisive shift from the escapist, self-absorbed youth of the prewar era, best typified by the German *Wandervögel* (youth movement). Youth no longer had the luxury of rebelling; it was recruited and mobilized, its rebellious nature harnessed by middle-aged activists.

Following the national AF's lead, which was the prototype for interwar recruitment of youth, many Alsatian youths joined the Camelots du Roi, the "elite of the Catholic, educated youth." Founded in 1908, the Camelots had a history of violence, with canes the preferred weapon, although many also owned revolvers, truncheons, and brass knuckles. The role of the Camelots in Alsace should not be underestimated. They broke up meetings of the Faisceau, protected AF gatherings, and beat up Germanophile communists and Catholics. In short, the Camelots served as a Praetorian Guard capable of defending the cause and attacking the enemy.[22]

The early Alsatian AF, and especially the Camelots, drew heavily on university students.[23] In fact, recruitment began even before the university. About fifty "undergraduates, *lycéens,* and high school students" formed a subgroup of the AF, which met regularly. When the AF attempted to start a new group in Graffenstaden (Bas-Rhin), the only recruits were youths between the ages of seventeen and twenty, presumably attracted by the activist tenor of the movement. Youth and privilege were overrepresented.[24]

Women were also represented in the AF. In 1925, the Jeunes Filles Royalistes du Bas-Rhin was formed. Its forty members were drawn from the university, the postal service, and the banks. Clearly, these women, like their male counterparts, were not working-class or peasant. Although some may have joined because their husbands belonged, the fact that so many came from the university, or were employed, suggests that many women joined out of support for the Church's influence on French politics. Although they clearly did not directly influence the leadership and did not even make up 50 percent of the AF, the participation of women was not insignificant.[25]

The AF's appeal in Alsace had certain limitations. Rural Catholics remained unmoved by its royalist philosophy, tending instead to support the autonomist movement. The foundation of a branch of the Ligue d'Action Française in Graffenstaden, for example, failed to attract the majority of Catholics, despite the militancy of a few local lay notables. Since the local curé did not support the AF, even "the fiercest of the extreme right" were "indifferent" to the League in Graffenstaden.[26] At the same time, non-Catholics had little reason to join. Any Jew who joined the AF was clearly an exception. Protestants, whether Lutheran, Anabaptist, or Calvinist, were generally not welcome, although the AF had an organization, the Association Sully, which claimed to embrace Protestant royalists.[27] Apathy characterized the AF's attitude toward Protestants. At one Strasbourg meeting, someone pointed out the existence of royalist Protestants in Alsace. Jacques Denisane, one of the Alsatian AF leaders, responded that "the present government attacks above all the Catholics," implying that the AF was not going to make any real effort to recruit Protestants.[28] Alsatian Protestants tended, in any event, either to favor the Germans or to accept the status quo.

The inclination of the French authorities played a huge role in defining the geographically irregular success of fascism. As a result, the number of public figures who were content with the Third Republic constituted a major factor in blocking the consistent spread of the AF. Compared with Germany, where very few officials supported Weimar, the Third Republic appears to have had a striking resiliency.[29] The importance of the local curé in shaping the politics of his flock, for example, was an important factor for defining the political geography of Alsace. Wherever the local curé instructed his parishioners to avoid a particular movement, that movement had almost no chance of success.

Conversely, the importance of the local curé could also fuel the AF's rare rural successes. In the small community of Logelheim, near Colmar, the curé was a royalist. As a result, a significant proportion of the village (twenty-five out of ninety-two voters) belonged to the AF. Undoubtedly, a few curés supported the AF but on the whole the local priests found the autonomist movement more attractive. Raised and educated in Germany, most of the younger clergy saw France as the country of anticlericalism. The curés (who were, after all, the closest to the *Volk*) were more sensitive to the regional, local, and linguistic-cultural needs of rural Alsatians than either the French government or the AF.[30]

Another important local figure was the mayor. In Dessenheim (Haut-Rhin), the mayor succeeded in founding a local chapter with about forty members. Municipal councillors could also provide key support for the AF. Thus, the vice president of the chapter in Saverne was a municipal councillor.[31] Support by the local police was also possible and the AF often tried to recruit highly placed officers. One Strasbourg police officer complained in his report of the "cynicism" of the AF in inviting the director of the police to a meeting of the League. The AF also frequently sought the support of editors of local newspapers.[32] If the local authorities were opposed to the AF, however, the creation of a viable local chapter was virtually impossible. This made the geographic success of the AF random.

For many Alsatians, the AF's royalism seemed anachronistic. In an influential article Charles Didio, a Catholic intellectual affiliated with Strasbourg Cathedral and with sympathies for the autonomist movement, gently attacked the premises of the AF. Didio expressed sympathy for the AF and declared, "no newspaper, no party direction in Paris has shown as much understanding and courtesy for our regional uniqueness" as had the AF.[33] Conceding that a monarchy would be an improvement over the existing republic, Didio nevertheless argued that monarchism was not particularly popular and therefore not a realistic possibility. Even more important from the Alsatian point of view, Didio pointed out that the French monarchy had always stood for centralization, not for regionalism, which made royalism problematic for the regionally minded Alsatians and which cast doubt on the integrity of the AF's appeal to Alsatian regionalism. Didio articulated the regional concerns of a great many Alsatians who leaned toward autonomism and who distrusted the centralist tendencies of the AF. Yet, Didio and the AF shared a disdain for republican government and a radical impulse to overthrow the status quo.

The AF proved to be the breeding ground for most of the French fascist groups in the 1920s and 1930s, linking them ideologically with conservative parties.[34] Indeed, the AF's ideological goals were compatible with all the fascist groups, even those (such as the Faisceau) with which it quarreled. Despite the clearly fascist character of the AF, it also had numerous connections with the established parties in Alsace. Some leaders of the UPR's assimilationist wing, including Joseph Pfleger and Alfred Oberkirch, affiliated themselves closely with the AF.

The Alsatian AF was not afraid to represent itself as fascist. If a fascist, one prominent article argued, was someone who refused to buckle in to the "valets of Moscow" and who answered a "slap with two solid punches," then, "oui, Messieurs, we are fascists." In the same article, the AF defined its version of clericalism as "resolutely ready to defend itself" and not "timid." Fascism, clericalism, and reactionary ideology shared the joint task of lifting the state out of the "mud" into which the Republic had lowered it.[35] Anti-Bolshevism and violent activism, common to all fascist parties, were openly espoused. At best, the AF was confused about its relationship with fascism. More likely, the AF saw a clear connection between its goals and fascist goals. Those who would brand the AF as clerical or reactionary should note that, in this instance, the AF had a very specific and militant view of what those terms meant, a view more fascist than conservative.

One hallmark of fascism is the merging of nationalism and socialism. For the Alsatian AF, once France absorbed the lesson that the nation, and not foreign interests, should be the focus of economic endeavor, then the social question could be addressed. The AF repeatedly stressed that "the Republic is the government of the foreign powers."[36] This, of course, implied the manipulation of France by Jews, Freemasons, and other assorted international plutocrats. The social problem was attributed to their baleful international influence on France. Xenophobia became the scapegoat for social inequity.

Alsace was a propaganda bonanza for the AF's national leadership. The return of the eastern departments provided a test case for the reassessment of the secular state. If Alsace and Lorraine could resist Herriot's maladroit attempt to extend France's anticlerical legislation to them, then the national struggle for religious liberty and the restoration of Catholicism as a pillar of French society would be given a shot in the arm. In the first issue of *Le National d'Alsace*, Léon Daudet castigated the Republic, which he believed "would quickly molest the Alsatians."[37] The Republic would inevitably renege on its promises to refrain from extending the laic laws to Alsace. Instead of simply disagreeing with the Republic and its anticlericalism, the AF violently assailed the whole system in the most offensive terms, taking refuge behind the motto "We do not confuse France with the present government."[38]

Maurras also stressed extreme anti-Germanism. This was a standard propaganda position for the national AF. According to Henri d'Halys, a frequent contributor to *Le National d'Alsace*, "France stands before two dangers that threaten it simultaneously . . . these are communism and Germany." As a result of this Germanophobia the AF often made wild accusations, as when Daudet claimed that "the laic laws, ostensibly from the Republic, are in reality of *boche* origin." The patent absurdity of such statements often alienated the Alsatian-speaking population. Nevertheless, it expressed quite succinctly the attitude of the pro-French urban bourgeoisie and it reinforced the AF's sense of mission and internal community by providing a clear and ever-present enemy.[39]

In response to the autonomist movement's powerful appeal, the local AF had to articulate its own regional platform, which it hoped would attract Alsatians. Pitting autonomism against regionalism, the AF argued that autonomism meant "detachment from France" and reintegration with Germany. Regionalism, however, was "the demand to destroy . . . centralization, in order to fully reliberate the provincial uniqueness and customs for the good of the entire land." Regionalism would also reconcile opposing classes "through the assertion of provincial, cultural, and religious commonalities." The advocacy of regionalism by no means represents an opposition to *étatism* as Eugen Weber would have it.[40] The centralized state that the AF opposed was the "jacobin" centralism of the parliamentary parties, not the firm rule of the king. To an Alsatian autonomist the "regionalism" of the AF was just another form of assimilation.

In order to attract Alsatians to its version of regionalism, the AF had to take a stand on the locally important issue of language in the school system. Declaring that "Herriot was not France," the Alsatian AF argued that imposing French as the only language taught in Alsatian schools was part of a broader attack on "devout Alsace."[41] The AF welded the defense of religion, family, language, and local customs into a circle of elements that constituted a community. Alsace should become bilingual, which would preserve the linguistic traditions of the area while binding Alsatians closer to France.[42] As early as 1920 the AF maintained that "in order to learn a language it is not necessary to kill the other that has always been spoken."[43] The ultimate goal was to bind Alsace to France. The AF pampered regional sensibilities as long as they did not conflict with the formation of a national community under the leadership of the Duc d'Orléans. Forcing the elimination of German would only have alienated the Alsatians from France, which served no French purpose.

The Alsatian AF suffered a serious blow on December 20, 1926, when the pope declared that Catholics should neither join the AF nor read its publications because it put politics before religion. One of the leading figures in the AF of Haut-Rhin, Fernand Heitz, articulated the AF's frustration with the pope's ruling in his correspondence with Bishop Ruch, a French veteran and "fervent patriot."[44] "Happily," wrote Heitz, "the church is eternal, its servants are mortal and the wind blows past the dome of St. Peter as always." Heitz was incensed. Only recently Bishop Ruch had praised the AF, yet now he painted the AF as a danger to the church.[45] The AF extended its duty to the Church to protecting it from itself and saw itself as more eternal than the pope. This pompous formulation was compelling to most of the AF faithful in Alsace, but not to the wider Catholic public.

Curiously, the AF refused to admit its political character. This, of course, was a common tendency of fascist movements, all of which equated politics with parliamentary parties and not with political ideology. The Alsatian AF resented that it was censored for putting politics before religion, while nothing was said about the Zukunft movement, which was nothing if not political.[46] Although Bishop Ruch condemned *Die Zukunft* in early December 1926 for the same reasons the pope condemned the AF, Ruch's malediction did not carry the same weight. The royalists even implied that the Church itself was political, since it allowed the UPR, clearly a political party, to organize Catholic youths "in a clearly political sphere," while forbidding the same Catholic youths from participating in the apolitical Camelots du Roi.[47] The Church used to represent eternal values but by the act of banning the AF it had proved itself to be practically on the same level as the Republic, leaving the AF the sole defender of France.

Despite the AF's public claims to the contrary, the papal renunciation of the movement was a devastating blow. Not that the party stalwarts lost heart; in fact they remained remarkably consistent and loyal. The Alsatian AF lost ground to the other more mainstream right-wing groups such as the UPR. *Le National* had ceased circulation by 1930 and the AF started a new paper, *La Province d'Alsace*. The police described royalism as "dead in Alsace" at the time of *Le National*'s disappearance and its replacement by *La Province d'Alsace*. Coupled with Poincaré's return to power, the loss of official Catholic support put the Alsatian AF into a period of limbo from which it never recovered.[48]

THE LÉGION

The first fascist group to challenge the AF was the Légion led by Antoine Rédier, a decorated veteran of the Great War. While the AF was expanding locally, the Légion initiated a radicalization of right-wing politics at the expense of the AF by demanding more immediate change and taking the military as its organizing model. Although more radical, the Légion's ideology was not inherently incompatible with that of the AF, or of other newly emerging right-wing groups. Initially loosely connected to the Jeunesses Patriotes, the Légion merged with the Faisceau in November 1925, after little more than a year of activity.

Founded in June 1924, the Légion originally consisted of only veterans but quickly expanded its membership to include civilians and even women. Civilian participation notwithstanding, the experience of World War I remained essential to Rédier's ideology. In his book *Comrades in Courage*, originally published in 1915, Rédier argued that the war revived a set of values that had been lacking in France since the revolution. Duty, bravery, authority, sacrifice, honor, and the common bond of *la patrie* were forged in the exclusively male confines of the trench. The battleground was no place for liberty. Nor was civil society, since it too required an attenuated and coordinated social effort in order to achieve victory. Rédier notes, "The war has changed them [the soldiers] profoundly. It has made good soldiers of them as well as good men. Will the miracle last forever?" Rédier hoped it would and that the lessons of Verdun would extend to peacetime. Thus, in 1915 Rédier was already arguing, "We must give authority and hierarchy, in turn, our unfailing devotion and accept with philosophy some hard constraints."[49]

Rédier's wartime experience shaped the political program of the Légion almost ten years later. Above all, Rédier objected to the liberal Third Republic and especially the Cartel des Gauches for its lack of discipline and authority. Parliament was a weak and indecisive "talking machine" that had the additional inherent flaw that the Cartel des Gauches could gain control of it.[50] Thus parliament, which included socialists, could officially promote the idea of a society divided along class lines. For those Frenchmen whose formative political experience had been the trenches (where equality in the face of death and the irrelevance of social division predominated), the idea of a class-oriented, political debating society was anathema. The Légion determined to arrest this apparent decadence and "unite under one authority" all of France, just as French soldiers had submitted to military authority.[51]

The Légion had a great deal in common with the so-called conservative leagues. In its programmatic statement, it clarified its relationship to the other national leagues. Its motto was simple: "No enemies on the right." The real enemy was the shared threat from the left. The Fédération Castelnau, the Union Civique, the Ligue des Patriotes, and the Anciens Combattants were too inert to be capable of "political action" but were "otherwise excellent" defensive leagues. The Ligue Millerand, associated with the Radical Party, contained "too many old parliamentarians" for Rédier's taste. The venerable AF had the right nationalistic attitude, but its royalism was fundamentally incapable of uniting all the French.[52] The goals of the conservative leagues and the Légion were the same, but in a typically fascist fashion the Légion stressed that its activism set it apart. The Légion promised to be more vigorous and to unite all the French instead of just those committed to royalism. Although it had no objection to conservative parliamentary activity, it preferred to restrict (or as the fascists saw it, to expand) its activity to the extraparliamentary arena.

The Légion drew its strength primarily from the provinces and did not compete well in Paris with the AF, the Faisceau, and the Jeunesses Patriotes, which by January 1926 had become significant forces in the capital. Actually, the Légion proved strongest in Lyons, Roubaix, Le Havre, Rouen, Angers, Saumur, Cholet, Châteauneuf-sur-Sarte, Enghien-les-Bains, Marseille, and of course Strasbourg. The police estimated that at the time of its merger with the Faisceau in November 1925 the Légion consisted of about ten thousand members, mostly from the provinces.[53]

As with the AF, the participation of the Alsatian social elites in a newly formed political movement such as the Légion was vital to its success. Deputies, leaders of existing vigorous political parties, members of the press, and officials in veterans' groups served a vital role in legitimizing an otherwise ephemeral movement. They provided contacts, respectability, and publicity. Above all, they protected the Légion from an apathetic and indifferent reception that would have banished it to utter obscurity.

Rédier's first visit to Strasbourg on January 12, 1925, to organize the movement in Alsace was attended by many notables in Alsace. One group that Rédier believed essential to ensure a sizable initial audience was the Union Nationale des Combattants (Groupe d'Alsace). Important figures from other local institutions were also recruited. Aloise Pfister, the secretary of the conservative, nationalist journal *L'Alsace Française*, was an *assesseur* on the guiding committee and had the task of spreading propaganda for the movement.[54] Other interested Alsatians included Joseph Weydmann, a general councillor and president of the Ligue des Catholiques d'Alsace, and Jules Jaeger, the director of the *Journal de l'Est* and *L'Alsace Française*. Jaeger also had the distinction of being tied to Millerand's Ligue Nationale Républicaine. A professor at Strasbourg University briefed Rédier on the subtleties of Alsatian politics in preparation for the March 5 inauguration meeting.[55]

Pierre Schmidt-Le-Roi, a leader in the UPR and later the leader of the APNA in Bas-Rhin, discussed with Rédier's local representative, J. M. Marty, the possibility that the UPR deputy Joseph Pfleger would support the Légion. Schmidt-Le-Roi himself was "very determined to continue, as much as possible," his support for the Légion. Involved in industry, Schmidt-Le-Roi at the time was also the chief of personnel at the Compagnie de Navigation Française Rhénane. Schmidt-Le-Roi claimed that the intensely pro-French Pfleger "did not oppose" the Légion and that he even "recognized the interest that it merited."[56] This was the same Pfleger who supported the AF. Although somewhat standoffish, Pfleger clearly did not oppose the Légion in the early part of 1925 and probably encouraged the participation of Schmidt-Le-Roi.

Another important personage listed as a dues-paying member of the Légion was the ex-deputy Anselme Laugel. Laugel was the type of public figure who, by virtue of his age, career, and commitment, commanded the necessary respect to legitimize the Légion. At the age of seventy-three, Laugel provided a tie to the prewar cultural autonomist movement. Laugel had left Alsace in 1870 but returned in 1891 to take over the family ironware business. He then served as *Conseiller général* in the village of Rosheim and was in the *Landesausschuss* (state commission) representing the town of Molsheim under the Germans. Laugel was the president of the Parti Républicain Démocratique et Social (Bas-Rhin section), until April 1924 when he resigned after the members voted to support the UPR. The example of Laugel, whose age and respectability belie the supposed youthful orientation of the fascists, underscores the importance of socially acceptable and conservative support to the Légion. These were the men with the money, ability, and influence necessary for a non-working-class movement to achieve success.[57]

The inconclusiveness of age as an ideological or organizational factor in the Légion is borne out by the age distribution of the core membership in Strasbourg. Members ranged in age from nineteen to seventy-three. Curiously, given the commonly held belief that the fascist movement was youth-oriented, four out of the ten whose age was given were over sixty. Youth certainly held its own; five of the ten were under thirty. No age was given for the other eighteen members, whose ages probably ranged from twenty-five to sixty. Although generalization is risky with such scanty data, youth did not seem to be a decisive social factor in this instance.

If there is a decisive social factor to be teased out, it is the lack of working-class support for the movement. The few members whose occupation can be traced included a merchant, an employee of the Mines de la Sarre, a teacher, an engineer, a hatter, a trainee at the Banque de France, and one departmental head at the Comptoir des Combustibles d'Alsace et de Lorraine.[58] Despite a fair amount of social diversity across the middle classes, few working-class representatives seem to have enrolled.

Just as the fascist appeal to the working class was more for the benefit of the bourgeois classes than for the blue-collar workers, the Légion's attitude toward women was more attractive to men than to women. In 1925, Rédier penned a brochure for a meeting of the Alsatian women's section, which laid out in greater detail his *Kinder, Küche, Kirche* (children, kitchen, church) prescription for female political and social behavior. The Légion's policy toward women was so morally and socially constricting that its appeal to women must have been limited. Women who evaded their social responsibility to reproduce would not be "tolerated" in the Légion. Women should not "have to enter into public life" but should find their "supreme consolation" in the Church. In addition, Rédier demanded a very strict code of behavior for women, because they "are responsible for the soul of tomorrow's French." Toward this end, he admonished women to "watch with severity your private life" and to act more like mothers than whores.[59] The *Kinder, Küche, Kirche* stereotype expressed a pervasive acceptance of dual spheres, which divided the world into two mutually exclusive domains based on gender: the household and public society. The attempt to preserve a nineteenth-century bourgeois perception of gender relations reinforces the argument that the Légion was middle-class.

The Légion showed a typical fascist ambiguity about women, even within the context of its belief in the superiority of the woman in the household. Rédier argued that society is hierarchical, which meant that women are inevitably subservient to men. Political activity by women should be limited to the advising of male family members "that there is a hierarchy of interests and that an honest man puts the highest before the least and those of the state before those of his own."[60] Not only does this statement imply that the position of women in the hierarchy is lower than that of men, it touches on the fundamental premise of fascism that each individual—man, woman, or child—must remain subordinate to the communal good (invariably defined as the state) and accept their "natural" position in society. The liberal principle that elevates the idea of individual liberty above the communal good (for the communal good) is thereby expressly negated. Women's suffrage as an extension of liberal philosophy is likewise rejected, even though many on the right believed women would support the clerical right.[61] Rédier expressed some of the most openly antifeminist sentiments of any of the revolutionary right, even going so far as to deny women the right to vote, a relatively unusual position for the French right.

Disgruntled at the "authoritarianism" of the Jeunesses Patriotes, Rédier and his ten thousand activists joined the Faisceau in November 1925.[62] The Légion's short life might seem to warrant the conclusion that it was an insignificant phenomenon or that fascism was strictly a fringe movement. Its significance, however, transcended its membership. The Légion was the first fascist movement that protested against the flabbiness of its parent right-wing parties, including the established AF. The existence of a more activist movement on its right prodded the AF to defend its position and become more radical. In conjunction with the AF, the Faisceau, and the JP, the activity of the Légion popularized and exploited popular Alsatian discontent with the government in Alsace.

THE FAISCEAU

On November 11, 1925, Georges Valois and a group of his followers commemorated the valor of French World War I veterans by solemnly gathering at the Arc de Triomphe in Paris to inaugurate the Faisceau. Dedicated to the radical overthrow of the French parliamentary system, the Faisceau had evolved out of Valois's weekly journal, *Le Nouveau Siècle*, founded in February 1925 under the auspices of the AF. Like the JP, the Légion, the Alsatian autonomist movement, and the AF, the Faisceau was a direct response to the right-wing fear of the left after the May 1924 elections. Following a surge of support from December 1925 to June 1926, the Faisceau showed real signs of nationwide popularity. The first Alsatian chapter opened in March 1926 and the Faisceau grew very quickly, especially in Haut-Rhin. Yet by 1927 the Faisceau had faded into obscurity and Valois had moved on to greener pastures.

The first trace of Faisceau activity in Alsace came in the spring of 1926, somewhat later than the national movement, of which the first growth spurt took place in December 1925 and January 1926. By mid-January the national movement registered about fifty new members per day. About three hundred people attended the inaugural meeting on March 15, 1926, in Mulhouse, but only twenty joined. In spite of a lag behind some other regions, the Faisceau had considerable success in the eastern provinces, largely because of a "lively discontent in the region," due to economic and nationality problems.[63]

The Alsatian Faisceau quickly caught up with the national movement, however. The national leadership—Georges Valois, Philippe Barrès, and Jacques Arthuys—spread their message during a two-day tour of the recovered provinces. Meetings in Mulhouse and Strasbourg on April 14 and 15, 1926, attracted a total of nearly thirty-five hundred sympathizers and were among the largest rallies in France. These rallies were at a time of great hope for the Alsatian fascist movement since the Faisceau's national leadership "counted heavily on Alsace and the Alsatians to set off the movement."[64]

Smaller meetings also effectively recruited activists, although they lacked the presence of the national leadership that was so critical in the mass rallies. On July 16, 1926, for example, somewhere between 250 and 300 Colmariens attended a meeting of the Faisceau sponsored by the Mulhouse chapter. As in the larger rallies, a local Alsatian speaker gave a synopsis of the talks in dialect, in order to reach out symbolically to Alsatians who were attracted to the autonomist movement. It is doubtful whether very many of the audience spoke only Alsatian, since a synopsis of the talks in dialect would have hardly been worth sitting through the tedium of several hours of incomprehension, despite all the fascist pageantry.

The precise size of the Faisceau is uncertain. Unlike the AF, the Faisceau did not publish a regional paper, which makes it difficult to assess the strength of the movement in the recovered provinces. This was a curious omission in an age when newspapers flourished and since the national leadership considered the eastern departments to be key regions. The national leadership focused on selling papers in Paris and campaigned vigorously in the Nord and Pas-de-Calais, using a very selective regional approach.[65] Perhaps given another year, the Faisceau would have established an Alsatian paper, but limited financial resources and hard political choices may have relegated the development of Alsace to a low priority, despite the relative enthusiasm of Alsatians for the movement. The failure to spread its message through a regional journal was a critical mistake for the Faisceau and may have been part of a systematic propaganda failure that contributed to the Faisceau's early demise.

Nevertheless, an estimate of the relative strength of the Faisceau in Alsace is possible. In December 1925, shortly after the official founding of the Faisceau, national membership stood at around five thousand.[66] The Faisceau expanded rapidly. By June 1926 there were about forty thousand on the rolls, of which twenty thousand were *légionnaires,* and another twenty thousand in the corporate organizations and the *faisceaux civiques*.[67] Since many of the *légionnaires* also joined the civilian branches, the actual number of fascists was probably much lower, perhaps as low as twenty-five thousand. Considering that Paris accounted for around fifteen thousand members, that Alsace held between six hundred and one thousand members (around a tenth of the regional membership) would have made it a major regional power.[68]

The Faisceau's social composition, like that of the AF, the JP, and the Légion, was skewed toward the middle and upper-middle classes. Despite the party's insistent rhetorical appeal to the lower classes, none of the Alsatian members were factory workers or even peasants. But the Faisceau's roots reached deep into the propertied classes. Most research on the Faisceau has focused exclusively on ideology, which unfortunately has obscured the relationship between ideology and social support. As a result, historians such as Zeev Sternhell mistakenly characterize the Faisceau as originating in the left, because they place too much value on a literal reading of the propaganda without critically examining whom the propaganda was directed toward and why.[69] Valois's books and his articles in *Le Nouveau Siècle* (the national newspaper), for example, emphasized the leftist aspects of the movement, not because this genuinely reflected its roots but because he sought to co-opt and recruit the left in order to validate the upper classes' belief in the viability of an organic, hierarchical, and harmonious society. Only recently (in Soucy's book, *French Fascism: The First Wave*) has a truer picture of the conservative origins of the Faisceau emerged.

Industrialists were an important source of money for Valois. Five out of the eight sponsors of *Le Nouveau Siècle* were industrialists. François Coty, the perfume magnate who later subsidized the Solidarité Française, donated more than 1 million francs.[70] Coty's support for the Faisceau was not accidental; he indiscriminately underwrote virtually every radical right movement from the AF to his own Solidarité Française. Given the prominence of industrialists in the national movement, the support of Alsatian industrialists is not surprising. When Jacques Arthuys reminded his Mulhouse audience that he "too was an industrialist," he was explicitly soliciting this class in the expectation that they were in attendance.[71]

Although factory owners and the haute-bourgeoisie played a key role in the party's funding, the rank and file drew primarily from the professional middle classes. The audience of a meeting in Sélestat, for example, consisted "principally of small bankers, bank officers and administrative officers."[72] At the Strasbourg mass meeting in April 1926, police described the crowd of between fifteen hundred and two thousand as consisting of "interior French, government bureaucrats, numerous engineers from the Pechelbronn mines, some women, and ecclesiastics in their cassocks."[73] The following day the national leadership of the Faisceau completed its tour of Alsace-Lorraine by holding a meeting in Metz. Attending this meeting were a significant number of notables. Several priests, lawyers, doctors, merchants, "numerous" lycée professors, and members of the Ligue de la République were prominent at this meeting. Communists, railroad employees, and members of the AF were not allowed to attend.[74] The Faisceau excluded leftists because they feared disruption of their meeting and because they did not expect to gain any converts.

The middle- and upper-middle-class orientation of the Alsatian Faisceau mirrored the composition of the national movement, which was predominantly middle- and upper-middle-class. Several municipal councillors lent their prestige to an exceptionally well-attended meeting in Versailles, showing again the importance of elite support. In Melun, not far from Paris, in a meeting composed of about three hundred members and sympathizers of the Faisceau, the police noted that "many *commerçants* were present."[75] According to the police, "The members came from all milieus of 'patrons,' factory managers, a majority of veterans, retired officers, a few, very few, old provincial aristocrats. The greatest number come from the middle classes: engineers, accountants, some workers."[76] About ninety engineers showed up at an organizational meeting in Paris for the Union Corporative des Ingénieurs, an affiliate of the Faisceau. Engineers were prominent in the Faisceau largely because of their uncertain economic status, and their technocratic bent. Alienated from decision making by the parliamentary system, they perceived themselves as an elite class that knew how to get things done.[77]

Valois's appeal to the workers reads much more like an appeal to the propertied classes than a serious attempt to convert the proletariat. "Fascism is the only movement able to serve the workers' interests without leading the workers into useless revolts, sterile strikes, or unemployment," wrote Valois. Fascism "is the regime of production rationally organized."[78] Rational organization was a buzzword for control from above. Those middle- and upper-class Frenchmen who sought order were more likely to be reassured by a philosophy that argued for a form of quietism than were the workers, many of whom seem attracted to the left precisely because it offered them control over their own destiny (perhaps for the first time) and also permitted activism.

For the industrialists, professionals, engineers, bureaucrats, and bankers who chose to support the Faisceau, the idea of an organic society—where the elite equaled the head and the working classes equaled the arms—was attractive because it sanctioned the existing relationship between classes. Hierarchy within the nation was both reactionary, because it was a sort of reimposition of the status quo, and revolutionary, because it demanded a new dedication to the state and modern forms of corporate representation. In neither case was this threatening to the middle- and upper-class individuals who supported fascist movements like the Faisceau. In times of crisis, they were more willing to accept the fascist notion of a modern, non-neutral state that would define, impose, and maintain the social and political norms and equilibrium.[79] The imposition of an ideology that encouraged all classes to accept their place in the state hierarchy reduced the possibility of a Bolshevist appropriation of private property and justified the oppression of dissent. Although Valois, like most fascists, argued for a redefinition of the elite along more democratic lines (and, above all, by the strength of their allegiance to the nation-state), this was scarcely threatening to the propertied classes. After all, they already held the powerful positions in society and had the best access to the education and knowledge that ensured social and political success. Allowing a few men of talent to rise from the laboring classes did not fundamentally threaten a group that already considered itself superior. The ideas of discipline and order also appealed to the conservative and radical right. The Faisceau's organization, which stressed obedience and a military chain of command as a means of ensuring a decisive government (in contrast to the Third Republic), was more attractive to those members of society who felt they belonged in the upper echelons of command.

Valois's firm espousal of a strong, central state also appealed to the middle and upper classes, although, paradoxically, in Alsace this was complicated by an appeal to decentralization. Unlike most French fascist leaders, Valois praised the French Revolution because it was "the first attempt at the creation of the modern state." The Faisceau, of course, was to be the second and more successful attempt at establishing the modern state. "The unitary state, which has one leader" was Valois's ideal.[80]

Nevertheless, the Alsatian members sought to increase the local appeal of the Faisceau by altering the national movement's advocacy of an authoritarian, centralized state to the advocacy of a state that was dependent on, and responsive to, regional representation. At a meeting in early October 1926 the head of the Strasbourg chapter, Edmond Schiffmacher, advocated a "regionalism based on a pervasive decentralization." Even the national leadership toned down its centralism for Alsatian consumption. Philippe Barrès, for example, told the audience of a Mulhouse rally that the Faisceau was "against the overly rapid assimilation of Alsace-Lorraine."[81]

Two conclusions can be drawn from this, particularly if the Faisceau is still to be considered fascist. First, the fascist ideal of a totalitarian or authoritarian state was a flexible one, dependent more on regional membership and views than either the Nazi or the Italian model would suggest.[82] Second, Alsace was dominated by the assimilation-versus-autonomy debate, and the Faisceau, like the other fascist movements, had to placate regional sensibilities.

Family values and the insistence on the sovereignty of the *chef de la famille* (head of household) provided a moral bulwark for social quietism. In the Verdun program, Valois demanded that the nation have a "true representation of national interests, under the form of two assemblies: an Assembly of professions (delegates from the corporations), and an Assembly of the heads of families (delegates from the communes)." Corporative representation was supposed to unite the "heads of enterprises and the workers" in a common effort to raise productivity, profits, and provide a trickle-down benefit to the workers of higher wages.[83] The elevation of the family head to the status of regional deputy would have favored respectable and propertied males.

Although Valois was adamant about the inclusion of Jews into the Faisceau, they were notably absent from the Alsatian membership rolls. Valois, in theory, held that believers of any religious faith could become, indeed were, good Frenchmen; he insisted that Jews were acceptable as members of the French nation. In any event, he explicitly argued that other solutions—such as killing all the Jews, sending them to Palestine, or setting up a separate government for Jews—were untenable. In this he differed from Maurras and the AF, who paid lip service to the unifying principle of *la France* but, in reality, espoused a virulent form of antisemitism and made the Church a necessary support for the foundation of a harmonious France. The nation, not the Church, was the unifying force for Valois.

The characterization of the Faisceau as philosemitic must be taken, however, with a grain of salt. Valois conceded that there was some justification for antisemitism and tacitly opposed the influx of foreign Jews. Ultimately, he argued that "there are Jews in France. It is necessary to live with them and to ensure that the communal life not be a dupery for anyone." This scarcely reads like an enthusiastic embracing of Jews into the corporate state. Unlike most fascists, Valois lauded pious Jews, whose virtues and morality were a plus for the nation. He attacked, however, the "emancipated Jews, who are the new adorers of the golden calf and whose dissolute lifestyle is a scandal for believers of all faiths."[84] His obvious ambivalence about Jews and the way he defined who was an acceptable Jew ultimately do not support the claim that Valois was not an antisemite.

Unquestionably, some working-class men and women joined the national Faisceau. Nevertheless, the working classes were largely aware of the party's inherent bias against them and consequently joined in disproportionately low numbers. The Faisceau's constant rhetoric that workers must be incorporated into the Faisceau had little effect on the bulk of Alsatian blue-collar workers. Although the Faisceau made a very vocal and visible appeal to the working classes, and was more successful than the AF or the Légion in attracting workers, lower-class members did not join in their capacity as workers but as veterans, youths, activists, or simply to impress their supervisors. It is ironic that, at a small meeting of party stalwarts, Schiffmacher lectured on the importance of the workers to the Faisceau's cause before an audience consisting of an inspector general of a social insurance organization, two *représentants de commerce,* a salesman, a manager of a store, and the son of the director of the Minoteries Alsaciennes. None of the young men attending were either blue-collar workers or farmers. They agreed in principle to the inclusion of "elite workers" in the hierarchy of the Faisceau, but their commitment to this ideal did not extend to actual practice.[85]

The lack of lower-class support can be deduced from the occupations of the members of the local Faisceau about whom we have information. Virtually none of the leaders of the movement in the recovered provinces were from a communist or socialist background.[86] This differs only slightly from the national membership, which had a token number of ex-leftists and working-class representatives. Converts to the Faisceau from communism—as in the famous case of Marcel Delagrange, the former communist mayor of Périgueux—were often already pariahs in their own parties and were searching for a means to continue their ambitious political careers. Men like Delagrange were obviously not representative and served primarily a symbolic value. In fact, the oft-cited perception that the Faisceau grew more leftist was probably not so much because of an inherent leftist orientation of the movement but because of the growing desperation of the Faisceau to regain its activism by proving it could unify the nation. Without proof of its activism, it could not sustain momentum for their movement. None of this mattered in Alsace, where there was little confusion or change in the political orientation or the sociological composition of the party over time. The leaders of the Faisceau repeated to a top-heavy middle- to upper-class audience that they intended to be a national, classless movement.

Finally, the peasants, usually considered a mainstay of European fascism, were noticeably absent from the Alsatian Faisceau. A fundamental linguistic and cultural gulf separated the peasants from Valois. Most Alsatian peasants spoke only a form of Alsatian dialect, so the linguistic, cultural, and class bias of the Faisceau toward France was foreign to them. In any event, the peasants found better representation in the UPR or in the autonomist movement, both of which catered directly to the regional sensibilities of the farmers.

Support for the Faisceau varied significantly according to department. Bas-Rhin, traditionally the more German of the two departments, was a relatively barren field for recruitment. The city of Strasbourg only mustered between 150 and 200 members at the time of the huge mass rally in April 1926.[87] Apart from Sélestat, there was very little organization outside Strasbourg. Recruitment in Haut-Rhin could be erratic, yet on the whole was more successful than in its northern neighbor. As of the beginning of April 1926, Colmar had no organized branch of the Faisceau.[88] This was probably because of the strength of the autonomist movement in Colmar, and the resistance of the local notables to a rabidly pro-French organization. Colmar continued to lag behind Mulhouse, in spite of repeated attempts by the Mulhouse chapter to organize meetings and create a separate section there.[89]

In sharp contrast, Mulhouse, which appeared to be a stronghold for the Faisceau, was the base of organization for Haut-Rhin. The first signs of Faisceau activism in March 1926 were in Mulhouse. The Mulhouse chapter had sufficient resources to go from house to house visiting all those who had enlisted in the army *(engagés volontaires)* rather than rely on the cheaper and more labor-efficient method of visiting a meeting of the veterans' associations or holding a rally.[90] Although less information is available on the size of the Mulhouse chapter than on that of Strasbourg, it clearly was the largest and most influential section in Alsace.

Both locally and nationally the summer of 1926 was the high point; from then on the movement disintegrated. The Alsatian and national Faisceau were now coordinated and the causes of their respective collapses closely related. After a mass rally in Rheims, attended by some twelve thousand fascists, the national Faisceau lost momentum. By September 1926, the number of those in the Faisceau's Légions (as opposed to Rédier's Légions) in Bas-Rhin was around one hundred, down considerably from April 1926.[91] The membership of the Strasbourg chapter and the Bas-Rhin were probably very close to synonymous. Police reported that the Faisceau in Strasbourg had managed to accumulate about three hundred members in June 1926, but that by September it had lost ground as a result of restrictions placed on reserve officers and the withdrawal of almost the entire contingent from the Pechelbronn mines.[92]

It was the Faisceau's inability to sustain its local activity that caused defections.[93] The all-important student activists were on vacation, more interested in sight-seeing or relaxation than political adventurism. As a result, the Faisceau failed to build on its initial local successes over the summer, and the local organization languished. In part this was due to Poincaré's firm rule and the elimination of the threatening Cartel des Gauches. More important, however, was the Faisceau's inept and rudderless national leadership. Over the course of the fall, members waited for some sign that the Faisceau retained its dynamic character, but they were repeatedly disappointed. In this sense, the vicissitudes of the national party had a major impact on the local chapter. With the changed national circumstances and the vacillation of the Faisceau's leaders, the Alsatian movement languished.

By November 1926, the movement had fallen off even more. A mere forty to eighty attended a Strasbourg meeting on November 18.[94] The movement, at least in Bas-Rhin, was dead by February 1927, well before Valois began to disassociate himself from the Faisceau. Doubtful that the Faisceau would follow through on its promise of activism and aware of the declining fortunes of the movement, most members quit the Faisceau and rejoined the old standby, the Action Française. At least the AF had longevity and tradition to recommend it, and since the Faisceau's activism had proved itself a hoax, the justification for leaving the AF was gone. Members of the Faisceau simply ceased paying their dues. Within six months, the national movement had also "totally disappeared from the preoccupations of the French public."[95] Without public attention, the Faisceau could not maintain its momentum. Out of sight, out of mind. Although this is true of any political party, it was doubly true for a fascist party predicated on activist revolutionary principles. The Faisceau's success in Alsace was limited to about nine months, from March to November 1926.

A number of historians have argued that the Faisceau faded away because of the disenchantment of its financial backers over the increasingly leftist tendencies of Valois.[96] Valois, however, had always stressed the evils of the financiers and the two hundred families whose tyranny allegedly oppressed the French economy. This was not seen as particularly problematic by industrialists when they decided to support the movement. From the very beginning, the Faisceau expressed a desire to incorporate the working class in a way that was not threatening to the propertied classes. Even when Valois grew impatient with fascism and moved toward syndicalism, his view of the solution to France's problems remained much the same.[97]

It is true, however, that the industrialists—and, for that matter, the rank-and-file membership—became disillusioned with the Faisceau and began to back away. The scales, however, did not suddenly fall from their eyes allowing them to perceive the leftist nature of the Faisceau. They knew all along what the Faisceau stood for and what it intended to do; that is why they joined in the first place. The real reason for the deflation of the movement was its failure to produce results. When Valois turned out not to be a Mussolini and the Faisceau proved to be no better than the AF, its raison d'être ceased to exist and money and membership vanished. Poincaré proved more effective than Valois at countering the socialist threat. In this context, it is significant that many of the disenchanted members of the Faisceau rejoined the AF.

Part of the disillusionment of the financial sponsors of the Faisceau was a direct result of the intense pressure applied by Maurras and the AF. This manifested itself in practical terms when, for example, François Coty withdrew his support for fear of offending the AF. Most members of the Faisceau were longtime AF members and sympathizers, who, when faced with a choice between loyalty to the old party or to the new, opted to stick with the old. Had Valois been able to orchestrate his departure from the AF without personally antagonizing its leadership (a virtual impossibility given the overlap in membership, which directly threatened the organizational viability and the ideological sovereignty of the AF), then perhaps the Faisceau could have continued to garner financial sustenance for years to come. Valois in effect initiated this conflict by insisting that the raison d'être of the Faisceau was to take up the flag of radical right-wing activism from the dying hand of the deaf Maurras. He gambled that the AF was so moribund he would be able to seize the initiative and unify the right before the AF could respond. This was a gamble that he lost, and the protracted struggle between the AF and the Faisceau had a corrosive effect on the unity of the right.

The Alsatian Faisceau lost its ability to define the political discourse through ideological inadequacy and through organizational deficiency. It is ironic that a movement which prided itself on having streamlined decision making through the imposition of a rigidly hierarchical organization should have lost its momentum through a lack of decisiveness, responsiveness, and flexibility on the part of the authoritarian leadership. The local movement became so pathetic that, in the fall of 1926, Schiffmacher tried unsuccessfully to revive its flagging fortunes by taking up the regional themes of the Heimatbund.[98]

. . .

The Légion and the Faisceau arose in Alsace out of a dual hostility to the Third Republic and to the *Heimatbewegung*. In this context the AF did not initially seem to be determined enough to adequately defend nationalistic ideology from the autonomists or, for that matter, to present a class defense of the bourgeoisie against the economic and governmental dithering of the Republic. Rédier and Valois represented fresh approaches, which offered a more profound commitment to attacking the Cartel des Gauches and to tightening the nation's communal bonds. The Légion and the Faisceau struggled against their parent, the AF, to improve the radical right's message and to move beyond the AF in terms of organization. By 1927 the organizational initiatives of French fascism had petered out: the AF was on the defensive because of the papal condemnation; the Légion had disappeared; and Valois had left fascism to dabble in syndicalism. The failure of the Faisceau was not a result of the ephemeral nature of the fascist movement but of the successful defense by the older fascist and conservative groups of their superior position and the changing political and economic environment that defused the activism of many conservatives.

Although their activism in Alsace arose concurrently, the AF, with its Dreyfus era roots, was in a sense the ancestor and the Faisceau, with its almost modernist attempt at organizational fratricide, was the offspring. It is not an accident that the Faisceau was an offshoot of the AF. The struggle between the parent and the child, however, represented the first powerful push of French fascism.

In explaining both the rise and the fall of the first generation of fascism in 1924–1926, one factor seems particularly notable. The fascisms of this period were far more sedate, technocratic, and ultimately middle-class than their 1930s successors. Impressed by Mussolini's apparently successful amalgamation of radical and populist dynamism with conservative interests, French conservatives embraced fascism and shaped it in their own image. The 1920s fascists were less populist than they aimed to be, and less revolutionary than "hegemonic"—adapting populist rhetoric and the model of Italy to maintain and legitimize the status quo, and their place in it.

The middle-class and conservative membership of these three groups reacted radically to the Cartel des Gauches, the explosion of separatism, and the uncertainty of economic and social life after World War I by creating and joining fascist movements. When radical activity produced nothing and the political situation was alleviated by Henri Poincaré's rise, these groups beat a retreat from the radical abyss to the relative comfort of the AF or the mainstream parties. They were no less fascist for backing away. The fundamental instability of the Third Republic in the form of a critical lack of commitment by the propertied French in Alsace remained and boded ill for the future. The underlying support for fascism had not evaporated and would resurface in the 1930s.

THE SECOND GENERATION OF FASCISM

PART TWO

The 1930s

BEEFSTEAK NAZIS?

THE ALSATIAN COMMUNIST AUTONOMISTS

In general, conversions from communism to fascism have been a source of historical controversy. Were ex-communists, like the "beefsteak Nazis" in Germany, "brown on the outside, red on the inside"?[1] This interpretation posits that conversion to Nazism was superficial and opportunistic and implies that fascism had its roots in communism. Opposing this view is the idea that fascism was largely a right-wing phenomenon. According to this interpretation, communists who converted to fascism jettisoned their Marxist ideology and became well-done Nazis, brown all the way through. The case of the communist autonomists, the only group in Alsace that did not come to fascism from the right, substantiates the latter argument.

The term *communist autonomist* refers to those Marxist Alsatians whose affinity for Germany caused them to place the issue of Alsatian autonomy above the traditional Marxist concern for class conflict.[2] Although not a contemporary term, the label *communist autonomist* enables the reader to follow this group through various incarnations with a sense of its continuity, and in fact, the term semantically mimics the group's transformation from communist to autonomist. Unfortunately, the label obscures the fact that Charles Hueber and his cohorts began as dedicated communists. Hueber, for example, rose to prominence in the German socialist party, founded the PCF in Alsace, and held a leadership position within the PCF as a deputy to the National Assembly. Yet to call the group Alsatian communists would confuse the Alsatians who remained faithful to the PCF after 1929 with the group surrounding Hueber. Nor would the label autonomist communist fit, since the PCF remained committed to autonomism long after the communist autonomists had drifted away from communism. Implicit in the use of *communist autonomist* is the crucial transformation from communism to Nazism that motivates this chapter. At the same time, the modifier *communist* maintains an important distinction from the clerical and right-wing autonomists, who arrived at Nazism by a different path.

Under Charles Hueber, the charismatic leader of the Alsatian communist autonomists, the PCF became the most vigorous advocate of autonomism in the mid-1920s, calling for the severance of all ties with France and a return to Germany. Their commitment to autonomy led them to migrate ideologically from communism to fascism in search of a German identity. In so doing they foreshadowed the transformation of more prominent socialists and communists into fascists, such as Marcel Déat, Hendrik de Man, and Jacques Doriot, who all abandoned the centrality of class for the pursuit of a national community.[3]

The evolution from communism to Nazism took place in two stages, which illustrate the difference between the 1920s and the 1930s. The first stage took place between 1918 and 1929, when the communist autonomists shed their affiliation with the French communists. During this period Hueber and his followers dropped the centrality of economics and class as the driving force of revolution in favor of cultural affinity for Germany, which in their view constituted the impulse for revolution in Alsace. The second stage took place in the mid-1930s when the communist autonomists became Nazi.

FROM FRENCH COMMUNISM TO OPPOSITION COMMUNISM, 1918–1929

Hueber's formative political experience, like that of most communist autonomists, took place during the period of German control over Alsace.[4] Born in 1883, Hueber opened the first Alsatian section of the metalworkers syndicate in 1900 and, in 1910, became the general secretary of the Alsace-Lorraine branch of the German socialist party. During World War I Hueber served in the German army, reaching the rank of sergeant. When revolution broke out in Germany in 1918, Hueber was prominent among the leaders of the Strasbourg soldiers' council.[5]

Immediately at war's end, Hueber advocated "neutralism," which sought to turn Alsace-Lorraine into an independent, free state that would act as a bridge between Germany and France. The quixotic idea of a neutral Alsace had its roots in prewar German socialist policy, which, accepting the legitimacy of German interest in the region, had promoted the idea that Alsace should become a neutral area guaranteed by Germany.[6] Once the Treaty of Versailles officially reincorporated Alsace-Lorraine into France, Hueber's neutralism became separatism, which advocated breaking away from France.

Hueber had a strong mercenary motive for his early support of separatism. Indeed, the question of finances played a persistent role throughout the interwar period, strengthening his ties to Germany and facilitating his decision to support Nazism. According to the French police, Hueber was in the pay of a separatist who dispensed German money to Alsatian autonomists in 1919.[7] Hueber's take amounted to a thousand francs a month, with occasional demands in special circumstances for as much as ten thousand francs. German money enabled Hueber to sustain a consistent level of activism in the form of strikes, meetings, and pamphlets.[8] Such support was certainly not forthcoming from the French left. Reliance on money from Germany and his evident Germanophilia continued to haunt Hueber and the communist autonomists but did not at this juncture constitute an irrevocable turn toward Nazism. The German nationalism of the communist autonomists in the early years of French rule was a germ that, nurtured by the Alsatian malaise, contributed to their transformation into Nazis.

Hueber's radicalism continued into the 1920s when he led the movement among Alsatian socialists to join Lenin and the Third International. The majority of Alsatian delegates to the December 1920 Congress of Tours voted, like Hueber and most members of the French socialist party, for the creation of the Parti Communiste Français (PCF).[9] This pattern was consistent with the general split in France between the socialists and the communists, where the communists had the overwhelming majority of members, but the socialists retained most of the leaders. Despite losing control of the local socialist paper to the moderate socialists, Hueber had built a viable new party journal, *Die Neue Welt,* by the end of January 1921.[10] In its first year the Communist Party in Alsace consisted of six thousand card-carrying members and another thousand in the communist youth group.[11] At this point, Hueber's position at the head of the Alsatian communists was unassailable. The regional branch of the PCF seemed poised for growth.

Alsatian members of the French socialist party, the Section Française de l'Internationale Ouvrière (SFIO), joined the Third International for different reasons than their interior French counterparts. Their roots in the German socialist party with its Marxist tenor and tight organization differentiated the Alsatian socialists from their French comrades. Rosa Luxemburg and Karl Liebknecht were more familiar to the Alsatians than the French revolutionary syndicalists or Jean Jaurès. Most Alsatian socialists had served in the German army, which alienated them from French socialists who had supported the French war effort. Many Alsatian veterans, moreover, had fought on the eastern front and had witnessed, or even participated in, the Russian Revolution.[12] Finally, many Alsatian socialists, including Hueber, formed Alsatian soviets in the wake of the unsuccessful German revolution of 1918.[13]

Of the two departments comprising Alsace, support for the Communist Party was much stronger in Bas-Rhin than in Haut-Rhin. In September 1920, before the formation of the PCF, the Haut-Rhin chapter of the SFIO had 4,300 members, slightly more than the 3,000 in Bas-Rhin. A year later, the number of communists in Bas-Rhin had catapulted to 4,600, owing to the dynamism of Hueber's leadership and his effective mobilization of the cultural dissatisfaction of German-speaking workers, particularly in Strasbourg. This figure represented the fifth-highest departmental total in France. Haut-Rhin, however, evolved in the opposite direction. Of the 4,300 socialists in 1920, only 1,500 had become communists a year later. Haut-Rhin's lack of enthusiasm for communism stemmed from the department's relatively pro-French disposition as compared to Bas-Rhin.[14]

The nucleus of communist support in Bas-Rhin came primarily from Protestant and urban areas. Lutheran Alsatians had a strong cultural affinity for Germany that favored the Germanophilia of the communists, even when they despised communism. Drulingen, for instance, a predominantly (over 75 percent) Protestant canton in northwest Bas-Rhin, had an unusually high percentage of support (between 15 and 25 percent) for the Communist Party between 1924 and 1928. Brumath and Schiltigheim, bordering on Strasbourg, had significant Protestant populations and were also strongholds of the Communist Party.[15]

Until the outbreak of autonomist discontent in 1924, French and Alsatian communists fundamentally agreed on policy. Indeed, Hueber and his followers during this period could be more aptly described as Alsatian communists than as communist autonomists, because they hewed so closely to the party line. Alsatian communists, for example, denounced clericalism as a bourgeois tool of oppression, a position they reversed after 1924. Above all, the Alsatian communists worked assiduously to advance the cause of the proletariat, attacking in turn socialists, conservatives, the state, and the Church.[16] Hueber's prominence as leader of one of the party's largest branches, editor of the regional edition of *L'Humanité,* and one of the few communist deputies in the National Assembly was indicative of the extent of the communist autonomists' assimilation into the PCF.

Sometimes regional and national party concerns meshed, as in the case of education. Both the Alsatian and the French communist leadership opposed the officially imposed "direct" method, which banished German and Alsatian from the classroom. Autonomists, and in fact most Alsatians, rejected the elimination of German in a region where over 80 percent of the population spoke a German dialect.[17] The peasants and working classes would labor under a considerable educational disadvantage vis-à-vis the more Francophone middle class. The direct method merely increased the cultural and class schism within Alsatian society to the disadvantage of working-class Alsatians.

Responses to the French occupation of the Ruhr in 1923 epitomized the complex relationship between Alsatian and French communists. On the one hand, Alsatians became spokesmen for the PCF in an important international issue and led the French party in advocating international solidarity with the German working classes. Hueber's stature in the party rose as a result of his participation in an international communist meeting in Essen to formulate strategy for German resistance to the French occupation. Arrest by the French authorities for undermining French diplomacy further enhanced his reputation within the PCF.

On the other hand, the Ruhr controversy had a special relevance for Alsace. Alsatian communists were uniquely suited to confer with the Kommunistische Partei Deutschland (KPD) because they were ex-German socialists and shared an opposition to arbitrary French occupation. Hueber supported German armed resistance against the French army because the situation in the Ruhr was analogous to Alsace's. The Ruhr controversy generated considerable interest within Alsace, and Hueber's arrest endowed him with a local notoriety that contributed to his election to the National Assembly the following year.[18] Alsatian communists simultaneously solidified their affiliation with the French and the German communist parties, while subtly advancing regional concerns.

The emergence in 1925 of Alsatian autonomism as a French issue meant that the PCF, like all the parties in Alsace, had to take a stand.[19] In September the party finally endorsed the position that Alsace suffered under the dual oppression of the French nation and the bourgeoisie. At the Congress of Strasbourg the PCF declared, "The police, officers, authorities, and bureaucrats of German imperialism have been replaced by the police, officers, authorities, and bureaucrats of French imperialism."[20] With the blessing of national leaders such as Maurice Thorez, the delegates at the congress espoused self-government, withdrawal of the French presence, and abolition of financial and economic exploitation by France. This was to be followed by a free plebiscite to determine the fate of Alsace. The French communists stuck to this position, remaining just as autonomist, and even separatist, as the Alsatians until the formation of the Popular Front in 1934.[21]

Despite apparent ideological compatibility, the PCF expelled the communist autonomists in 1929 in a move that cost the party popular and organizational support in Alsace. The break resulted ostensibly from tactical differences in electoral politics. On a deeper level, however, the rupture involved the evolution of a differing order of priorities. For the communist autonomists, autonomism superseded all other questions. The exploitation of the working classes by the bourgeoisie could only be addressed after the resolution of the national question. The French communists, however, viewed the Alsatian malaise as a secondary manifestation of bourgeois French imperialism.

Hueber's inflammatory speech in Alsatian dialect to the National Assembly on December 8, 1927, typified the communist autonomists' approach to the Alsatian question. Supported by the communist deputies, Hueber declared "German is my mother tongue and that of the majority of Alsace-Lorrainers." With the full support of the French communists, Hueber made clear that the Third Republic was a deceitful hoax whose real function was to oppress the working classes and to colonize Alsace-Lorraine.[22] Hueber's vituperative attack on French language and culture so shocked the members of the French National Assembly that they expunged significant portions of his address from the record. Stung by the cultural insult of his speaking German in the National Assembly, French patriots attacked the entire autonomist movement on the grounds that Hueber and other Alsatians were in the pay of the Germans.[23]

The PCF, while supportive of Hueber's position, differed on the significance of Alsatian cultural identity, preferring to stress economic exploitation. In 1933 Maurice Thorez, as a representative of the party in the National Assembly, contended more dispassionately than Hueber that "Alsace-Lorraine has been more severely affected by the economic crisis than France."[24] Supported by a host of figures, Thorez analyzed the suffering in the different sectors of the Alsatian economy in order to demand self-determination for Alsace. He avoided employing linguistic, administrative, and religious arguments, which might have evoked the Germanic concept of *Volk* and *Kultur,* to establish Alsace's fundamental alienation from France. Instead he presented culture as only one part of a systematic exploitation in Alsace that represented a fatal flaw in the French capitalist system. At bottom, Thorez believed that culture was a secondary manifestation of economic exploitation, whereas Hueber believed it was the central issue in Alsace.

The beginning of the end of mutual cooperation came on August 22, 1926, the so-called Bloody Sunday, when the Colmar section of the Catholic UPR and the Communist Party tried to hold a joint meeting to protest the central government's attempt to prevent autonomists from initiating any political activity.[25] By ensuring that political discourse in Alsace centered exclusively on the issue of autonomy versus assimilation, Bloody Sunday legitimized Hueber's interpretation of the centrality of cultural identity. Moreover, the flow of blood radicalized and polarized popular opinion on the issue of autonomism. The image of communist and Catholic workers fighting together encouraged the communist autonomists to support the idea of a revolutionary Alsatian *Volk* as opposed to a revolutionary proletariat. The elevation of *Volk* over class marked the beginning of an irreparable split between Hueber and the PCF. The communist autonomists had become visibly and irretrievably connected to the clerical autonomists.

The Colmar trials of the leading autonomists in May 1928 demonstrated the fragility of Alsatian loyalty toward the French state, further aggravating the communist autonomists' dilemma. French repression merely confirmed autonomist accusations that France was insensitive to regional concerns. Although the PCF took pains to demonstrate solidarity with the autonomist movement by providing the Colmar defendants with legal counsel, the violent popular response to the guilty verdict nudged the communist autonomists toward a firmer alliance with the clerical autonomists in order to ride the wave of regionalist sentiment. The autonomist communists had to decide between remaining affiliated with the PCF, which seemed uninterested in the revolutionary potential of the autonomist movement, or joining forces with the clerical autonomists, a move that would seriously compromise their support in the communist community. Driven by local politics (autonomism was an immensely powerful regional issue until 1929), the communist autonomists could not extricate themselves from their commitment to the centrality of autonomy for fear that a reversal would alienate them from the mainstream of Alsatian opinion and cause them to miss a crucial revolutionary moment.

In the wake of Bloody Sunday and the Colmar trials, the PCF still endorsed entente between all the autonomist factions in Alsace. Never comfortable with this alliance, Jacques Doriot, then a spokesman for the PCF, admitted that it had supported "certain petit-bourgeois, anti-imperialist formations" out of necessity.[26] Collaboration or even agreement with the clerical autonomists had always embarrassed the PCF national leadership, because it conflicted with party directives against political alliance with bourgeois and chauvinistic factions. Particularly striking is the fact that the tumultuous events of Bloody Sunday in 1926 were not reported in *L'Humanité* until well over a week after the event, when most other manifestations of violence against communist activity were immediately noted.

Hueber's electoral tactics in the municipal election of May 1929 brought differences that were simmering between the interior communists and the communist autonomists to a boil. In Strasbourg, the PCF rose from 14.4 percent of the vote in 1925 to 21.75 percent in 1929, whereas the French socialists, previously the dominant party in Strasbourg under the leadership of the Francophile mayor Jacques Peirotes, fell from 41.7 to 25.5 percent. The French communists won eleven of the thirty-six municipal council seats in Strasbourg and constituted the largest block of the twenty-two elected autonomists. On the basis of this sharp jump, Hueber formed an alliance with the clerical autonomists, who secured his election as mayor of Strasbourg with Michel Walter, a leader of the clerical UPR, as his adjunct. Hueber remained mayor until 1936. Hueber justified this maneuver by arguing that all Alsatian autonomists—communist and clerical alike—were fundamentally anti-imperialist. This pattern of close alliance with the clerical autonomists was echoed with varying degrees of success throughout Alsace.[27]

The communist autonomists confirmed their decision to share power with the clerical autonomists by withholding support from a French communist candidate in favor of the autonomist Paul Schall in a June by-election for the municipal council and followed this act of insubordination by reopening *Die Neue Welt* in early July. Their decision to publish a rival paper to *L'Humanité* forced the PCF to expel Georges Schreckler, an up-and-coming communist autonomist and editor of *Die Neue Welt,* and Jean-Pierre Mourer, the leader of the communist autonomists in Haut-Rhin. The schism was a fait accompli at this point, although Hueber was not expelled until the fall.

The argument between orthodox communists and dissident Alsatians centered on the interpretation of autonomism and its precise role in the revolutionary struggle. In a tightly disciplined party such as the PCF, mavericks were impermissible, especially if they violated party directives against compromise with bourgeois parties. Jacques Doriot condemned the communist autonomists as "opportunistic elements" that had finally been caught "red-handed" in the forbidden act of allying themselves with the petty bourgeoisie.[28] As Doriot himself would find out half a decade later, no one was indispensable to the Communist Party if he contradicted orthodoxy.[29]

Hueber's crime was that he had disobeyed party policy in the municipal elections. Doriot (correctly) objected to Hueber's claim that the communist autonomists were expelled because they had supported the autonomists, pointing out that the PCF and the Comintern had always supported the autonomist movement. "We reproach you above all," Doriot criticized, "for having voted for Michel Walter and [Alfred] Koessler, a UPR sympathizer."[30] The PCF wanted to maintain "full independence" from other parties and objected to a tactical alliance with the clerical autonomists on the grounds that "the national liberation of Alsace-Lorraine could only be definitively solved by the proletarian revolution." Any disagreement with this formulation smacked of revisionism. Furthermore, French communists believed that the growth of the party in the last election at the expense of the "social-chauvinistic" SFIO showed that religion had become secondary and that the groundswell of Alsatian autonomism could be channeled into the Communist Party.[31] All that was required was party discipline and patience, neither of which Hueber and the communist autonomists possessed in great abundance.

Hueber's perennial lack of financial purity also contributed to the Communist Party's mistrust. As a result of his election, Hueber owed over twenty-four thousand francs, which should have prohibited him from commencing publication of a journal competitive with *L'Humanité.*[32] This raised the Communist Party's suspicions, since neither Comintern nor French communist coffers had provided the money used for *Die Neue Welt.* Money from any other source could only mean alliance with the bourgeois enemy. These suspicions proved well founded. According to the police, the payment of outstanding debts to the employees and creditors of *Die Neue Welt* in August 1929 "coincided with Mayor Hueber's return to Strasbourg" from Freiburg where he had met with German agents.[33]

BEEFSTEAK NAZIS? • 77

The communist autonomists believed that the PCF was responsible for the split, and that the only difference between them was the Alsatian issue. The founding congress of the Kommunistische Partei-Opposition (KPO), which was affiliated with the German dissident communist group the Internationale Vereinigung Kommunistische Opposition (IVKO), in October 1929 finalized the rupture between the communist autonomists and the French communists.[34] Looking back on the paper's expulsion from the PCF, *Die Neue Welt* remarked bitterly:

> We remain, as always, the communist party of Alsace. As such we differ from those who have sought the division of the constant and unbroken Alsatian party . . . solely on the question of tactics, not in the basic tenets and goals—with the exception of the Alsace-Lorraine problem in which the differences with the dissidents reach back to the basic principles of Marxism.[35]

The new party also linked the regional insensitivity of the French communists "to the bureaucratization and to the dictatorship of the leaders in Moscow and Paris."[36] As the PCF had wholeheartedly supported autonomism during the Colmar trials, this attempt to depict it as ignorant and uninterested in local issues had limited success.

The PCF neither understood nor cared that local politics had impelled the communist autonomists to support the clerical autonomists in the Volksfront (the political alliance of all autonomist factions) or risk marginalization.[37] The surge in support for the PCF in 1929 resulted largely from the public's perception that the PCF was at the forefront of the demand for autonomism. Mourer put it most clearly:

> What would have happened if, in view of the election results, we would have followed to the letter the watchword: "class against class" imposed during the last world communist congress? This tactic would have had the result of isolating us and assuring the victory of the bourgeois and chauvinistic parties. In Alsace, nationalism can only be vanquished by the unique front of all anti-imperialist parties.[38]

Local politics victimized the communist autonomists because it reduced all political discourse to the simple dichotomy of autonomism versus assimilationism. Dedicated to revolutionary change in society, the communist autonomists believed that the best chance for revolutionary action lay in alliance with the clerical autonomists and not with the PCF. They had no way of knowing that autonomism would cease to be the central issue in Alsatian political discourse within a year, as a result of a change in the French government's attitude toward legitimate Alsatian concerns and the rise of Nazism.

FROM OPPOSITION COMMUNISM TO NAZISM

The next turning point for the communist autonomists, irrevocably severing them from the Marxist camp, came between 1934, when they were expelled from the IVKO, and 1935, when they formed the Elsäßische Arbeiter- und Bauernpartei (EABP). Hueber and the communist autonomists chose to rally around the issue of autonomism instead of antifascism. By refusing to oppose fascism, Hueber consciously turned a blind eye toward Nazism. By embracing autonomism, he showed that he still preferred Germany to France, which left his followers fatally stranded between Nazi Germany and their Marxist origins. The break with the IVKO exiled the communist autonomists from any Marxist affiliation and left them with little choice but to create an independent party that eventually united with the Alsatian Nazis.

As a dissident communist organization, the KPO maintained a tenuous connection with Marxism until 1934. Mourer's statement, in July 1929, that "to us a communist party comrade is closer and much more dear than a bourgeois" remained valid. *Die Neue Welt* continued to worship Rosa Luxemburg and Karl Liebknecht on the appropriate anniversaries. Mussolini's "italianization" campaign in Southern Tyrol, which "bore great similarity to the frenchification of Alsace-Lorraine," drew sharp criticism from the KPO.[39] The KPO identified fascism with the tendency to "strengthen central authority even more." Nazis were included in this critique of fascism, when the communist autonomists denounced the violence of Nazi storm troops in 1932 and stressed that capitalists financed Hitler.[40]

Nevertheless, the KPO's continuing divergence on key issues undermined its commonality with the PCF and Marxism. As one observer put it, Hueber and his followers were "communists who were not communists."[41] In particular, the KPO objected to rigorous adherence to the party line emanating from Moscow. The French communists' lack of internal party dialogue and their inability to respond flexibly to regional issues seemed ineffective and unreasonable to the KPO leaders. They also opposed the French communists' unwillingness to accept the centrality of French imperialism, by which they meant the oppressive exploitation of non-French territory by the French nation. All of these issues involved the KPO's ongoing fundamental inability or unwillingness to subordinate the interests of the Alsatian *Volk* to the class struggle.[42]

Comparison of the PCF and the KPO between 1929 and 1934 shows that the latter lost considerable working-class support. Doriot claimed that the PCF held up quite well, managing to reconstitute forty-four out of fifty-four sections in Alsace. Possessing a more dispersed electorate with representation in Erstein, Hagenau, Strasbourg, Colmar, and Mulhouse, the PCF maintained several organizational advantages through its national backing and its traditional system of recruitment.[43] Nevertheless, the loss of Hueber, Schreckler, and Mourer left the local PCF bereft of leadership with either name recognition or charisma. In national elections from 1928 to 1932, the PCF's share of voters dropped from 20.1 to 8.2 percent in Bas-Rhin and from 13.3 to 7.8 percent in Haut-Rhin. In 1929 alone, the circulation of the French communist daily *L'Humanité* fell by almost half. The communist autonomists, however, picked up only 8.3 percent of the vote in Bas-Rhin and 0.6 percent in Haut-Rhin—a sure sign that by 1932 they had failed to translate their superior leadership and intimate under-standing of local issues into a decisive victory over the French communists.[44]

The KPO reached its apogee in 1932. The core membership consisted of about 1,300 activists, very few of whom came from Haut-Rhin.[45] Out of a total of 11,254 voters for the KPO in Bas-Rhin, 7,916 were from Stras-bourg. By 1935 *Die Neue Welt*'s circulation, at an inflated figure of 2,800 and 3,000 (considerably higher than its actual subscription rate), had not risen substantially, and it ran an estimated deficit of about 10,000 francs per month.[46] This debt was covered by German funds. With their con-stituency slipping away, the communist autonomists reformulated their strategy to exploit Hueber's mayoral status, in hopes of attracting support throughout Alsace to a visible Strasbourgeois party.

The KPO failed to translate Hueber's high profile into popular success. The better-organized PCF systematically disrupted KPO meetings and suc-cessfully planted doubts in the minds of many working-class Alsatians about the consistency of Hueber, calling him a "communist of circumstance."[47] The French communists were joined by a cross section of Francophile groups, from the socialists to the right-wing Jeunesses Patriotes and the Ac-tion Populaire Nationale d'Alsace.[48] Although the communist autonomists derived some advantage from appearing to be an autonomous David pitted against the assimilationist Goliath, the determination of this anti-Hueber coalition cast doubt on his efficacy as mayor of Strasbourg. Detached from the PCF, the opposition communists found that alliance with the clerical au-tonomists put them at a significant disadvantage in their attempts to recruit on the left without bringing in new supporters from the right.

Events in Germany played a disproportionate role in the politics of the communist autonomists. Shortly after Hitler's seizure of power, the KPO split into factions representing German refugees and Alsatian autonomists. The leadership of the Kommunistische Partei Deutschland Opposition (KPDO, the German chapter of the IVKO) fled Germany as a result of Nazi attacks on Marxist and working-class organizations. Many emigrated to Strasbourg where, as early as March 1933, they set up committees to di-rect resistance against Hitler from abroad. The Alsatian KPO gave the refugees access to jobs, travel money, and shelter from the authorities. When police pressure forced the Strasbourg foreign committee to resettle in Paris in the summer of 1933, many KPDO members remained in Alsace to facilitate contacts between the foreign committee and party members still in Germany.[49]

The refugees, understandably, were engrossed in their personal and political struggle against Nazi Germany and fascist ideology. Typical of the refugees' activity and influence on the party was their participation in a large antifascist rally, attended by the French communists and the socialists, in June 1934. Antifascist agitation by the refugee faction in *Die Neue Welt* became so vigorous that Germany in April 1933 banned its sale in the Reich. From their key positions in *Die Neue Welt* the refugees attacked the Nazis, calling Nazi Germany a "terrorist state." In November 1934 an article in *Die Neue Welt* characterized Hitler's repudiation of territorial demands for Alsace-Lorraine as a lie.[50]

Indigenous communist autonomists chafed at the influence of German refugees. The IVKO was defunct, complained one article in *Die Neue Welt*, and therefore this ungrateful "emigrant group" should have no jurisdiction over the KPO in Alsace. Although the Alsatians had faithfully assisted their comrades' escape from Germany, they resented the tendency of the emigrants "to set the fight against Hitler's Germany above all other political questions."[51] On the contrary, the communist autonomists refused to drop their autonomist agenda "just because (as a result of the failure of the German socialists and party-line communists) Herr Adolph Hitler rules in Berlin."[52]

On the whole, the leading communist autonomists remained faithful to the issue of autonomism. When they changed their name to the Elsäßische Arbeiter- und Bauernpartei in 1935, the communist autonomists complained that their critics within the KPO "have remained loyal to the name and have betrayed the program, the idea," while "we prefer to give up the name and remain loyal to our program." The communist autonomists' obsession with the autonomous "program" grew increasingly out of touch with the social and political tendencies of Alsatians at a time when leftists and Catholics alike were more concerned about the immediate danger of fascist revolution. The autonomist issue, so pressing in 1929, had receded from public view as a result of the government's more regionally responsive position. The obsession of communist autonomists with autonomism was fast becoming obsolete.[53]

August Friedrich Hirtzel, a prominent communist autonomist and a Strasbourg municipal councillor, realized the anachronistic nature of his colleagues' dogged adherence to the Alsatian Volksfront. In the face of the oppressive nature of the newly victorious Nazi Party in Germany, Hirtzel believed that a cultural political coalition such as the Volksfront could no longer defend Alsatian interests. Hirtzel was also concerned that the leaders of the allied autonomist parties had been seduced by fascism. The fear that certain elements of the autonomist Volksfront had become fascist was well founded. During late 1932 and 1933, the Landespartei, a participant in the Volksfront, conducted an internal debate over whether it displayed its Nazism too openly.[54]

Hirtzel was not alone in his concern that the communist autonomists were flirting with fascism. In May 1934, an anonymous contributor to *Die Neue Welt* disagreed with those complacent autonomists who proclaimed that autonomism was opposed to fascism. This critic claimed, "fascist trains of thought of Hitlerian stamp have already deeply penetrated the ranks of the autonomists." The demand for a "surmounting of party ego-tism" through a belief in a "unity of the *Volk*" was a "fundamental idea of fascism and national socialism."[55]

Antifascism found resonance in the French communist and socialist de-cision to form a Popular Front, opposing the revived activism of the fascist leagues that had taken to the streets of Paris in the riots of February 1934. In fact, after 1934 the primary political question in Alsace, as in France, was fascism versus antifascism, as the Popular Front moved to the fore-front of national and regional politics. This, of course, further marginal-ized Hueber's group.

In January 1934 the conflict between the Volksfront faction and the an-tifascist faction came to a head. At the KPO assembly in Strasbourg, Al-fred Quiri, the chief editor of *Die Neue Welt*, pleaded for the rejection of the alliance with the clerical autonomists. The delegates overwhelmingly voted to maintain the Volksfront in what constituted a major defeat for the remaining communists in the party. The antifascist and refugee wing left the KPO and responded by expelling Hueber and his followers from the IVKO that summer, claiming that "the French working class is now the most important ally of the Alsatian working masses." Hans Mayer, a Ger-man refugee who had worked as an editor of *Die Neue Welt*, bitterly remi-nisced that the Volksfront faction "could not clearly distinguish where jus-tified criticism of French domestic policy stopped and high treason began." The incipient division between communists and autonomists, refugees and native Alsatians, and anti-fascists and fascists was now a fact.[56]

Although Hueber and the communist autonomists expelled Quiri and his ideological colleagues, they retained the official name of Kommunistis-che Partei-Opposition and accepted the de facto standoff until September 1935. The dissolution of the Volksfront by the UPR in the 1935 municipal elections eliminated Hueber's coalition in the city council and forced him to relinquish the position of mayor, ending the KPO's state of limbo. The party officially changed its name to the Elsäßische Arbeiter- und Bauern-partei and openly acknowledged its raison d'être to be autonomism.

Throughout this transition period between 1933 and 1935, the Alsat-ian political community noted the nazification of the KPO. Maurice Thorez, speaking for the Alsatian branch of the PCF, mused that "certain parties that advertise themselves as belonging to the Volksfront reflect the influence of Hitler." The socialist newspaper *Freie Presse* pointed out that Hueber and Jean-Pierre Mourer had in their language "become identical" to the pro-Nazi Alsatian Landespartei. *La Dépêche de Strasbourg* envi-sioned for its Radical Party readers the merger of the pro-Nazi journal the *Elsaß-Lothringer Zeitung* and *Die Neue Welt* four years before it actually happened. Although their involvement in the Popular Front made these opponents of the KPO acutely sensitive to the slightest hint of fascism, their accusations of Nazism were accurate.[57]

One way to determine the communist autonomists' attitude toward Nazism is to examine their usage of the term *fascism*. For example, they labeled their assimilationist foes fascist, but not the Nazis. Like his Volksfront cohorts in the pro-Nazi Landespartei, Hueber did not attack French fascism "because it is fascism, but because it is *French* fascism."[58] It was not, as it was for the majority of the Marxist left in France after 1934, a term signifying the radical right-wing, militant minions of the bourgeoisie. Communist autonomists repeatedly associated French chauvinism and assimilationism with fascism. Accordingly, they considered fascist any group that resisted the idea of an Alsatian *Volk* affiliated with Germany or any group that imposed Frenchness on Alsatians. Thus, socialists and members of the Radical Party found themselves lumped together as fascists with genuinely fascist groups such as the AF and the JP. In an attempt to bypass the increasingly important question of fascism versus antifascism, the communist autonomists completely revised the idea of fascism, ignoring its chief characteristics, so that it would refer only to their enemies. The KPO's willful distortion of the term *fascism* reflected its unwillingness to attack Nazism.

Communist autonomists also associated fascism with anyone who supported war. "Fascism Is War!" warned one headline in *Die Neue Welt*.[59] In a revealing inversion, the communist autonomists considered the Popular Front's insistence on combating fascism as the real threat to world peace. Unlike the refugees in the IVKO, who realized that fascism had to be actively combated, the communist autonomists objected to the antifascist struggle.[60] Instead they claimed to be pacifists, crassly redefining fascism in order to capitalize on Alsatian fears. Pacifism had a special appeal to Alsatians, who not only shared the painful memory of World War I with most Europeans but also faced the possibility that war might result in yet another social and political transformation in Alsace.

Despite occasional genuflections before Marxist icons, after 1935 the communist autonomists became even more fascist than ever. In their view, the harmony of the Alsatian *Volk* outweighed the need for a rectification of social inequities caused by class advantages. "We proclaim the unity of peasants and workers," wrote *Die Neue Welt*. "They are Alsatians, they belong to the laboring people *[schaffenden Volke]* and they must maintain a solidarity with the laboring people in other countries."[61] The substitution of the term *schaffenden* for the more Marxist-sounding *arbeitenden* constituted a redefinition of the notion of "work." Work no longer implied a proletariat, distinct from the rest of society by virtue of its relationship to the means of production. Communist autonomists now accepted a broader definition of work, which extended to everyone who earned money and was consistent with the Nazi ideal of a corporative, harmonious, hierarchical, and racially pure national community. The newly formed EABP slogan even omitted all reference to the working class, emphasizing instead the common problems of the *Volk*. The slogan read:

> Against capitalism and imperialism,
> Against capitalist exploitation and nationalist repression,
> For language and homeland rights,
> For self-determination in Alsace-Lorraine![62]

The communist autonomists also attacked the Soviet Union and Stalin, arguing that "the Soviet Union ranged itself in the ranks of the capitalist and imperialist states." As Doriot was to do in his fascist Parti Populaire Français, the Alsatian communists retroactively criticized "party-line communists" and the autocratic nature of the Comintern's decision making.[63] Such rhetoric went considerably beyond their previous stance under the IVKO, which objected to the bureaucratization of the international communist movement and to the assumption that the Russian experience was a useful model for the rest of Europe. They no longer merely disagreed over the implementation of Marxist ideology, they moved toward a fascist categorical opposition to socialism.

By early 1938 the EABP openly favored the Nazi Party. Reporting on Hitler's Reichstag address, the EABP attacked the international press for its negative view of Hitler. The party also uncritically reported Hitler's assertions about the economy and his peaceful intentions. Statements by Hitler such as "The German *Volk* is soldierly, but not warlike," were accepted at face value. Further proof that the EABP had drifted away from the central concerns of the Alsatian public and toward fascism was its unqualified support of the Austrian Anschluß.[64] The implications were clear: both Austria and Alsace were predominantly Catholic, culturally German communities bordering on but not belonging to Germany. Politically conscious public opinion in Alsace therefore watched the Anschluß unfold with concern. The fact that the EABP, along with the other autonomist organizations, supported the Anschluß on historical and cultural grounds unmistakably signaled that the party had no reservations about joining Hitler's Germany. The EABP's subsequent support for the absorption of the Sudeten Germans into Nazi Germany on the basis of self-determination, coupled with its increasingly strident pleas for peace, seem explicable only on the basis of its unshakable desire to join Hitler's Germany.[65]

After splitting from the IVKO, the EABP became extremely ambivalent on the Jewish question. Articles in *Die Neue Welt* seesawed between antisemitic diatribes and attempts to prove the EABP's philosemitism. For several years the EABP could not decide whether to give up on its pre-1935 constituency, which included Jews, or to recruit aggressively from its autonomist constituency. One article in *Die Neue Welt* concluded that foreigners, especially the Polish, were taking over Alsace. It resolved, "The foreigner is endured here, but the foreigner does not command. This is the will of the Alsatian Heimatfront!" The Polish were a convenient racial catchall category that included all Slavs and, significantly, Jews. Yet in the 1936 elections, Hueber responded to criticisms of antisemitism by making a direct appeal to Jewish voters as the candidate who had sheltered German Jewish refugees from the Nazi regime: "Therefore, worthy fellow citizens, I cannot be an antisemite."[66] There is a defensiveness in this assertion that suggests Hueber and the EABP were already acting in an antisemitic manner. A scant two years later, the EABP characterized the murder of a German diplomat in Paris that "precipitated" the infamous Crystal Night pogrom in Germany as "the result of a carefully prepared action by certain circles," implying the existence of a Jewish conspiracy. Since the "moral responsibility" for this act lay with international Jewry, the EABP concluded that the Crystal Night was an appropriate response.[67]

The communist autonomists' espousal of Nazism accompanied an increasingly close financial collaboration with the Nazis. According to testimony from 1939, Jean-Pierre Mourer acted as the principal conduit for money from Nazi Germany to the leaders of the Alsatian Landespartei throughout the 1930s. As early as June 1935, Mourer operated out of the office of the Landespartei's journal, the *Elsaß-Lothringer Zeitung.* Mourer's connection with Germany included numerous meetings with Robert Ernst, a "150 percent Nazi" and head of the German-based *Elsaß-Lothringen Heimatstimmen,* and his representative Albert Bongartz. Hueber, as we have already seen, had been accepting money from Germany all along. Given the process of disbursement, he probably had a personal relationship with Ernst at least as early as 1929, before Ernst became a Nazi.[68]

The EABP represented the penultimate humiliation of the communist autonomists. Exiled from all Marxist parties, the party struggled for survival in a wilderness of autonomist and Marxist parties. It could not effectively compete with existing autonomist parties for a shrinking number of dedicated activists. At the same time, the party was unable to claim greater dedication to the working-class cause than the PCF, the SFIO, or even the largely defunct IVKO. Having crossed the Rubicon from Marxism to autonomism and considering the hard times the EABP had fallen upon, it was almost inevitable that the party would merge with the pro-Nazi Landespartei. By 1939, almost nothing remained of the original 1921 constituency of railroad and postal employees, miners, and workers.

Eventually the communist autonomists ceded all doctrinal independence and merged *Die Neue Welt* with the *Elsaß-Lothringer Zeitung* in April 1939, consummating a de facto marriage. The EABP and the Landespartei officially joined forces at the end of July 1939, becoming the Elsaß-Lothringische Arbeiter- und Bauernpartei. Firm governmental action in banning the *Elsaß-Lothringer Zeitung* in August 1939 left the communist autonomists without a public voice.[69] When most of the autonomist leaders were arrested for espionage in 1939, officials left Hueber off the list because of his bad health. His colleague Mourer, however, was arrested and imprisoned with the other Nazi autonomists. Between his health and close police surveillance, Hueber kept a low profile until the Germans occupied and annexed Alsace. As the price for Hueber's support, the Nazis reinstalled him as mayor of Strasbourg in 1942—a position he held until his death in 1943. Mourer, rescued from French prison by the victorious Germans, also regained political prominence under the Nazis as the chief administrator for the Mulhouse district.

. . .

As the case of the communist autonomists shows, communists and socialists who became fascist were not motivated by an inherent similarity between fascism and communism. Far more important was the substitution of nationalism for communism—*Volk* for class. Between 1918 and 1940, the communist autonomists converted from communism to Nazism. At the heart of this conversion was the communist autonomists' rejection of class struggle as the basis of their political ideology in favor of a cultural struggle for German national identity. Autonomism served as an ideological bridge that carried the communist autonomists from the left bank to the right. The transformation took place in stages. In 1929 they embraced the preeminence of autonomism without completely rejecting the class struggle. By 1935, however, Hueber and his followers had shed all vestiges of Marxism in order to strengthen their ties to the autonomist movement.

In the process of adhering to the autonomist agenda, the communist autonomists frittered away much of their support. A succession of schisms from close to a third of the electorate rendered the movement insignificant. To be sure, the high number of voters in 1920 represented an artificial alliance of socialist and communist voters, which could not possibly survive the split between socialist and communist factions. Still, the PCF was larger than the KPO, which in turn was larger than the EABP. When Hueber and his followers made their last migration from the KPO to the EABP, only a handful of supporters remained. The collaboration of Hueber, Mourer, and a few other EABP leaders with the Nazi government during the war reflected personal motives, for by then they had no popular support. Over the course of twenty years Hueber and the communist autonomists had managed to relegate their movement to the margins of Alsatian politics.

The transformation from communism to Nazism reflected the changed context of the 1930s. The success of first Mussolini and then Hitler brought many to the conclusion that fascism was the wave of the future. The social groups turning to fascism in the 1930s were different from the earlier groups, as the communist autonomists clearly demonstrated. Despite the steady diminution of Hueber's German-speaking, working-class constituency, the fact remains that a fascist movement had appeared which purported to represent their interests. The spread of fascism to new social groups was not restricted to the communist autonomists. Peasant and urban lower-middle-class Alsatians also developed their own fascist vehicles.

REGIONAL FASCISM

THE BAUERNBUND

In 1947 Joseph Bilger, head of the Alsatian Bauernbund (BB), stood trial for his role in the Nazi annexation of Alsace-Lorraine. Bilger's defense argued that he had used his positions as *Ortsgruppenleiter* (NSDAP-captain), *Gauredner* (district spokesman) of the *Elsäßischer Hilfsdienst* (Alsatian help service), and propaganda chief of the Lorraine Nazi paper, the *Deutsche Volksgemeinschaft,* to oppose the Nazis and to protect Alsatian interests from within.[1] Against the prosecution's claim that Bilger and the BB constituted a fifth column for German penetration of Alsace, Bilger countered that he had always been pro-French and that he was a scapegoat for French postwar nationalism. Unconvinced, the court found him guilty and sentenced him to ten years of hard labor.

Bilger's decision to support Nazism was consistent with his entire political career. For Bilger, fascism (regardless of nationality) was the end, whereas for many other fascists in Alsace, a particular national identity was the end. Although he had unimpeachable pro-French bona fides in the form of alliances with Dorgères's Front Paysan and the AF, he had equally strong ties to the Alsatian autonomist movement and clearly began to support the Nazis sometime between 1938 and 1940, if not before. The only constant was his unflagging devotion to a radical right-wing political agenda centered on a defense of the Alsatian peasantry. Even after World War II, with a jail term for collaboration behind him, Bilger continued to agitate for a fascist solution. Banned from Alsace, he went to Algeria where he became a leader of the Mouvement Populaire du 13 Mai, a national, Catholic, imperialist organization that attracted nearly ten thousand members in opposition to Algerian independence.[2]

As Bilger went, so went the Bauernbund. His control over the BB was so complete that he virtually embodied its ideology. Certainly no one else exercised much voice in the movement's direction or editorial pages. As much as they denigrated his thick-headedness, contemporary observers also had to acknowledge his charisma.[3] Bilger undoubtedly reflected the views and prejudices of many Alsatian peasants. Charismatic he may have been, but his thought was frequently garbled, ambiguous, and contradictory. The contentious and confused nature of his personality contributed significantly to the nature of the BB. Bilger was a doer not a thinker, so his actions often lacked logic. This partially explains his muddled and violent approach to Alsatian identity.

The contradictions between the Bauernbund's espousal of German culture and Nazi ideology and its willingness to be part of France and to work with the French radical right suggest an ambiguity in the national orientation of the BB that was lacking in all the other fascist groups in Alsace. Bilger, to be sure, did not always steer successfully between the German Scylla and the French Charybdis, as his postwar trial clearly demonstrates. Nevertheless, he emulated and manipulated the larger national movements for Alsatian gain.

The Bauernbund's constituency was limited to the peasantry of Alsace-Lorraine. Despite Bilger's pretensions to leadership over a wider region, the BB never transcended the boundaries imposed by the Rhine and the Vosges. Nor did the party ever successfully expand its social base. Hampered by cultural, geographic, and social restrictions, the BB failed to make the transition to a Nazi-style mass party, even though it became the largest fascist movement in Alsace. The result was an autochthonous Alsatian fascist party precariously situated between the monoliths of French fascism and German Nazism.

Although historiography traditionally defines fascism as a nationalist movement, the case of the Bauernbund demonstrates that fascism could accommodate itself to regional identity. "Fascism is not only the martial music of the devotees of the nation-state," according to Bernard-Henri Lévy, "it can also speak patois, dance to the rhythm of an Auvergne folk dance, or march to Breton bagpipes."[4] Lévy could easily have added that fascism can also sing Alsatian folk songs.

Fascism posits the existence of a community that supersedes and encompasses the needs and actions of the individual. Such a community is always viewed as a harmonious, organic, and hierarchical entity in which each individual is a respected—but replaceable—cell. The state must embody this community. As most forms of fascism revolve around a national community, fascism has generally come to represent an equivalence between nation and state, where the state has the power to enforce national homogeneity and act for the body.

The parameters of the community, however, are not immutable, a point that becomes especially clear in border regions. Although French and Italian fascists considered the nation to be the appropriate entity, the Nazis insisted on the preeminence of a racial community. Instead of making nation or race the operative organism, Bilger limited his horizons to Alsace-Lorraine. In a sense, he merely substituted a smaller national community (Alsace) for a larger one (France or Germany). Bilger's regionalism, however, differed from the nationalism of Germany and France. The Bauernbund's smaller size and sense of locality and uniqueness often put it at odds with the national fascists' cultural and political critique of smallness and heterogeneity. For the BB, Alsace was a viable community that could not be entirely absorbed or subsumed into either the French or the German national polities. In a sense, this was the difference between a mass culture advocated by the German and French movements and popular culture as embodied by Alsace.

Thus, during the 1930s the Bauernbund emerged as a purely regional fascist movement that borrowed heavily from fascist ideology and organizational techniques and applied them to regional ends. This phenomenon can best be characterized as regional fascism. This was a marked departure from the 1920s, when fascist movements co-opted regionalism. Under the leadership of Joseph Bilger, the BB incorporated and appropriated Nazi *Blut und Boden* (blood and soil) ideology, racial antisemitism, and fascist organizational techniques. Throughout the 1930s, the BB vacillated between Nazism, French fascism, and Alsatian autonomism, while consistently adhering to its own fascist ideology. The BB demonstrates the existence of regional fascism in the interwar era and proves that fascism is not simply an expression of hypernationalism.

. . .

Rural life in Alsace had undergone a radical transformation since 1850. The proportion of agricultural workers in Bas-Rhin fell from 65 percent in 1910 to 44 percent in 1936. Not only was the birthrate in decline, it was lower than in most industrialized nations.[5] The Bas-Rhin birthrate plummeted from thirty births per thousand in 1905 to sixteen per thousand in 1938. Like most movements on the radical right, the Bauernbund evinced deep concern for the falling birthrate.[6] At the same time, better transportation, better education, and the expansion of national government broke down the barriers between urban and rural worlds. Preindustrial peasant village society gave way to "a mixed way of life" characterized by the "worker-farmer," who commuted to the city for employment but still owned land. Peasant children left their family farms to pursue opportunities in the cities or towns as factory workers, artisans, domestic servants, or government employees.[7] These disruptions went to the very heart of peasant life and created social and cultural uncertainty even when they brought material advantages. This uncertainty became a source of support for the BB.

André Gestermann, a professor of agriculture in Colmar, founded the Bauernbund in February 1924 to protect and defend peasant interests at a time when economic development was undermining traditional life. Low prices on foodstuffs, the result of a flood of imports, placed an onerous burden on farmers. Under Gestermann, the BB's activity was restricted to Haut-Rhin, where it presented itself as an alternative to the established, pro-French Fédération Agricole, which reflected the interests of the rural notables, who combined large landholdings with local political power. In contrast, the BB was clearly affiliated with the autonomist camp. A list of the BB's demands sent to the prefect of Haut-Rhin in 1926 included the repeal of the legal right to hunt on private property, the creation of an agricultural office run by a knowledgeable official, and financial support from the Crédit Agricole for viticulture. These demands show the Bauernbund's initial emphasis on self-help for the small farmer, who was pitted against both urban industrial interests and the rural notables. They also illustrate the peculiar contradictory mixture of reactionary and modern ideals that characterized the BB.[8]

In 1928 twenty-four-year-old Joseph Bilger succeeded the ailing Gestermann as the animating spirit of the organization. As secretary general, Bilger immediately put his stamp on the party by expanding it to Bas-Rhin. For the first three to five years, Bilger continued to represent peasant interests without overtly involving the Bauernbund in the debate over autonomism versus assimilationism. In the 1932 elections, for example, the BB endorsed candidates from both the autonomist and the Francophile wings of the UPR purely according to their commitment to rural issues.[9] Gradually, however, Bilger shifted the focus from interest group representation to political ideology.

Much has been made of Bilger's affinity for Nazism. Socialists, for example, referred to him as the "Führer Hitler-Bilger."[10] As a representative of a German-speaking peasantry with strong ties to the German cultural nation, Bilger found the "blood and soil" aspect of Nazism attractive. Several months after Hitler became chancellor, Bilger favorably critiqued the Third Reich, which he held responsible for "the unification of all German peasants" and which would "undoubtedly realize the path to professionally unified organization." Further, Bilger wrote, "we follow the events in Germany in the certainty that our native peasantry will also overcome all the chains of liberal alienation [Überfeindung], and the artificiality and corruptness of our present system."[11] In short, from the beginning of the Nazi regime, Bilger admired what the Nazis had achieved and shared with them an extreme revulsion against liberal democracy.

The fundamental similarity between the Nazis and the BB became most apparent when the Elsaß-Lothringisches Bauernblatt responded to oft-repeated charges that it was Hitlerian. The *Bauernblatt* concluded that "the abusive slurs [by the local liberal and socialist press, which accused the BB of Nazism] merely prove that we are on the correct path." Bilger vowed to "break terror with terror!" and crush liberal and socialist opposition.[12] The BB's respect and admiration for Nazism remained constant throughout the 1930s.

Not only did the BB sympathize with the Nazi movement, it drew much of its ideological content from Nazism. This was the root of accusations that its program was "the exact copy of that of Walther Darré, the [Nazi] minister of Agriculture."[13] Thus, in 1936, although the BB was still loosely affiliated with Dorgères's Peasant Front, Bilger claimed that "the peasant as the source of the people's power" demanded the institutionalization of "the law of life, which is based on the immutability of 'Blood and Soil'" and "would never tolerate on this earth the principles of liberal capitalism and collective Marxism."[14] Such rhetoric, especially when considered in conjunction with the extreme antisemitism of the BB, clearly derived from Nazism.

Bilger wanted to return the peasantry to its rightful place at the center of society. Although Bilger claimed a Christian corporatist component to his ideology, the binding force was not the medieval religious Weltanschauung that gave each member of society a place in God's hierarchical structure, but the more modern idea of a *Volksgemeinschaft* (racial community). For the Bauernbund, parliament was a travesty because selfish bourgeois interests dominated the parties and decided all peasant and rural issues without giving peasants a voice. Addressing local vintners in 1932 Bilger declared, "Industrial capitalism is on the verge of collapse. It seems to want to secure a safer field for its rapacity *[Raubfeld]* in agriculture." Marxism was equally odious to Bilger, since the class struggle blocked "Christian and economic solidarity" by pitting one class against another. Social harmony could only be achieved through the creation of a "corporative parliament" that would ensure the "collaboration of the laboring classes" in government. Liberal parliament should therefore be replaced by a professional trade parliament with "direct and unadulterated representation of the productive peoples' power."[15]

Not only was Bilger corporatist, certain aspects of his notion of corporatism followed the same development as in Germany. In an article entitled "From the *Standesgemeinschaft* [corporative community] to the Volksgemeinschaft," Bilger argued that the Bauernbund sought the unity of all France—to make France into a Volksgemeinschaft—through the imposition of the same sort of political coordination that was taking place in Germany.[16] Corporatism for Bilger meant loyalty to "the *Heimat,* the Volksgemeinschaft, Christian morals, and cultural rights" and rejection of the party system "in favor of organized corporative work, within which the coming socially regulated state *[Ordnungsstaat]* should be built."[17] As with the Nazis, the notion of interest representation was subservient to the rejection of parties and the acceptance of the Volksgemeinschaft.

Like the Nazis, the Bauernbund made antisemitism a central rallying point. One paper claimed that Bilger lifted his antisemitism straight from *Der Stürmer,* Julius Streicher's notorious antisemitic Nazi paper, dryly noting that although the BB rallied around the *Croix d'Arc* (Cross of [Jeanne] d'Arc), it evoked the swastika.[18] Even Bilger's postwar apologists admitted the centrality of antisemitism when they disingenuously argued that "Bilger's antisemitism . . . was clearly an Alsatian species (the Alsatian peasantry has traditionally been anti-Jewish)," and therefore presumably not as heinous as the racial antisemitism of the Nazis.[19] Although antisemitism was rampant in Alsace and undeniably present in all the fascist movements, it was not the essential keystone in the AF, the Faisceau, the JP, or even in the Francistes that it was for Bilger, who could not imagine any acceptable Jew.

The Bauernbund's ubiquitous antisemitic diatribes turned "the Jew" into a symbol for all that was corrupt, evil, and wrong with modern society. Bilger repeatedly contrasted the purity of Christianity with the decadence of Judaism. "The oriental Talmud-immorality," he wrote, "stands against the deep morality and honesty of genuine Christendom."[20] Bilger's outbursts against Jews were attacks against what he perceived as the anomie of the modern world. The obverse of such religious zeal against the decadence wrought by industrialization, technological progress, and democratization was a striving for a moral regeneration of society along Christian lines. All the French fascist groups from the Faisceau to the PPF shared this commitment to a purification of society, although they did not always use antisemitism to highlight it.

Capitalism—specifically finance capital—was another of Bilger's favorite targets. Since the Bauernbund and the Volksständischen Arbeiterfront (VAF) represented peasant and artisan interests rather than the managerial and more elitist constituency of the AF and the Faisceau, they adopted a more radical stance toward the oppressive nature of capitalism. "The bloodthirsty beast of prey must be exterminated," Bilger exhorted at a 1932 rally, "in order finally to clear the path" for new, antiliberal forms of government.[21] Antisemitism was a convenient means of focusing rural resentment and distrust of capitalism. Jews were, according to Bilger, intimately associated with the anti-French, antipeasant, and immoral accumulation of excess profit. "The Jew becomes fat through the *Groschen* [penny] you bring to him," the *Volk* admonished in an article complaining that Jews dominated commerce, "and Christ becomes scrawny through the *Groschen* you take away from him."[22]

At the same time, the divisive aspects of socialism were also the fault of the Jews. "Everyone knows," wrote a contributor to *Volk,* "that the socialist party is completely controlled by Jews." The national prominence of Léon Blum and the local visibility of Salomon Grumbach, whom he called "Salami Groumbich," in the socialist party served only to stoke the racist fire. In a typically fascist argument, the Bauernbund objected to Marxism on the grounds that class warfare promoted societal conflict. Communism promoted selfish instead of community interests, when it should be "Gemeinnutz vor Eigennutz" (common good before self).[23]

Although Bilger's ideological affinity with Nazism is indisputable, he took pains to stress that he did not necessarily accept Germany as the locus of Alsatian fascism. "We are loyal French citizens," Bilger declared at a 1935 rally, "which does not prevent our being good Alsace-Lorrainers."[24] Despite the Bauernbund's ideological convergence with Nazism, very little evidence can be found to support the contention that it was a German fifth column. Much of the controversy over Bilger's precise role as a Nazi collaborator stems from a misunderstanding of his relationship to Germany. His detractors, on one hand, claim that his acceptance of Nazi ideology meant he was necessarily pro-German. His defenders, on the other hand, argue that his reticence about Germany constituted an all-important divergence from Nazism. The truth lies somewhere in between. Bilger emulated Nazism and flirted with pan-Germanism, but his fairly consistent acceptance of French nationalism justifies a certain amount of doubt about his role as a collaborator before the war.

Bilger's touchstone was always Alsace and not Germany. There is even some evidence that certain elements of the Nazi Party opposed Bilger.[25] Bilger had very little to do with Robert Ernst, who was responsible for much of the German support for the Alsatian Nazis. Bilger was, however, apparently a close personal friend of Prince August Wilhelm of Prussia, who was an SA Obergruppenführer (lieutenant-general). If this friendship began before the war, it might indicate some SA support for the BB. Competitive bureaucracy characterized Nazi rule and often led to situations where the SA, the German foreign office, the SS, and the Wehrmacht played out their rivalries in arenas that were not directly supervised by Hitler. For example, SS Obergruppenführer Werner Lorenz, as head of the Volksdeutsche Mittelstelle (Liaison Office for Ethnic Germans), represented a more national socialist point of view than that of Robert Ernst and his supporters in the Volksbund für das Deutschtum im Ausland (Association for Germans Abroad), both of which dealt with German minorities outside of Germany. Ernst claims that his faction was out of favor after 1936, when Lorenz asserted control over the foreign German movement. In stark contrast to the communist and clerical autonomists and the Alsatian Nazis, for example, Bilger stood outside the flow of payments from Robert Ernst and the Nazis to the clerical and communist autonomists.[26]

One aspect of the BB's ideology that epitomized its unique regional focus was the BB's revolutionary ideal. Bilger was not inspired by the French Revolution but by the Bundschuh Rebellion, a violent peasant movement that in 1493 attempted to reassert the traditional corporate rights of the peasantry against the secular and ecclesiastical authorities. One of the chief symbols for the BB was the green flag of the Bundschuh movement.[27] Bilger used the memory of this bloody peasant uprising as a vehicle for the medieval values he hoped to instill in his movement.

On the surface this would appear to mark the BB as reactionary, since it harked back to a distant past. On further reflection, however, it was the revolutionary content of the Bundschuh Rebellion that the BB sought to evoke. The BB "is a movement of renewal for the rural people," according to the *EBB,* "truly the biggest since the Bundschuh."[28] The BB updated this premodern or preindustrial symbol to make it relevant to contemporary circumstances. The original Bundschuh Rebellion resulted in the murder of hundreds of landowners and notables. A recurring demand was the elimination of the servitude to monks and bishops.[29] As a devout Catholic, Bilger never emphasized this aspect of the Bundschuh Rebellion. The raising of the Bundshuh flag, however, represented a willingness to resort to personal violence against any authorities who opposed the realization of corporate peasant demands.

Bilger deliberately revised and co-opted the Bundshuh Rebellion (actually a more widespread southern German event) to evoke an Alsatian consciousness and an Alsatian community. The Bundschuh was certainly not a historical precedent for the French fascists, nor was it prominent in Nazi revisionist history. The French Revolution was the touchstone for the French fascists, who either claimed to be its inheritors or rejected it outright as the source of modern liberal decadence. The Nazis, for their part, largely ignored both the Bundshuh Rebellion and the French Revolution. Ernst Renan's remark about nationalism holds true for Bilger's regionalism: "Getting its history wrong is part of being a nation."[30] For Bilger, the Bundshuh was a uniquely Alsatian event, which set Alsace apart from both Germany and France.

Autonomists from the Landespartei circle looked favorably on the BB during the early 1930s. The Landespartei enthusiastically greeted the founding of the Elsäßer Jungland (Alsatian Youth), the original Green Shirts, because the group would "recruit young, corporate-conscious leaders for our movement, who no longer woo the favor of the government."[31] Bilger's newspaper, the *Elsaß-Lothringisches Bauernblatt,* was printed at Alsatia, the autonomist press, and after 1935 by the René Hauss publishing house, another autonomist press.[32] This was an important link between the autonomists and the BB, for the extremely partisan autonomist presses would never have extended such hospitality to non-autonomists and may have even acted as a conduit for German money. Another instance of BB and autonomist connivance occurred at a violent BB demonstration in December 1936 that had been banned, when Landespartei leader René Hauss and communist autonomist Jean-Pierre Mourer led the crowd in singing "O Straßburg" and German military songs while Bilger was being arrested.[33] Typical of the BB's ambiguous national stance was the fact that the demonstrating peasants apparently also sang the "Marseillaise" and chanted "France for the French!"[34]

Bilger's relationship to the clerical autonomists of the UPR was complex. He began his career as a journalist for the Haut-Rhinois Catholic daily, *Der Elsäßer Kurier,* which was part of the Haegyist cartel directed by the autonomist Abbé Haegy.[35] His early collaboration with the autonomists is a clue to his persistent adherence to Alsace as his frame of reference. Although Bilger and the autonomists were not always allied, their respective political development followed similar paths, drifting toward Nazism over the course of the 1930s. During the first few years of Bilger's reign, the BB remained closely allied to the UPR. Even after Bilger ran his own candidates against those of the UPR in 1935 and allied himself more closely with the French radical right, the UPR supported a BB candidate in cantonal elections. Nevertheless, the radical weekly *La République* reported in 1935 that Bilger was no longer Joseph Rossé's protégé and that he no longer served "the cause of political autonomism."[36] An attempted merger between the two parties in March 1938 failed. Afterward, the UPR autonomists distanced themselves from Bilger, either for fear that his ambitious mobilization of the Alsatian peasantry would undermine their political strength in rural Alsace or because Rossé leaned too much toward the PSF.[37]

Bilger's apparent coolness toward autonomism coincided with a major shift in his nationalist orientation that took place between 1933 and 1936. During this period, Bilger allied with Francophile extremists, declaring himself prepared "to work in the regional cadre for the interest of the entire nation."[38] In November 1933 the BB held its first meeting under the auspices of the Parti Agraire. Joseph Rossé spoke at this meeting, which indicates that Bilger's drift into the Francophile camp was a gradual one. Autonomists in the Landespartei lost patience in autumn 1935 with Bilger's increasing acceptance of France.[39]

At the same time, Bilger's political ambitions became more transparent. No longer content to manage the Bauernbund as a peasant interest group, Bilger founded the Völkständischen Arbeiterfront in 1935 in an attempt to expand his movement to Alsatian cities and create an ideological alternative to the existing party system. Like most fascist leaders, Bilger hoped to use his constituency as a springboard to the creation of a mass party under his control. The Green Shirts (founded on February 28, 1932) served as a paramilitary force policing rallies and promoting a publicly activist image intended to impress the public with the VAF's dynamism.[40] An increase in membership and participation facilitated the restructuring of the BB into a more Nazistic mass party.

One of the earliest meetings to discuss the creation of the VAF attracted over five hundred participants comprised of representatives from the seamen's association, canal navigators, artisans, horse breeders, and a large contingent of farmers.[41] The idea was simple: unite the working professions through the motto, "Common enemy, common work."[42] Workers and farmers shared a belief in "family, work, home, Fatherland, and Christendom." The VAF declared itself "against the obsolete, disgraceful party racket, against the hell-spawned lodges and international Jewry, against capitalism and anonymous feudalism." It fundamentally opposed liberalism and Marxism and called for the creation of "the Fourth Republic of peasants and workers."[43] Although these goals were present in the BB before Bilger took control, he focused them into an unmistakably fascist platform that he hoped would garner enough social support to overthrow the existing government.

Despite Bilger's attempt to broaden his movement into a socially diverse mass party, the BB and the VAF remained largely peasant. These were not tenant or sharecrop farmers, but *cultivateurs,* who owned land and made a respectable living from farming. Interviews with residents of several villages just south of Colmar revealed that "large landowners," not subsistence farmers, joined the BB.[44] Families in that district whose landholdings were so marginal that at least one member of the family had to work in the nearby potash mines tended to support the communists. Such social splits within the village between the prosperous and the poor shaped the composition of the BB.[45] The moderately well-off farmer, who made a decent living from his property but fell far short of the profits and influence of the wealthy landowner, was attracted to the BB's social philosophy emphasizing the stability and importance of his class.

The VAF failed to attract non-peasants. Those few urbanites who joined were not working-class. Redefinition of socialism to mean a concern for the family "as the first socialist cell" generated little enthusiasm among workers.[46] A few low-level officials in Mulhouse supported the movement for awhile. Some artisans expressed interest, but they soon found better representation elsewhere.[47] Urban fascists such as the AF, the JP, and the Francistes had a more cogent appeal to lower-middle- and middle-class city dwellers. At the same time, the UPR proved more effective as a mass party than the Bauernbund could ever hope to be. In short, after a brief stint as a novelty party, the VAF failed to extend its social base.

In any event, Bilger's agricultural platform precluded urban support. He complained that the government was responsible for low agricultural prices, which forced farmers to leave the countryside and seek higher wages in the cities, thus disrupting village life.[48] Bilger's attacks on the government had some validity. In many ways, the French government was unable or unwilling to stimulate agriculture, preferring to gamble that strong industrial growth would trickle down.[49] Prices divided the city dwellers, who invariably wanted lower food prices, from the farmers, who wanted higher prices. Bilger's demand for higher prices on agricultural goods irritated urban consumers as well as policy-makers and industrialists, who believed that low food prices stimulated industry and profit by dampening down inflation.

Well over half of the Bauernbund's membership came from Haut-Rhin; the rest were thinly spread out over Bas-Rhin and Lorraine. At six thousand members, the BB's core of activists represented a twenty-fifth of the eligible voters (150,000) in Haut-Rhin.[50] The number who voted for the Bauernbund in Chambre d'Agricole elections was higher. Six thousand activists, moreover, compared favorably with the other radical right-wing groups. The AF, for example, in all of Alsace comprised at its peak only three thousand die-hard royalists.

The Bauernbund won over whole villages in the district. In the canton of Huningue, bordering on Switzerland, the BB comprised about 350 members and another 100 sympathizers in early 1936. In the 1936 elections to the Chambre d'Agricole d'Alsace-Lorraine, 14,000 Huninguers voted for the BB. In the cities of Mulhouse, Altkirch, and Thann, the party had a combined total of 72 syndicates with approximately 2,400 members. The BB was also a force in the area around Colmar, with a following of approximately 1,200 strong. The district of Guebwiller, the BB's stronghold, had 1,700 adherents.[51]

Judging from attendance at rallies and the publication figures of the *Bauernblatt* and *Volk,* the Bauernbund's membership surged between late 1936 and the fall of 1937, profiting from the anti-Marxism engendered by the success of the Popular Front. At the end of 1936, the BB printed 8,000–9,000 copies of its journal, the *Bauernblatt,* which were distributed not just in Alsace but throughout Lorraine as well. Publication reached its peak between March and September 1937 when the *Bauernblatt* hovered between 18,000 and 25,000 copies and *Volk,* the AF's bimonthly "battle publication," maintained a consistent printing of 8,000 copies. By December 1937, the *Bauernblatt* had dropped to 9,500 copies and *Volk* to 5,500.[52] The low number of copies per issue, compared to large local newspapers such as *Les Dernières Nouvelles de Strasbourg,* which printed as many as 128,500 copies daily, did not necessarily reflect a small membership, since peasants rarely subscribed to a journal that could be read at the village café. In any event, the figures for Bilger's papers were above average for the partisan press in Alsace.[53]

Like the other fascist movements, the BB encountered the hostility of several key groups. Specifically, three important institutions opposed the BB. The Comice Agricole, long the chief representative of rural interests, defended itself against the upstart movement. The UPR became concerned in the mid-1930s that the BB would undermine its rural support.[54] Even the Catholic Church proved lukewarm. These established groups had existing constituencies and interests in rural Alsace that Bilger threatened to co-opt. Given the institutional strength and diversity of Bilger's opponents (defenders of the religious, political, and corporative status quo), the BB faced serious restrictions on its ability to expand.

Local curés' lack of enthusiasm for Bilger's movement limited the BB's appeal.[55] Village priests were caught up in their own struggle with the bishop. This struggle was part of a larger rift within the Alsatian Catholic Church between the rural, Germanophile curés and the urban, Francophile elements centered around Bishop Ruch. Indeed, the division between the rank-and-file priests and the upper echelon of the hierarchy created political tension within the UPR.[56] The BB, despite its apparent religiosity, did not address this problem, but as the BB appealed almost exclusively to Catholics, the hierarchy's apathy presented a barrier to expansion.

In February 1936 the Bauernbund mounted a serious challenge to the Comice Agricole for control of the Chambre d'Agricole. The BB profited from popular resentment of the Comice's complacency, as many Alsatian farmers thought the Comice no longer aggressively defended peasant interests. In Bas-Rhin alone, officials estimated that the BB garnered close to twenty thousand votes in the Chambre d'Agricole elections. There are those who would argue that this larger group of twenty thousand were not actually fascists, that they voted according to a narrow range of issues. This is a weak argument intended to diminish the range of fascism and the strength of the fascist movement. As Hannah Arendt intimated through the use of the expression "the banality of evil," support for fascism could be shockingly mundane. Furthermore, there is no reason to assume that fascism was not a mainstream ideology. Nevertheless, the reasons for supporting a group such as Bilger's included economic as well as cultural and political motives.[57]

Dairy farmers were an important source of support for the Bauernbund. According to the police, Bilger "skillfully exploited" the gap between the price of milk paid by the consumer and the money received by the dairymen. To replace the middleman, Bilger founded dairy cooperatives in early 1938 that successfully raised milk prices in some areas, attracting the support of many dairy farmers. At the same time, he openly criticized the Comice for not guaranteeing milk prices.[58] When the Comice countered by forming its own dairy cooperatives, dairy farmers found themselves awkwardly caught between the two warring peasant organizations. Many tried to take advantage of both by enrolling simultaneously in the Comice's and the BB's cooperatives, in hopes of being on the winning side.[59]

The Comice fought to retain its hold over Alsatian farmers and firmly resisted the BB's strategy of "sapping" the Comice by flooding its assemblies with BB partisans. In Sélestat the Comice "energetically combated" the BB well enough to prevent its growth, at least through 1936.[60] When the BB attempted to establish a dairy cooperative in the region around Barr and Obernai, representatives of the Comice "called upon the farmers not to let themselves be duped by the BB."[61] They hinted at financial impropriety and unfulfilled promises. The local press accused Bilger of funneling money from the dairy cooperative into his political party. Although not necessarily opposed to the BB's political agenda, most dairy farmers may have preferred to see the Comice adopt the cooperative mentality of the Bauernbund rather than finance Bilger's political ambitions. In this case, the farmers opted to create a "neutral cooperative" that would remain genuinely apolitical and not act as a source of funds for the BB. By January 1939 the BB's dairy cooperatives were on the defensive. Despite resorting to sabotage and attempts to stop dealers' trucks, the Bauernbund was unable to prevent competition from the Comice cooperatives.[62]

In the mid-1930s Bilger sought to bypass, defuse, or overpower his opposition by allying himself with the Front Paysan and the French radical right. His sympathy for such movements illustrates his commitment to linking his rural movement to a complete restructuring of the political world. Bilger also hoped to profit from the success and dynamism of these national movements by showing that he was neither a Nazi nor an ignorant peasant, but that his ideas found resonance in France as well. Similarly, his adulation of the Belgian Rexist Léon Degrelle and the recently martyred head of the Rumanian Iron Guard and "hero of his race," Corneliu Codreanu, drew attention to the international scope of his ideology.[63]

Founded in 1934, the Front Paysan was a coalition of French peasant groups—including the Comité d'Action Paysanne, the Parti Agraire, and Henri Dorgères's Ligue des Paysans de France—for the purposes of unifying and organizing the defense of peasant interests. Bilger's success, in addition to linguistic and cultural barriers, ensured that the national peasant groups could not directly transplant their own organizations to Alsace. As early as 1933, officials noted that the Parti Agraire had "little chance of success in Haut-Rhin."[64] Bilger's alliance with Dorgères began in 1935 as part of the latter's effort to build a national constituency based on peasant activism. After attending one of the BB's rallies in Colmar, Dorgères was so impressed by the discipline and effectiveness of a hundred of Bilger's Green Shirts in silencing three hundred protesters, that he decided to copy the idea. "Seduced" by "the idea of some sort of uniform for the peasant youth" that would alleviate their "inferiority complex," Dorgères set up his own Green Shirt battalions to bolster and defend the Ligue des Paysans de France.[65]

Bilger's motives for linking forces with Dorgères remain murky. He welcomed the mass mobilization of the French peasantry by the Front Paysan in response to the "sickness" of the liberal party system. Their goals, however, were not exactly the same. Bilger did not simply seek the unification of his movement with like-minded rural interest groups in France, especially not as a junior partner, but the creation of "a corporative work-state." With this objective always in mind, the Bauernbund was willing to adopt "elastic tactics," including alliance with Dorgères. There was, ironically, little difference between Bilger's stated objectives and those of the Front Paysan. Dorgères, for example, capped his appeal to the voters of Blois in 1936 with the slogan, "Long Live the Corporative and Familial Republic!" Dorgères and Bilger differed primarily in their definition of community; Dorgères envisioned a French community, Bilger an Alsatian one. Their personal ambitions may have also generated mutual distrust.[66]

Bilger's political activity extended beyond the Front Paysan to include close ties with the entire French radical right. The Alsatian branch of the Jeunesses Patriotes, for example, endorsed the Bauernbund in 1936. "We have had the joy of hearing the regional leader of the Front Paysan last December fourth," reported the JP's short-lived regional paper, *Le National Populaire d'Alsace*. The BB's "doctrine was based on natural realities: Family—Work—Region—Christianity." The JP particularly lauded the BB's anti-Marxism and Bilger's leadership qualities. Bilger was "not simply a remarkable orator but a first-class organizer." Although marginal in Alsace, the JP represented the most elitist wing of the intensely French radical right. Consequently, its endorsement of the BB during the mid-1930s indicated deep ideological compatibility between the regionally oriented Bauernbund and the Francophile fascists.[67]

The Parti Populaire Français, run by the erstwhile communist Doriot who advocated a form of French national-socialism, made a brief and largely unsuccessful bid to win support in Alsace. One of its admirers was Bilger. "The onetime communist Doriot," Bilger's paper *Volk* commented, "has said some reasonable things and defends a foreign policy position that we have already advocated here."[68] Like the JP, the PPF's lack of regional success prevented mutual understanding with the BB from deteriorating into competitive acrimony.

Marcel Bucard's Francistes and the BB were more circumspect in their relations, largely because similarities in their ideology made them competitors. One Alsatian Franciste warned of "the next Peasant War" if the government did nothing about the low prices of agricultural products. He concluded that "Francisme wanted: 1. The power of peasants in its own corporation. 2. The power of this corporation in the state."[69] This rhetoric, especially the reference to the Peasant War, could have come straight from the pages of the Bauernbund press, where Bilger exhorted peasants to make a revolution against the liberal system. Likewise, the Francistes utilized antisemitism to attract peasants to "the corporative agricultural organization within the framework of an authoritarian, fascist state."[70]

The AF also endorsed Bilger. In June 1938 the AF sponsored a banquet in Strasbourg commemorating and featuring Charles Maurras, just days before his election to the Académie Française. The speakers at the banquet constituted a quorum of Francophile fascists. On the same dais with representatives from the Etudiants Royalistes de Strasbourg and the Haut-Rhin chapter of the AF were representatives from the Protestant royalist Association Sully, the PPF, and Joseph Bilger. Insisting that he was not a royalist himself, Bilger nevertheless "recognized in Maurras the founder of a social, corporative, and political doctrine that could save the country." Bilger especially praised Maurras's efforts to rescue France from "the control of international Jewish finance."[71]

The local and national press immediately attacked the AF for supporting Bilger, whose Nazi sympathies seemed at odds with the Maurras's anti-Germanism. The AF dismissed accusations that Bilger's program closely resembled Nazism as merely the result of "certain similarities in vocabulary, natural enough . . . in a land of German speakers." In any event, the AF was not careless enough to invite someone without "serious guarantees of his loyalty." Bilger, moreover, was to be preferred to Alsatians such as Herman Bickler, the head of the Nazi Jungmannschaft, who were "guilty of high treason" against France. "The vigorous nationalism and antisemitism of the Alsatians are eclipsing the Jewish Republic. Do not seek to discredit the best Frenchmen there," admonished the AF, "by favoring confusion with a Hitlerian squad."[72] As long as Bilger claimed loyalty to France, any similarity to—or sympathy for—Nazism was irrelevant to the royalists.

The 1938 banquet was the last known date of Bilger's collaboration with the Francophile right. Sometime between June 1938 and the outbreak of war, Bilger drifted from the French to the German camp. He no longer saw any advantage in remaining affiliated with French nationalist groups. Munich marked the inevitable turn toward war—a war that Bilger probably believed Germany would win. His goal was to be on the side of the victor, pressing for the corporate rights of Alsatian peasants.

A general collapse of the party accompanied the BB's shift in 1938 from a French to a pro-German stance. The UPR and the Comice's successful defense of their role in Alsatian rural politics, in addition to the spectacular growth of the PSF, deflated the BB's momentum. The Elsäßer Kurier, the UPR autonomists' chief voice in Haut-Rhin, claimed to have gained 250 subscribers and lost only 2 as a result of an editorial attack on the BB. Irate farmers accused Bilger of being a "traitor to the dairymen" and a "stool-pigeon for the Prefecture seeking to divert the peasants."[73] In June 1939 the court sentenced Bilger to one month (suspended) in prison and a 2,500 franc fine for speculating in milk prices. The type of crime undermined Bilger's credibility. Indeed, the local press began to speculate about Bilger's financial support, wondering whether he paid for the freely distributed copies of Volk by skimming off the top of the dairy cooperative movement or with money taken directly from the Nazis. Bilger's increased extremism resulted in frequent arrests between 1936 and 1939 and was symptomatic of his diminishing influence.[74] Sometimes he was arrested for antisemitic and anti–Third Republic rhetoric in his paper. Other times Bilger ran afoul of the law for misuse of cooperative and political funds. He also kept himself in the public eye by getting himself arrested for holding a rally despite a governmental ban. His personal lawyer in these cases was Pierre Pflimlin, who later became mayor of Strasbourg, prime minister of the Fourth Republic, and president of the European parliament in postwar Europe.[75]

An indication of Bilger's shift to Germany lay in his return into the good graces of the Landespartei, which by this point was totally committed to Nazism. At a time when the extreme autonomists in the Landespartei, the Jungmannschaft, and the EABP were solidifying their relationship with the German Nazis, Bilger's return to the autonomist fold represented a final turn toward Nazism. It is ironic that Bilger did not immediately join the Nazi occupation in June 1940, because he was a prisoner of war in Germany.[76] Called up for service, Bilger dutifully fought for the French army. Indeed, it is probably significant that he was not arrested by the French government in 1939 along with the other autonomists, since the hypersensitive and vigilant French officials arrested all the other pro-German leaders. Nevertheless, Bilger merged the Bauernbund into the German organizations shortly after his return from POW camp, sanctioning the German political coordination of all Alsatian corporate and political groups. This was a voluntary act in return for which Bilger became *Ortsgruppenleiter* in Ingersheim. In February 1941 he then left this position in Ingersheim to become the chief of propaganda in Lorraine. Bilger's selection for this position clearly indicates that the Nazis considered him ideologically sound.

Bilger then grew disenchanted with the Nazis when they turned out to be less sensitive to regional issues than he had expected. In June 1942 he had to leave his post as a result of his opposition to the resettlement of Lorrainers in the east. The Nazis used resettlement to break local resistance to their rule by sending Alsatian and Lorraine families to eastern Europe as punishment for individual draft evasion or even passive resistance to the regime. Bilger moved to Hamburg, where the Nazis kept him under surveillance.[77] Protected by Prince August Wilhelm of Prussia, Bilger survived and returned to Metz, but he remained out of public life for the duration of the war. In 1943 he met with Alsatian representatives of the Action Française in southern France, who bitterly opposed the German occupation of Alsace-Lorraine, but nothing came of this meeting.[78] Bilger's activity during the war was typical of his entire career. Ideologically, he was strongly attracted to Nazism, which the Nazis acknowledged by giving him extensive powers to formulate propaganda in Lorraine. Yet eventually he turned away from the party because of his commitment to Alsace and even entered into relations with the Resistance.

· · ·

Through the figure of this obscure regional fascist we can glimpse the broad interconnection between Nazi and French fascist groups. Fascists may have quibbled over the definition of the national *Volk* or, more prosaically, over the maintenance of their political turf. Dorgères, for example, trusted neither Bilger's Nazism (meaning his German orientation) nor his determination to forge his own empire. But as long as a fascist social order was implemented by somebody, and as long as the interests of the Alsatian peasantry were safeguarded, Bilger did not care whether Alsace found itself a part of Germany or of France.

Bilger's application of fascist ideology on the regional level was symptomatic of the difference between the fascism of the 1920s and that of the 1930s. Unlike the fascist movements of the 1920s, which were nationalist in orientation, the new groups focused on the social and political agenda of fascism. The ideological emphasis within fascism had shifted subtly from one decade to the next. The case of Bilger and the Bauernbund may be exceptional because he represented a regional, rather than national, frame of reference. Nevertheless, the mere existence of a regional fascism, based in this instance on the idea of a unique Alsatian community, should serve as a reminder that fascism was—and is—far more flexible and adaptive than we assume.

THE ALSATIAN NAZIS

The most obvious example of the new direction taken by fascism in the 1930s was the emergence of an Alsatian Nazi movement. The "Alsatian Nazis" distinguished themselves from the clerical autonomists, the communist autonomists, and the Bauernbund activists by their relatively direct and uncomplicated espousal of the Nazi cause. No longer content to argue for administrative autonomy within France, frustrated at the post-1929 apathy toward German cultural issues, and inspired by the success of Hitler in Germany, many of the 1920s autonomists turned to Nazism as the best vehicle for their pro-German agenda.

Founded in 1927 at the height of the autonomist movement, the Unabhängige Landespartei für Elsaß-Lothringen focused the Alsatian malaise into a political party whose chief goal was separation from France. The desire for separation, however, with its pro-German agenda, could easily drift into acceptance of Nazism, which was, after all, the most vociferous nationalist voice in Germany. Even in the 1920s the Landespartei had a far deeper attachment to Germany than any other party. At the same time, the autonomists in the Landespartei drew their chief ideological inspiration from Mussolini. The two threads—fascist ideology and German nationalism—began to come together around 1929 when a significant faction of the Landespartei espoused Nazism. By the mid-1930s, the Landespartei had become a Nazi vehicle.

The change in the official autonomist movement from a popular movement representing

Alsatians' legitimate grievances at France's heavy-handed administration to a Nazi mouthpiece can best be seen in the career of the Alsatian Landespartei's leader, Karl Roos. In 1924 Roos became involved in the *Heimatbewegung*, eventually becoming the head of the Landespartei. The author of several books on Alsatian culture, Roos's political activity stemmed from an unshakable belief in the Germanness of Alsace. His dramatic trial for pro-German activity in 1929 marked the acme of autonomism; from that moment on the movement lost momentum. Like many other autonomists, Roos became convinced that only Nazi Germany could liberate Alsace from France. Roos failed, however, to mold Alsatian Nazism into a unified movement, and throughout the 1930s it was characterized by internecine struggles. Nevertheless, collaboration between German Nazis and the Landespartei grew during the 1930s. When World War II started, the French government arrested Roos and executed him for high treason.

Roos was by no means the most extreme of the Alsatian Nazis. Just as the relationships of the communist autonomists and the Bauernbund to Nazism were fundamentally different, so too, variety characterized the Alsatian Nazi movement. Led by Hermann Bickler, a small group of dedicated Nazis challenged the Landespartei to forge even closer links to German Nazism. Eventually this group organized and became the Jungmannschaft, a sort of advance guard for the German SS. Thus, a hierarchy of Nazism in Alsace emerged, consisting—in descending order of commitment and radicalness—of the Jungmannschaft, the Landespartei, the communist autonomists, the Bauernbund, and the clerical autonomists.

· · ·

The connection between the Alsatian autonomists and Germany was extensive. Between 100,000 and 150,000 refugees from Alsace settled in Germany after 1918, forming a sizable reservoir of support within Germany for the regaining of Alsace.[1] Emigrant Alsatians banded together in the Hilfsbund der vertriebenen Elsaß-Lothringer im Reich (Welfare Union of Exiled Alsace-Lorrainers in the Reich); they published news from their homeland in the *Elsaß-Lothringischen Pressedienst* and sponsored scholarly research through the Wissenschaftliches Institut der Elsaß-Lorrainer im Reich (Scholarly Institute of the Alsace-Lorrainers in the Reich). Broader-based German cultural organizations, such as the Verein für das Deutschtum im Ausland (Society for Foreign Germans) and the Deutscher Schutzbund für die Grenz- und Auslandsdeutschen (German Protective Union for Border and Foreign Germans), a German organization dedicated to the maintenance of German culture abroad, also took an interest in Alsace. Alsatian émigré Robert Ernst, who became responsible for transmitting funds to Alsatian autonomists during the 1920s and 1930s, parlayed his early experience in the Alsatian refugee groups into a prominent role in the German cultural organizations.[2]

Furthermore, autonomism's growth depended on money from Germany.

Operating through a network of Alsatian refugees in Germany and Swiss intermediaries, the German foreign office disbursed 2 million marks to the autonomist movement between 1925 and 1933. From its inception in 1926, the autonomist publishing house, the Erwinia Verlag, received heavy subsidies from the Deutscher Schutzbund. Abbé Joseph Fasshauer, an editor at Erwinia and codefendant in the Colmar trials, made monthly trips to Switzerland collecting money for Erwinia.[3]

Few in Germany accepted the frenchification of Alsace. The historian Hermann Oncken, for example, lectured that Alsace-Lorraine was part of the German cultural community and that the sole purpose of France's occupation of Alsace was the destruction of Germany.[4] German newspapers portrayed Alsace as an occupied territory garrisoned by "black troops," compelled against its will to become French.[5] Despite Hitler's occasional renunciations of German rights in Alsace-Lorraine, German Nazis perpetuated the struggle for the return of the region. Indeed, in *Mein Kampf*, Hitler excoriated prewar German policy for not "once and for all pulverizing the French Hydra with a cultural fist" in Alsace-Lorraine. Shortly after Hitler came to power, about 350 national socialists marched along the border singing "Deutschland über Alles," leaving little question as to the intentions of the new leaders of the German regime toward Alsace-Lorraine.[6]

Belief in Alsace's intrinsic Germanness was not limited to Germany; the Alsatian autonomists also believed that Alsace was part of Germany. Roos, a professor of German, stated baldly, "We are German. Over the centuries our people have remained German." Convinced that Alsatians were happy before the war, Eugene Ricklin, a former Reichstag deputy, asked, "Does France believe that a people, like that of Alsace-Lorraine, which is racially German due to its language and which has prospered for nearly fifty years under the German regime can become French overnight?" Ricklin had, of course, a prosperous political career prior to 1918 as mayor of Dannemarie, president of the *Landtag,* and deputy to the *Reichstag.* Nevertheless, he expressed widespread resentment at the French attempt to turn Alsatians into compliant French citizens. The Landespartei consistently maintained that "France was never, and is not now, the Fatherland of the Alsatian people," and that Alsace had joined France against its will.[7]

In addition to financial and cultural affiliations, strong religious ties bound many Alsatians to Germany. Not all Protestants were Nazi, nor did they all insist on returning to Germany. Nevertheless, Lutherans felt culturally closer to Germany than most Catholic Alsatians did, because of their religion. Consequently, Lutheran Alsatians were susceptible to Nazi arguments about German culture and nationalism and were prominent in the Landespartei and the Nazi movement.

The other denominations did not embrace Nazism as directly as the Lutherans. Although the Anabaptists were also represented in the Nazi movement, they by no means played a central role. Hermann Bickler, the leader of the Jungmannschaft, for example, was born and raised in

Lorraine by an Anabaptist grandfather.[8] Calvinists, for their part, tended to be pro-French and in any event concentrated in Haut-Rhin. Catholic Alsatians were underrepresented in the Alsatian Nazi movement, although they played an important role in the autonomist struggle. The more Nazi the Landespartei became, the less interested the Catholics became. This was because of a general revulsion at the secularization policy of the Nazi *Gleichschaltung* (political coordination) and the fact that Catholics had alternative outlets for their radical right-wing activity, including the "left wing" of the UPR, the Bauernbund, and the various French fascist groups.

The Landespartei and the Jungmannschaft genuinely despised the bourgeoisie, even though Alsatian Protestants tended to be bourgeois.[9] By bourgeoisie, however, they meant pro-French or Jewish urban entrepreneurs who profited from the cultural repression of German-speaking Alsatians. Alsatian Nazis had a cultural motivation for their hatred of the upper classes, since these represented assimilation into French culture. "Our Alsatian bourgeoisie," Paul Schall argued to an audience of almost two thousand, "is partly responsible for the Alsatian malaise." Bickler also singled out the bourgeoisie as the class whose power must be "broken."[10] Correct-thinking shopkeepers and lawyers, however, were not included in this critique. Indeed, many Alsatian Nazis were disenchanted intelligentsia who had joined Germanophile fraternities in university during the 1920s and held positions as archivists, librarians, or teachers. Roos, for example, was a German folklorist and Hermann Bickler was a lawyer. Such embittered intellectuals represented a significant, if not essential, group capable of articulating a cultural alternative to France.[11]

Another source of support for the Landespartei came from rural areas. Many farmers, especially in Bas-Rhin, attended rural meetings of the Landespartei. In contrast to Joseph Bilger's Bauernbund, which recruited from the Catholic peasantry of Haut-Rhin, the Landespartei drew primarily from the Protestant peasantry of Bas-Rhin. Given its stronger cultural and religious affinity for Germany, it is not surprising that Bas-Rhin provided the overwhelming majority of the Nazis. Many may have been veterans of the German army, as Roos himself was.[12]

The year 1928–1929 was a turning point, a time when autonomists nearly succeeded in matching their political ideology to public opinion.[13] The 1928 Colmar trials had transformed the Alsatian malaise into a raging epidemic by publicly demonstrating the anti-Alsatian spirit of the French government. When the National Assembly refused to seat Joseph Rossé and Eugene Ricklin, the Alsatians defied the government by returning two more Colmar defendants, René Hauss and Marcel Stürmel. To the applause of the extreme left and right in the Assembly, Hauss denounced the insensitivity of the government and demanded minority rights for Alsace. Over the course of the year, the UPR's pro-German left wing gained power within the party, declaring itself ready "to march hand in hand . . . not only with the autonomists but also with the communists to defend the *Heimatbund*'s point of view."[14]

Autonomists feverishly agitated throughout 1928 and 1929. At the height of their popularity, autonomists drew large numbers to their rallies. One of the largest was a rally held in Strasbourg on July 31, 1928, attended by six thousand Alsatians.[15] The result was the Volksfront, an autonomist bloc of all political hues, which faced the National Front, a coalition of all parties that stressed integration into France (including the APNA, SFIO, Democrats, and Radicals).[16] Included in the Volksfront were the Landespartei, the Elsaß-Lothringische Fortschrittspartei, the communist autonomists, and the UPR. As an electoral alliance, the Volksfront produced notable victories in the October 1928 cantonal elections and the May 1929 municipal elections. The new Strasbourg municipal council, for example, consisted of twenty-two autonomists against fourteen assimilationists.[17]

The creation of the *Elsaß-Lothringische Zeitung* in December 1929 best symbolized the collaboration of autonomist parties. This was not simply a regional paper; it combined the moral, cultural, and political essence of the autonomist movement into a single persuasive daily created from the amalgamation of the Landespartei's biweekly, the *Volkswille,* and the Progressive Party's weekly, the *Freie Zeitung,* edited by Camille Dahlet. And although the communist autonomists had their own paper, Mourer had an office at the *Elsaß-Lothringische Zeitung* for a short period.[18] Although dominated by the Landespartei, the *Elsaß-Lothringische Zeitung,* like the Volksfront, was a model for the construction of a harmonious Alsace that stood above petty party differences.

The new journal did more than criticize the Third Republic—it categorically opposed parliamentary democracy. One contributor argued that "democracy and parliamentarianism were responsible for the terrible financial conditions" of the depression years. Furthermore, according to the same author, "democracy at present does not grip the entire life and death interests of the nation."[19] Despite opposition to Italy's ongoing oppression of the Sudtirol, the autonomists approved of the way in which Italian "fascism had done away with the parties." Editor Paul Schall, whose Nazi sympathies were already evident in 1931, excoriated both the UPR and the APNA because, at bottom, "they are governmental parties."[20]

The idea that parliamentarianism and democracy were corrupt and inefficient was pervasive in autonomist circles. Even a relatively moderate autonomist cleric, such as the UPR's Charles Didio, believed that "state authority must do away with the party agitation that reigns in France."[21] The solution was to eradicate the decadence of parliamentary politics in favor of the "idea of the *Volksgemeinschaft,* the willingness to sacrifice, and self-discipline." Indeed, the Volksfront, which spanned clerical, communist, and Radical parties, embodied this transcendent approach to politics.[22]

Even before Hitler's seizure of power, autonomists in the Landespartei accepted the universality of fascism. Reviewing the history of Italian Fascism, one *Elsaß-Lothringische Zeitung* contributor quoted what he thought was one of the Duce's "most significant speeches," in which he argued that "fascism as an idea, doctrine, and realization is universal." A unified Europe, "which solved the modern state problem of the twentieth century in a fascist sense," was attractive to Alsatians who thought of their region as quintessentially European.[23]

The *Elsaß-Lothringische Zeitung*'s position toward Hitler was clearly favorable. As early as 1929, the Landespartei referred to Hitler as "this extraordinary patriotic man." Although striving to maintain the facade of neutrality toward Hitler, Schall clearly endorsed the Nazis for wanting the "renewal of Germany" and "the formation of Greater Germany based on the *right of self-determination*," and because they opposed parliamentary democracy.[24] Not only did Schall support the Nazi's repudiation of the Treaty of Versailles to create a greater Germany, his reference to self-determination linked Alsace, which never had a plebiscite, with the national-socialist revision of European boundaries.

The *Elsaß-Lothringische Zeitung* published an illuminating pamphlet in July 1933 entitled, "What Is Our Position Regarding Hitler's Germany?" France's obsession with turning Germany into "a second-class nation," opined the *Elsaß-Lothringische Zeitung*'s editors, necessitated the rise of Hitler. Furthermore, the "German revolution" (meaning Hitler's revolution) resembled the French Revolution because both were "national and social" and resulted in necessary "encroachments to the disadvantage of certain citizens." Hitler had revived Germany, making it an equal of France. If only France and Germany could work together (implying that France should adapt a similar form of government), then Alsace could become a bridge between the two.[25] The *Elsaß-Lothringische Zeitung*'s consistent assessment of Hitler during the critical period between 1930 and 1933 was, to put it charitably, favorable. It was also at odds with the rest of France, which hardly would have accepted the idea that the rise of Hitler was both a good thing and France's fault.

The high point for the Landespartei came in late 1928 and early 1929 when Karl Roos triumphantly returned from Switzerland to stand trial for his pro-German activity. Smuggled across the border, the folklore professor arrived in Strasbourg on November 9, 1928, where communist autonomists sheltered him. The following evening he gave a dramatic speech at a mass rally, climaxing in the raising of a huge red-and-white flag with the cross of Lorraine and the singing of "O Straßburg."[26] Following the rally, the police arrested him and sent him to Besançon for trial.

Roos's trial proved a brilliant manipulation of the French government's ambivalence. Claiming disingenuously that the "cultural movement" was not political and that he knew many German nationalists from his university days, Roos forced the prosecution on the defensive.[27]

In much the same way that Hitler turned his 1924 trial for treason into a trial of the German government, Roos succeeded in forcing the government to defend its policy toward Alsace. The prosecution failed to present a strong enough case, in part because the government no longer favored a repressive administration, so Roos was acquitted. Roos's acquittal constituted a major victory for the Landespartei and the autonomist movement. On the evening of his acquittal Roos addressed six thousand autonomists in the Palais des Fêtes. Weak attendance at a counter rally held by the assimilationists in Colmar the next day merely served to highlight Roos's victory.[28]

Support for the party dissipated almost immediately. A senatorial by-election in Haut-Rhin held on October 20, 1929, signaled the ebbing of the Volkfront's fortunes. Abbé Xavier Haegy, the popular éminence grise behind autonomism, ran against Joseph Pfleger, a leading spokesman for assimilation. On the eve of the election an exchange between the candidates underscored the central issue of the election. When asked if he was a Frenchman or a German, Haegy responded, "I am an Alsatian." To the same question, Pfleger asserted, "I am first of all a Frenchman."[29] Despite Haegy's advantages of press, prominence, and personality, Pfleger won by a narrow margin. Summing up various explanations for Haegy's defeat, the police claimed, "The autonomist propaganda of Abbé Haegy went too far and turned off precisely those that it sought to win over."[30]

Autonomists were at a loss to explain Haegy's defeat, especially since they could not accept the limitations of autonomism. As a result of the loss of autonomist momentum, the Landespartei suffered from dissension and "indifference" from 1929 to 1931.[31] Roos repeatedly commented on the poor attendance at Landespartei meetings and rallies.[32] Some members blamed flagging enthusiasm on the party's penchant for unilateral decisions. The rank and file also criticized the "poor organization of the party and the absence of a program." Roos was not immune from criticism and several activists accused him of lacking vigor.[33]

The party's collapse also resulted from the autonomists' failure to offer a realistic alternative. Many Alsatians agreed with Robert Redslob, a professor at the University of Strasbourg, when he described Alsace's cultural, political, and economic situation under France as "good, even excellent."[34] France had turned Strasbourg into an important port and virtually every sector of the economy prospered. Union with Germany grew less attractive and less necessary (however much autonomist leaders advocated it) the more the Alsatian economy flourished. Especially after the onset of the depression in 1929, the French economy seemed more viable than the German.

Part of the problem was that the Landespartei had lost touch with its Catholic constituency. Bishop Ruch, who had been so instrumental in mobilizing the initial defense of regional rights in 1924 and 1925, circulated several pastorals within his diocese criticizing the autonomists for allying themselves with communists and for placing politics before God.[35] Ruch opposed the German orientation of the autonomists. Since the village curés constituted a core of autonomist activism, Ruch undermined the movement by forcing them to choose between corporate obedience and ethnic identity.

Above all, the French government adopted a conciliatory attitude toward Alsace. After the public debacle at Colmar the government realized the futility of simply suppressing Alsatian regionalism. As a result of Roos's acquittal and the amnesty extended to the convicted defendants of Colmar, popular resentment directed toward France dissipated. The prefect of Bas-Rhin noted a drop in complaints about "governmental arbitrariness" in April 1929 and that political parties were distancing themselves from autonomism. He foresaw "a more tranquil period in Alsace." This was quite a transformation from six months earlier, when the prefect described the situation in Alsace as "troubled."[36] After 1929 the government was loathe to take any action that might alienate Alsatians. It is worth noting that French policy toward Alsace could preserve some semblance of continuity because of the way Alsace was administered. Paul Valot (who was such a consummately faceless bureaucrat that almost no information on his personal life or political views exists) directed the Services d'Alsace et de Lorraine, which oversaw all administrative matters and advised the government on matters Alsatian. Moderation by the central government on almost all regional issues resulted in growing popular acceptance of French rule.

Whatever the cause, the ebb of autonomist enthusiasm and the disarray in the Landespartei resulted in an internal power struggle. The younger members of the party chafed at the lack of progress on the part of the "old party bosses."[37] Led by Hermann Bickler, a new generation of "young hotheads *[Stürmer]* of the Jungmannschaft" nudged "their elders toward an increasingly German national socialist extremism." "Domestic difficulties" between autonomists continued to characterize relations until Bickler transformed the Jungmannschaft into the Elsaß-Lothringische Partei (ELP) in 1937.[38]

Hermann Bickler was the driving force behind Alsatian Nazism.[39] From 1924, when he founded the Studentischen Heimatbund (a student corporation at the University of Strasbourg opposed to the assimilationist policies of the Cartel des Gauches), to 1978, when he published his memoirs, Bickler believed in a Nazi Alsace. Bickler joined the Landespartei immediately upon its formation in 1927 and remained a member until 1937. By 1931 his insistent, strident voice exercised a growing influence within the party. In the process, Bickler earned the explicit trust of the Nazis, who appointed him *Kreisleiter* (county executive) of Strasbourg in September 1940 and let him enter the SS at the rank of colonel. Furthermore, he became the head of Section VI of the *Sicherheitsdienst* (security service) in Paris in 1943, responsible for political intelligence in France, including collaboration with all French fascist groups.[40]

On January 10, 1931, Bickler launched the pro-Nazi *Jungmannschaft,* a controversial supplement in the *Elsaß-Lothringische Zeitung*. Intended as a fortnightly supplement, the *Jungmannschaft* appeared irregularly after its first four installments.[41] The supplement was not especially popular with the readers of the *Elsaß-Lothringische Zeitung*, which still reflected the integrative Volksfront approach and was not yet the Nazi mouthpiece it later became. An in-house survey taken in July 1931 revealed a polarized readership. Criticism was severe enough that the *Elsaß-Lothringische Zeitung* eventually distanced itself from the *Jungmannschaft*, which "did not, properly speaking, constitute a supplement of the *Elsaß-Lothringische Zeitung*, but an open forum that it had put at the disposal of a group of young Alsatians."[42]

Undeterred, the following year Bickler transformed ideology into organization. Divided into local cells, the new Jungmannschaft organization included activists between the ages of eighteen and forty-five (although Bickler admits that, despite its name, many members were much older).[43] Bickler did not intend the Jungmannschaft to be a mass movement. "The unanimity of the movement," Bickler reminisced, "was only possible because from the beginning it had included an elite and not the masses." The idea was to form a revolutionary vanguard of "the most outstanding and virtuous" elites, whose very example and leadership would guide Alsatians to an understanding of their Germanness. The Jungmannschaft disdained "to parliamentarianize," instead forming a racially and ideologically pure nucleus that represented what Alsace should be and that had the resolve to impose a revolution from above to make it so.[44]

The Jungmannschaft's selectiveness and political tactics were adaptations to the Alsatian political situation. Bickler was well aware that Alsatian public opinion was too apathetic toward Nazism to support the development of a mass party. Bickler admitted, for example, that after 1933 the bulk of the UPR lost interest in autonomism for religious reasons.[45] A German Nazi Party had, in any event, little future in the French National Assembly.

Instead, Bickler organized the Jungmannschaft to extend the principles of national socialism to Alsace.[46] In this, the Jungmannschaft was much more aggressive than the Landespartei, which, although it was pro-Nazi, showed a greater proclivity for building a mass party in conjunction with other groups. Unlike the Bauernbund or clerical autonomists such as Joseph Rossé, who merely found Nazi ideology worthy of imitation, Bickler and his Jungmannschaft were the real thing. In a 1941 letter to Director of the Party Chancellory Martin Bormann, Gauleiter Robert Wagner of Baden wrote, "Bickler's group must be treated as completely national socialist. The Jungmannschaft was nothing other than a camouflaged SA."[47] Indeed, the disguise was quite thin—its proposed uniform, consisting of a brown shirt, was "an imitation of the Hitlerian S.A.'s tunics," although the Jungmannschaft dropped this color for fear it would be too obvious. Members of the Jungmannschaft attended Hitler Youth rallies in Germany on an unofficial basis during the 1930s.[48]

Not only did the Jungmannschaft have overt connections with the German Nazi Party, its ideological program was pure Nazi. Above all, the Jungmannschaft believed in a state that reflected the concerns of the *Volk*. Unlike more regionally oriented groups (such as the Bauernbund and the clerical autonomists), the Jungmannschaft explicitly defined Alsatians as Germans.[49] The Jungmannschaft's idea of *Volk*, as with the Nazis, was essentially a racial concept. Unlike the French fascists, for whom *Volk* was a cultural concept, the Alsatian Nazis sought to unite the nation and to create homogeneity on the basis of race. The Jungmannschaft objected, for example, to the influx of African colonials, asserting that "a policy of clear separation" between the races would be in the interests of blacks and whites, since it would merely "respect the differences made by nature itself."[50] Common membership in a race ameliorated class conflict and social disharmony.

The Jungmannschaft, therefore, defined unacceptable members of the community through the strict litmus test of race. In particular, the Alsatian Nazis targeted Jews, turning them into symbolic foreigners, the antithesis and enemy of everything German. "Don't buy from Jews!" advised one *Frei Volk* flyer dated September 1938. In November 1937 *Frei Volk* mocked the reelection of "the Jew La Gardia [*sic*]" as mayor of New York City, implying that America's decadence was the fault of the Jews. Another article, dated November 5, 1938, declared that "the Jews are in general natural enemies of the people and especially of our Alsace-Lorraine *Volk*." Even the world of sport was not immune; in July 1937 the Jungmannschaft claimed that an international Jewish conspiracy prevented a bout between Joe Louis and Max Schmeling that would prove the validity of "Hitler's theory" of the superiority of the Aryan race. (This, of course, was written before the famous June 22, 1938, rematch took place, which resulted in an embarrassing first-round knockout of Aryan supremacy.) The consistent message was that Jews constituted an international—and therefore powerful—force that was racially inferior to members of the German race and that was responsible for all the evils perpetrated on the Alsace-Lorraine *Volk*.[51]

Bickler shared the Nazis' antipathy toward Christianity. On the one hand, he wanted to found the Jungmannschaft on "a large Christian base capable of encompassing as much of the world as possible." Ostensibly Christian, the language of this sort of appeal suggests a crass and cynical manipulation of religion rather than genuine belief. On the other hand, Bickler defended the *Gleichschaltung* of the Catholic and Protestant churches in Germany on the grounds that a powerful state had the right to suppress "elements of trouble and disorder." Everything, including religion, had to be subservient to the state.[52]

The group surrounding Bickler was not the only Alsatian representative of Nazism. Another youth group, the Bund Erwin von Steinbach, had close ties to the Jungmannschaft. The Bund took the name of the Gothic German architect of the Strasbourg Cathedral to remind its members of the close cultural ties between Alsace and Germany. Founded in 1926 by two autonomist Protestant pastors, the Bund Erwin von Steinbach languished until 1931 when Friedrich Spieser moved to Alsace from Germany and took over its direction. Under Spieser's leadership, the Bund organized frequent trips to the Vosges, "popular educational evenings," and the singing of folk songs.[53]

Although the Bund was a Nazi organization, its function differed slightly from that of the Jungmannschaft. Where the Jungmannschaft constituted a paramilitary political elite, Spieser's organization performed a cultural missionary role. Through campfires, song fests, and the monthly journal *Straßburger Monatshefte*, Spieser popularized Germanic culture in Alsace. In a letter to Robert Ernst, at that time director of the German Schutzbund, written sometime in 1933–1934, Spieser declared that the goal of the Bund was to convert peasants, women, and the half-educated to "a natural, deep-rooted attachment to the *Volkstum* [nationality]."[54]

The ultimate goal of Spieser's cultural propaganda is clear, not only from his correspondence with Ernst at this time but also from the articles he published in his journal. Without mentioning Nazism, Spieser's job was to predispose Alsatians to Nazi culture and to politicize all aspects of culture. Interspersed among pieces on culture, folklore, and art were political essays such as Hermann Bickler's "On the Present Situation in Alsace-Lorraine."[55] French authorities viewed Spieser's political assault on culture with trepidation. Despite its relatively small circulation (one thousand copies per issue), the government banned it in August 1939.[56] Resurrected by the Nazis in the fall of 1940, the *Straßburger Monatshefte* continued its cultural mission with contributions from Robert Ernst, Paul Schall, and other Nazi autonomists.

Publicly, Spieser strenuously denied any affiliation with the Nazis or the Germans.[57] His close contacts with the Nazi movement, however, dated back to the 1920s. At the universities of Göttingen and Marburg, Spieser had attracted the attention of Ernst, who probably paid for his education in Germany.[58] In addition, Bickler and Spieser belonged to the same Strasbourg Protestant student fraternity, Argentina, in 1927. Openly autonomist and Germanophile, Argentina included about three hundred students with a heavy concentration in Protestant theology. Bickler attended Spieser's wedding to a wealthy German countess in 1931. Spieser's friendship with Bickler extended to the public sphere, as the former was "one of the principal collaborators in the supplemental periodical *Jungmannschaft*." Essentially the Jungmannschaft and the Bund were interchangeable.[59]

The formation of the Jungmannschaft and the activity of the Wanderbund Erwin von Steinbach created organizational animosity toward the Landespartei. The Jungmannschaft disapproved of "the Roos-Schall-Walter-Mourer collusion," that linked the Landespartei, the UPR, and the

EABP.[60] Schall, concerned about the success of Bickler's Jungmannschaft, formed the short-lived Bund der Elsäßischen Wanderfreunde in July 1933.[61] Instead of flying the *Wolfangel*, the Jungmannschaft's swastika equivalent, the Wanderbund resurrected the Bundschuh symbol from the sixteenth-century peasant revolt. The overt parallel with the Bauernbund suggests Schall may have hoped either to establish links with Bilger or to kill two birds with one stone by co-opting some of the Bauernbund's membership. Although for the most part this was a struggle over tactics and party control—a dispute among ideological brothers—it nevertheless divided the Nazi movement.

The rise of Nazism in Germany and Alsace disrupted the harmony of the Volksfront. The various components of autonomism—communist, clerical, Catholic, progressive, and Nazi—split over the issue of fascism. The opposition communists underwent a bifurcation between 1934 and 1935 (see Chapter 4). Camille Dahlet, a radical-socialist autonomist from Saverne and coeditor of the *Elsaß-Lothringische Zeitung*, was unable to square the separatist and Nazi ideology of his Landespartei colleagues with his belief in administrative autonomy. Claiming "unbridgeable differences of opinion," Dahlet resigned his position at the *Elsaß-Lothringische Zeitung* in the fall of 1933.[62] The Nazi autonomists fumed that his Progressive Party was simply a "petty bourgeois club of atheists and freemasons." As far as Nazi autonomists were concerned, the movement was better off without such weak-kneed moderates.[63]

Other dedicated Landespartei members found the growing Nazism of the party unacceptable. The Protestant pastor Charles-Philippe Heil quit the Landespartei in 1934 out of distaste for its pro-Hitler slant and formed a short-lived political alternative called the Parti Régionaliste Alsacien. He continued to share many goals with the Landespartei—rapprochement between France and Germany, reform of the state, and autonomous administration of Alsace—with one key exception: Heil was now willing to accept that Alsace remain part of France.[64]

The UPR, similarly, backed away from the Volksfront. Rapprochement between the UPR and the Francophile APNA blossomed after the two parties joined forces to combat an attack by the central government on religious education. In June 1934 the UPR noted that its Christian principles made it difficult to maintain alliance with other parties in the Volksfront.[65] As a result, the front's electoral unity dissolved during the municipal elections of 1935, when the UPR supported Charles Frey, the democratic candidate for mayor, instead of the incumbent communist autonomist Charles Hueber. Over the strenuous objections of the UPR's left wing, led by Rossé and Stürmel, the Volksfront ceased to exist.

The Landespartei made a small comeback in 1936, largely as part of the percolation of right-wing activity in response to the Popular Front, Germany's economic recovery, and the apparent threat of Bolshevism. Prior to 1936 the Landespartei and the *Elsaß-Lothringische Zeitung* had lost considerable support and languished in a state of "negligible influence." In the 1936 national elections, however, the Landespartei garnered 11,801 votes—all from Bas-Rhin, prompting Bickler to declare in November 1936 that membership had doubled since the summer.[66]

When the communist autonomist paper, *Die Neue Welt,* dropped all pretense of Marxist orientation and officially merged with the *Elsaß-Lothringische Zeitung, Les Dernières Nouvelles de Strasbourg* wryly commented that, "In reality, close collaboration between the Landespartei and the worker and peasant party . . . was established long ago."[67] Shortly after the papers merged in July 1939, the two parties became one. As desperate as the communist autonomists were for money, influence, and credibility by 1939, the Landespartei was equally uncertain about its future. Persecuted by the French police, at odds with the Jungmannschaft, and without much public backing, the Landespartei and the EABP combined forces in a hopeful effort to revivify their political fortunes.

The Jungmannschaft, despite its avowed hatred of parties, became the Elsaß-Lothringischer Partei (ELP) in 1937 with its own newspaper, the *Frei Volk.* Bickler had little choice; the Popular Front's ban on leagues and non-political movements threatened the Jungmannschaft with dissolution. The ELP grew out of the tactical split between Bickler and his Jungmannschaft, on one hand, and Schall, Hauss, and the leaders of the Landespartei, on the other. Their disagreement revolved around how overtly to support the Nazis. Bickler appeared to have been a genuine Nazi, whereas Schall, Hauss, and the other "moderates" were Nazis out of convenience.

Their disagreement reflected different sources of support within Nazi Germany. Robert Ernst, a dedicated Nazi and indefatigable agitator for the germanization of Alsace-Lorraine, supported the Landespartei and the Volksfront.[68] His support can best be seen in his reportage of Alsatian events in the *Elsaß-Lothringischer Pressedienst* and the *Elsaß-Lothringen Heimatstimmen,* both edited by Ernst during the 1930s.[69] As an official of the private Volksbund für das Deutschtum im Ausland, Ernst competed with a number of private, party, and governmental organizations that purported to deal with foreign Germans. Judging from his organizational and ideological approach, Bickler and the Jungmannschaft probably got support directly from the SS. There is unfortunately no smoking gun irrefutably demonstrating the connection between the SA and/or the SS and the Jungmannschaft. Nevertheless, Bickler's prompt assumption of high rank in the SS in 1940 and the similarity of their objectives suggest that this connection existed. Friedrich Spieser used his wife's considerable fortune to subsidize the Erwin von Steinbach Bund and may have had closer ties to the party or the SA. Such organizational competition was rife in the Nazi system.

Bickler turned out to be the most radical of the young turks among the Nazi autonomists with the inside track on German Nazi support. The journal *Frei Volk* attacked the timidity of other separatists. Nevertheless, the Landespartei activists—Schall, Schlegel, and Hauss—"resolved to make a major effort to oppose the success of the Bicklerian competition."[70] *Frei Volk,* which began publication in 1937, was not printed at the printing press controlled by Schall and Emil Brumder. Division continued to mark the Nazi autonomists throughout 1938.

Most Alsatians were unmoved by the Nazism of *Frei Volk* and the *Elsaß-Lothringische Zeitung,* largely because of the opposition, not only of the Francophile radical right but of the press. *Les Dernières Nouvelles de Strasbourg,* by far the largest daily in the region and the most neutral, was very clear about its disgust with Nazism. It pointed out, for example, that "it is not in France that one must look for concentration camps." Oscar de Férenzy, editor of the pro-French radical right-wing Catholic paper *La Voix d'Alsace et de Lorraine,* wrote an article entitled "After the Jews, the Catholics?" in which he pointed out that Nazism's antisemitism and anti-Catholicism were two sides to the same coin. Férenzy feared that regional antisemitism, such as that espoused by Bickler would lead Alsace into the arms of Nazi Germany.[71]

Declining interest in autonomism and widespread provincial suspicion of Hitler forced the autonomists further right. The Landespartei and the Jungmannschaft had to become increasingly shrill in order to make themselves heard. In turn, their radicalism and Nazism soured the public in what became a cycle of opposition to the German variety of fascism. *Frei Volk,* for example, admonished those Alsatians who gave their children French names "such as Eliane, Roger, Jeannine," when they could have given them "Alsatian" names that "sound much better" such as "Adelheit, Hildegrunde, Greta, Gutlinde, Richardis, Siegfried." A year later the Nazi administration took up the same name theme in what turned out to be an absurd and bitter cultural struggle over Alsatian names. Such demands did little to conciliate the wider public.[72]

Consequently, the Alsatian Nazis never became a mass party. To be sure, they could not openly pursue their political goals under the watchful eye of the French police. Even so, the maximum number of Alsatian Nazi publications in circulation in 1938 did not exceed 8,500.[73] The *Elsaß-Lothringische Zeitung* normally printed between 3,000 and 4,000, although the figure was frequently higher whenever the Landespartei wanted to distribute free copies. The *Frei Volk* had about 1,500 subscribers and printed 3,000 copies. At around 1,000 copies, Spieser's *Straßburger Monatshefte* had a much smaller audience. The actual number of Nazi activists was much lower, probably around 4,000, since many Alsatian Nazis would have subscribed to all three papers. Moreover, the Alsatian Nazis were concentrated in a few areas within Bas-Rhin. In short, it is easy to exaggerate the Nazi threat in Alsace.[74]

If the Alsatian Nazis appeared divided and marginal, with 4,000 activists in 1938 they were nevertheless one of the largest fascist strands. If one includes the communist autonomists, the Rossé faction of the UPR, and the Bauernbund, the overall Nazi movement (as opposed to the fascist movement) in Alsace was considerable, reaching around 15,000 in the late 1930s. Nazism, however, was not a unified movement in Alsace. Each group espoused a different version of Nazism and had varying degrees of commitment to Hitler. Indeed, Rossé and Bilger did not even embrace Nazism openly and can only be included as sympathizers—and competing ones at that.

The outbreak of World War II forced the French police to take measures against the autonomists. Given police knowledge about the Alsatian Nazis, the government surprisingly refrained throughout the 1930s from actively prosecuting them. Until 1939 the government contented itself with monitoring the activities of the Alsatian Nazis and hesitated to interfere, for fear that any action might result in a resurgence of Alsatian discontent. In September 1939, however, the government could not ignore the threat posed by the Alsatian Nazis, as a potential fifth column, and it arrested fifteen of the most prominent Nazi sympathizers. Those arrested represented a cross section of the autonomist movement, including Joseph Rossé and Marcel Stürmel of the UPR, Hermann Bickler of the Jungmannschaft, Karl Roos and Paul Schall of the Landespartei, and Jean-Pierre Mourer of the communist autonomists. Friedrich Spieser fled to Germany. The prisoners were moved to Nancy, tried, and convicted. Although several received the death sentence, only Karl Roos stood in front of a firing squad before the German army liberated them.[75]

Liberation by the Germans brought the Alsatian Nazis out of obscurity and into positions of power. The arrested autonomists signed the resolution of Trois-Epis, encouraging Alsatians to accept Nazi rule. Even in death, Karl Roos served Hitler as a martyr for the Nazi cause, when the party honored his exhumed remains in an ostentatious ceremony held on June 19, 1941. Spieser returned with the German troops and became the "court jester who could freely speak the truth" to Gauleiter Robert Wagner. Rather than accept an administrative position, Spieser opted to open a well-funded publishing house to continue his propaganda battle.[76] Bickler became a highly placed administrator and intelligence officer. Many other Nazi autonomists, like Bickler, took positions in the SS or the SA. Thus, Rudolf Lang, a founding member of the Jungmannschaft, became the county administrator of Saverne.[77] Molsheim and Guebweiler also had former Jungmannschaft activists as county administrators. Paul Schall took over the editorship of the *Straßburger Neueste Nachrichten,* the German version of *Les Dernières Nouvelles de Strasbourg,* and became a *SS-Sturmbannführer* (major) and official advisor to the *Gauleitung* (district administration) on the Alsatian *Volkstum.*[78]

. . .

Autonomism deteriorated from the 1920s, when it encapsulated the essence of Alsatian discontent at French rule, to 1940, when its leaders openly paraded as Nazi officials. Autonomist leaders became increasingly dogmatic and shrill during the 1930s the more they accepted Nazism. Given the cacophony of the 1930s, Alsatians ironically grew deaf to the note struck by the Alsatian Nazis. Alsatians would not have voluntarily agreed to a German-Alsace-Lorraine Anschluß in 1940, as Robert Ernst would have us believe.[79] On the contrary, Alsatians were recalcitrant subjects of the Nazis during the war.

The Alsatian Nazis themselves were a disparate group, just as German Nazis were. The uniforms created an artificial homogeneity, disguising innumerable ideological, personal, and organizational conflicts. Close examination of any totalitarianism reveals cracks and fissures in the monolith. The differences between Roos and Schall on one side and Bickler and Spieser on the other reflected different notions and expectations of Nazism. The latter accepted the racial ideology of Nazism and believed that Alsace was immutably German. The former faction, however, understood that the inherent centralism of the Nazi state would suffocate and crush Alsatian peculiarities. Although Roos and Schall worked for the imposition of Hitler's regime in Alsace, they had a stronger commitment to the idea of an Alsatian community than Bickler, who saw the world only in terms of Germans and foreigners. Hence their disagreement over participation in the Volksfront.

Roos, Schall, and the Landespartei stood closer to Nazism than the Germanophiles of the UPR led by Joseph Rossé. Rossé accepted Nazism as part of joining Germany, but his belief in Catholicism and traditionalism muted his enthusiasm for Nazism. The Landespartei, comprised primarily of lapsed Protestants, actively sought the imposition of Nazism in Alsace. Roos and Schall seemed to think it would strengthen the Alsatian community, whereas Bickler thought it would strengthen Germany.

CHAPTER SEVEN

Between 1927 and 1933–1934 French fascism labored in obscurity. Hitler's seizure of power, the riots in Paris on February 6, 1934, and the election of the Popular Front in 1936 provided the impetus for a new fascist initiative. The character of these new fascists differed from that of the previous generation. Much more radical and violent, the new French fascists emanated from a slightly different social stratum than their predecessors. Rather than the middle- and upper-middle-class technocratic constituencies of the AF, the PSF, and the Faisceau, new organizations such as Marcel Bucard's Francistes, Jacques Doriot's PPF, and a host of ephemeral movements catered to lower-middle-class discontent. And, within limits, they extended fascism to what the Nazis called the *schaffenden* or "producing" classes.

Tremendous fluidity between Alsatian fascist groups characterized the 1930s. Some groups were so marginal that they only lasted about a week. Failure did not daunt the most idealistic leaders; they simply formed or joined a different movement. In their search for a genuine fascist solution, many French fascists proved willing to solicit funds from the Nazis. Whereas, in the 1920s, French fascists had laid greater stress on the importance of French national identity, in the 1930s they emphasized social and political ideology.

Earlier versions of French fascism persisted into the 1930s, their role and influence somewhat diminished. The AF weathered a papal condemnation and maintained a steady, if unspectacular, level of activism.[1] Its political influence was negligible; a rival paper complained that the AF existed solely "to vituperate and to insult." Although the AF continued to hold meetings up until the outbreak of war, its core of young, urban, middle-class activists remained static, and the party served more of a propagandistic than a revolutionary role.[2]

The JP also sustained a low level of activity from 1925, when it opened a branch in Alsace, through the 1930s. Even more than the national JP, the Alsatian JP catered to a bourgeois clientele. Because of its elitist orientation, the movement held small lectures attended by students and military personnel instead of large rallies. JP members did very little proselytizing specifically for their own movement. Instead they directed their energy into the AF, the Solidarité Française, and/or the Croix de Feu.[3]

FÉDÉRATION DES CONTRIBUABLES

Among the movements that succeeded the first generation of fascism was the Alsatian branch of the Fédération des Contribuables. The first issue of the movement's weekly, *Der Steuerzahler,* appeared in August 1933 and lasted until December. The last issue published an article proclaiming that the *Protocols of the Elders of Zion* exposed "what international Jewry will destroy in order to seize world domination." After objections by *La Tribune Juive* and as a result of a general lack of interest, *Der Steuerzahler* ceased publication and reconstituted itself as *Le Combat.* Under the continuing guidance of Marcel Eschbach, *Le Combat* grew ever more extreme. Composed mostly of unemployed youths, who adopted a black-shirt uniform with a *Flammenkreuz* (cross of fire) insignia, the movement was marginal at best. A cartoon depicting a uniformed youth holding a pack of Jews at bay with a whip gives an indication of the appropriate attire.[4]

The Steuerzahler movement was not, as one historian would have it, simply one of "agitators and demagogues" and therefore not fascist.[5] In the first place, *Der Steuerzahler* insisted on a "national revolution" that would abolish the liberal state. Reforms or constitutional revision would not suffice, and the paper repeatedly incited its readers to overthrow the government. Moreover, in lieu of a liberal, parliamentarian republic, *Der Steuerzahler* wanted a "national state," endowed with authority in the person of a "Führer," who would "subordinate all private interests to the national interest." In this new state, society would be organized along hierarchical lines with "the intellectual, political, economic, social, and working elite" making decisions for the masses. Although *Der Steuerzahler* may not have had the paramilitary troops to back it up, its rhetoric was unquestionably fascist.[6]

Its successor *Le Combat* went even further, calling the Republic a "government of assassins" after the February 1934 riots in Paris. This was, to be sure, demagogic agitation, but of a sort that contributed to the malaise, insecurity, and blockage of French political life and habituated Alsatians to the idea of a fascist takeover. *Le Combat* did in fact plan a paramilitary force called Steuerzahler-Milize for right-thinking youths, but enlistment was negligible.[7]

Antisemitism became the chief ideology for *Der Steuerzahler* and subsequently for *Le Combat*. Headlines urged "France for the French!" and warned Alsatians that Jews were overrunning France.[8] The lead article for the October 1934 issue, titled "Jewish servitude!!" declared that the Jewish menace had existed since the time of the first Jew. "Jews are our danger, Jews are our misfortune," Eschbach lamented.[9] With each passing month, Eschbach made antisemitism more central to the group's ideology. *Le Combat* even went so far as to accuse Marcel Bucard's Francistes of failing to be antisemitic.[10] The grounds for this claim are incoherent but seem to revolve around the fact that Bucard stole the name Francisme from a genuinely antisemitic party headed by Henry Coston. Bucard may have appeared somewhat dilatory on the Jewish question until 1936 because he advocated a secular state that would stand above sectarian differences, nevertheless he attacked "foreigners" and stateless people, which included Jews.[11]

In the middle of 1934, the subheading of *Le Combat* changed from "Organ of the National Party of Taxpayers" to "Organ of the New Generation," indicating a decisive shift from the French Fédération des Contribuables to a purely antisemitic movement.[12] *Le Combat* proposed to continue the lifework of Edouard Drumont, the nineteenth-century antisemitic agitator who elevated hatred of Jews to a systematic ideological critique of modernity through his paper, the *Libre Parole*.[13] Much of the Alsatian press considered *Le Combat* to be pro-Hitler because of its antisemitism. And in fact some members of the movement expressed "great admiration for Hitler and his method of government." Eschbach went to Germany early in 1935 for the purpose, according to the police, of soliciting money for his faltering movement.[14] A contributor to Julius Streicher's antisemitic rag, *Der Stürmer,* came to Alsace in November 1935 and held several meetings with Eschbach to coordinate and pool information and techniques. Although *Der Stürmer* apparently did not give money to Eschbach, preferring that his movement "be spontaneous," it had an abiding interest in Alsatian antisemitism.[15] Despite *Le Combat*'s extensive links with the German Nazis, however, it never became overtly Nazi in the way that the Jungmannschaft did. Eschbach always espoused unity with the French national community.

Popular support for *Der Steuerzahler* and *Le Combat* never amounted to much. *Der Steuerzahler* published 3,000 copies of its first issue in September 1933 (most of which were for free distribution) and folded in December without having amassed a faithful readership. Initially a weekly, *Le Combat* became an erratic monthly. Eschbach had persistent financial problems as a result of overprinting.[16] *Le Combat*'s print run of 7,500 per issue in 1934 and 3,500 for its last issue in 1936 far outpaced its subscriptions.[17] Alsatian response to *Le Combat*'s antisemitism was lukewarm. Public provocation by Eschbach's group in August 1934 resulted in an "anti-national-socialist and anti-Hitlerian" crowd response.[18] Opposition from the Jewish community, either in the form of Jewish gangs that beat up hawkers of *Le Combat* or as political requests addressed to the government to ban the paper, contributed to the paper's irregularity.[19]

Not least among the factors inhibiting *Le Combat*'s success was the intense government scrutiny of Eschbach, which led the police to conclude that *Le Combat* was "a newspaper sustained by the initiative of Germany and German funds." The police were particularly sensitive about any contact with Germany and tended to exaggerate any evidence of pro-German activity. Although unwilling to ban the paper after the experience with autonomists in the mid- to late 1920s, many government officials were anxious to suppress Eschbach's activity. As a compromise they harassed the movement and arrested Eschbach several times for graffiti and incitement to murder. The last issue of *Le Combat* was dated January 1936. Eschbach floundered around for the rest of the year searching for a means of revivifying his movement, without success.[20]

Unfortunately not enough sociological data exists to obtain an accurate profile of the Combat movement. The group comprised somewhere between thirty and a hundred members, most of whom were urban youths. It is safe to assume that the upper- and middle-class support that was typical of the Faisceau, PSF, AF, and JP did not materialize for the Combat. Unemployment may have provided a psychological prod toward violent antisemitism. According to his mother (who may have been a trifle unrealistic), Eschbach's activism would have ceased if he had had a real job.[21]

Der Steuerzahler/Le Combat bridged the German-French identity crisis through antisemitism. The group's leaders had at one time been part of the AF, yet they had close contacts with the most rabid of the German Nazi antisemites. Emphatically pro-French, *Le Combat* nevertheless published in German. The police catalogued a number of meetings between the editors of *Le Combat* and representatives of Julius Streicher's paper *Der Stürmer*. Yet the paper violently attacked the "Streicher disciples" among the Alsatian Nazis for betraying France. Numerically insignificant, the Combat movement nevertheless constituted a new and more vociferous transitional fascism no longer confined by the nationality question.[22]

THE SOLIDARITÉ FRANÇAISE

Another transitional fascist movement, the Solidarité Française, surfaced in 1933, although in Alsace it went by the name of Staatsreform. In September 1933 local sympathizers began publishing a bilingual newspaper called *Die Staatsreform*.[23] Although the subtitle called for "a republican reform of the state," *Die Staatsreform*'s intention was the substitution of an authoritarian, corporative state for a republican one. It particularly demanded the abolition of parties.[24] Within a month, *Die Staatsreform* inaugurated the Force Nouvelle (Neue Front), which declared, in its opening manifesto, that it would unite the postwar generation against "the hypocrisy of the parliamentary system," "the arrogance of interest groups," and "the incoherence and anarchy that ruins our economy."[25] Like other fascist parties, the Staatsreform specifically called for the participation of the younger generation that would "sooner or later flood and submerge those who today desperately cling to their sinecures under a revivifying wave of energy, health, and youth."[26]

The Solidarité Française—like its patron, the millionaire perfumer François Coty—was well connected with the other French fascist movements.[27] Coty himself had supported the AF, the Faisceau, the PSF, and the Croix de Feu before financing his own movement. Coty also tried to bring the fascist message to the masses by selling his daily, *L'Ami du Peuple,* at the low price of ten centimes. Not only did the various fascist movements share Coty as a benefactor, they shared ideology and activists. Jean Renaud, who directed the Solidarité Française, noted that JP president Taittinger was "at heart with us" and had sent two of his deputies to address a party rally. Most of those in attendance at one of the Solidarité Française's founding meetings already belonged to the JP or the Croix de Feu.[28]

The same pattern of collaboration between the Solidarité Française and other radical right-wing, fascist movements extended to Alsace. Pierre Pflimlin, one of the founders of the Alsatian branch and collaborator of the journal, exemplifies the crossover among the French fascist parties. As Joseph Bilger's personal lawyer, Pflimlin kept busy throughout the 1930s defending the excesses of the Bauernbund. His name also appeared on the membership rolls of the PSF.[29] Another key figure in the JP who turned up as leader of the Alsatian Solidarité Française was Pierre Schmidt-Le-Roi.[30] Both Pflimlin and Schmidt-Le-Roi were leading members of the APNA and therefore linked mainstream Alsatian politics to the fascist movements.[31] Joseph Weydmann of the APNA, and at that time president of the Ligue des Catholiques d'Alsace, was also involved in the Staatsreform movement.

Members of the Alsatian Solidarité Française also had links with the newer, more radical fascist movements. Camille Riegel, the editor of *Die Staatsreform,* for example, later collaborated with Gustave Hervé to publish a German language version of Gustave Hervé's national socialist weekly, *La Victoire Dimanche,* entitled *Neue Front,* in 1935.[32] That the name was the same as the Staatsreform movement signified their ideological closeness. In addition, Hervé and the old activists of the Force Nouvelle agreed to work together during the 1935 municipal elections to secure the election of corporative city councils that were not composed of "political parties that flourish under discord, but of vital forces in the city that prosper together." Like many other such experimental alliances this one did not last; it disappeared by September.[33] Another key Staatsreformist named Sauner, editor of the APNA's *Mülhauser Bote,* also directed the Mulhouse chapter of the Francistes.[34] Sauner's antisemitism led Jewish merchants in Mulhouse to threaten to withhold advertising if he remained on the *Bote's* staff.

However much the Staatsreform had in common with other organizations, the members of the Alsatian branch of the Solidarité were not a "pretorian cohort . . . recruited from the marginal proletariat and the unemployed."[35] While Renaud may have formed his personal Parisian storm troopers, in Alsace the movement adopted an elitist pose. Dependent as it was on leadership from the more traditional French fascist parties, the Neue Front inevitably reflected the same social bias. Attendance at Staatsreform meetings substantiated the middle-class orientation of the movement.[36]

Only lasting from 1933 to 1934, the short-lived Staatsreform made no real effort to form a mass party but was content to exert an intellectual influence through its paper. Continuing the elitist tradition of the 1920s radical right, *Die Staatsreform* posited that France had to decide between a "reform of the state in a corporative direction" or "Bolshevist revolution." The Staatsreform/Neue Front attempted to revive the authoritarian corporatism of the AF, the PSF, and the Faisceau at a time when the radical right seemed to be flagging. Actually, *Die Staatsreform* claimed that it went "one step farther [than the Solidarité] by not only demanding 'a corporative solidarity with the French nation,' but also setting the goal of realizing the integral, corporative state—the corporate state *[Ständestaat].*"[37] Corporatism for the Staatsreform was a form of patronization that openly appealed "to the officials and artisans, to the businessmen and tradesmen, to the intellectuals, industrialists, and financiers." Alsatians should understand "that it is natural law that the strong, the powerful, and the well-to-do are required to shield and protect the small, the weak, and those of moderate means, not like a shrub protects the violets, but like the mighty full-grown oak, which permits the ivy to strive upward."[38]

By September 1934 the Force Nouvelle had run its course. The paper *Die Staatsreform* ceased publication in July 1934 as a result of internal dissention and a lack of funds. In any event the movement had dwindled to around two hundred members in Mulhouse and none in Bas-Rhin.[39] An emissary from the Solidarité's central office visited Strasbourg in an attempt to convince Pierre Pflimlin and Pierre Schmidt-Le-Roi, the founders of the Alsatian branch, to redouble their efforts. Concerned about financial improprieties by Jean Renaud and acutely aware that funds for a renewed propaganda drive were not available (as a result of Coty's death in July), Pflimlin and Schmidt-Le-Roi demurred.[40] By whatever name, the Solidarité Française, Staatsreform, or Force Nouvelle faded out of existence in Alsace, as it did in France.

THE FRANCISTES

Somewhat more successful was Marcel Bucard's Franciste movement. Everyone agrees that the Francistes were genuinely fascist. Indeed, the sub-heading of the German language edition of *Le Franciste* described the movement as the "French Fascist Movement" and much of its funding came from the Italian Fascists. Inaugurated at 11:00 P.M. on September 29, 1933, at the Arc de Triomphe in Paris, Francisme espoused the sort of militarized revolutionary society that is commonly associated with fascism. The blue-shirted Francistes believed that fascism was "the new creed of the whole world."[41] Although Paris was the center of Bucard's movement, as it was for virtually all the French fascist movements, the eastern provinces, especially Alsace-Lorraine, provided the "most disciplined of his troops."[42]

Bucard's life is virtually a history of the French fascist movement. After a courageous and meteoric career in the army during World War I, Bucard turned to politics. Under the patronage of André Tardieu, Bucard ran unsuccessfully for election to the National Assembly in 1924. Disappointed at his loss and the success of the left, Bucard joined the Légions and then the Faisceau. He became a valuable publicist for Georges Valois and spent a considerable portion of 1926 in Alsace-Lorraine, where he helped popularize the Faisceau. After the Faisceau quietly folded, Bucard took up with Coty and became an editor of *L'Ami du Peuple*. In 1932 he offered his services to Gustave Hervé and the Parti Socialiste National. Involved in the founding of the Croix de Feu, Bucard ended his participation because of personal, not ideological, differences.[43]

The Alsatian Francistes are a good example of the cross-pollination between fascist movements of all ilks. Although zealous in defense of its role as the standard-bearer of fascism, Francisme showed sympathy for other fascist movements. Bucard asserted his brotherhood with all European fascist movements when he wrote, "It is a deeply held belief of Franciste doctrine that only an alliance with all fascist lands can free Europe and the world."[44] Within France, *Le Franciste* expressed admiration for Doriot's firm stand against communism. Bucard even attracted autonomists. According to the socialists, the Francistes "obtained the membership of several autonomists, including one Colmar defendant." "It is true," Bucard confirmed, "that more and more of our members consider themselves Alsatians who previously belonged to the autonomist party."[45]

The *Freie Presse* came into possession of a letter from a Franciste to a priest, which asserted autonomist conversions. The letter may have been a fake. Nevertheless, it elicited extensive debate and discussion about the similarity between Nazis and French fascists. And if the letter was fabricated by the Francistes, it indicates a desire on their part to attract autonomists. Although the local press leapt to the conclusion that "it is evident the French fascists are in the pay of Hitler," it seems more plausible that the Francistes and the Nazis merely shared enough key ideological points that conversion was possible. Bucard underscored this when he identified the chief autonomist complaints—"imbecilic sectarianism," domination by the Freemasons, and the erosion of spiritual traditions—as much the same as his.[46]

Still, some Francistes ended up on Hitler's payroll. The French court sentenced Emile Gillmann, a onetime official in the Franciste Party, to twenty years for German espionage. Gillmann was also involved with the National Socialistes (Nasos) in their subsequent incarnation as the Parti Réaliste Français (PRF) as a contributor to the party's paper, *Le Fanal*. Although Gillmann had left the Franciste Party at the time of its dissolution in 1936 (by the Popular Front) and no longer officially represented the party, his case showed the ease with which "the most Franciste of the Francistes, that is to say, the most French of the French," could become a German spy.[47]

Although often considered inspired by Mussolini's Fascist Party rather than by the German Nazis, the Francistes also imitated Hitler's movement. Bucard received money from the Italians and lifted Nazi-style uniforms and pageantry straight from Hitler.[48] In fact, the national Franciste movement also had close ties with the Nazis. Armand Grégoire, a lawyer at the Cours d'Appel de Paris and a Franciste activist, had an extended correspondence with Dr. Herbert Scholze, a political advisor for the SA, beginning in 1934.[49]

At the same time, the Francistes had numerous ties with the PSF. Movement between the two parties was not uncommon; ex-PSF members joined the Francistes, and disenchanted Francistes turned to the PSF. Ex-PSF members were among those listed as contributors to *Le Franciste*. Again, this could have been an invention by the editors of *Le Franciste*. Nevertheless, the intent and the expectation of attracting PSF members was there. When Francisme began to wane, many members switched to the PSF. Crossover flourished despite the vigorous attack on the PSF by the Francistes. Bucard and his followers justified their attack on nonideological grounds. De La Rocque, according to them, was "a demagogue who only had his personal career in mind." Their main substantive criticism of the Croix de Feu was that it lacked revolutionary zeal and masqueraded as a fascist imitator.[50]

Unlike the other French fascist groups—notably the Faisceau, the AF, the Staatsreform, and even the Croix de Feu/PSF—the Francistes did not draw solely from the middle and upper classes. Among the leaders of the Strasbourg chapter were a railroadman, an employee, a merchant, a chemist, a commission agent, and a chief cook. Collaborators on *Le Franciste*, Bucard's local journal, included an ex–police secretary and an electrotechnician for the railroad.[51]

Another indication of Bucard's support can be seen in a section of *Le Franciste* entitled "Our Battle Fund," which appeared in most issues and listed reader donations with a short quote from the donor. Whether these were genuine excerpts or fabrications made up by the editors, they at least show who the party wanted to join. Among the contributors were city workers, a country vicar, students, construction workers, a roofer, some unemployed, a gamekeeper, a chauffeur, some plasterers, some farmers, and a number of widows. Another sign of the party's commitment to the lower-middle and even working classes was the paper's employment listings. Errand boys, locksmiths, and businessmen advertised their services, while businesses looked for cabinetmakers, mechanics, apprentice bakers, and electricians.[52]

The industrial working classes (that is, the Marxist proletariat) were virtually nonexistent in the Francistes. Francisme was composed of laborers and artisans, not factory workers. The Francistes' social appeal to blue-collar workers mirrored that of the German Nazis.[53] Bucard's incessantly violent anti-Marxism sufficed to deter most Marxists—at least in Alsace, although he claimed that from 25 to 30 percent of his national following came from the Communist or Socialist Party. Franciste supporters "should not be riff-raff, proletarians, or dispossessed, but proud, self-conscious workers, members of the same racial family [*Volksfamilie*], who fulfill their duty in the interest of the state and the entire racial community." Violent anticommunism was a common refrain in the donors' comments: "Down with communism!" "Not a class-conscious prole, but a worker proud of his place!" or "Enemy of the CGT! [Confédération Générale du Travail]" were typical expressions of antisocialism.[54] To be sure, some of these working antisocialists may have previously been members of a left-wing party, but more research needs to be done to determine if their affiliation with Marxism or their status as proletarians was the aberration in their lives.

The social composition of the Francistes notwithstanding, upper and middle classes had an effect on Bucard, at least on the national level. Although Bucard himself came from a provincial petit-bourgeois family, his wife was the daughter of an industrialist. More important, substantial funding came from the same sort of right-wing industrialists as had subsidized the Faisceau. According to one historian, Bucard attracted 200 million francs from financial figures such as Ernst Mercier, who also had close contact with Colonel de La Rocque of the Croix de Feu. This meant that Francisme's ideology as dictated by Bucard was compatible with that of the frustrated right-wing elite. As happened in the case of the Faisceau, industrialists and notables supported the Francistes as an alternative to socialism that would sustain the social and political status quo or, at the very least, not threaten to upset it as much as Marxism did. "We do not fight the employer," one article explained, "since we do not want to kill off the energy of the leading men in the field to the detriment of all."[55]

Accordingly, Bucard demanded the creation of a corporative state that would reestablish "the solidarity that ought to exist between the different elements of the economy." In a typically fascist formulation, Bucard argued that the political parties had created complete anarchy and that "authority is the only security for freedom." Bucard hoped to co-opt workers through specific worker demands such as a minimum wage, reasonable wages, yearly vacations, old-age pensions, and easing of work conditions.[56] The specificity of these demands was an advance over the theoretical assertions of the Faisceau and consequently resulted in a more varied social membership. But the demands remained closely tied to the imposition of an obligatory corporative state that would have favored owners, who would inevitably have come to represent and control the individual corporations. With equal representation in the regional corporative committees, the owners could count on an institutionalized nondemocratic imbalance that would prevent their ever being outvoted, as might happen in the parliamentary system.[57]

Regionalism was an important aspect of Francisme's ideology. Provincial autonomy would complement bureaucratic centralization by stimulating local economies and nurturing traditional values and lifestyles. Francisme insisted on "absolute political loyalty" to France based on a reciprocal respect for Alsatian culture.[58] Thus party activists in Alsace demanded the "protection of the mother tongue, culture, morals, and customs in addition to the local legislation." "Autonomism, No! Regionalism, Yes!" read the headline of one article, which explained that Francisme called for the destruction of the "artificial wall" between France and Alsace and explicitly rejected the pro-German orientation of autonomist groups.[59]

THE NASOS AND THE PRF

Hitler spawned some other unusual imitators in Alsace. The Parti National-Socialiste Français (Nasos), a small, short-lived radical group founded in 1935, rejected a return to Germany while wholeheartedly accepting the Nazi model. "We want a France belonging to the French," declared the Nasos. In their program, the Nasos demanded the "abolition of class struggle in favor of the collaboration of workers in a corporative regime." Somewhat confused, they guaranteed the right to private property but called for the installation of "the dictatorship of the worker." A clever substitution of "worker" for "proletariat" might appear to be paying homage to communism. In fact, the Nasos could not have been less concerned with class interests or the proletariat. They were, however, extremely interested in work as a virtue.[60]

Like all fascists, the Nasos detested parliamentary government and wanted to replace it with "an authoritarian and responsible government." Everything from banks to schools must submit to the idea of France. Under a Naso regime, banks would not be allowed "to be institutions of illicit speculation." "Culture being the patrimony of all, education will be free at all levels," one point of the program elaborated, implying that education entailed the creation and maintenance of a national culture.[61] Unlike most fascist parties in Alsace, the Nasos insisted on a unitary French state and French culture. Their propaganda was in French, not German, and ignored Alsatian regionalism. Their inflexibility on this point contributed to their marginality.

Antisemitism was the bulwark of the Nasos. The Nasos claimed to favor peace between peoples, but "this peace will only be possible when everyone has understood that it is necessary to be national before being international." This was a thinly disguised appeal to local antisemitism. The Nasos' hatred of all forms of socialism also relied heavily on antisemitism. According to Luchont (probably a pseudonym), the party's would-be Hitler, socialism was the party of Jews, not workers.[62]

Like the Francistes, the Nasos' social composition was lower-middle-class. The party's leadership, for example, consisted of a grocer, a locksmith, an unemployed business employee, a factory representative, a student, an engineer, a young shopkeeper, a builder, a draftsman-photographer, and several French veterans.[63] Comparison between the Nasos leadership and that of the Faisceau, the AF, the PSF, and the Staatsreform, shows a completely different class composition. Some overlap existed—all these groups were primarily urban, and they shared a technocratic element in the form of engineer participation—but essentially the Nasos represented a more lower-middle-class constituency.

By the end of 1936 the Naso movement had run its course. Disregard for regional sensibilities, close governmental scrutiny, and competition from other more viable fascist movements contributed to the party's demise. Undaunted, Luchont regrouped his forces in 1937 as the Parti Réaliste Français (PRF) with its own monthly, *Le Fanal,* which appeared irregularly and which the police deemed "insignificant" at 1,500 copies per issue and confined to Strasbourg.[64]

Vehemently opposed to the "divisive works of an exploitative and putrid capitalism," Luchont specifically called upon "workers, peasants, and soldiers" to complete a "revolution of work." Luchont demanded work, old-age pensions, accessible education, and tax reform.[65] Luchont now wrote in German, having learned his lesson that Alsatians, especially those from the social milieus from which he wanted to recruit, could be reached only in German. To ensure these benefits, Luchont attacked Jews, who were "bloodsuckers," and international high finance, which crippled the little man. He also insisted on the establishment of corporative representation in an "authoritarian and completely responsible government."[66] Working within accepted fascist discourse, Luchont managed to express genuine working- and lower-middle-class concerns. The PRF, however, met with as little success as its predecessor and had disappeared by the summer of 1937.

THE PARTI POPULAIRE FRANÇAIS AND OTHERS

Another notable fascist party, the Parti Populaire Français (PPF), had limited success in Alsace.[67] Jacques Doriot, the charismatic ex-communist who led the party, had a credibility problem in the region. During 1928–1929, when the Alsatian malaise was at a fever pitch, Doriot had been a spokesman for the French communists when they expelled the Alsatian communist autonomists. Accordingly, he looked faintly ridiculous to many Alsatians as the head of a new party that had broken with Moscow.

Despite his obvious inconsistency—turning from communism to fascism—the Alsatian right-wing political elite graciously received Doriot. In the full knowledge that the PPF would never amount to much in Alsace and that Doriot's defection constituted an important setback for the communists, papers such as the Catholic pro-French *Elsäßer* approved of Doriot's call "to restore the country's soul." The AF "sincerely extended its hand to Doriot's friends in Alsace" who shared the goal of anticommunism.[68] The local PPF reciprocated by sending a representative to a banquet honoring Charles Maurras. Landespartei autonomists grudgingly admitted respect for the PPF, whose "promises were more concrete than those of Colonel de La Rocque."[69]

Such a favorable initial impression was the result of intensive organizational groundwork. Doriot had substantial funds at his disposal, thanks to generous donations from banks, management associations, and industrialists that found the Popular Front threatening. With this money, the party published a local German-language weekly, *Die Stimme der Parti Populaire Français*. Its first issue appeared in March 1937 and contained between 7,000 and 10,000 copies for free distribution. By the end of the year 4,000 copies per issue were printed.[70] Despite its auspicious start, however, the PPF did not leave a lasting impression on Alsatian politics. *Die Stimme der Parti Populaire Français* ceased publication and the national party went into decline in 1938.

The Alsatian PPF represented an unusual linkage between ex-communists and industrialists. The ex-communists provided organizational and propaganda expertise, while the businessmen provided money and, to a certain extent, ideology. *Die Stimme der Parti Populaire Français*'s editorial director was René Heck, a municipal councillor and ex-associate of Charles Hueber's. Another key activist of the Alsatian PPF had been expelled from the French Communist Party for "indiscipline." On the national level, the use of communist agitators to disseminate fascism with a communist vocabulary had more success than any of the preceding fascist movements in attracting workers. At least this is what Doriot asserted when he wrote, "our party is composed of all sorts of men from all walks of life." Whether this was also true in Alsace is unclear as the movement itself was extremely short-lived.[71]

Although ex-communists orchestrated the cultural program, funds for the publication of *Die Stimme der Parti Populaire Français* came from a number of local industrialists, brewers, and manufacturers.[72] The patronage of wealthy anti–Popular Front businessmen and associations meant that the PPF's ideology, like that of its predecessors, was an attempt to make bourgeois concerns palatable to the public. The pattern here is familiar: partnership between ex-communist and capitalist factions was unequally weighted toward the source of funds.

The high point of the second generation of French fascism came in 1935–1936. Responding to the Popular Front's success and primed by the economic, political, and intellectual crises that beset the 1930s, groups such as the Francistes and the PPF proliferated and militated for an antiliberal resolution of France's problems. The Bauernbund and the Alsatian Nazis also stepped up activity at this time. At times bitterly divided by a narrow range of differences in national identity and social philosophy, these groups nevertheless shared more than they admitted.

Typical of the guarded support and connections between the various groups was the career of Dr. Marcel Gillmann. Gillmann appeared at Naso and Franciste meetings to express sympathy and encouragement. Indeed, in early 1936 the police identified Gillmann as a "departmental delegate" for the Francistes. By the end of the year, Gillmann had been arrested, along with Bilger, at an illegal Bauernbund demonstration.[73] Then, during 1937, he flirted with the short-lived Terre d'Alsace movement, which proposed to unite peasant and anticommunist movements into a single bloc that would prevent a French version of the Spanish Civil War. Elected as the general councillor for the canton of Obernai in 1938 with the help of the UPR, Gillmann continued to represent the Bauernbund.[74] Gillmann's facile movement from party to party, including the UPR, was by no means an isolated phenomenon and illustrates the extent of compatibility and mutual support that existed between the diverse French fascist movements.

Momentum for the new French fascist parties quickly dissipated, however, in favor of the PSF, which gradually combined the various strands of French fascism under its auspices. By 1938 at the latest, the Francistes, the PPF, and the Nasos had dwindled to insignificance. In addition, the acceleration of the European diplomatic crisis as Hitler pursued his revision of the European world order with growing impunity changed the orientation of many Alsatians. The language of and about fascist activity altered considerably as the chief issue shifted from the Popular Front and the emergence of left-wing politics to Hitler, war, and the emergence of right-wing politics. The Spanish Civil War also negatively influenced the French fascist movement by forcing many right-wing intellectuals to confront the consequences of their violent rhetoric and souring much of the public on the ability of either right- or left-wing extremists to resolve social and political issues equitably.[75] At the same time the Spanish Civil War confirmed the extreme right's belief in the instability and violence of the left. As a result, the fascist majority moderated and moved toward the PSF while the radical fringe became even more extreme and marginal than ever.

One group that epitomized the flamboyant and ephemeral character of the French fascists on the eve of war was Jean-Charles Legrand's Front de la Jeunesse, which, according to one observer, followed in the antisemitic tradition of Bilger, Bucard, and Darquier de Pellepoix. Despite vigorous prosecution by the authorities, Legrand managed to trumpet antisemitism at a number of meetings and organize fascist demonstrations in the streets beginning in late 1938.[76] Dressed in red shirts, Legrand and his followers harangued audiences about the Jewish menace. Legrand apparently had connections with the German Nazis, especially the antisemites of *Der Stürmer*. The Alsatian Nazis, however, vehemently objected to Legrand because he threatened to undermine their viability. At the same time, Legrand's followers attended a Strasbourg meeting held by the notorious French antisemite Darquier de Pellepoix.[77]

If Legrand's national orientation was unclear, it was because of his incoherence on the Alsatian issue. His assimilation of Nazi style, including above all antisemitism, and intensely violent antirepublican rhetoric that exceeded the fascist norm led many observers to believe that he was pro-German. Yet in his newspaper, Legrand declared that Alsace was completely French. "The only Hitlerian menace in Alsace," he wrote, "is the sick politics of France."[78]

In May 1939 another fascist band made its presence felt in Alsace. Headed by several Parisians, the Faisceau d'Alsace brought in "a certain number of boxers from Montmartre" to create a "uniformed shock troop" that would crack the heads of autonomists.[79] One of the leaders had recently had a falling out with Legrand and used his troops to break up the latter's meetings. Not to be confused with Georges Valois's Faisceau, this new Faisceau represented the most extremely violent and destabilizing fascist movement of all. It called for the assassination of Bickler and Legrand, ransacked Bickler's office, and disrupted meetings.[80] This too led to nothing.

. . .

Ultimately, these fascist groups failed to live up to their promise to unite the French polity. In one important respect, however, they did advance beyond the 1920s fascist movements by couching their ideology in terms that were more acceptable to lower-middle-class and working Alsatians. They did this by imitating communist style more directly—even, in the case of the PPF, by using ex-communists as hired guns. Key ideological premises such as corporatism held new, more radical, meanings for fascists in the Steuerzahler, Staatsreform, Franciste, and Naso Parties. That is to say, the new French fascists developed a form of corporatism that spoke to social constituencies hitherto untouched by fascism. In turn, the salesmen, shopkeepers, apprentices, and laborers that joined these groups vigorously applied their own frustrations to the idea of corporatism. For the growing numbers of lower-middle-class members, fascism offered jobs, stability, more respect, and better political representation. Accordingly, corporatism became a vehicle for revolutionary change rather than for a preservation of the status quo.

Heading most of the new French fascist movements, however, were the same people who had led the 1920s movements. Bucard, for example, had been an important propagandist for the Faisceau. Funding either came from abroad, as in the case of the Francistes, or from the same techno-cratic, upper-middle-class milieu that had characterized the first generation of fascism. The only group that genuinely emanated from the lower-middle class—the Nasos—quickly collapsed without the money or the expertise to spread its message. The agenda of the new French fascist leaders was much the same as it had always been: the reestablishment of society on moral, organic, and hierarchical grounds, and the reimposition of a social order that was necessary to maintain or even to advance their interests. The main difference was their flexibility in their search to create the social di-versity that would validate their views.

Although the new French fascist experiments advanced the partnership between notables and the masses, none of the movements discussed in this chapter succeeded in becoming a mass party. The French fascist groups were clearly less successful than the Alsatian Nazis or the Bauernbund, both of which could draw more heavily on regional insecurities and dis-content. Even the PPF, commonly considered a "mass party," failed to sus-tain its political promise in Alsace.[81]

Several factors militated against their success. First, the government kept close tabs on each movement and frequently intervened at the na-tional, prefectural, cantonal, and municipal levels to block their activity. The best example was the national government's outlawing of the leagues in 1936. Second, the extensive interaction between the various movements did not translate into unanimity. The ambitions of leaders such as Bucard and Doriot placed their respective organizations in competition with each other. Third, the fascist movement was fractured along social, geographi-cal, and cultural lines. Language, religion, patronage, national identity, and economics created a patchwork of conflicting political affiliations. From one town to the next, fascism could vary from Francisme to Bauern-bund to Nazism. Finally, the radical, extremist nature of the new fascist leaders also hampered their success. Impatient for quick success, the lead-ers themselves often turned elsewhere after a few setbacks.

Fascism simultaneously dominated Alsatian politics and splintered into ephemeral and often vehemently opposed factions. This apparent paradox occurred because the new French fascists were willing "to descend into the streets" to project a shrill and insistent message that alienated the public yet demanded attention.[82] However, these groups constituted only a part of the fascist phenomenon of the 1930s. Considered together, the sum of the fascist movements was indeed larger than any of its parts. Moreover, the parts were to a surprising extent interchangeable. Former communist autonomists played key roles in the Alsatian PPF; Landespartei autonomists joined the Francistes; members of the UPR, Landespartei, Jungmannschaft, EABP, Bauernbund, or Francistes had no qualms about collaborating with the Nazis after 1940; and radical antisemites dabbled in both Nazi and French fascist organizations. The stage was now set for the Parti Social Français to forge the disparate fascist parts into one single entity.

MASS FASCISM

THE PARTI SOCIAL FRANÇAIS

All of the Alsatian fascist movements lacked the intellectual and social force to attract a socially diverse following. Yet each tried to build its limited constituency into a mass party because the fascist goal of social, national, and state harmony necessitated universal participation. The AF, for example, was unable to move beyond its urban bourgeois constituency and in the 1930s, of all the groups under discussion, seemed the most content with its role as an oppositional force. Similarly, the Bauernbund built a strong peasant constituency on the basis of its dairy cooperatives. Urban dwellers, however, remained largely unmoved. The PPF, the Francistes, and the Nasos all believed they alone held the key to a right-wing synthesis built on a lower-middle-class constituency. At a meeting of the Parti National-Socialiste Français, which had some Francistes in attendance, Luchont, the leader of the Nasos, proclaimed, "Only one party in France should exist and that is the Parti Socialiste National Français [sic]." To which, a Franciste rose and averred with equal certainty that Francisme was "a universal party."[1] Competition between movements precluded fulfillment of their corporatist aspirations for an inclusive national community, even when they could agree on which nation.

Only the Croix de Feu and its successor the Parti Social Français (PSF) made the transition from an oppositional interest group to a mass party.[2] Its national and regional membership and level of political activity rose steadily from its inception in 1927 until its dissolution in Alsace in 1940. Unlike the other French fascist parties, the Croix de Feu/PSF transcended partisan interests to include substantial representation from all sectors of society, especially after 1936 when it became a parliamentary party—the PSF. Despite a typically fascist distortion in favor of lower-middle- to upper-middle-class constituencies, by 1938 the PSF had become the largest party in France. The Croix de Feu/PSF's transformation from a small extraparliamentary, radical right-wing opposition group into a large, dynamic, antiliberal parliamentary party mirrored the evolution of the Italian Fascists and the German National Socialists.

Until recently, historians have viewed the Croix de Feu/PSF as a fundamentally conservative organization firmly rooted in the French mainstream. René Rémond, one of the first historians to analyze the French right, insists that "there was no French fascism." He admits, however, that his argument would fail if it could be proved that the Croix de Feu/PSF was fascist.[3] Rémond's refusal to acknowledge the fascist character of the Croix de Feu/PSF has shaped subsequent debate so much that historians prefer to ask why it was not fascist, rather than whether it was. Only recently have William Irvine and Robert Soucy reopened the question.[4]

The most tenacious shibboleth concerning the Croix de Feu/PSF, shared by analysts from both the right and the left, is that it was not fascist but part of "a Caesarian-Bonapartist tradition that had only a formal resemblance to fascism."[5] Clinging to a narrow definition of fascism, this interpretation maintains that Colonel François de La Rocque's movement was too authoritarian, too conservative, or too pusillanimous to be considered fascist. The PSF was merely the latest in a series of right-wing French movements that linked a charismatic leader with the conservative, authority-craving masses against the progressivism of liberalism.

The Bonapartist interpretation of the PSF suffers from a number of serious misconceptions. Neither Bonaparte was particularly antiliberal or corporatist. To be sure, Bonapartists shared a disdain for parliamentary structures with the twentieth-century movements. Bonapartism, however, had a respect for democratic institutions, or at least the illusion thereof. Most French historians agree that the Radical Party was the inheritor of Bonapartism. The Bonapartist Party had a far more mixed political ideology than the leagues of the 1930s. It combined the notion of a strong government overseeing a well-ordered society with the idea of democracy, using plebiscites to fortify the authority of the ruler. None of the fascist movements, including the PSF, shared Bonapartism's commitment to democracy. Furthermore, Bonapartism depended on the viability and continuity of its ruler. The party disintegrated after 1870 as a result of an insufficient organization and the lack of a credible leader.[6] On this basis alone, the PSF clearly diverges from the original Bonapartism. Furthermore, de La Rocque may have evoked the historical memory of Napoleonic myth, but in so doing he was not reviving a nineteenth-century worldview but creating a new one, in which the Bonapartist myth stood for the eradication of liberal democracy and the establishment of a state-mediated, corporative, authoritarian, and organic society. Such usage was not unusual among fascist movements.[7]

The Bonapartist interpretation also assumes that participation by notables in a movement automatically exempts it from being categorized as fascist. This is the view of Jean Plumyène and Raymond Lasierra who argue that "the right will always refuse to be identified with fascism" and that elites "would have found it [fascism] far too risky and adventurous."[8] Such was demonstrably not the case with the Alsatian Faisceau, Italian Fascism, or for that matter German Nazism, where notables were prominent.[9]

A related argument is that fascism had its roots in the left. The most sophisticated advocate of this position is Zeev Sternhell who argues that French fascism evolved out of the leftist intellectual tradition.[10] Looking solely at the intellectual development of French fascism and ignoring inconvenient movements such as Francisme and the Front Paysan, Sternhell stresses the antimaterialist and revolutionary nature of fascism. This makes little sense, since the social composition of all fascist movements either lacked, or significantly underrepresented, the working classes.[11] In fact, fascism's chief supporters came from the middle classes, who wanted to overthrow the political system in a way that would solidify and reaffirm their position in society. A few intellectuals such as Karl Hueber, Jacques Doriot, and Marcel Déat made the journey from communism to fascism, but only by abandoning Marxism. At best they carried with them a commitment to revolutionary action, but they harnessed it to completely different ends; instead of seeking to liberate the individual for society, these nouveaux fascists confined the individual in order to liberate society.

The PSF's notable lack of working-class support conformed to the general pattern of fascist movements. As a rule, fascist movements drew heavily from the middle classes. Like most rules, however, such was not always the case. The PPF under Doriot apparently had a loyal working-class constituency, which converted in order to follow their charismatic leader/patron. The PPF was the exception that proved the rule, rather than the other way round. As many recent criticisms have shown, Sternhell's argument does not adequately explain the overall fascist movement.[12]

The Croix de Feu/PSF fits all the criteria for a fascist movement.[13] Organizationally and socially, it represented the only radical right-wing mass party that co-opted the social and political aspirations of a wide range of French citizens under the vague rubric of a revolutionary restructuring of French political life. This was comparable to the Italian Fascist Party and the NSDAP, whose transition from an oppositional extraparliamentarian movement to a parliamentary party increased their popularity and ultimately undermined republican institutions. The PSF's repeated protestations of "loyalty to the republic" must be viewed skeptically, since they referred to the party's chief strength—the realistic possibility of changing the French political system from within. Moreover, de La Rocque insisted on distancing himself from the parliamentary process by promising never to head a republican government. This is commonly interpreted as a Boulanger-like weakness, but it was probably an expression of contempt for the Third Republic. Thus, Rémond errs when he concludes that the PSF was not fascist precisely because of its growth as a parliamentarian party.[14]

Even though the PSF promised the abolition of liberal government by legal means, the threat of violence was integral to the party's success. Inherent in the name, purpose, and evolution of the movement was militarism. The Croix de Feu (literally, cross of fire) glorified a baptism by fire that turned French boys into men and separated hardened, serious veterans from insincere, frivolous civilians. Implied was a belief in the superiority of military organization and experience as a guide for political affairs. Colonel de La Rocque accepted violence as a necessary political tool against cultural (that is, non-French) and political opponents. Indeed, one Alsatian activist, Charles Munz, died in a skirmish with communists.[15] Such a view was common throughout interwar Europe, from the Italian Arditi to the German Freikorps, and had its strongest French expression in the writings of Antoine Rédier and Drieu La Rochelle.[16] *Authority, hierarchy, closed ranks, camaraderie,* and *combat* were watchwords for a militarization of politics. By applying combat experience to politics, de La Rocque and the Croix de Feu helped normalize interwar political violence.

Bolstered by a fundamental belief in militarism as a metaphor for society, the Croix de Feu/PSF advocated replacing the Third Republic with a state that eliminated liberalism and redrew political representation along corporatist lines. Like all fascist movements, the Croix de Feu/PSF believed that communal society was an organic body whose disparate parts needed to work in harmony. Liberalism, according to the PSF, promoted disorder, atomization, and greed.[17] Society, not the individual, was the center of PSF (and fascist) philosophy. Workers should work, intellectuals should think, leaders should lead, and everyone should accept their position in society. Although it grudgingly accepted the idea of individual social mobility on the basis of talent, the PSF advocated the maintenance of the social status quo. Croix de Feu members accordingly saw corporatism as a more logical form of representation that, unlike parliamentary government, could harmonize social conflict and bring order to an apparently disintegrating society.[18]

The Croix de Feu/PSF employed the language of corporatism in an extremely vague way in order to attract as many supporters as possible. Indeed, its supporters criticized the PSF for its lack of precision.[19] Different social groups tended to have different notions of corporatism. Farmers favored a corporatism that elevated the peasantry as the highest moral and cultural ideal; workers stressed corporate representation of their interests; and middle and upper classes wanted corporatism to reaffirm their positions at the pinnacle of society. The PSF embraced all of these notions, however contradictory. Within limits, the PSF was opportunistic—rather like the Nazi Party and the Italian Fascists.

Anticommunism was a central feature of the Croix de Feu/PSF. Class divisions, even more than liberal individualism, represented a threat to communal harmony based on inequality, authority, and national homogeneity. Individuals could be atomized and prevented from finding common cause, but socialism presented a specific and potentially powerful means of overcoming inequities. Communism, in the Croix de Feu/PSF's view, was a bloody, frightening, and disruptive force that would appropriate private property and destroy the traditional way of life. On the front page of the first issue of the PSF's regional paper, *Le Flambeau de l'Est*, the editors encouraged readers to contemplate the atrocities of the Spanish Civil War, asking if they "wanted to become exposed to this sort of misery." De La Rocque considered his party to be the only one that could effectively combat communism, because it consisted of a disciplined, elite cadre of veterans.[20]

. . .

At first the Croix de Feu seemed like just another run-of-the-mill veterans' organization. Founded in 1927 by Maurice Hanot as an association for wounded French veterans with a nationalist orientation, the Croix de Feu was initially a narrow interest group with a mere five hundred members.[21] Its political range and potential membership remained limited as long as it only included wounded veterans who had received the Croix de Feu for valor. In 1929 the Croix de Feu established the Association des Briscards, open to any veteran who had served on the front for a minimum of six months. When Lieutenant-Colonel François de La Rocque assumed control of the Croix de Feu in 1931, he quickly expanded the scope of the group. Through the establishment of auxiliary organizations—such as the Sons and Daughters of the Croix de Feu (1930); the National Volunteers (1933), for men too young to have fought in the war; and the National Regroupment (1933), which extended membership to all sympathizers—de La Rocque gradually opened the movement to nonveterans. Eventually, the Croix de Feu/PSF extended its social and political organization into music clubs, fairs, charity work, and other leisure activities in much the same way as the German Social Democrats and, for that matter, the Nazis did.[22] National membership in the Croix de Feu and its affiliates climbed from insignificance in the 1920s to 35,000 members at the time of the riots of February 6, 1934. A year later, Croix de Feu membership had ballooned to 200,000, with between 25,000 and 30,000 in Paris alone.[23] In July 1936 the Croix de Feu took one more step toward reaching an ever-widening audience by reconstituting itself as the PSF.

Unlike any other right-wing party operating in Alsace, the Croix de Feu/PSF capitalized on its national audience, advertising itself as "the only large national party that is capable of rescuing our Christian and Latin civilization."[24] Those who sought to crush the left saw in the PSF a national instrument that had greater clout than any regional party and that had showed continuous growth from the late 1920s until 1939. In its first year, the national PSF had 600,000 members, easily outstripping the combined 484,000 active communists and socialists. Estimates set the party's size in 1937 anywhere between 700,000 and 1.2 million.[25] *Le Flambeau de l'Est* probably exaggerated its success by claiming that it had 2,650,000 members by July 1937. When World War II began, the PSF had eleven deputies, 198 *conseillers généraux,* 344 *conseillers d'arrondissement,* 2,692 mayors, and 10,257 municipal councillors across France. These figures were up from July 1938 when the PSF counted 185 *conseillers généraux,* 222 *conseillers d'arrondissement,* and 2,819 mayors.[26] This growth is especially astonishing in light of the absence of national elections after 1936. Had Vichy not intervened, the PSF probably would have become the dominant party in France, if it was not already. In a sense, Vichy was the victory of the PSF made possible by the Germans instead of by electoral success.

Alsace initially held little promise of success for the Croix de Feu. The majority of Alsatian veterans had, after all, served in the opposing German army. Once it opened its doors to Alsatian veterans in 1933 who had served in the Reichswehr, however, the Croix de Feu was able to do what no other radical right-wing party could: break down the barriers of national and regional identification.[27] Opening membership rolls to Reichswehr veterans fit the pattern of expansion developed by de La Rocque. But even after this major conciliatory step, the Croix de Feu found its major source of support among pro-French elements. Indeed, its party statutes specified the "brotherly collaboration of all Frenchmen in order to secure the prosperity and greatness of the fatherland." Nevertheless, Reichswehr veterans who had perfunctorily fulfilled their obligation to the Wilhelmine state but who supported—or at least accepted—France could join the Croix de Feu/PSF in good conscience. Indicative of Alsatians' changing attitude toward France was an autonomist meeting held in April 1936 in which a PSF representative was "vigorously applauded" for criticizing an autonomist speaker for not placing "France first."[28]

The Croix de Feu/PSF attracted Alsatians through a rehash of radical right-wing regionalism. Indeed nothing distinguished it from the regionalism of the AF. According to the PSF, each province (including Alsace) loved France, and the best way to liberate regional loyalty was to cultivate regional rights. France, however, must "become itself again" before regionalism could be profitable. Croix de Feu officials emphasized the importance of maintaining Alsatian dialect while remaining "convinced of French unity." Regionalism, in the PSF's view, was a means of purifying the French nation of degenerate secular and divisive elements. This attempted blend of regionalism with nationalism elicited a polarized response. The Alsatian Nazis hated it, as did all the Marxist parties, because it denied Alsace's German heritage. The Catholic, conservative, and even mainstream press, however, were enthusiastic.[29]

By the mid-1930s, the Croix de Feu had built a sizable following in Alsace. The number of members and sympathizers in the district of Mulhouse alone reached forty-three hundred in March 1936. Although no figure is given, the police described the Colmar district's Croix de Feu as "important" and in some areas "very active."[30] Numerous meetings held in the Wissembourg (Bas-Rhin) district increased membership, and similar growth occurred throughout Alsace. As a result, Haut-Rhin became one of the top ten *départements* in terms of established sections shortly after the national elections.[31]

The year 1936 marked an upsurge in radical right-wing activity throughout France and Alsace. The Croix de Feu accelerated its regional activity in anticipation of the 1936 national elections. Although the Croix de Feu ostensibly remained aloof from party politics, it exercised enormous influence over local electoral results. Bitterly anti-Marxist, the Croix de Feu urged its members and sympathizers to oppose categorically all Popular Front candidates. About 120 members with automobiles toured the rural communities distributing a list of acceptable antisocialist candidates. The Croix de Feu also published a brochure that condemned liberalism for its "murderous materialism."[32]

Meetings and rallies built to a crescendo before the election. Colonel de La Rocque spoke in Strasbourg on March 1, 1936, concluding to thunderous applause that the Croix de Feu would protect France against "fascist and Hitlerian copies" (meaning the Alsatian Nazis) that would lead to Red revolution.[33] This was an interesting manipulation of the concept of fascism—turning it on its head by identifying it with Red revolution. Here are the roots of the interpretation that France had no fascism. By creating a wholly imaginary form of fascism that propagated Bolshevism, it has been easy then to argue that such a movement did not exist.

The victory of the Popular Front put the Croix de Feu on the defensive, especially when Léon Blum's government banned all leagues and paramilitary organizations. Unlike the Cagoule ("hoods," the nickname of the Comité Secret d'Action Révolutionnaire), which assembled militant right-wingers in a clandestine organization, de La Rocque decided to turn the Croix de Feu into a parliamentary party. On July 11, 1936, the PSF officially replaced the veterans' league. Despite the official change, the new PSF retained a hierarchical, paramilitary structure, organized into *poignées* (fists) of five men, troops of five *poignées,* clans of five troops, tribes of five clans, and legions of five tribes.[34] What originally seemed a setback actually provided, in the end, a convenient pretext for further expansion of de La Rocque's political power. Had the government not dissolved the Croix de Feu, it might well have gone the way of the other French extraparliamentary movements and gradually disintegrated.

The PSF made enough headway in Alsace to merit opening a German language weekly, *Le Flambeau de l'Est,* in September 1936. Within two months it was publishing five thousand copies per issue, which made it one of the most successful fascist papers in the region. By 1937 it regularly printed sixteen thousand copies per week. At least one issue reached twenty thousand copies.[35] This made *Le Flambeau de l'Est* the second-largest weekly in Alsace, behind only the *Travailleur Syndicaliste* put out by the Popular Front. No other local fascist weekly printed more than five thousand copies. These figures echoed the national trends; de La Rocque's *Le Petit Journal* (two hundred thousand) effortlessly outstripped the AF (forty thousand) and Doriot's *La Liberté* (thirty thousand).[36] With three times the circulation of any other regional fascist paper, *Le Flambeau de l'Est*'s popularity points to a change in the nature of radical right-wing politics. The PSF had broken through the numeric limit that kept other fascist movements on the political margins.

The Alsatian PSF did more than just transcend journalistic marginality; it achieved significant electoral results. The PSF did surprisingly well in the 1937 cantonal elections. In two cantons, Lapoutroie and Saales (both of which were over 70 percent French-speaking), PSF candidates were elected. Only four cantons in Alsace were more than 50 percent French-speaking, which suggests that the PSF's appeal was strongest among the culturally French. Nevertheless, even in German-speaking areas such as Schiltigheim, on the outskirts of Strasbourg, the PSF candidate garnered one-fourth of the votes. De La Rocque's party only ran seven candidates locally in the 1937 elections, opting to compete exclusively in areas with strong Popular Front candidates. If its candidate lost in the first round of voting, it threw its support behind the remaining anti-Marxist candidate.[37] Thus, the PSF's influence on Alsatian politics extended beyond the election of its candidates to support for other successful anti-Marxist candidates.

The Alsatian PSF's growth manifested itself in other ways as well. At the time of the Croix de Feu's dissolution in June 1936, for example, the main towns in the Sélestat district (Erstein, Obernai, and Sélestat) counted about 530 de La Rocque supporters. By November 1936, PSF membership in the same towns had reached at least 750, not including extensive support in smaller villages. One village became so enamored of de La Rocque that it named its main street after him. Entire organizations converted to the PSF. The "Family League," for example, enlisted so many PSF members that it fell under PSF control. De La Rocque continued to draw huge crowds right up to the beginning of the war. By 1939 the Alsatian PSF had an estimated 27,000 members organized into 165 sections.[38]

The PSF's steady growth reflected its success in appealing to a wider social range than any other fascist party. This was in keeping with the party's declaration that it was "not the party of one class, but of all classes; it is the party of the family, the most primitive and irreducible social cell." According to PSF figures, the national party's composition in 1937 was 25 percent professionals, 23 percent farmers, 18 percent workers, 18 percent white-collar employees, and 16 percent shopkeepers. To be sure, workers and farmers were underrepresented in comparison to the white-collar middle class.[39] In addition, the PSF may have juggled these figures to produce a socially heterogeneous but politically and culturally homogeneous image. Acknowledging these distortions does not change the fact that the fusion of town and country, owners and employees, into a fascist party was new in France. The PSF represented an advance in this regard over the Croix de Feu. According to Pierre Milza, the Croix de Feu consisted of "25 percent bourgeois representatives and high-ranking officials, 41 percent members of the middle classes, 28 percent technicians, office workers, workers in the tertiary sector and only 5 percent farmers."[40] Note the feeble participation of farmers and the absence of factory workers.

Although precise figures are not available, a similar pattern extended to Alsace. Like the national party, the Alsatian branch was heavily weighted toward the middle classes. Police reports note that "engineers, factory directors, lawyers, reserve officers," and government employees figured prominently in the movement. Those farmers belonging to the Croix de Feu tended to be the "most important viticulturists" or prosperous farmers.[41] Skewed as it was, the social composition of the Alsatian PSF was much broader than any of its competitors or predecessors. Indeed the PSF, with between twenty and thirty thousand activists, compared favorably to the UPR, which had around fifteen thousand party members. Additionally, the party had a significant lower-middle-class contingent, many of whom had previously belonged to the Francistes or some other fascist group.[42]

The PSF built itself into a mass party through a social policy that in many ways presaged postwar developments. Like many conservative parties, the PSF had a deep concern for social problems, as its name might suggest. Vehemently opposed to communism and socialism—which it thought demanded an unrealistic and unfair "abolition of private property" or "transferral of all means of production to the general public, i.e. the state"—the PSF was willing to resort to violence to protect property. Nevertheless, the PSF accepted the proactive reality of "direct state factories" and "compulsory syndicates" as a defense "against the doctrine of absolute individualism."[43]

The PSF's agricultural program sought to attract farmers through a direct appeal to their interests. In competition for farm support with the UPR, the Bauernbund, and the Landespartei, the PSF needed farmers to validate its pro-Christian, organic philosophy. Like the German Nazis, who idealized the peasant in their *Blut und Boden* philosophy, the PSF declared that its "chief duty" was to place the peasant "at the pinnacle of the nation and the national economy." Arguing that "independence does not mean discordance," the PSF insisted that it fundamentally agreed with Dorgères on peasant policy. Concrete proposals consisted of a reform of inheritance taxes, lower interest rates for farmers, control of middlemen's profit, tax reductions for necessary goods, professional organization, stable prices, lowering of production costs, and production planning. In addition, the PSF advocated upgrading or installing hygienic water lines, roads, and electrical lines in rural areas. Although farmers in many areas of Alsace were hesitant to join "a political party that they did not know well enough," the PSF achieved some rural success especially in wine-growing communes, where crop failures and a change in national markets predisposed inhabitants to support more radical political organizations.[44]

Middle and upper-middle classes dominated the PSF, holding most of the key propaganda and leadership positions. In Mulhouse, for example, the PSF leadership consisted of an industrialist, three engineers, a doctor, an entrepreneur, and a merchant. Similarly, the Colmar Croix de Feu was led by "very cultivated and active people (engineers, factory managers, lawyers, reserve officers) enjoying considerable sympathy among the military and administrative milieus."[45] The majority of the Strasbourg university section of the PSF were students in medicine or law. The local leaders of the Croix de Feu/PSF bore a striking similarity to the leadership of the Faisceau in the 1920s. The editors of Le Flambeau de l'Est, for example, were lawyers and industrialists. The party's leaders were virtually all industrialists, lawyers, engineers, accountants, prosperous shopkeepers, and landed cultivators.[46] Technocratic, well-to-do, and well-positioned socially, the PSF directors in Colmar and Mulhouse had no intention of fundamentally disrupting their situation, except perhaps to improve it.

Although dominant, the middle and upper-middle classes did not monopolize the party leadership. Other elements of society held some positions of power in the PSF—more so than the other fascist parties. The professions of the party's leaders in the area of Saint-Louis, located in southernmost Haut-Rhin, for example, show the PSF to be socially flexible. Among the leaders were an accountant, a dyer, a restaurateur, a farmer, a tailor, a postman, and an office employee. Most were native Alsatians, although one was born in Basel and another in Rouen. Saint-Louis, a rural area, had little industry, which explains the lack of working-class participation. This sample suggests a strong lower-middle-class character to the Croix de Feu. In Sélestat, one of Bas-Rhin's larger towns, an office worker was the head of his section.[47] The PSF's candidate in the Woerth cantonal elections was a railway worker. Among the local party leaders were several barbers, a railroad employee, a locksmith, and some office workers. Factory workers, however, were almost entirely absent, a state of affairs that the PSF made little effort to alter.[48] Despite the participation of non-notables, socially diverse leadership was the exception, not the rule.

The greatest obstacle faced by the Alsatian PSF in its drive to become a right-wing mass party was the UPR, which also laid claim to a broad social constituency. Indeed, with its long history, dating to before 1918, and its perennial electoral success, the UPR was a formidable opponent. In some ways the UPR presented greater competition to the PSF in Alsace than the Radical Party did in the rest of France, since the UPR modeled itself after the disciplined German Center Party.[49]

Fear of electoral losses led the UPR to be critical of the PSF. Despite the

UPR's attempts to discredit it, however, the PSF claimed, "at bottom our goals and positions are the same, with the exception that we do not confine our interests to Alsace-Lorraine alone."[50] Both parties, for example, defended Catholicism as a bulwark of French and Alsatian society. Although there was a grain of truth in this, conflict and rivalry better describes their relations. The UPR had a greater sensitivity to Alsatians' affection for German culture. Unfortunately, the UPR's "German" constituency was diminishing and the PSF represented a more viable pro-French vehicle.[51] Although the UPR prospered during the 1936 national elections and the 1937 cantonal elections, the PSF's activism as well as that of the Bauernbund threatened the UPR's dominance over Alsatian politics. The PSF was well on its way to challenging, if not overtaking, the UPR.

The radical right added its voice to that of the UPR in uncertain opposition to the PSF. Although it shared the PSF's antisemitism, French nationalism, and antiparliamentarianism, the venerable AF found the success of the PSF unnerving. Royalists argued that the PSF's electoral success would split the right and help the Popular Front. They still quixotically hoped to act as the guiding force of the radical right. Discomfort turned into action when royalist youths tore down PSF posters and placards, calling de La Rocque a traitor.[52] Likewise, the Francistes found themselves losing momentum as the Croix de Feu grew. In a feeble attempt to discredit its competitor, *Le Franciste* called de La Rocque a "demagogue, who only looks for personal glory."[53]

The national frictions between Doriot's PPF and the PSF existed in Alsace as well. Doriot wanted to join forces in an anticommunist "Liberty Front." De La Rocque, however, insisted on organizational independence and his party continued to grow while Doriot's party languished.[54] The Alsatian JP, whose goal was to recruit elites in a loose political and ideological alliance, allowed its members to join the Croix de Feu (and the AF and the Solidarité Française)—at least before 1936.[55] The JP undoubtedly grew jealous as the PSF continued to expand.

The Alsatian PSF embarked on a uniquely antisemitic course within the party; in most *départements* antisemitism was not overt.[56] Algeria was an exception, as was Alsace. Two types of antisemitism—cultural and racial—struggled for dominance. The first, espoused by de La Rocque, accepted Jews, but only if they conformed to an essentially non-Jewish culture. Acculturated, patriotic French Jews could even join the PSF, whereas foreign, capitalist, or socialist Jews (those Jews who did not accept their place in society) elicited distaste and opposition. In one article de La Rocque, speaking of a "Jewish rabble" headed by Blum, asserts that Western civilization is "founded on a Christian basis" but then claims that, just because everyone must serve this Christian culture, this does not mean he objects to the religious rights of "non-Christians and foreign races." In another article, he states that "Patriotic Jews" were welcome, but they should do something about Léon Blum who catered to "a mostly revolutionary, often German and recently naturalized, and almost always ostentatious and indiscrete Israelite clientele."[57] No wonder the Alsatians believed de La Rocque would support their antisemitism.

The second form of antisemitism rejected Jews on racial grounds in addition to cultural ones and, if taken to its logical extreme, insisted on rigorous ghettoization, forced expulsion, or the annihilation of all Jews. Extremist Alsatian members espoused this view and trumpeted antisemitism from the local paper. *Le Flambeau de l'Est* boldly declared unequivocal opposition to the acceptance of émigré Jews from Germany: "We in Alsace have had too much of this immigration." The same issue contained a tasteless cartoon depicting Léon Blum—France's first Jewish head of state—in a Nazi uniform ornamented with the Star of David instead of the swastika, giving a Nazi salute to thousands of jackbooted Jews who were shouting, "One Volk! One Reich! One Führer! Heil Blum!" In the following issue, the editors argued that Jews were fundamentally inferior because "the Jew" was an "economic vulture." These were not isolated expressions of antisemitism. In the 1936 elections, the PSF had put up placards in Mulhouse warning Alsatians that "the Jew kills your parents," "steals your goods," and "poisons your race."[58]

Such an escalation of antisemitism by Alsatian PSF members reflected Nazi influence. It also suggests that the PSF collected a hodgepodge of unaffiliated fascists from the other fascist groups, for whom antisemitism was an end in itself. Antisemitism was a particularly important issue, because many thought that the PSF could gain even more support in Alsace if it rode the wave of anti-Jewish sentiment resulting from Blum's election. Outside the PSF, antisemitism was rife during the 1930s, fed by the political ideologies of the Bauernbund, the Alsatian Nazis, the UPR, and a host of ephemeral fascist movements. All of these groups were heavily indebted to German national socialist antisemitism. Although 1930s Alsatian and particularly PSF antisemitism had strong French precedents in the violent rhetoric of Count Gobineau, *La Gringoire*, Edouard Drumont, and Darquier de Pellepoix, it drew primarily on Nazi sources.[59] Contemporary observers noted the German connection when they compared an unnamed "young Strasbourgeois orator of the PSF" to Julius Streicher, the German editor of the notorious antisemitic *Der Stürmer*. The national leadership, however, refused to bar Jews from membership, and antisemitism continued to be a battleground over the locus of authority within the party.[60]

Aggressive antisemitism was part of a larger debate within the Alsatian PSF over the nature of the party. Radical members of the party intended to reveal its fundamental compatibility with other European fascist parties, especially Nazism. "Shouldn't we also restore national unity," as the Germans under Hitler have done, one writer mused. The Popular Front had created an unusual situation in Alsace, where the Nazi Jungmannschaft and the PSF formed a temporary alliance. One PSF leader loudly declared at a Strasbourg brasserie, "It is necessary to come to terms with Hitler, thus it is necessary to come to terms with the autonomists." This alliance was not long-lived, but it does indicate the turbulence within the PSF.[61]

Essentially, the national leadership attempted to expand on the basis of a vague corporatism and anticommunism. In the wake of the Popular Front, the PSF successfully attracted a wide range of radical right-wingers precisely because it did not articulate the finer points of its political philosophy in any way that might alienate specific classes. Consequently, many Alsatian PSF members simultaneously belonged to other organizations such as the Bauernbund, on the grounds that the former offered the best opportunity to advance their cause politically whereas the latter catered to their immediate corporative interests.[62] Local activists, however, sought to fill the intellectual vacuum with their own agenda. Without much guidance from above, Alsatian activists pursued a number of ideas, including extreme antisemitism and even Nazism, until de La Rocque clarified the party's position.

One way the PSF's national leaders reasserted control over Alsatian extremists was by rejecting Nazism. Sticking to its goal of "national reconciliation," the party insisted that it remain nominally open to Jews who were not "international." The party's local political bureau resolved to "fight against all foreign national movements, including Jewish nationalism."[63] *Le Flambeau de l'Est* became increasingly critical of Nazi Germany. After visiting Germany, a PSF commentator remarked, "It is no longer the land of laughter, it is the land of silence." Another article pointed out the "difficulties faced by Christian churches on the other side of the Rhine." The PSF's chief objection was on national grounds; Hitler's Germany posed a serious threat to French security. Accordingly, the PSF also attacked the Alsatian Nazis, whom it considered pro-Hitler and not representative of Alsatian opinion.[64]

Although the party subscribed to a social order similar to the Nazis, its priority was the pulling together of the hitherto fragmented radical French right. Thus, the PSF hewed more closely to a French nationalist agenda than the other 1930s fascists. The Bauernbund, the Francistes, and the other new French fascists made fascist social and political philosophy more central than national identity. Although many PSF members (especially the extreme antisemitic ones) did collaborate with the Nazis when the war broke out, the Germans recognized that the PSF was opposed to a German Alsace and banned it.[65]

The PSF profited from Alsatian anxieties at the time of the Czechoslovakian crisis in September 1938. Mobilization seriously disrupted economic life in the region, when panic induced many Alsatians to migrate to the interior and many businesses and banks to relocate for fear of expropriation by German troops. In this trial run for real war, Alsatians experienced dislocation, deprivation, and uncertainty well before many other Europeans and tended to lay responsibility for failure at the door of the French government. The PSF played up material losses, demanding that France should pay for the damages.[66] Failure to do this, claimed the PSF, would be the responsibility of the Third Republic. Forced to choose between France and Germany, Alsatians found themselves more than ever favorably inclined toward France. Yet the PSF managed to blame the international crisis on the Third Republic's inherent flaws. The PSF analysis that only a strong France could have stood up to and prevented German aggression grew increasingly popular.

. . .

The PSF appeared considerably more moderate than its fascist competitors. It repeatedly claimed that it was a "republican" party.[67] De La Rocque rejected a Streicher-like antisemitism and he steered away from the pro-Nazi implications of some of the more radical Alsatian activists. This apparent moderation, however, does not mean that the PSF was not fascist. From 1936 when the Croix de Feu became the PSF, the party pursued the single-minded goal of becoming the sole political representative of the radical right, with a view toward legally transforming the system, as Mussolini and Hitler did.

Fascism in prewar Alsace culminated in the PSF, which successfully transformed itself from a movement of extremes to a mainstream party. The PSF made fascism a palatable political alternative to the Popular Front and the chaos of the 1930s. Unlike all the other French fascist movements, from the AF to the Francistes, the PSF transcended social barriers to form a mass party. Even the Alsatian- and German-oriented autonomist movements (the Bauernbund, the Landespartei, and the Jungmannschaft) proved unable to unify diverse social classes in a single, radical, right-wing movement. As German-Alsatian fears of cultural discrimination and persecution waned during the 1930s, many erstwhile autonomists continued their struggle against anticlericalism, liberalism, and communism from within the PSF.

THE WAR AND BEYOND

At 12:20 on the afternoon of June 19, 1940, the German army raised the swastika over the Strasbourg Cathedral, opening a new chapter in the history of fascism in Alsace. The following week, Hitler triumphantly entered Strasbourg. The contrast with the French repossession of Alsace in 1918 could not have been greater. Many Alsatians (the Germans estimated about 40%) had already evacuated to central France, leaving the city streets desolate. No crowds cheered the incoming troops. A contemporary joke best expressed the Alsatians' attitude toward their new rulers. "Admit it," a German says, "the French are incompetent. After more than twenty years they have not succeeded in making Alsace French!" To which an Alsatian replies, "That's true, it only took you fifteen days to convert us completely to Frenchmen!" The German retaking of Alsace merely punctuated an already declining enthusiasm for Nazism, and subsequent German actions stoked Alsatian antipathies. Had Germans entered in 1926, 1933, or even 1936, the response might have been more favorable.[1]

Pro-Nazi sentiment was fairly widespread in Alsace until 1938, when the Munich crisis unequivocally demonstrated Hitler's aggressive intent. Throughout the 1930s, however, Alsatian Nazism was fragmented into groups with varying degrees of commitment to German Nazism. These included the clerical autonomists in the UPR, the Bauernbund, the Landespartei, the communist autonomists, and the outright Nazi affiliates, the Jungmannschaft and the Bund Erwin von Steinbach. Social support came from rural Catholics, pro-German Protestants, culturally disenchanted white-collar workers, and professionals, and it spanned both departments.

Around 1938, however, support for Nazism began to erode. The Munich crisis and the ongoing *Gleichschaltung* of the Catholic Church in Germany seriously dampened local enthusiasm for the Nazi cause and sparked interest in the French fascisms. Above all, the mobilization during the crisis had devastating effects in Alsace. Half of Strasbourg evacuated to France, including many industrial, financial, and commercial institutions. The same pattern held true throughout Alsace.[2] The Alsatian economy never fully recovered from the dislocation of its economy, and the prospect of war weighed heavily on the Alsatians. With access to German radio and newspapers, Alsatians were better informed about Hitler than most Europeans. And as French citizens, they were more critical of Nazism than the Germans. As a result, most Alsatians recast their allegiance with France in a favorable light.

From the beginning of their rule, the Germans knew that Alsatians were not overwhelmingly in favor of the Third Reich.[3] On the German side an us-versus-them mentality developed in which the *Reichsdeutsche* (Reich Germans) ruled and looked down on the Alsatian *Volksdeutsche* (Ethnic Germans) whose loyalty to the Reich was questionable. A barrage of regulations designed to convert Alsatians into Germans soured German-Alsatian relations. Towns, streets, businesses, individuals, and families all had to germanize their names.[4] Cultural signifiers became matters of life and death, as in the case of the Nazi ban of French berets, the wearing of which Gauleiter Robert Wagner believed constituted an "expression of Western and French sentiments" punishable by a stay in a concentration camp.[5]

The cynicism of the Nazis about Alsace can be seen in the way they dealt with the Alsatian autonomists, Karl Roos's fellow prisoners, who still languished in the Nancy prison at the time of the armistice between German and France. As part of the spoils of war, Hitler demanded that the prisoners be turned over to the German army, which the French government dutifully did on July 14. Still confined, the autonomists remained prisoners of the Germans for forty-eight hours until they all signed the declaration of les Trois-Epis, which exhorted all Alsatians to "proceed . . . to the integration of their *Heimat* within the Great German Reich."[6] Their liberation, as it turned out, was a prelude to the de facto annexation of Alsace by Germany. Not all the signatories were enthusiastic about signing a document that committed them unequivocally to endorsing the new regime. All of them, however, received sinecures during the war, in addition to their liberty, for signing. In this way the Nazis sought to legitimize their authority through the elevation of the autonomist leaders to visible positions of authority in Alsace.

The goal of German policy in Alsace was the forcible conversion of the local population to Nazism. Unlike the rest of France, which was "merely" occupied, Hitler integrated Alsace directly into the Third Reich by attaching it to Baden. This annexation was not formally ratified by treaty; nevertheless the government subjected Alsace to a more rigorous policy of germanization and *Gleichschaltung* than the rest of Baden. Gauleiter Wagner, who was prone to castigate the recalcitrant Alsatians for their failure to understand that Nazism existed for the benefit of Alsace, typified the heavy-handedness of German policy. Wagner thought he was best serving Alsace by forcing it to share all the responsibilities of the Reich, including military service.[7]

For their part, most ordinary Alsatians stubbornly opposed the new regime. Public opinion toward the Third Reich, according to Nazi intelligence reports, was "irregular and uncertain." Catholic priests encouraged their parishioners not to let their children join the Hitler Youth.[8] Gauleiter Wagner's order to dissolve all Catholic organizations and confiscate their property did little to alleviate Catholic resistance. Mass deportation of undesirable Alsatians further alienated the population.[9] Remaining Alsatians lived in constant fear of resettlement and resented the use of deportations to enforce compliance with Nazi cultural policies. Resistance—in the form of singing satirical songs, wearing berets, posting fliers, or simply not joining—was rife. Alsatians satirized the germanization policy by replacing the street name "Rue du Sauvage" with "Rue Adolph Hitler," or "Where the Fox Preaches to the Ducks" with "Rue du Dr. Goebbels." One Strasbourg resident perfectly expressed the lamentable frustration and misery experienced in Alsace for the duration of the war when he wrote, "I wish I had another place to live in; but there isn't anywhere."[10]

The only German policy that met with general local approval was the promise that Alsatians would not have to serve in the armed forces. Such a promise compares rather unfavorably with that of General Joffre's 1918 promise that France would protect Alsace's regional uniqueness. In any event, Gauleiter Wagner rescinded the German promise on August 25, 1942, when he instituted obligatory military service. "There is no neutrality in this war," Wagner argued, therefore Alsatians had a duty to fight.[11] Posters exhorted Alsatian youths to enroll in the Wehrmacht or the SS because, "As long as the German and European youth fight for their ideals, the Alsatian youth is not permitted to be absent."[12] The reimposition of the draft capped a series of measures—compulsory participation in the *Reichsarbeitsdienst* (Reich Labor Service) in May 1941, the official introduction of the Nazi Party into Alsace in October 1941, and compulsory membership in the Hitler Youth in January 1942—that laid the burden of being German on the Alsatians.[13]

Alsatians resisted by evading both the labor service and the draft, often fleeing to southern France or Switzerland.[14] On February 13, 1943, the Germans captured fourteen Alsatians who were attempting to escape military service by crossing into Switzerland at Ballersdorf. That same week, riots took place over conscription in several Haut-Rhin villages. The subsequent execution of the youths exposed the hostility between the rulers and the ruled. Even when they complied, the Alsatian conscripts sometimes voiced their dissatisfaction by singing the "Marseillaise" as they left the train depot.[15] Would-be draft evaders faced the unenviable choice of conscription, execution, or knowing that their families would be deported to eastern Europe.[16] As a result, many Alsatians found themselves dragooned into the SS where they became participants in atrocities such as the massacre of 642 villagers at Oradour on June 10, 1944.[17] In the end, a half-million inhabitants were deported from Alsace-Lorraine, 130,000 Alsatians and Lorrainers served in both Axis and Allied armies, and 37,000 died.[18]

Against this somber backdrop, the history of fascism in Alsace staged its third act. Those French fascists who favored the national part of national socialism became *résistants*. The illegal annexation of Alsace and the oppressive cultural war fought against Frenchness directly violated the beliefs of patriotic Frenchmen. Thus, one of the leaders of the Alsatian AF wrote, "I can not, I will not resign myself to defeat."[19] Another royalist, Robert Heitz, spent eleven months in prison for resistance activity and only avoided execution through the intervention of Joseph Bilger. The Nazi administration identified the AF and the Croix de Feu as "inimical to Germany."[20]

In addition, those interwar fascists who remained devoted to Catholicism opposed Nazism for its unremitting secularism. The Nazis' turning Strasbourg Cathedral into a Nazi museum, closing all the denominational schools, and expelling the majority of the clergy deeply offended Catholic Alsace. The Catholic clergy led resistance to Nazi pressure by facilitating the escape of draft-age men and teaching French during religious instruction.[21] As a result, the Catholic Church became a symbol of resistance to both the populace and the Nazi hierarchy. Catholic autonomist leaders such as Joseph Rossé and Marcel Stürmel who collaborated with the Nazis became isolated from the main current of Catholic opinion.

Those Alsatians who remained committed either to a return to Germany or to the socialist part of national socialism generally chose to collaborate. The Jungmannschaft, the Landespartei, and the EABP fell into the former category, as did the pro-Nazi wing of the UPR. In addition, some Francistes and PSF members collaborated out of an unshakable belief in the rightness of the Nazi social order. Similarly, Joseph Bilger led his Green Shirts into the Nazi Party.[22]

Over the course of the war, however, the ideologues—the fascists who collaborated—lost whatever support they had. This was particularly true of the autonomists, whose call for union with Germany as the best guarantor of Alsatian rights was no longer credible. Part of the autonomists' disenchantment stemmed from the 1941 Nazi proclamation: "henceforth the question of an autonomous Alsace, even within the cadre of the Reich, may no longer be posed."[23] Even without such a bald condemnation of autonomism, it was clear from their germanization policy that the Nazis completely rejected everything the autonomists had worked for. Bilger, Rossé, and others recognized that their base of support had eroded and belatedly opposed the Nazi regime. Bilger, by 1942 an official in Lorraine, opposed the deportations of Alsatian families to eastern Europe, realizing that such a policy would permanently alienate Alsatians from Germany. As a result, the Nazis put him under house arrest in Hamburg. Joseph Rossé used his wartime publishing empire to print both Nazi propaganda and anti-Nazi and religious tracts and used his influence to intervene on behalf of many Alsatians who ran afoul of the Nazis. The resistance activity of these autonomists, however, was too little too late.[24]

The postwar purges were relatively light in Alsace. The courts only sentenced thirty-three Alsatians to death, many in absentia.[25] Among those sentenced to death were Jean-Pierre Mourer, Hermann Bickler, Paul Schall, and Friedrich Spieser, although Mourer was the only one to stand before a firing squad. An additional eleven received life sentences for their actions during the war. Robert Ernst, Joseph Rossé, Marcel Stürmel, and Joseph Bilger served limited sentences of hard labor.[26] Obviously, those convicted came from the ranks of the Alsatian Nazis and the collaborators. Nobody from the AF or the PSF found themselves on trial.

By successfully resisting the Nazis, the Francophile fascists distanced themselves from the negative aspects of fascism and preserved their positions in society. The best example of survival is Pierre Pflimlin, who parlayed his heroic resistance into a prominent role in Alsatian, French, and European politics, despite his earlier participation in a wide range of fascist organizations.[27] Although Pflimlin probably genuinely converted to democratic ideology during the war, his activity in prewar fascist organizations and his postwar political success indicates a widespread blindness to selective fascisms. It would be unreasonable to accuse him of practicing postwar fascist politics, but nevertheless, Pflimlin's case raises the question as to whether fascist continuity exists between the 1930s and the present.

Fascism survived the war and still plays a role, albeit a reduced one, in Alsatian politics. In the 1980s fascism resurfaced as a public philosophy. Jean-Marie Le Pen recently garnered 25 percent of the presidential vote in Alsace—well above the national average. Pockets of pro-German Alsatians still exist, although their voice is muted. Antisemitic rowdies have desecrated Jewish cemeteries. The continuity with the interwar era and the sporadic revival of fascism clearly show that World War II did not permanently discredit fascism.

. . .

Fascism in Alsace defies easy generalization since it was a highly variable and diverse phenomenon. The flexibility of European fascism appears most clearly in Alsace, where different national cultures clashed. Unlike the Nazis or the Italian Fascists, who focused fascist energies into single, coherent, mass parties, fascists in Alsace explored the full range of possibilities. To date, the examples of Italian Fascism and German Nazism have dominated our understanding of fascist ideology and practice. This has seriously distorted the nature of fascism as success has become the definitional yardstick. Moreover, the focus on conventional national forms of fascism as seen from Berlin, Rome, or Paris conveniently simplifies the fascist phenomenon by avoiding the question of interaction, competition, and variety. Only the study of such border regions as Alsace can challenge this bias toward the center. And it is precisely in these border areas that fascism faces its deepest contradictions and its greatest complexity.

The fascist phenomenon in Alsace seriously undermines many cherished beliefs about fascism. Many observers, for example, argue that fascism is a populist movement.[28] Such a view assumes that fascism tends to be organized from the bottom up and depends on mass participation for legitimation. In Alsace, however, many of the fascist movements were far from populist. The Faisceau and most of the other French fascist groups were the clearest examples of elite-oriented fascism. Even Nazism, which in Germany was populist, eschewed a populist strategy in Alsace in favor of a revolutionary vanguard one. At the same time, some Alsatian fascist movements were populist, most notably the Alsatian Bauernbund, so it would be equally incorrect to argue that fascism was never populist. The absence of a uniformly populist trend in Alsace suggests that it is not a necessary characteristic.

Another confounding conclusion is that fascism could have a regional orientation—an aspect of fascism that has hitherto eluded the attention of scholars. Hypernationalism certainly played an important role in Alsatian fascism. Nevertheless, the case of Alsace—and especially the Bauernbund—demonstrates that fascism was also rooted in regionalism. This occurred in two ways: fascist regionalism and regional fascism. Movements such as the AF, the Faisceau, the Nazis, and even the Francistes attempted to co-opt regionalism in order to attract support in what might be called fascist regionalism. Their regionalism was at odds with the heavy stress on central authority, cultural homogeneity, and nationalism of all these parties. The Faisceau, for example, espoused a radical right-wing centralization of the French state but in Alsace used dialect speakers at its rallies. For their part, the Nazis (whose totalitarian bent is well known) financially supported the Alsatian regionalists and repeatedly advocated regional rights.

More significant, regionalism began to co-opt fascism, drawing on fascist ideology and techniques to advance the interests of the region. This regional fascism was the dubious achievement of the Bauernbund, which adopted an unquestionably fascist ideology culled from both Nazi and French fascist sources, yet was indifferent as to which nation Alsace should belong. Instead, the Bauernbund's ideal was an Alsatian community. The implications of this are broad. It means that fascist ideology has been and can be tied to a wide variety of cultural communities. If regional fascism existed, then the nation is not the sole ideal fascist community, which in turn implies that fascism extends potentially well beyond traditional nationalist movements. It also extends the notion of how fascism could be co-opted for all sorts of purposes.

Each fascist group had its own social niche. The only class that lacked much of a fascist option was the working class, which was far more effectively represented by the Marxist parties. The Bauernbund built a strong following among Catholic peasants. The AF, the Faisceau, and the PSF appealed largely to professional and upper-middle-class Alsatians. The new fascists—the Francistes and the Nasos—spread the fascist message to the urban lower-middle class. The Alsatian Nazis appealed to middle-class and rural Protestant Alsatians. The fact that almost every social group had developed its own fascist alternative by the 1930s undermines the idea of a single definition of fascism. Each fascist movement articulated a slightly different fascist ideology. A completely different picture of fascism emerges, depending on which fascist group one focuses on—a problem clearly reflected in the definitional literature. Moreover, explanations of fascism that identify fascism as uniquely lower-middle-class simply do not hold water in a situation in which a wide range of social groups had their own version of fascism.[29]

Some would argue that the diverse social appeal of fascism reflects its amoral tendency to seek power without regard for ideology. According to this view, the quest for and use of power defines fascism, and fascist leaders such as Mussolini and Hitler would say or do anything to gain power.[30] A related argument suggests that fascism insinuates itself only where there is a political vacuum.[31] Both of these arguments represent the social constituencies as passive in their response to fascism. The case of Alsace, however, suggests a different possibility. Different classes co-opted fascism for their own purposes. Fascism was an ideology or a spirit that simultaneously criticized the liberal, Marxist, and even conservative ideologies and constructed an alternative solution. Although achieving power was more desirable than not, power was not the defining characteristic of fascism for the rank and file. Each social level had its own version of what the new order should be, and elements of all social levels willingly embraced and commandeered fascism.

The relationship between women and fascism merits greater attention than this study has given it. Clearly, gender played a powerful role, especially since women could not vote at this time. Men dominated the movement and in many respects the patriarchal, frequently violent, hierarchical, and militaristic tendencies of the various Alsatian fascists reflected male issues and attitudes. In extreme form, fascists such as Antoine Rédier delineated a fairly strict division between domestic and public spheres and essentially held women up as models for passivity and obedience to the state. This, of course, was consistent with European reactions to the changed gender map of the interwar era, which saw men become fearful of the effects of women workers, bobbed hairstyles, and the decadence of the Roaring Twenties.

Women, however, did participate in fascist movements and their concerns occasionally surfaced. Female support for the fascist movements is nearly impossible to quantify, because they did not vote, but it is likely that many supported tradition, family, and order. Women were less involved with the more violent aspects of fascism. Police reports and newspapers noted their presence at rallies, particularly of those movements that had acquired a certain respectability such as the AF and the PSF. The number of pro-Nazi women may have been low, but support for the Bauernbund, the AF, and the PSF might have been more substantial. Although barred from leadership, women—or perhaps more precisely, women's issues—influenced some fascist policies. The PSF, for example, advocated daycare centers for working mothers, women's suffrage, and equal pay for equal work. Its rationale was typically fascist; children had to be raised nationalistically, women were thought to vote right-wing, and there was a surplus of women in the workplace as a result of World War I. Those women who had to work because of the shortage of men were not to be penalized in the expectation that when they married they would take up their traditional role. These measures, in other words, were consistent with the idea that women should, where possible, stay at home, raise children, and virtuously educate their families to be patriotic. Women were not wholly integrated into fascist organizations, but their treatment served as a model of obedience and submission to the hierarchy for men.

Another aspect of fascism revealed in the study of Alsace is the clear change in the nature of fascism over time. Fascism went through several generations between the 1920s and 1945. Here Alsace was probably fairly representative of European-wide trends. The 1920s fascisms in Alsace were heavily influenced by the example of Mussolini and the specific question of national identity. Mostly upper-middle-class in origin, 1920s French fascists saw fascism as a means of criticizing and blocking both Marxism and liberal democracy and reasserting their control over French society. The neo-Marxist argument that fascism was an attempt to reimpose bourgeois hegemony has considerable validity for the 1920s.[32]

In the 1930s, fascism ceased to be the prerogative of the upper-middle class. The depression, Hitler's mercurial rise, and the permeation of fascist discourse into society contributed to the change in fascism. The transformation of the autonomists into Nazis, the conversion of the communist autonomists into Nazis, the rise of the peasant Bauernbund, and the proliferation of urban, lower-middle-class, pro-French groups such as the Francistes and the Nasos all point to the radicalization and the social diversification of fascism. The ideologies changed correspondingly. Where the traditional fascists of the 1920s articulated a corporatism that emphasized the expertise and paternalistic authority of the well-educated and technocratic elite, the second generation of fascists presented conflicting visions

THE WAR AND BEYOND • 157

of peasant corporatism, violent anticapitalist corporatism, and Nazi-style racial *Volksgemeinschaft.*

Toward the end of the 1930s, yet another evolution took place in the overall fascist movement. The PSF, under de La Rocque, unified the first- and second-generation fascists, creating the first and only fascist mass party in Alsace. Although the PSF did not integrate very many of the Alsatian Nazi activists, it managed to pull together the diverse elements of the French fascist movement. The war interrupted this development and ushered in a new era of fascism, in which fascists had to weigh the cost of collaboration with the Nazis against their cultural identity as either Alsatians or Frenchmen and women. The end of the war by no means marked the definitive end of fascism's evolution.

Local context also shaped fascism, as the case of Alsace shows. After all, over time, the local conditions changed. Underlying the organization of this study is the rich context of Alsatian life from 1918 to 1945. Local circumstances had profound effects on the organization and even the ideology of fascism, contributing to its diversity. The role of religion and religious identity, for example, differentiated fascism in Alsace from elsewhere. The simultaneous influence of German Lutheranism and French Catholicism created a situation in which both religions had affiliations with fascism, with the Catholics in the majority. This was quite different from Germany, where Catholics tended to remain loyal to the Center Party and, as a minority, remained suspicious of the centralizing and totalitarian aspects of Nazism. The French fascist movements, like those of Austria, placed Catholicism at the center of national identity. Unlike either Germany or France, fascism in Alsace reflected the influence of both religious communities. Alsace's peculiarities do not make it a sui generis case with little bearing on the wider phenomenon. On the contrary, they suggest that every region has its own context, its own discourse, and its own historical development, all of which strengthen the conclusion that fascism did not manifest itself uniformly.

Alsace's religious sociology lends itself to some conclusions about the relationship between religion and fascism in interwar Europe. Undoubtedly, the truly religious tap into a different tradition and sensibility than the fascist; and some fascisms, most notably Nazism, were notably anti-Christian. Nevertheless, religion was compatible with fascism. In particular, religious institutions often seized on fascism as a weapon against godless communism or liberal materialism. Many Catholics and Protestants found aspects of fascism attractive—especially the notion of cultural conformity and the reimposition of order—and at this time the idea of God and country facilitated the acceptance of fascism by religious individuals. Conversely, fascists usually had few qualms about co-opting religion as a pillar of society. Thus, the inclusion of either Catholics or Protestants in a movement or government does not disqualify it from being considered fascist. The exact nature of the relationship between religion and fascism, however, depended heavily on whether it was Catholic or Protestant, during the 1920s or 1930s, and within national or local contexts.

Another significant aspect of the local context was the way that the political structure of Alsace (and France) simultaneously stimulated diverse movements and inhibited the emergence of a fascist consensus. Mayors, village priests, and important individuals influenced the success or failure of a given movement at the local level. These individuals reflected the way that local religious, class, national, and linguistic divisions manifested themselves. The result was the arbitrary and unsystematic implantation of fascisms.

Little research has been done on the interaction of fascist movements.[33] Instead, historians have focused on mainstream national movements and have assumed that nationalism was an insurmountable barrier between movements. Nevertheless, the study of border regions such as Alsace reveals the byzantine nature of competing fascisms. One aspect that emerges is that clear distinctions between fascist groups are rarely apparent. To decontextualize Alsatian fascism—to pluck out a single group—is to miss the larger picture where interaction was the rule. Thus, members of the mainstream UPR legitimized Nazism, Marxist autonomists shared office space with Alsatian Nazis, and the Bauernbund garnered ideas and support from pro-German and pro-French groups. The list could go on.

Rarely in the interwar era did fascists overtly describe themselves as operating within an international movement. Their association of internationalism with socialism, communism, and plutocratic exploitation and the importance of nationalist and expansionist ideologies inhibited any sort of call for international cooperation. The only attempt at a fascist international was the abortive 1934 meeting in Montreaux.[34] What was commonplace, however, even ubiquitous, was the suggestion that what had worked in Italy or in Germany could strengthen Alsace or France. Repeated expressions of profound respect for Mussolini's and Hitler's achievements point to a deep-rooted acknowledgment of a fundamental commonality across national lines.

Movements that shared national identification demonstrated ideological and organizational tensions. In these cases, the conflict revolved around who would become the Führer. Members of the Francistes, the Nasos, and the PSF, for example, often attended each other's rallies but argued over such seemingly trivial symbolic issues as who had the right to use the fascist salute.[35] Similar internecine bickering marked the Alsatian Nazi movement, which was divided among the Bauernbund, the left wing of the UPR, the Landespartei, and the Jungmannschaft. Yet within national orientations a tremendous amount of fluidity existed. The career of Marcel Bucard—who worked with the Faisceau, the Solidarité Française, the Croix de Feu, and Gustave Hervé's National Socialist Party before he founded the Francistes—is just one example of the extent of cooperation across the French fascist movement.

The pattern of individual participation substantiates the deeply contradictory interactions within the overall fascist movement. Conversion or joint membership across German and French fascisms was rare until the mid-1930s. As the Alsatian public grew more comfortable with accommodation with France, more pro-Germans switched to a pro-French position. The Croix de Feu's opening of its membership to *Reichswehr* veterans perhaps best illustrates this process. In the 1930s some groups and individuals crossed the nationalist barrier in search of a fascist order. The Bauernbund is just one example of this with its intellectual debt to German *Blut und Boden* and antisemitic ideology, its advocacy of a French Catholicism, and its vacillating affiliations with German and French groups. Many of the ephemeral antisemitic movements of the mid- to late 1930s combined French orientation with support from the notorious Nazi propagandist Julius Streicher. Thus, nationalism was, at least at times, a permeable barrier.

Taken together, the fascist movements in Alsace influenced political discourse in other ways, affecting how Alsatians viewed their problems and polarizing them around a nexus of issues relating to their identity. The local political parties, for example, rushed to imitate the militarization of fascism. Even liberal parties saw fit to join in the spirit of the times and create their own paramilitary troops. Another innovation pioneered by the fascists that became popular across the political spectrum was youth. Everyone became obsessed with youth, forming uniformed youth groups and constantly referring to the younger generation, vigor, and renewal in their literature. Finally, Mussolini and Hitler, in their capacity as fascist icons, became conduits for discontent. If only there were a comparable leader in Alsace or France, many disgruntled Alsatians argued, then life would be better. In short, fascism permeated Alsatian political life to a degree that transcends quantification.

That fascists failed to bridge the barriers of national culture in favor of a unified fascist political agenda points to the possibility that culture—the complex of human artifacts that shape individual behavior and identification—deserves greater attention as a motivating force behind fascism. The relative success of fascism in Alsace bears out the significance of cultural identity (in this case the problem of identification with national cultural traditions) for fascist activity. Although the lack of unity was a notable failure, when considered in sum, fascism in Alsace garnered more support than in the rest of France and much of Germany. The reason for this was Alsace's status as a border region and the importance of national identity in an area subjected to intense pressure from Germany and France to become a showpiece of their respective nations. In this context, the different fascisms represented alternative hypernational identities and linked local problems to mutually exclusive hypernational solutions. The fascist parties channeled the regional political discourse in Alsace into confrontational and violent directions. The evolution of the discourse into vehemently opposed French and German camps effectively ended the pluralist compromises that had marked Alsatian life for centuries and hindered consideration of more moderate alternatives.

In fact, the homogeneity espoused by the fascists never existed in Alsace, which was split along national, religious, linguistic, and class lines. All of the fascisms rejected the variety of Alsatian life and forced Alsatians to choose between the French, German, or Alsatian camps. French-speaking upper-class Alsatians leaned toward the French fascist groups, if they were attracted to fascism in the first place. The German-speaking population—consisting of the petite bourgeoisie, rural elements, and the urban working classes—supported the autonomist movement and favored the Nazis. Protestant fascists tended to join the pro-German fascist groups, whereas the Catholics were more divided. Alsatians in Haut-Rhin were consistently more pro-French than the Bas-Rhinois, which was reflected in their participation in the various fascist groups. The irony is that the diversity of the fascist movements reflected the realities of Alsatian life, even though each strenuously denied Alsatian heterogeneity.

Differing versions of national identity did not necessarily preclude cooperation and interpenetration between fascist groups. In the 1930s many fascist leaders ceased to dwell on a specific (French or German) identity and recognized that state manipulation of mass culture could retroactively build acceptable cultural identities. The success of the Italian *doppolavoro* (leisure) and the Nazi *Kraft durch Freude* (strength through joy) organizations demonstrated the burgeoning possibilities for social control through state action. Accordingly, some fascist leaders focused on the political goals of fascism without connecting them to either France or Germany. The way that the Bauernbund vacillated between German and French fascism during the 1930s illustrates this process. A number of individuals bridged the French and German movements, showing up at a variety of rallies, switching allegiances, and borrowing Nazi ideology—especially antisemitism—for pro-French purposes.

. . .

Rather than call for a "narrow definition of fascism," it seems obvious that fascism needs to be recast much more broadly if it is to encompass the full range of fascisms present in Alsace.[36] The exclusionary definitions that have become the norm selectively dwell on highly subjective criteria and miss the breadth of the fascist movement. The idea of a generic fascism, which seems to rectify this problem, ends up being equally exclusionary because it implies that any movement lacking one or more of the "defining" characteristics is not actually fascist.

All of the movements in this study were unmistakably fascist. Many of them openly embraced the label, as in the cases of the Faisceau, the Francistes, the Bauernbund, and the Alsatian Nazis. The diversity among these groups alone is enough to demonstrate the problems with narrow, exclusionary definitions. The other groups, including the AF, the PSF, the pro-

German wing of the UPR, and the Croix de Feu/PSF, were at times just as fascist, although for legal and contextual reasons they often chose not to draw attention to it. To argue that the latter groups merely imitated fascism downplays their fundamental similarity and interaction with the overtly fascist organizations.

Fascism is a *political* philosophy that posits the universal subservience of the individual to the nation (or community), and the equation of the nation with the state and/or party. In the words of the French fascist Marcel Bucard:

> Our fathers wanted liberty; we demand order. . . . They preached fraternity; we demand discipline over feelings. They professed equality; we affirm the hierarchy of values. . . . For them, the individual is a sacred entity, fundamentally natural to the state. For us, the individual only exists as a function of his family and place of birth.[37]

Only through devotion to the state, as representative of the nation, can individuals find fulfillment. Thus, Mussolini rejected individualism, writing that fascism "accepts the individual only in so far as his interests coincide with those of the State, which stands for the conscience and the universal will of man as a historic entity."[38] Moreover, fascists argue for a closed cultural circle enforced by the state—a set of cultural absolutes and truths—unlike liberals and socialists who argue for a more universal humanity, and conservatives who cling to an elitist view of culture. For fascists, the defining cultural characteristic can vary—it can be race (Nazis), nation (Italian Fascists), or region (the Alsatian Bauernbund)—but it always carefully delineates those who belong from those who do not, and it does so in a way that, at least theoretically, transcends class and individual differences and enhances the authority of the state.

This definition is deliberately broad and inclusive; it does not mean that each of these fascisms was the same. Contextual factors such as region, national orientation, religion, social level, time, and relationship to land (to name just the most salient variables in Alsace) formed a complex equation that shaped the nature of each fascist organization. Thus, each fascist group's interpretation of community, state, and representation varied according to the sum of these various parts. Additionally, the different fascist movements affected each other, which is why fascism became so significant in the 1930s and why they gradually moved toward conformity. What makes Alsace so interesting is that its peculiar, mixed cultural setting resulted in an array of fascist adaptations and interactions that bore greater similarity to the European-wide diffusion of fascism than to the linear evolution of individual fascist parties in Germany, Italy, and elsewhere. The diversity and complexity of these interactions points to a fascism that was neither monolithic nor comprised of isolated strands.

Fascism in Alsace was neither a single comprehensive ideology nor an isolated deviant in interwar politics but, rather, a somewhat flexible ideal that contrasted with the political status quo. Without a source text or theorist, Europeans were free to imagine their own versions of fascism, which led to a multitude of fascisms. Fascism gripped the imaginations of Europeans as the wave of the future, the "third path," or as "neither right, nor left."[39] As such, it permeated the political discourse and influenced popular and elite perceptions of local, national, and international events.

NOTES

1. Although the idea of "Alsace-Lorraine" has become a commonplace, the linking of the two provinces is, for the most part, arbitrary. The term *Alsace-Lorraine* did not originate until 1871 when the Germans annexed them. After 1918 the French consistently referred to them as "Alsace *and* Lorraine" or the "recovered provinces." Nevertheless, the French did administer them jointly through the Services d'Alsace et de Lorraine. When the Germans rolled in again in 1940, the two were again separated. In short, Lorraine was different; and it makes more sense in this study to focus solely on Alsace and leave Lorraine to some future scholar.

2. Henry Rousso, *The Vichy Syndrome: History and Memory in France since 1944* (Cambridge, Mass., 1991), 8, 300.

3. Christian Baechler, *Le Parti Catholique Alsacien, 1890–1939: Du Reichsland à la République Jacobine* (Paris, 1982), 743–46.

1: THE ALSATIAN MALAISE AND THE AUTONOMIST MOVEMENT

1. This Alsatian (Strasbourgeois) folk song is quoted from Frédéric Hoffet, *Psychanalyse de l'Alsace* (Colmar, 1973), 14. Hans in Schnokeloch was a popular culture figure representing the archetypical Alsatian. The pro-German Karl Roos, executed in 1940 for treason, popularized Hans in Schnokeloch in the 1920s.

2. Archives Nationales (AN), F7.13398, Strasbourg, Sept. 28, 1929, "Les autonomismes alsacien, breton, corse et flamand." See also Alain Déniel, *Le mouvement breton, 1919–1945* (Paris, 1976); Jack Reece, *The Bretons against France: Ethnic Minority Nationalism in Twentieth-Century Brittany* (Chapel Hill, 1977); and Suzanne Berger, *Peasants against Politics: Rural Organization in Brittany, 1911–1967* (Cambridge, Mass., 1972).

3. *Elsaß-Lothringer Zeitung (ELZ),* Aug. 4, 1930. Unless otherwise noted, all translations are my own.

4. The German Rhenish movement and the Alsatian separatist movement were traveling in opposite directions. The former sought to leave Germany, the latter to join it, which created odd bedfellows. The AF, for example, was somewhat supportive of the Rhinelanders whereas it was bitterly opposed to Alsatian autonomists. The French government supported the Rhenish movement as a means of weakening the German state, while acting to suppress Alsatian regionalism. By 1924 the momentum of the Rhenish movement in Germany had largely dissipated, at the very moment when Alsatian autonomism became an issue. Again, this suggests a lack of convergence between the two movements. Alsatians were interested

in and favorably inclined toward the Rhenish movement, but cooperation aimed at a larger Rhenish state was not really an issue. See Klaus Reimer, *Rheinlandfrage und Rheinlandbewegung (1918–1933): Ein Beitrag zur Geschichte der regionalistischen Bestrebungen in Deutschland* (Frankfurt am Main, 1979), for a description of the Rhenish movement.

5. Joseph Rossé, Marcel Stürmel, A. Bleicher, F. Dieber, and J. Keppi, eds., *Das Elsaß von 1870 bis 1932* (Colmar, 1932), 4:422, doc. 44, quoting the *Journal Officiel Débats* meeting of June 17, 1924.

6. John E. Craig, *Scholarship and Nation-Building: The Universities of Strasbourg and Alsatian Society, 1870–1939* (Chicago, 1984), 1.

7. Maurice Barrès, *Colette Baudoche: The Story of a Young Girl of Metz* (New York, 1918).

8. Benedict Anderson, *Imagined Communities: Reflections on the Origin and Spread of Nationalism* (New York, 1991); Karl-Heinz Rothenberger, *Die elsaß-lothringische Heimat- und Autonomiebewegung zwischen den beiden Weltkriegen* (Frankfurt am Main, 1975), 23 (quotation).

9. Jack Morrison, "The Intransigents: Alsace-Lorrainers against the Annexation, 1900–1914" (University of Iowa, 1970), 207. For an example of the earlier *Heimat* scholarship, see Wilhelm Heinrich Riehl, *Die Naturgeschichte des deutschen Volkes* (Leipzig, n.d.). George Mosse, *The Crisis of German Ideology* (New York, 1981), discusses the spread of the *völkisch* movement and its influence on German political consciousness. The work of writers such as Julius Langbehn, as described by Fritz Stern, *The Politics of Cultural Despair: A Study in the Rise of Germanic Ideology* (Berkeley and Los Angeles, 1961), encouraged this trend.

10. Pierre Maugué, *Le particularisme alsacien, 1918–1967* (Paris, 1970), 59.

11. Rothenberger, *Heimat- und Autonomiebewegung,* 19; Fernand Braudel, *The Identity of France* (New York, 1988), 1:104; Hoffet, *Psychanalyse de l'Alsace,* 35–84.

12. Paul Lévy, *Histoire linguistique d'Alsace et de Lorraine* (Paris, 1929), 2:477. Figures are from Rossé et al., *Das Elsaß,* 4:199, table 95, and represent the number of Alsatians who used French regularly in ordinary conversation, not the number of those who could actually communicate in French. *Le Temps* published different language figures for 1932: 996,578 French-speaking Alsatians as opposed to 1,525,043 German-speaking Alsatians (Bas-Rhin [BR]), AL98.1105, July 4, 1932, referring to *Le Temps,* July 2–3, 1932). Maugué, *Le particularisme alsacien,* 47, points out that in 1918 very few Alsatians (2 percent) used French with any degree of regularity. Some have argued that the number of French speakers was up from prewar figures. To be sure, the number of French speakers in Strasbourg rose from 4,850 in 1910 to 25,411 in 1926 (*Alsace Française,* Jan. 11, 1931). Given the change in nationality and the resultant influx of "interior Frenchmen," however, such a figure scarcely seems significant. Any figure that purports to settle definitively the number of French and German speakers should be taken with a grain of salt. Despite the muddiness of the figures, it should be clear that German was the dominant language, and that Alsace was deeply divided linguistically.

13. *Der Komplott-prozeß von Besançon vom 10. Juni bis 22. Juni 1929: Gesammelte Verhandlungsberichte* (Colmar, 1929), 26.

14. Hans Ulrich Wehler, *Sozialdemokratie und Nationalstaat: National-itätenfragen in Deutschland, 1840–1914* (Göttingen, 1971). Compare David Blackbourn, *Class, Religion and Local Politics in Wilhelmine Germany: The Center*

Party in Württemberg before 1914 (New Haven, 1980); or Dan S. White, *The Splintered Party: National Liberalism in Hessen and the Reich, 1867–1918* (Cambridge, Mass., 1976), for criticism of the centralized view of the Wilhelmine state.

15. Rossé et al., *Das Elsaß*, 1:24.

16. Maugué, *Le particularisme alsacien*, 11, 23.

17. Dan P. Silverman, *Reluctant Union: Alsace-Lorraine and Imperial Germany, 1871–1918* (University Park, Pa., 1972), 148–49, 163; Marcel Stürmel, *Die Autonomie Elsaß-Lothringens auf Grund der Verfassung von 1911* (Colmar, 1931), 2; Jean-Marie Mayeur, *Autonomie et politique en Alsace: La constitution de 1911* (Paris, 1970).

18. The regionalism of France has been commented on by numerous authors: R. K. Gooch, *Regionalism in France* (New York, 1931); Theodore Zeldin, *France, 1848–1945* (Oxford, 1973), 2:29–85; Lawrence Wylie, *Village in the Vaucluse* (Cambridge, Mass., 1957); William Brustein, *The Social Origins of Political Regionalism: France, 1849–1981* (Berkeley and Los Angeles, 1988); Christian Gras and Georges Livet, eds., *Régions et régionalisme en France du XVIIIe siècle à nos jours* (Vendôme, 1977), to mention just a few.

19. Hermann Hiery, *Reichstagswahlen im Reichsland: Ein Beitrag zur Landesgeschichte von Elsaß-Lothringen und zur Wahlgeschichte des deutschen Reiches, 1871–1918* (Düsseldorf, 1986).

20. Karl Liebknecht, "Polen, Elsaß-Lothringen, Irland," in vol. 9 of *Gesammelte Reden und Schriften* (Berlin, 1968), 355.

21. William Irvine, *French Conservatism in Crisis: The Republican Federation of France in the 1930s* (Baton Rouge, 1979), 27–65.

22. Baechler, *Le Parti Catholique Alsacien*, 552.

23. BR, AL121.102, "Affaires politiques: Partis, élections, esprit publique," Strasbourg, March 8, 1921, Rapport "Etat d'esprit" by the Direction de la Police Strasbourg.

24. Rothenberger, *Heimat- und Autonomiebewegung*, 19; Maugué, *Le particularisme alsacien*, 17.

25. BR, AL98.1283, folder "Haut-Rhin," Colmar, Préfet du Haut-Rhin à M. le Sous-Secrétaire d'Etat à la Présidence du Conseil, June 17, 1925.

26. Rossé et al., *Das Elsaß*, 1:30–32 (32).

27. Craig, *Scholarship and Nation-Building*, 255–56; Baechler, *Le Parti Catholique Alsacien*; François Igersheim, *L'Alsace des notables (1870–1914): La bourgeoisie et le peuple alsacien* (Strasbourg, 1981).

28. Rossé et al., *Das Elsaß*, 4:228, table 119, and 4:222, table 114; Alfred Wahl, "Patrimoine, confession et pouvoir dans les campagnes d'Alsace, 1850–1940," *Etudes Rurales* 63–64 (July–Dec. 1976): 235–45.

29. Henri Strohl, *Le protestantisme en Alsace* (Strasbourg, 1950), 458. Strohl estimates that about 50 Lutheran pastors stayed in Germany. There were 203 Lutheran pastors in 1918 (see Rossé et al., *Das Elsaß*, 4:223, table 115b).

30. Stuart R. Schram, *Protestantism and Politics in France* (Alençon, 1954), 130; Rossé et al., *Das Elsaß*, 4:223, table 115b.

31. Rudolf Heberle, *Landebevölkerung und Nationalsozialismus: Eine soziologische Untersuchung der politischen Willensbildung in Schleswig-Holstein, 1918–1932* (Stuttgart, 1963).

32. For a thorough description of Jewish national identity from 1870 to 1918, see Vicki Caron, *Between France and Germany: The Jews of Alsace-*

Lorraine, 1871–1918 (Stanford, 1988); and Paula Hyman, *The Emancipation of the Jews of Alsace: Acculturation and Tradition in the Nineteenth Century* (New Haven, 1991). For an overview of the Jewish experience in Alsace, see Freddy Raphael and Robert Weyl, eds., *Juifs en Alsace: Culture, société, histoire* (Toulouse, 1977).

33. Rossé et al., *Das Elsaß*, 4:222, table 114.

34. Craig, *Scholarship and Nation-Building*, 115, quoting memorandum from Pierre Bucher enclosed with Bucher to Wittich, April 20, 1900.

35. AN, F7.13395, Strasbourg, March 19, 1927, "Rapport sur le mouvement autonomiste" and "La propagande antifrançaise en Alsace et Lorraine: Le mouvement autonomiste depuis 1918," by Bauer. See also Rothenberger, *Heimat- und Autonomiebewegung*, 58–70.

36. AN, F7.13383, Strasbourg, Commissaire Spécial à M. le Préfet du Bas-Rhin, Oct. 20, 1926.

37. General Joffre cited in Paul Schall, *Elsaß gestern, heute und morgen?* (Filderstadt-Bernhausen, 1976), 154.

38. Colmar, Collection Fernand-J. Heitz, 2J.226.1, no date, c. 1927–1928, untitled "Mémoire" on post-1918 Alsace, p. 2.

39. National Archives, Washington, D.C., MID, RG165, 2655-C-191, Aug. 23, 1923, "Report on Econ. Situation in A&L from a lecture M. B. Berninger, Dir. of Commerce and Industry at Strasbourg." Alexandre Millerand, *Le retour de l'Alsace-Lorraine à la France* (Paris, 1923), 48, has different figures for Alsace, but the picture remains much the same: 135 factories were destroyed and 14,145 buildings were totally or partially damaged.

40. Michel Hau, *L'industrialisation de l'Alsace, 1803–1939* (Strasbourg, 1987), 283.

41. Rossé et al., *Das Elsaß*, 2:253; Joseph Weydmann, "L'évolution de la législation sociale en Alsace-Lorraine de 1870 à 1918," in *L'Alsace contemporaine: Etudes politiques, économiques, sociales*, comp. Société Savante d'Alsace et des Régions de l'Est (Strasbourg and Paris, 1950).

42. Rothenberger, *Heimat- und Autonomiebewegung*, 37.

43. Irmgard Grünewald, *Die Elsaß-Lothringer im Reich, 1918–1933: Ihre Organisationen zwischen Integration und "Kampf um die Seele der Heimat"* (Frankfurt am Main, 1984), 29.

44. Out of a total of 12,934 marriages taking place in Alsace-Lorraine in 1910, there were 1,544 in which one partner was German and the other Alsatian. Rossé et al., *Das Elsaß*, 4:55, table 15.

45. For a full description of the transition in 1871–1872, see Alfred Wahl, *L'Option et l'émigration des alsaciens-lorrains, 1871–1872* (Paris, 1974). See also Caron, *Between France and Germany*, for information on Jewish emigration in comparison with overall emigration patterns in Alsace. Lothar Kettenacker, *Nationalsozialistische Volkstumspolitik im Elsaß* (Stuttgart, 1973), is perhaps the most thorough account of the Nazi reannexation, although Marie-Joseph Bopp, *L'Alsace sous l'occupation allemande, 1940–1945* (Le Puy, 1945), is a moving account of the war years in Alsace. Rothenberger, *Heimat- und Autonomiebewegung*, 37, claims that approximately 150,000 Germans and several hundred "Old Alsatians" left Alsace for Germany at this time.

46. BR, AL121.855, "Intérieur Police: Rapports généraux, 1918–1925," Strasbourg, Aug. 10, 1921, "Rapport sur l'activité des Services de Police d'Alsace

et de Lorraine pendant le mois de juillet 1921," signed "Sebille." Camille Dahlet, *La République,* Oct. 19, 1924, cited in Rossé et al., *Das Elsaß,* 4:414, doc. 42, has a useful discussion of the "Beamtenproblem."

47. For Alsace as a colony, see Dr. Brumder, "Elsaß-Lothringen: 'Deutsche Kolonie im französischen Einheitstaat?'" *ELZ,* April 8, 1931; for the cartoon, see *Volkswille,* Aug. 28, 1929.

48. For the direct method, see Edouard Helsey, *Notre Alsace: L'enquête du "Journal" et le Procès de Colmar* (Paris, 1927), 53–54; for bilingual education, see Steve Harp, "Learning to Be German: Primary Schooling in Alsace-Lorraine, 1870–1918" (Indiana University, 1993), chap. 4; for the autonomists, see "Schulbildung und Volkselend: 'Bildung macht frei!'" *Die Neue Welt,* Dec. 13, 1921.

49. Rossé et al., *Das Elsaß,* 4:528–29.

50. Craig, *Scholarship and Nation-Building,* 100–135, 249–90.

51. On Millerand, see his *Retour de l'Alsace-Lorraine à la France.* The Alsatian economy did relatively well until 1925. See Hau, *L'industrialisation de l'Alsace,* 265.

52. Rothenberger, *Heimat- und Autonomiebewegung,* 86. For Bishop Ruch see Rossé et al., *Das Elsaß,* 4:422–23, 426–29. For Strasbourg, see Rothenberger, *Heimat- und Autonomiebewegung,* 84, and Maugué, *Le particularisme alsacien,* 53.

53. Rossé et al., *Das Elsaß,* 4:205. Alsatians expressed their opinion in a referendum held in 1924.

54. For Bilger, see Rothenberger, *Heimat- und Autonomiebewegung,* 84; for Haegy, ibid., 85, quoting *Die Heimat* (1925).

55. "Nationalstaat oder Nationalitätenstaat," *Die Zukunft,* March 6, 1926. Rothenberger, *Heimat- und Autonomiebewegung,* 92, claims that neither the refugee organization Alt-Elsaß-Lothringern im Reich nor the Auswärtiges Amt provided enough money to get *Die Zukunft* off the ground. He bases his claims that the money came from private German sources on interviews with Robert Ernst. The fact that the money did not emanate from official sources does not mean that the German government did not tacitly support *Die Zukunft.* It merely meant it wished to disassociate itself from direct sponsorship. Moreover, the alacrity with which private, non-Alsatian refugee sources coughed up funds suggests that Alsace's autonomist movement and Alsace's role as a German national symbol were highly relevant to nationalist Germans. Grünewald, *Die Elsaß-Lothringer im Reich,* 190, notes that the Alsatian refugee organizations in Germany aided the autonomist movement and helped influence the German government's willingness to support the Alsatians for short-term disruption of French domestic politics.

56. Rossé et al., *Das Elsaß,* 4:501.

57. Rothenberger, *Heimat- und Autonomiebewegung,* 135, quoting the party program.

58. For UPR see ibid., 132; for Wolf see *Das Neue Elsaß,* April 14, 1927.

59. Jean-Paul Mourer, *Heraus aus der Sackgasse! Warum elsäßische Arbeiter- und Bauernpartei?* (Strasbourg, 1935), 30.

60. Rossé et al., *Das Elsaß,* 4:449; Hiery, *Reichstagswahlen im Reichsland,* 45. French officials promulgated the décret in 1895 to ban an unwanted Italian paper published in Nice.

61. *Der Komplott-Prozeß von Colmar vom 1. bis 24. Mai 1928: Gesammelte Verhandlungsberichte* (Colmar, 1928) gives a full account of the trial itself.

62. Jean Dumser, *Bekenntniße eines waschechten els.-loth. Autonomisten: Das Hauptquartier der elsäßischen Autonomiebewegung: Berlin-Frankfurt* (Strasbourg, 1929), was written after the Colmar trial by a Lorraine autonomist. With the support of the AF, Dumser testified that he himself had participated in the transfer of funds from Germany to Alsace, and that the Erwinia publishing house was largely subsidized by the Germans.

63. BR, AL98.1283, Prefectural Reports, folder "Ae.28.XIII.3," Strasbourg, Préfet du Bas-Rhin à M. le Président du Conseil, May 30, 1928.

64. Ibid; *Der Komplott-prozeß von Besançon;* Samuel Goodfellow, "From Germany to France? Interwar Alsatian National Identity," *French History* 7, 4 (1993): 450–71.

65. See Marcel Bucard, *Les tyrans de la IIIe* (Paris, 1937), 32, 66.

2: LEGITIMIZING NAZISM

1. Philip Bankwitz, *Alsatian Autonomist Leaders, 1919–1947* (Lawrence, Kans., 1978), 108. Rossé was serving a sentence of fifteen years hard labor, twenty years local banishment, and confiscation of personal property.

2. BR, AL98.1109 (March–June 1933), citing *Freie Presse,* May 13, 1933, French language supplement.

3. AN, F7.13395, Directeur des Services Généraux de Police d'Alsace et de Lorraine à M. le Procureur Général près de la Cour d'Appel, Colmar, March 30, 1927. Haegy, Rossé, Fashauer, Keppi, Gromer, and Herber are cited.

4. Baechler, *Le Parti Catholique Alsacien,* 743–46.

5. Ibid., 244, quoting Nicolas Delsor, "Am Bau der Zukunft," *Der Elsäßische Volksbote,* April 9, 1919.

6. Martin Blinkhorn, ed., *Fascists and Conservatives: The Radical Right and the Establishment in Twentieth-Century Europe* (London, 1990), 9.

7. Irvine, *French Conservatism in Crisis;* Robert Soucy, *French Fascism: The First Wave, 1924–1933* (New Haven, 1986), 219.

8. Rossé et al., *Das Elsaß,* 4:357, citing a letter by G. Sigwalt published in *Der Elsäßer,* Nov. 6, 1919.

9. For a thumbnail sketch of Dr. Charles Didio's life see Baechler, *Le Parti Catholique Alsacien,* 723.

10. Dr. Didio, "Die Action Française im Elsaß!" *Die Heimat* 5, Sept. 9, 1925, p. 251, and Oct. 10, 1925, p. 281.

11. Haegy cited in AN, F7.13393, Mulhouse, Feb. 9, 1930, Rapport; Schmidt-Le-Roi cited in AN, F7.13399, "Alsace 1932–1933, Autonomisme Alsacien," Strasbourg, Jan. 11, 1932, Rapport.

12. BR, AL98.1137, Jan. 25, 1937, referring to *La Dépêche de Strasbourg* and *La République,* Jan. 24, 1937, "L'Alsace et les fascismes."

13. *Die Gottlosenbewegung: Ihr Wesen und ihre Tatigkeit in dem verschiedenen Ländern,* Flugschriften der Elsäßischen Volkspartei—Nr. 8 (Colmar, 1931).

14. *Nein! Herr Blum, Niemals! Die Antwort auf die Kriegserklärung an das christliche Elsaß-Lothringen* (Colmar: Editions Alsatia, 1937).

15. BR, AL98.1137, Feb. 11, 1937, citing *Freie Presse,* Feb. 8, 1937.

16. Baechler, *Le Parti Catholique Alsacien,* 659. See also my chapters on the Action Française and the Faisceau.

17. Baechler, *Le Parti Catholique Alsacien,* 347.

18. *Le National d'Alsace,* July 18, 1926, p. 2 (quotation); Nov. 21, 1925, p. 1 (Pfleger article).

19. AN, F7.13208, Strasbourg, Commissaire Spécial à M. le Préfet du Bas-Rhin, April 1, 1925 (see also Chapter 4); Baechler, *Le Parti Catholique Alsacien,* 594–96.

20. AN, F7.13233, Jeunesses Patriotes (JP), dossier "JP.1926," Saverne, Commissaire Spécial à M. le Sous-Préfet de Saverne, Oct. 20, 1925; ibid., Paris, March 13, 1925, "Meeting organisé par les Jeunesses Patriotes."

21. Gilbert Struss, *Die APNA: Wie sie kam, was sie will* (Colmar, 1931), 36–37.

22. The APNA's program was reprinted in ibid., 100–103. Rudy Koshar, ed., *Splintered Classes: Politics and the Lower Middle Classes in Interwar Europe* (New York, 1990), 5–9, recapitulates the historiography linking the lower-middle classes to fascism. See also Detlef Mühlberger, *Hitler's Followers: Studies in the Sociology of the Nazi Movement* (New York, 1991).

23. Oded Heilbronner, "The Failure That Succeeded: Nazi Party Activity in a Catholic Region in Germany, 1929–1932," *Journal of Contemporary History* 27, 3 (July 1992): 531–49.

24. John Pollard, "Conservative Catholics and Italian Fascism: The Clerico-Fascists," in Blinkhorn, *Fascists and Conservatives,* 41.

25. "Rede des H. Dr. Pfleger auf der Gründungsversammlung der Elsäßischen Volkspartei, 13. Februar 1919," in Rossé et al., *Das Elsaß,* 4:484–86.

26. See Pierre Lorson, *Pax Alsatia: Charles Ruch, évêque de Strasbourg* (Strasbourg and Paris, 1949).

27. Haut-Rhin (HR), Collection Fernand-J. Heitz, 2J.213, Fernand Heitz to Mgr. Ruch, July 23, 1927, objecting to Ruch's condemnation of the AF. Rossé et al., *Das Elsaß,* 4:426–29, is a copy of Ruch's appeal to the Alsatian clergy dated June 22, 1924.

28. See David Schoenbaum, *Zabern 1913: Consensus Politics in Imperial Germany* (Boston, 1982).

29. Dreyfus, *La vie politique en Alsace,* 97; Helsey, *Notre Alsace,* 115. For a succinct biography of Abbé Haegy see Baechler, *Le Parti Catholique Alsacien,* 591–94.

30. Baechler, *Le Parti Catholique Alsacien,* 706, 707, 708. Other publications controlled by Haegy include *Der Elsäßer, Das Gübweiler Volksblatt, Der Unterländer Kurier, L'Echo de Wissembourg,* and *Der Volksfreund,* to name just a few. BR, AL121.855, Intérieur Police, "Rapports généraux, 1918–1925," Sept. 25, 1923, signed "Sebille," reports that the clerical press already consisted of "sixteen dailies with 100,000 subscribers; seven weeklies or biweeklies with 35,000 subscribers; twenty-five political, social, and religious reviews with around 400,000 subscribers."

31. Baechler, *Le Parti Catholique Alsacien,* 610; Jean Hurstel, "Du pluralisme au monolithisme: Brève histoire de la presse alsacienne," *Objectif Alsace* 52, 7 (Oct. 19, 1987); and Jules-Albert Jaeger, "La presse en Alsace," in *Alsace depuis son retour à la France,* Comité Alsacien d'Etudes et d'Informations (Strasbourg, 1937), 3:191.

32. AN, F7.13383, Strasbourg, Commissaire Spécial à M. le Préfet du Bas-Rhin, Oct. 20, 1936.

33. Baechler, *Le Parti Catholique Alsacien,* 593; *Der Komplott-prozeß von Colmar,* 154.

34. Helsey, *Notre Alsace,* 252.

35. HR, Collection Fernand-J. Heitz, 2J.213.31, Abbé Haegy to Heitz, June 18, 1928. For Third Republic, see Dreyfus, *La vie politique en Alsace,* 97; for the anonymous pamphlet, see *Die Gottlosenbewegung,* 3.

36. For a succinct biography of Rossé, see Baechler, *Le Parti Catholique Alsacien,* 601–4; also Bankwitz, *Alsatian Autonomist Leaders,* 37–44.

37. BR, AL98.1121, July 11, 1935, citing *Freie Presse,* July 10, 1935.

38. BR, AL121.855, Intérieur Police, "Rapports généraux, 1918–1925," Strasbourg, Aug. 10, 1921, signed "Sebille," notes widespread discontent among the *fonctionnaires.*

39. Dreyfus, *La vie politique en Alsace,* 56–58.

40. *Die Amnestie für die Colmarer Komplottverurteilten und die Geschichte ihrer jahrelangen Verschleppung,* Flugschriften der Elsäßischen Volkspartei—Nr. 6 (Colmar, 1931).

41. BR, D286.350, Cabinet du Préfet Bas-Rhin, Strasbourg, Sept. 16, 1928, Rapport.

42. AN, F7.13398, Strasbourg, Commissaire de Police Becker à M. le Directeur des Services Généraux de Police d'Alsace et de Lorraine, Oct. 16, 1930; AN, F7.13399, "Alsace 1932–1933, Autonomisme Alsacien," Strasbourg, Nov. 25, 1933.

43. BR, AL98.1151, Nov. 7, 10, 12, 14, 15, 1938.

44. Bankwitz, *Alsatian Autonomist Leaders,* 83.

45. Ibid., 46–47.

46. Baechler, *Le Parti Catholique Alsacien,* 547. See also Grünewald, *Die Elsaß-Lothringer im Reich,* 159.

47. Bankwitz, *Alsatian Autonomist Leaders,* 88–89.

48. Robert Heitz, *A mort (souvenirs)* (Paris, 1946).

49. Marcel Stürmel, *Das Elsaß und die deutsche Widerstandsbewegung in der Sicht eines ehemaligen Abgeordneten der Elsäßischen Volkspartei* (Karlsruhe, 1980).

50. Baechler, *Le Parti Catholique Alsacien,* 514.

51. Ibid., 606.

52. Dr. Gromer, *Die Elsäßische Jungvolkspartei und die politische Jugendbewegung unsere Tage: Ein Orientierungsversuch,* Flugschriften der Elsäßischen Volkspartei—Nr. 17 (Colmar, 1935), 3.

53. BR, AL98.1121, July 1935, citing the article "Résolution lue par M. Rossé et votée à l'unanimité par le congrès des Jeunesses de l'UPR," *Der Elsäßer Kurier,* July 7–8, 1935.

54. BR, AL98.1123, Nov. 6, 1935, citing *Der Elsäßer Bote,* Nov. 5, 1935. The *Bote* was not criticizing the Jeunesses.

55. BR, AL98.1122, Sept. 24, 1935, citing "UPR et le corporatisme," *Der Elsäßer,* Aug. 21, 1935.

56. Gromer, *Die Elsäßische Jungvolkspartei,* 3; BR, AL98.1140, Aug. 3, 1937, citing *Les Dernières Nouvelles de Strasbourg,* Aug. 1, 1937.

57. BR, D414.213, Sous-Préfecture de Wissembourg, folder no. 1978, July 20, 1934, "Manifestations des Jeunesses UPR à Wissembourg le 8 juillet 1934—chemises grises." Baechler, *Le Parti Catholique Alsacien,* 606.

58. BR, AL98.1139, July 15, 1937, citing *Der Elsäßer Kurier,* July 14–15, 1937. This figure was probably inflated.

59. "Jungbauernschaft marschieren auf!" *Elsäßisches Bauernblatt (EBB),* Oct. 8, 1932. This figure is at best a guess.

60. Heinrich Baron, *Mit Karl Roos dem Blutzeugen des deutschen Elsaß: Die letzten Tage in der Todeszelle* (Strasbourg, 1940), 15–16; BR, AL98.1102, Jan. 26, 1931, citing *La Dépêche de Strasbourg,* Jan. 25, 1931.

3: THE FIRST GENERATIONS OF FRENCH FASCISM

1. BR, AL121.862 (AF 1919–1925), Strasbourg, Commissaire Spécial à M. le Commissaire de la République, April 14, 1919.

2. Ibid., Strasbourg, Dec. 31, 1920, Rapport (quotation); and ibid., Strasbourg, Commissaire Spécial, Gare de Strasbourg, à M. le Préfet du Bas-Rhin, Dec. 13, 1924.

3. For Chaumont-Guitry, see BR, AL121.862 (AF 1919–1925), Strasbourg, Dec. 31, 1920, Rapport, and Dec. 30, 1920, Rapport. For Valot, see ibid., Strasbourg, Commissaire Spécial, Gare de Strasbourg, à M. le Préfet du Bas-Rhin, Dec. 13, 1924.

4. François-G. Dreyfus, "L'Action Française en Alsace," *Etudes Maurassiennes* 3 (1974): 55; Maurice Pujo, *Problèmes d'Alsace et de Lorraine* (Paris, 1920).

5. Both Samuel M. Osgood, *French Royalism under the Third and Fourth Republics* (The Hague, 1960), and Eugen Weber, *Action Française: Royalism and Reaction in Twentieth-Century France* (Stanford, 1962), see 1923 as a key year for the national AF.

6. *Le National d'Alsace,* June 7, 1925.

7. For February 27, 1925, see BR, AL121.862 (AF 1919–1925), Strasbourg, Commissaire Spécial, Gare de Strasbourg, à M. le Préfet du Bas-Rhin, March 2, 1925. For the meeting in Colmar, see ibid., April 20, 1925. For June 27, 1926, see AN, F7.13200, AF. Several different police operatives give estimates varying from twenty-five hundred to three thousand. Not all of those attending came from Alsace.

8. BR, AL98.1091, *Le National d'Alsace,* Strasbourg, no date, 1927; BR, D286.349, Strasbourg, Commissaire Spécial à M. le Préfet du Bas-Rhin, Feb. 2, 1925.

9. For April 19, 1925, see AN, F7.13194, AF, "Chiffres de tirage, 1916–1926." For March 27, 1928, see AN, F7.13196, AF, Paris, April, 2, 1928.

10. For May 1925 estimates, see AN, F7.13194, AF, subfolder "Notes d'ensemble sur organisation et effectifs," May 1925, report "Action Française." For police estimates, see ibid., same folder, Paris, Nov. 24, 1924, and June 22, 1925; for quotation, BR, D286.349, Strasbourg, Commissaire Spécial à M. le Préfet du Bas-Rhin, Sept. 2, 1925; for growth figures, BR, D286.349, Strasbourg, Commissaire de Police à M. le Commissaire Central, June 27, 1926, and Commissaire Spécial à M. le Préfet du Bas-Rhin, June 28, 1926.

11. Osgood, *French Royalism,* 157.

12. Richard Hamilton, *Who Voted for Hitler?* (Princeton, 1982); Thomas Childers, *The Nazi Voter: The Social Foundations of Fascism in Germany, 1919–1933* (Chapel Hill, 1983); Henry A. Turner, *German Big Business and the Rise of Hitler* (New York: Oxford University Press, 1985); and David Abraham,

The Collapse of the Weimar Republic (Princeton: Princeton University Press, 1981); Mühlberger, *Hitler's Followers*. This list is not complete. By comparison, the historians of the French fascist movements have ignored the social composition of the radical right. Whether this is a result of an obsession with ideology or of the difficulty in gaining access to twentieth-century documents is immaterial. Robert Soucy, *French Fascism: The First Wave* and *French Fascism: The Second Wave, 1933–1939* (New Haven, 1995), is the first to begin to address this lack in a way that transcends unsubstantiated generalization.

13. BR, AL121.862 (AF 1919–1925), Strasbourg, Commissaire Spécial, Gare de Strasbourg, à M. le Préfet du Bas-Rhin, May 1, 1925. The underwriters of *La Province d'Alsace* in 1930 show a similar pattern. Out of nine listed, two were industrialists. A journalist, a lawyer, a commercial employee, a merchant, a baker, a doctor, and a retired frigate captain filled out this list. See AN, F7.13401, Strasbourg, April 4, 1930.

14. For Armbruster, see BR, D286.349, Strasbourg, Commissaire Spécial à M. le Préfet du Bas-Rhin, Jan. 27, 1925. Stephen Wilson, "A View of the Past: Action Française Historiography and Its Socio-Political Function," *Historical Journal* 19, 1 (1976): 156, presents a compelling argument that the royalist historiography of writers such as Jacques Bainville "was a paradigmatic justification for a social order based on inequality and inherited wealth." See also William R. Keylor, *Jacques Bainville and the Renaissance of Royalist History in Twentieth-Century France* (Baton Rouge, 1979), xxiii, who argues that Bainville aimed his prose at the bourgeoisie.

15. BR, D286.349, Strasbourg, Commissaire Spécial à M. le Préfet du Bas-Rhin, Feb. 2, 1925; Richard Wagner, *La vie politique à Mulhouse de 1870 à nos jours* (Mulhouse, 1976).

16. BR, D286.349, Strasbourg, Commissaire Spécial à M. le Préfet du Bas-Rhin, Sept. 2, 1925.

17. For Chaumont-Guitry, see BR, AL121.862 (AF 1919–1925), Strasbourg, Dec. 31, 1920, Rapport, and Commissaire Spécial, Gare de Strasbourg, à M. le Préfet du Bas-Rhin, Dec. 13, 1924. For women in banks, see ibid., Strasbourg, Commissaire Spécial, Gare de Strasbourg, à M. le Préfet du Bas-Rhin, Aug. 21, 1925.

18. Jack D. Ellis, *The Physician-Legislators of France: Medicine and Politics in the Early Third Republic, 1870–1914* (New York, 1990), 243, notes that doctors turned to the extreme right, including the AF, after World War I.

19. For banquets in Alsace, see Weber, *Action Française*, 266. For ideology, see Robert Proctor, *Racial Hygiene: Medicine under the Nazis* (Cambridge, Mass., 1988), 6.

20. Michael H. Kater, "Hitler's Early Doctors: Nazi Physicians in Predepression Germany," *Journal of Modern History* 59, 1 (March 1987): 52. See also Michael H. Kater, "The Burden of the Past: Problems of a Modern Historiography of Physicians and Medicine in Nazi Germany," *German Studies Review* 10, 1 (Feb. 1987): 40–41, which describes the medical profession as "the most heavily nazified professional group in Hitler's Germany."

21. Peter Loewenberg, "The Psychohistorical Origins of the Nazi Youth Cohort," *American Historical Review* 76 (Dec. 1971): 1473–76.

22. HR, 2J.213.1, Dr. Didio, "Die Action Française im Elsaß," *Die Heimat*, Sept. 9, 1925 (quotation). For choice of weapons, see AN, F7.13194, AF, Paris,

July 18, 1925. For the role of the Camelots, see AN, F7.13200, AF, Strasbourg, Commissaire Spécial à M. le Préfet du Bas-Rhin, March 28, 1926. Some "Camelots du Roi" armed with canes protected a meeting of about 250 on March 27.

23. BR, AL121.862 (AF 1919–1925), Strasbourg, Commissaire Spécial, Gare de Strasbourg, à M. le Préfet du Bas-Rhin, Dec. 13, 1924.

24. Ibid., March 10, 1925, and May 14, 1925 (quotation).

25. Ibid., Aug. 20, 21, 1925.

26. Ibid., March 10, 1925; BR, AL121.862 (AF 1919–1925), Erstein, Commissaire Spécial d'Erstein à la Police, March 23, 1925.

27. Weber, *Action Française*, 264.

28. BR, AL121.862 (AF 1919–1925), Strasbourg, Commissaire Spécial, Gare de Strasbourg, à M. le Préfet du Bas-Rhin, March 2, 1925.

29. This is quite different from Juan Linz's argument in Walter Laqueur, ed., *Fascism: A Reader's Guide* (Berkeley and Los Angeles, 1976), that fascism only succeeded where no other political movement had co-opted the political space. Linz is talking about democratic representation, the sense on the part of social groups that they remained unrepresented, whereas the issue here is the response of the sponsoring elites to radical movements without reference to the aspirations of the people.

30. For Logelheim, see BR, AL121.862 (AF 1919–1925), Colmar, Commissaire Spécial de Police de Colmar, Dec. 6, 1924. For younger clergy, see HR, 2J.213.60, Collection Fernand-J. Heitz, "La situation politique de l'Alsace au début de 1934," 15.

31. For Dessenheim, see AN, F7.13200, Colmar, Commissaire Spécial de Police à M. le Préfet du Haut-Rhin, Feb. 17, 1926. For Saverne, see BR, D286.349, Saverne, Sous-Préfet de Saverne à M. le Préfet du Bas-Rhin, July 23, 1925.

32. BR, AL121.862, AF, Strasbourg, Feb. 21, 1921, Invitation from the Ligue d'AF to hear Cauchois speak on "Le régionalisme et l'Alsace-Lorraine: Le problème harmonieusement résolu par la Monarchie" (quotation). Ibid., Saverne, July 19, 1925, Rapport, shows editors from two local papers were present at an AF meeting.

33. "Die Action Française im Elsaß," *Die Heimat*, Sept. 9, Oct. 10, 1925.

34. Philippe Machefer, *Ligues et fascismes en France (1919–1939)* (Vendôme, 1974), 8.

35. "Fascistes? Cléricaux? Réactionnaires?" *Le National d'Alsace*, Jan. 11, 1924.

36. Robert Murbach, "Sozial und National," *Le National d'Alsace*, March 13, 1926; "Im Dienst des Auslandes," ibid., Dec. 11, 1926 (quotation).

37. "Nationalisme et communisme," *Le National d'Alsace*, Jan. 1, 1925; Léon Daudet, "Salut au *National d'Alsace*," ibid., Dec. 24, 1924 (quotation).

38. Henri d'Halys, "L'opposition fantôme," ibid., Feb. 25, 1925.

39. Henri d'Halys, "Die Stimme der Vernunft," ibid., March 8, 1925; Daudet, "Salut au *National d'Alsace*."

40. Jean Pictave, "Regionalismus und Autonomie," ibid., June 21, 1925 (quotations); Weber, *Action Française*, 134.

41. *Le National d'Alsace*, March 15, 1928.

42. "Die Sprachenfrage in der Zukunft," ibid., Sept. 12, 1925.

43. Pujo, *Problèmes d'Alsace et de Lorraine*, 8.

44. *Encyclopédie de l'Alsace* (Strasbourg, 1984), 11:6550, s.v. "Ruch, Charles Joseph Eugène."

45. HR, Collection Fernand-J. Heitz, 2J.213.54, Heitz to Msgr. Ruch, Aug. 11 (quote), July 23, 1927.

46. "An die Katholiken Frankreichs! Verurteilung des Kurier, Elsässer, und Konsorten," *Le National d'Alsace,* Dec. 25, 1926.

47. Dreyfus, *La vie politique en Alsace,* 108–9; "Strasbourg: Die 'Jeunesses Populaires d'Alsace,'" *Le National d'Alsace et de Lorraine,* July 10, 1927 (quotations).

48. BR, D286.349, Strasbourg, Commissaire Spécial à M. le Préfet du Bas-Rhin, Oct. 14, 1928; BR, AL98.1098, Compte-rendu for the week March 28–April 4, 1930, p. 4.

49. Antoine Rédier, *Comrades in Courage* (New York, 1918), 16, 64.

50. AN, F7.13208, folder "Le mouvement fasciste: La Légion pour la politique et de la victoire," Strasbourg, Commissaire Spécial à M. le Préfet du Bas-Rhin, March 30, 1925.

51. AN, F7.13208, folder "Le mouvement fasciste *Le Nouveau Siècle,*" Strasbourg, Commissaire Spécial à M. le Préfet du Bas-Rhin, March 30, 1925, "Schéma de conférence sur '*La Légion*'"; Rédier, *Comrades in Courage,* chap. 4.

52. AN, F7.13208, folder "Le mouvement fasciste *Le Nouveau Siècle,*" Strasbourg, Commissaire Spécial à M. le Préfet du Bas-Rhin, March 30, 1925, "Schéma de conférence sur '*La Légion.*'"

53. AN, F7.13208, Paris, Jan. 11, 1926, "Au sujet du mouvement fasciste"; Soucy, *French Fascism: The First Wave,* 37; AN, F7.13208, no date.

54. AN, F7.13208, Strasbourg, Commissaire Spécial à M. le Préfet du Bas Rhin, April 1, March 30, 1925.

55. Soucy, *French Fascism: The First Wave,* 31; AN, F7.13208, Strasbourg, Commissaire Spécial à M. le Préfet du Bas-Rhin, March 30, 1925, Letter from J. M. Marty to Rédier.

56. Baechler, *Le Parti Catholique Alsacien,* 736; AN, F7.13208, Strasbourg, Commissaire Spécial à M. le Préfet du Bas-Rhin, April 1, 1925 (quotation).

57. For Laugel, see AN, F7.13208, Strasbourg, Commissaire Spécial à M. le Préfet du Bas-Rhin, March 30, 1925, List of the members of the Légion in Strasbourg; and Baechler, *Le Parti Catholique Alsacien,* 731.

58. AN, F7.13208, Strasbourg, Commissaire Spécial à M. le Préfet du Bas-Rhin, March 30, 1925, List of Légion members committed to paying their annual dues of twenty-five francs. This list has twenty-seven members. Biographical information is given in about half the cases.

59. AN, F7.13208, folder "Le mouvement fasciste: La Légion pour la politique et de la victoire," Strasbourg, Commissaire Spécial à M. le Préfet du Bas-Rhin, March 30, 1925, "Schéma de conférence sur '*La Légion.*'"

60. Rédier, *Comrades in Courage,* 217.

61. J. McMillan, *Housewife or Harlot: The Place of Women in French Society, 1870–1940* (New York: St. Martin's Press, 1981).

62. AN, F7.13208, no date.

63. AN, F7.13210, Mulhouse, April 5, 1926, Rapport "Le Faisceau ou les Légions"; ibid., Paris, Jan. 19, 1926, and Jan. 6, 1925.

64. Ibid., Mulhouse, April 15, 1926, Rapport "Le Faisceau."

65. AN, F7.13208, Paris, Jan. 16, 1926.

66. AN, F7.13209, folder "Le Faisceau 1926 A–N inclus," Paris, Dec. 12, 1925. Although the circulation of *Le Nouveau Siècle,* the Faisceau's daily, was two

hundred thousand in December 1925, this was probably part of a massive propaganda campaign. AN F7.13208, Paris, Dec. 10, 1925.

67. AN, F7.13208, Paris, June 11, 1926.

68. Soucy, *French Fascism: The First Wave,* 111.

69. See Zeev Sternhell, *Neither Right nor Left: Fascist Ideologies in France* (Berkeley and Los Angeles, 1986); Yves Guchet, *Georges Valois: L'Action Française, le Faisceau, la République Syndicale* (Paris, 1975); Allen Douglas, *From Fascism to Libertarian Communism: Georges Valois against the Third Republic* (Berkeley and Los Angeles, 1992). Ernst Nolte, *Three Faces of Fascism: Action Française, Italian Fascism, National Socialism* (New York, 1969), and Karl Friedrich and Zbigniew Brzezinski, *Totalitarian Dictatorship and Autocracy* (Cambridge, Mass., 1956), are part of a historical tradition that stresses the Bolshevist origins of fascist movements and downplays their conservative roots. Writers on French fascism such as René Rémond, Jean Plumyène, Raymond Lasierra, and Yves Guchet argue specifically that the Faisceau was leftist in origin. They attempt to disassociate the right from fascism in order to marginalize French fascism, and to whitewash subsequent conservative parties. This has led to a fundamental misunderstanding about French fascism, which has made it possible for extreme rightwing groups to make a rather vigorous comeback on the argument that the evil of fascism was totally external (Nazi), and/or Bolshevist. Michael Dobkowski and Isidor Wallimann, eds., *Radical Perspectives on the Rise of Fascism in Germany, 1919–1945* (New York, 1989), and Soucy, *French Fascism: The First Wave,* are part of an opposing historiography and pin the causes of fascism on the right. All these writers are concerned almost entirely with the ideological history of fascism. As a result, they do not look closely at the relationship between social support and ideology. Certainly in the case of the French fascist groups in the 1920s, the study of the social support and its ideology leads to the conclusion that the right dominated the orientation of the fascist movement.

70. AN, F7.13208, Paris, Nov. 1925, Jan. 14, 1926.

71. AN, F7.13210, Mulhouse, April 15, 1926, Report.

72. Ibid., Sélestat, Commissaire Spécial de Police de Sélestat, Nov. 20, 1926.

73. Ibid., Strasbourg, April 16, 1926, "Rapport succinct et urgent à Monsieur le Commissaire Central."

74. AN, F7.13209, folder "Le Faisceau 1926 A–N inclus," Metz, April 17, 1926, "Rapport du Commissaire Spécial Wagner sur une réunion privée tenue par le Faisceau à Metz le 16 avril 1926."

75. Weber, *Action Française;* AN, F7.13210, Versailles, Le Préfet de Seine-Oise à M. le Ministre de l'Intérieur, Feb. 8, 1926; ibid., Melun, Commissaire Spécial à M. le Contrôleur Général des Services de Police Administrative à Paris, March 13, 1926 (quotation).

76. AN, F7.13209, folder "Le Faisceau 1926 A–N inclus," Paris, Dec. 12, 1925.

77. Ibid., Dec. 23, 1925; Klaus-Juergen Müller, "French Fascism and Modernization," *Journal of Contemporary History* 11, 4 (Oct. 1976): 75–107.

78. Georges Valois, *Le fascisme,* Appendix 1, p. 116.

79. This is a point that Soucy makes forcefully, in *French Fascism: The First Wave,* 233–41.

80. Valois, *Le fascisme,* 36, 39.

81. For Schiffmacher, see AN, F7.13210, Strasbourg, Commissaire Spécial à

M. le Préfet du Bas-Rhin, Oct. 5, 1926; for Barrès, see ibid., Mulhouse, Commissaire Chef de la Sûreté à M. le Commissaire Central à Mulhouse, April 15, 1926.

82. Indeed, the Gauleiter and the ras were persistent flies in the authoritarian ointment of the respective parties. A growing historiography on Italian fascism points indirectly to the use of regionalism by fascist ideologues. See Anthony L. Cardoza, *Agrarian Elites and Italian Fascism: The Province of Bologna, 1901–1926* (Princeton, 1982); and Frank M. Snowden, *The Fascist Revolution in Tuscany, 1919–1922* (New York, 1989). Paul Jankowski, *Communism and Collaboration: Simon Sabiani and Politics in Marseille, 1919–1944* (New Haven, 1989), suggests that fascism in Marseille depended primarily on local issues, patronage, and ethnic identity.

83. AN, F7.13210, Mulhouse, April 6, 1926, Flyer distributed in Alsace. The Program of Verdun was elaborated by Valois at a mass rally in Verdun on Feb. 21, 1926.

84. Valois, *Le fascisme,* 56, 57.

85. AN, F7.13210, Strasbourg, Commissaire Spécial à M. le Préfet du Bas-Rhin, Sept. 30, 1926.

86. AN, F7.13208–12, have most of the information for this assertion.

87. AN, F7.13210, Strasbourg, Préfet du Bas-Rhin à M. le Ministre de l'Intérieur, April 16, 1926.

88. Ibid., Colmar, Commissaire Spécial de Police à M. le Préfet du Haut-Rhin à Colmar, April 3, 1926.

89. Ibid., July 17, 1926, Rapport.

90. AN, F7.13210, Mulhouse, April 5, 1926, Rapport.

91. Ibid., Strasbourg, Commissaire Spécial à M. le Préfet du Bas-Rhin, Sept. 30, 1926, and Préfet du Bas-Rhin à M. le Ministre de l'Intérieur Direction de la Sûreté Générale à Paris, April 16, 1926.

92. Ibid., Strasbourg, no date, probably late 1926.

93. AN, F7.13210, folder "Le mouvement fasciste 'Le Faisceau,'" "Copie de la circulaire du 20 septembre 1926."

94. Ibid., folder 3, "Faisceau 1926, 2e semestre, Dépt. O-Y," Strasbourg, Nov. 19, 1926, Rapport.

95. AN, F7.13212, Strasbourg, Commissaire Spécial à M. le Préfet du Bas-Rhin, Feb. 1, 25, 1927; ibid., Paris, Aug. 3, 1927 (quotation).

96. Most notably Soucy, *French Fascism: The First Wave,* and Guchet, *Georges Valois.* This has become the standard interpretation.

97. Georges Valois, *L'homme contre l'argent: Souvenirs de dix ans, 1918–1928* (Paris, 1928).

98. AN, F7.13210, Strasbourg, Commissaire Spécial à M. le Préfet du Bas-Rhin, Oct. 5, 1926.

4: BEEFSTEAK NAZIS?

1. Hans Bernd Gisevius, *To the Bitter End* (Boston, 1947), 105.

2. Bankwitz, *Alsatian Autonomous Leaders,* 29, is the first to use this term.

3. Philippe Burrin, *La dérive fasciste: Doriot, Déat, Bergery, 1933–1945* (Paris, 1986), 18.

4. *Encyclopédie de l'Alsace,* 7:4113–14, s.v. "Hueber."

5. BR, D286.353, Strasbourg, Cabinet du Préfet Bas-Rhin, March 8, 1920, Rapport.

6. Rothenberger, *Heimat- und Autonomiebewegung,* 58–59; Wehler, *Sozialdemokratie und Nationalstaat,* 52–85.

7. BR, AL102.87, Sûreté Générale, Strasbourg, May 22, 1929, Commissaire Spécial (signed Bauer) à M. le Préfet du Bas-Rhin; Rothenberger, *Heimat- und Autonomiebewegung,* 72–73.

8. AN, F7.13395, no date, Rapport "La propagande antifrançaise en Alsace et Lorraine," by Bauer; Grünewald, *Die Elsaß-Lothringer im Reich,* 163.

9. BR, D286.353, Strasbourg, Cabinet du Préfet Bas-Rhin, Dec. 14, 1920, Rapport, and Dec. 3, 1920, Rapport.

10. Bernard Reimeringer, "Un communisme régionaliste? Le communisme alsacien," in Gras and Livet, *Régions et régionalisme,* 362; BR, D286.352, Strasbourg, Cabinet du Préfet Bas-Rhin, Jan. 26, 1921, Rapport.

11. *Encyclopédie d'Alsace,* 10:5859, s.v. "Parti Communiste"; BR, AL121.855, Intérieur Police, "Rapports généraux, 1918–1925," Strasbourg, Sept. 12, 1921, signed "Sebille," Report dated Aug. 1921.

12. Reimeringer, "Un communisme régionaliste?" 365.

13. Robert Heitz, "La 'Révolution' strasbourgeoise de novembre 1918," in Société Savante d'Alsace et des Régions de l'Est, *L'Alsace contemporaine,* 373–82; Christian Baechler, *Les Alsaciens et le Grand Tournant de 1918* (Strasbourg, 1972); Jean-Claude Richez, "La révolution de novembre 1918 en Alsace dans les petites villes et les campagnes," *Revue d'Alsace* 107 (1981): 153–68.

14. For September 1920, see Dreyfus, *La vie politique en Alsace,* 74, 75. For Bas-Rhin one year later, see "Ein Jahr Kommunistische Partei," *Die Neue Welt,* Dec. 22, 1921. For Haut-Rhin one year later, see Wagner, *La vie politique à Mulhouse,* 114–16.

15. Dreyfus, *La vie politique en Alsace,* 186; "Konfessionskarte von Elsaß-Lothringen," in Rossé et al., *Das Elsaß,* 4:17.

16. Reimeringer, "Un communisme régionaliste?" 366–68.

17. "Schulbildung und Volkselend: 'Bildung macht frei!'" *Die Neue Welt,* Dec. 13, 1921.

18. BR, AL121.855, Intérieur Police, "Rapports généraux, 1918–1925," Strasbourg, Feb. 20, 1923.

19. BR, D286.348, folder "Questions d'Alsace et de Lorraine 11e volume commencé le 1 jan. 1925," Strasbourg, Préfet du Bas-Rhin à M. le Président du Conseil, Aug. 16, 1929; BR, D286.348, Cabinet du Préfet Bas-Rhin, Strasbourg, Préfet du Bas-Rhin à M. le Président du Conseil, Nov. 14, 1928; Solange Gras, "La presse française et l'autonomisme alsacien en 1926," in Gras and Livet, *Régions et régionalisme,* 355–59.

20. Pierre Zind, *Elsaß-Lothringen, Alsace-Lorraine: Une nation interdite, 1870–1940* (Paris, 1979), 334.

21. Jacques Doriot, "La lutte anti-impérialiste en Alsace-Lorraine," *L'Humanité,* May 29, 1929; Maurice Thorez, *Oeuvres de Maurice Thorez* (Paris, 1950–1965), 2:54, 5:77–78.

22. Charles Hueber, *Elsaß-Lothringen in der Kammer* (Strasbourg, 1927), 10.

23. Gras, "La presse française et l'autonomisme alsacien en 1926," 342; Hueber, *Elsaß-Lothringen in der Kammer,* 9.

24. "L'Alsace-Lorraine sous le Joug," April 4, 1933, in Thorez, *Oeuvres,* 5:62.

25. Baechler, *Le Parti Catholique Alsacien,* 371–74.

26. Doriot, "La lutte anti-impérialiste en Alsace-Lorraine."

27. For the French socialists, see Dreyfus, *La vie politique en Alsace,* 149; for the French communists' results, see Baechler, *Le Parti Catholique Alsacien,* 433; for Hueber on autonomists, see Dreyfus, *La vie politique en Alsace,* 150.

28. Doriot at the regional congress of September 22, 1929, quoted by Jean Diebold, "Auf frischer Tat ertappt," *Die Neue Welt,* Sept. 27, 1929.

29. Jacques Doriot, *La France ne sera pas un pays d'esclaves* (Paris, 1936). For a full account of Doriot's activities, see Dieter Wolf, *Die Doriot-Bewegung: Ein Beitrag zur Geschichte des französischen Faschismus* (Stuttgart, 1967); and Jean-Paul Brunet, *Jacques Doriot: Du communisme au fascisme* (Paris, 1986).

30. "Discipline communiste," *L'Humanité,* May 24, 1929. This was part of a series of articles published by Doriot in *L'Humanité d'Alsace-Lorraine.*

31. Doriot, "La lutte anti-impérialiste en Alsace-Lorraine."

32. BR, D286.358, Strasbourg, Commissaire Spécial à M. le Préfet du Bas-Rhin, July 10, 1929; AN, F7.13401, Strasbourg, Commissaire Spécial à M. le Préfet du Bas-Rhin, Sept. 17, 1930.

33. BR, AL98.1091, Strasbourg, Directeur des Services Généraux de Police d'Alsace et de Lorraine à M. le Conseiller d'Etat, Aug. 26, 1930.

34. See K. H. Tjaden, *Struktur und Funktion der "KPD-Opposition" (KPO): Eine organisationssoziologische Untersuchung zur "Rechts"-Opposition im deutschen Kommunismus zur Zeit der Weimarer Republik* (Meisenheim am Glan, 1964).

35. *Die Neue Welt,* Oct. 31, 1929.

36. BR, D286.358, Strasbourg, Commissaire Spécial à M. le Préfet du Bas-Rhin, Oct. 30, 1929, reports comments at the Congress of Dissident Communists held on October 27, 1929.

37. In order to prevent confusion between the Alsatian Volksfront and the better-known Popular Front of 1936 and to convey the importance of the mainte-nance of German culture to the autonomists, I have decided to leave the term *Volksfront* untranslated.

38. BR, D286.358, Strasbourg, Dec. 1, 1929, Rapport.

39. J. P. Mourer, "Von Opportunismus und Parteilinie," *Die Neue Welt,* July 9, 1929; "Südtirol unter Mussolini's Diktatur," *Die Neue Welt,* May 20, 1931.

40. "Wenn wir einen Landtag hätten!" *Die Neue Welt,* Feb. 3, 1934 (quota-tion); *Die Neue Welt,* July 1932; and "Die französische Großindustrie finanziert—Hitler!" *Die Neue Welt,* Feb. 17, 1931.

41. Hans Mayer, *Ein Deutscher auf Widerruf: Erinnerungen* (Frankfurt am Main, 1982), 1:175.

42. Reimeringer, "Un communisme régionaliste?" 378–80; Mourer, "Von Opportunismus und Parteilinie."

43. Doriot quoted in Dreyfus, *La vie politique en Alsace,* 152, 185.

44. Reimeringer, "Un communisme régionaliste?" 378; Dreyfus, *La vie poli-tique en Alsace,* 182.

45. BR, D286.358, Strasbourg, Commissaire Spécial à M. le Préfet du Bas-Rhin, Jan. 14, 1931, mentions 1,300 members. Hueber announced at a meeting that *Die Neue Welt* had a subscription of about 1,300 (ibid., Oct. 30, 1929). This

figure is corroborated by a police report on the overall subscriptions in Alsace, which puts the number of subscribers to *Die Neue Welt* at 1,200 (BR, AL98.1085, Presse, Organisation de la Presse, n.d.).

46. For KPO voters, see François-G. Dreyfus, "Les socialismes en Alsace de 1912 à 1962," *Bulletin de la Faculté des Lettres de Strasbourg* 44, 5 (Feb. 1966): 522. For *Die Neue Welt* circulation figures, see BR, AL102.109, Presse, Strasbourg, Commissaire Divisionnaire de Police Spéciale à M. le Préfet du Bas-Rhin, May 21, 1935, "Rapport de la presse."

47. BR, D286.358, Strasbourg, Commissaire Central à M. le Préfet du Bas-Rhin, Sept. 12, 1931; ibid., Strasbourg, July 26, 1930, Rapport; and ibid., Saverne, Feb. 1, 1930, Rapport.

48. AN, F7.13393, Strasbourg, Jan. 22, 1930, Rapport.

49. Tjaden, *Struktur und Funktion der "KPD-Opposition,"* 318, 325–26.

50. For the rally, see "Eindrucksvoller antifaszistischer Aufmarsch: Über 3,000 Arbeiter und Arbeiterinnen bekunden ihre Kampfbereitschaft gegen Faszismus und Krieg," *Die Neue Welt,* June 11, 1934. For Germany's banning the newspaper, see BR, AL98.1109 (March–June 1933), quoting *Die Neue Welt,* April 7, 1933. *Encyclopédie d'Alsace,* 10:5867, s.v. "Parti Communiste Opposition" (quotation); Jean Guy, "Hitler 'verzichtet' auf Elsaß-Lothringen," *Die Neue Welt,* Nov. 23, 1934.

51. "KPO-Elsaß und IVKO," *Die Neue Welt,* Aug. 21, 1934.

52. "Laßt doch Hitler u. de La Rocque aus dem Spiel!" *Die Neue Welt,* Feb. 13, 1937.

53. "Unser Landeskongreß: Ein Bekenntniß zur Arbeiterklasse, zu Volk und Heimat," *Die Neue Welt,* Oct. 28, 1935 (quotations); Goodfellow, "From Germany to France?"

54. *Encyclopédie de l'Alsace,* 10:5867, s.v. "Parti Communiste Opposition"; AN, F7.13399, "Alsace 1932–1933, Autonomisme Alsacien," Strasbourg, Nov. 16, 1933.

55. "Der autonomistische Parteitag und der Faszismus," *Die Neue Welt,* May 3, 1934.

56. Quiri was captured and hanged by the Nazis in 1944. See Bibliothèque Nationale et Universitaire de Strasbourg, Section des Alsatiques, M270.010, Armoire 3, undated placard. Reimeringer, "Un communisme régionaliste?" 389, citing a statement by the IVKO published in *Der Republikaner,* Aug. 17, 1934 (quotation); Mayer, *Ein Deutscher auf Widerruf,* 1:175 (quotation).

57. Thorez, *Oeuvres,* 9:31; BR, AL98.1121 (June–July 1935), citing *Freie Presse,* July 8, 1935; BR, AL98.1123 (Oct.–Nov. 1935), citing *La Dépêche de Strasbourg,* Oct. 13, 1935.

58. "Der autonomistische Parteitag und der Faszismus," *Die Neue Welt,* May 3, 1934 (italics in the original).

59. "Faschismus ist Krieg!" *Die Neue Welt,* April 8, 1937. Numerous articles in *Die Neue Welt* stress this antiwar theme, but perhaps the most glaring is "Nieder mit dem Krieg!" Sept. 28, 1938.

60. "An alle Antifaschisten und Friedensfreunde!" *Die Neue Welt,* July 5, 1935. The fact that this advertisement to participate in an antifascist rally on July 7 was buried on page 4 demonstrates the subtle change in priorities under the EABP. Hueber still hoped to woo members of the KPO so they did not unilaterally reject the issue of antifascism. See also "Waehlt elsäßische Heimatfront!" *Die Neue Welt,*

April 25, 1936, where it lists seven slogans, three of which deal with war: "Für Friede und Verständigung!"; "Für Abrüstung!"; and "Gegen die Kriegshetzer!"

61. "Der Bauerntag verboten!" *Die Neue Welt*, Dec. 12, 1936.

62. "Unser Landkongress: Ein Bekenntnis zur Arbeiter, zu Volk und Heimat," *Die Neue Welt*, Oct. 28, 1935.

63. "Antifaschistischer Imperialismus!" *Die Neue Welt*, Aug. 25, 1936 (quotation); Mourer, *Heraus aus der Sackgasse!* 39, 45.

64. "Hitlers dreistündige Reichstagsrede," *Die Neue Welt*, Feb. 22, 1938 (quotation); "Österreichs Zugehörigkeit zu Deutschland," *Die Neue Welt*, March 18, 1938.

65. Francis Sigrist, *Le problème de l'Anschluß et la presse alsacienne de la langue allemande, 1934–1938* (Université de Strasbourg, 1970); "Ja, sie verlangen die vollständige Autonomie!" *Die Neue Welt*, April 2, 1938.

66. "Sollen die Ausländer im Elsaß regieren?" *Die Neue Welt*, April 18, 1936. Hueber quoted from BR, D286.344, Cabinet du Préfet, "Kammerwahl 1936—Nachwahl."

67. "Das jüdische Problem: Die Reaktion Deutschlands auf das Pariser Attentat," *Die Neue Welt*, Nov. 23, 1938. This particular sentiment was in italics.

68. Bankowitz, *Alsatian Autonomist Leaders*, 50; *Encyclopédie d'Alsace*, 10:5867, s.v. "Parti Communiste Opposition"; Ronald M. Smelser, *The Sudeten Problem, 1933–1938: Volkstumspolitik and the Formulation of Nazi Foreign Policy* (Middletown, Conn., 1975), 126, citing Hans Steinacher, "Notizen," Aug. 1–2, 1935 (quotation).

69. BR, AL98.1087, *ELZ*, Aug. 27, 1939, Paris, "Note pour M. le Vice Président du Conseil de Georges Valot, Président du Conseil."

5: REGIONAL FASCISM

1. *Affaire Joseph Bilger* (1947): 11–16.

2. Ariane Chebel d'Appollonia, *L'extrême-droite en France: De Maurras à Le Pen* (Brussels, 1988), 302; Henry Coston, *Partis, journaux et hommes politiques d'hier et d'aujourd'hui* (Paris, 1960), 265. Bernard Reimeringer, "Un mouvement paysan extrémiste des années trente: Le Bauernbund," *Revue d'Alsace* 106 (1980): 130, also notes Bilger's participation in the Poujade movement and Henri Dorgères's postwar Rassemblement Paysan. See also Joseph Algazy, *La tentation néo-fasciste en France, 1944–1965* (Paris, 1984), 225–26.

3. "Le Front Paysan," *Le National Populaire d'Alsace*, Feb. 1936.

4. Bernard-Henri Lévy, *L'idéologie française* (Paris, 1981), 212.

5. Etienne Juillard, *La vie rurale dans la plaine de Basse-Alsace: Essai de géographie sociale* (Strasbourg, 1953), 395, 298.

6. "Bevölkerungsprobleme," *Elsaß-Lothringisches Bauernblatt (ELBB)*, Dec. 23, 1933.

7. Eugen Weber, *Peasants into Frenchmen: The Modernization of Rural France, 1870–1914* (Stanford, 1976); Juillard, *La vie rurale*, 394, 411 (quotations). Hau, *L'industrialisation de l'Alsace*, 432, argues that the poverty of the rural areas contributed to the growth of industry in the region.

8. For the Bauernbund and the Fédération Agricole, see Baechler, *Le Parti Catholique Alsacien*, 628; and Reimeringer, "Un mouvement paysan extrémiste,"

120. For the Bauernbund and the autonomist camp, see AN, F7, 13625, folder "Les congrès agricoles, 1909–1932," Colmar, Commissaire Spécial de Colmar à M. le Préfet du Haut-Rhin, Jan. 22, 1930. For the list of demands, see BR, AL98.1283, Colmar, Préfet du Haut-Rhin à M. le Sous-Secrétaire d'Etat à la Présidence du Conseil, June 7, 1926. Note the similarity of the demand for hunting rights with article 4 of the peasants' twelve articles of 1525. Peter Blickle, *The Revolution of 1525: The German Peasants' War from a New Perspective* (Baltimore: Johns Hopkins University Press, 1981), 19.

9. *EBB*, May 14, 1932.

10. Reimeringer, "Un mouvement paysan extrémiste," 113–34 (115); and the exchange in *Elan: Cahiers des ICS* 24, 5–8 (May–Sept. 1980).

11. Joseph Bilger, "In Hitlers 3. Reich: Die Einigung aller deutsche Bauern!!" *EBB*, April 15, 1933.

12. Joseph Bilger, "Die rote Front gegen die bodenständige Arbeit!" *ELBB*, April 22, 1934.

13. "Une campagne contre l'Alsace nationale?" *L'Action Française*, June 20, 1938, quoting *Le Vendu*.

14. J. Bilger, "Die volksständische Arbeitsfront," *Volk*, Feb. 16, 1936.

15. *EBB*, Sept. 17, 1932.

16. Joseph Bilger, "Von der Standesgemeinschaft zur Volksgemeinschaft," *ELBB*, April 7, 1934.

17. "Der Kampf um die Macht: Ein Aufruf der Agrarpartei—Vor den Generalratswahlen," *ELBB*, Sept. 8, 1934.

18. BR, AL98.1146, Feb. 15, 1938, citing *Der Republikaner*, Feb. 14–15, 1938.

19. *Affaire Joseph Bilger*, 7.

20. "Die volksständische Arbeitsfront," *Volk*, March 1, 1936.

21. *EBB*, Oct. 1, 1932.

22. *Volk*, March 1, 1936.

23. *Volk*, May 29, 1936 (contributor), and March 1, 1936 (Blum); Joseph Bilger, "Von der Standesgemeinschaft zur Volksgemeinschaft," *EBB*, April 7, 1934.

24. BR, AL98.1122, Sept. 19, 1935, quoting *ELZ*, Sept. 18, 1935.

25. Reimeringer, "Un mouvement paysan extrémiste," 118.

26. Smelser, *The Sudeten Problem*, 190–209, 258; and Robert Ernst, *Rechenschaftsbericht eines Elsäßers* (Berlin, 1954), 203.

27. *EBB*, May 27, 1933.

28. "Die Grüne Front in Elsaß-Lothringen," *EBB*, Sept. 3, 1932.

29. Gerald Strauss, ed., *Manifestations of Discontent in Germany on the Eve of the Reformation* (Bloomington: Indiana University Press, 1971), 144–49.

30. Renan, *Qu'est que c'est une nation?* 7–8, quoted in E. J. Hobsbawm, *Nations and Nationalism since 1780: Programme, Myth, Reality* (New York, 1990), 12.

31. "Gründung eines Jungbauernbundes 'Elsäßer Jungland,'" *ELZ*, Feb. 26, 1932.

32. BR, AL102.109, no date, c. 1936.

33. BR, AL98 (Dec. 1936), Dec. 20, 1936, citing *La République*, Dec. 20, 1936.

34. Ibid., Dec. 29, 1936, citing *La Province d'Alsace*, Dec. 24, 1936.

35. Hurstel, "Du pluralisme au monolithisme," Oct. 19, 1987; AN,

F7.13398, "Autonomisme Alsacien 1929–1931," Colmar, Commissaire Spéciale de Colmar à M. le Préfet du Haut-Rhin, Jan. 31, 1930.

36. BR, AL98.1123, Oct. 9, 1935, quoting *La République,* Oct. 8, 1935.

37. Baechler, *Le Parti Catholique Alsacien,* 631; Reimeringer, "Un mouvement paysan extrémiste," 128.

38. Dreyfus, *La vie politique en Alsace,* 240, quoting *Le National Populaire d'Alsace,* Feb. 2, 1936.

39. BR, AL98.1123, Oct. 8, 1935, quoting *ELZ,* Oct. 7, 1935.

40. *EBB,* March 5, 1932.

41. "Auftakt der Arbeit," *ELBB,* July 14, 1934.

42. "Gemeinsamer Feind, gemeinsamer Arbeit," *ELBB,* July 28, 1934.

43. *Volk,* Jan. 5, 1936.

44. BR, AL102.90, Saint-Louis, Commissaire Spécial à M. le Préfet du Haut-Rhin, Feb. 21, 1936, "Union Paysanne d'Alsace"; Geneviève Herberich-Marx and Freddy Raphael, "'Les Noirs' et 'les Rouges' au village: Mémoires de mineurs-vignerons de Haute-Alsace," *Saisons d'Alsace* 92 (June 1986): 93 (interviews).

45. AN, F7, 13625, folder "Les congrès agricoles, 1909–1932," Colmar, Commissaire Spécial de Colmar à M. le Préfet du Haut-Rhin, Jan. 22, 1930.

46. *Volk,* Jan. 5, 1936.

47. "Die Arbeitsfront im Volk," in ibid. See Stephen Zdatny, *The Politics of Survival: Artisans in Twentieth-Century France* (New York, 1990), 20. Koshar, *Splintered Classes,* 1–24, extends this point to Europe in general and includes an essay by Steven Zdatny ("The Class That Didn't Bark: French Artisans in an Age of Fascism," 121–41).

48. BR, D399.1, Sous-Préfecture de Strasbourg-Campagne, folder 4, Strasbourg, Commissaire Divisionnaire de Police Spéciale à M. le Sous-Préfet de Strasbourg-Campagne et Préfet du Bas-Rhin, Dec. 2, 1935, Rapport; BR, D391.6, Sous-Préfecture de Sélestat (ancien V-Z-2), Rhinau, May 8, 1937, Rapport.

49. Michel Augé-Laribé, *La politique agricole de la France de 1800 à 1940* (Paris, 1950), 384.

50. Baechler, *Le Parti Catholique Alsacien,* 630.

51. For 1936 elections, see BR, AL102.90, Saint Louis, Commissaire Spécial à M. le Préfet du Haut-Rhin, Feb. 21, 1936, "Union Paysanne d'Alsace." For the cities, see BR, AL102.90, Mulhouse, Commissaire Spécial, Chef de Service à M. le Commissaire Divisionnaire de Police Spéciale à Strasbourg, March 6, 1936. For the Colmar area, see BR, AL102.90, Colmar, Commissaire Spécial à M. le Commissaire Divisionnaire à Strasbourg, Feb. 27, 1936. For Guebwiller, see Baechler, *Le Parti Catholique Alsacien,* 630.

52. BR, AL102.109, Strasbourg, Commissaire Divisionnaire de Police Spéciale à M. le Préfet du Bas-Rhin, Dec. 10, 1936, "Rapport de la presse"; ibid., Strasbourg, Contrôleur Général à M. le Préfet du Bas-Rhin, March 10, Sept. 11, 1937; and Jan. 10, 1938 (Press figures for December 1937).

53. BR, AL98.1085, "Presse," no date, mid-1930s. *Les Dernières Nouvelles de Strasbourg* was by far the largest press; the closest daily, *Der Elsäßer,* had a printing run of 19,000. Partisan weeklies such as the AF's *La Province d'Alsace* (3,000), the PPF's *Stimme der PPF* (3,500), the Jungmannschaft's *Frei Volk* (3,000), and the Radical *La Dépêche de Strasbourg* (2,000) did not dwarf the BB's journalistic production.

54. Marcel Stürmel, *Landwirtschaftliche Organisation und die Elsäßische*

Volkspartei: Die "Grüne Front" in Elsaß-Lothringen, Flugschriften der Elsäßischen Volkspartei—Nr. 3 (Colmar, 1931).

55. BR, D286.344, Cabinet du Préfet, folder "Elections législatives, 1924–1936," Strasbourg, Préfet du Bas-Rhin à M. le Ministre de l'Intérieur, Jan. 25, 1936, "Renouvellement de la Chambre des Députés."

56. Baechler, *Le Parti Catholique Alsacien,* 3.

57. For Alsatian farmers and the Comice, see BR, D391.22, Sous-Préfecture de Sélestat, folder 212 "Bauernbund," Erstein, Commissaire Spécial à M. le Sous-Préfet à Sélestat, March 1, 1938. For the Bas-Rhin, see BR, D286.344, Cabinet du Préfet, folder "Elections législatives 1924–1936," Strasbourg, Préfet du Bas-Rhin à M. le Président du Conseil, Ministre de l'Intérieur, Feb. 20, 1936. Hannah Arendt, *Eichmann in Jerusalem: A Report on the Banality of Evil* (New York, 1965).

58. BR, D391.22, Sous-Préfecture de Sélestat, folder 212 "Bauernbund," Erstein, Commissaire Spécial à M. le Sous-Préfet à Sélestat, Feb. 8, March 1, 2, 1938; ibid., Marckolsheim, L'Inspecteur de Police Spéciale Gerum à M. le Commissaire Spécial à Erstein, March 1, 1938.

59. Ibid., Erstein, Commissaire Spécial à M. le Sous-Préfet à Sélestat, Feb. 8, March 1, 1938; BR, D391.6, Sous-Préfecture de Sélestat (ancien V-Z-2), folder 51, Erstein, Commissaire Spécial à M. le Sous-Préfet à Sélestat, March 19, 1938.

60. BR, AL98.1147, April 8, 1939, quoting *Les Dernières Nouvelles de Strasbourg* of the same date; BR, D391.6, Sous-Préfecture de Sélestat (ancien V-Z-2), Sélestat, Aug. 3, 1936, Handwritten note signed by the Sous-Préfet of Sélestat.

61. BR, D391.22, Sous-Préfecture de Sélestat, folder 212 "Bauernbund," Erstein, Commissaire Spécial à Ms. les Sous-Préfets d'Erstein et de Sélestat, Jan. 10, 1939; BR, AL98.1149, July 30, 1938, quoting *Der Republikaner,* July 29, 1938.

62. BR, D391.22, Sous-Préfecture de Sélestat, folder 212 "Bauernbund," Sous-Préfet à Sélestat à M. le Préfet du Bas-Rhin, Jan. 11, 7, 1939.

63. Léon Degrelle, "Das Absolute," *Volk,* Jan. 2, 1939; "Léon Degrelle berichtet über spanischen Rot-Mord," *Volk,* March 1, 1939. For a description of Degrelle's movement—Rexism—see Jean Stenger, "Belgium," in *The European Right: A Historical Profile,* ed. Hans Rogger and Eugen Weber (Berkeley and Los Angeles, 1966), 156–64; *Volk,* March 3, 1939.

64. L. Gabriel-Robinet, *Dorgères et le Front Paysan* (Paris, 1937), 57–60; AN, F7.13241 (Agrarian movements), folder "Parti Agraire et Paysan Français," Mulhouse, Commissaire Spécial à M. le Sous-Préfet de Mulhouse, Nov. 24, 1933 (quotation).

65. Henri Dorgères, *Au temps des fourches* (Paris, 1975), 197; interview with Dorgères, in Francis Bergeron and Philippe Vilgier, *Les Droites dans la rue: Nationaux et nationalistes sous la Troisième République* (Grez-en-Bouère, 1985), 151 (quotations).

66. Bilger cited from "Der Kampf um die Macht: Ein Aufruf der Agrarpartei—Vor den Generalratswahlen," *ELBB,* Sept. 8, 1934; slogan from Gabriel-Robinet, *Dorgères et le Front Paysan,* 34. For mutual distrust, see Reimeringer, "Un mouvement paysan extrémiste," 125, citing a letter from Dorgères.

67. "Le Front Paysan," *Le National Populaire d'Alsace,* Feb. 1936 (quotation). Soucy, *French Fascism: The First Wave,* 48–52, however, argues that, whereas the JP was led by upper-middle-class men, its rank and file were lower-middle-class. In Alsace the movement was so small it made no serious effort to

recruit from the lower classes, opting instead to restrict membership to influential politicians and esteemed members of society. See BR, AL102, Colmar, Commissaire Spécial à M. le Commissaire Divisionnaire à Strasbourg, Feb. 27, 1936, "Jeunesses Patriotes."

68. "Neues Leben aus den Ruinen? Junge Kräfte auf den Trümmern der Demokratie!" *Volk*, May 5, 1939.

69. *Le Franciste*, Aug. 1935. All references to this newspaper are to the German language edition.

70. Joseph Bilger, "Bauern revoltieren!" *ELBB*, June 24, 1933; "Bauer, hör her!" *Le Franciste*, Jan. 1933, supplement "Von der Arbeitsfront!" (quotation).

71. *L'Action Française*, June 7, 1938.

72. BR, AL98.1148 (May–June 1938), citing *La Dépêche de Strasbourg*, June 5, 1938, and *Der Republikaner*, June 8, 1938. "Une campagne contre l'Alsace nationale?" *L'Action Française*, June 20, 1938, cites *Le Vendu* as attacking Bilger.

73. BR, AL98.1151, Nov. 10, 1938, quoting *Der Elsäßer Kurier*, Nov. 10, 1938; BR, D391.22, Sous-Préfectoire de Sélestat, folder 212, Sous-Préfet à Sélestat à M. le Préfet du Bas-Rhin, Jan. 7, 1939 (farmers).

74. BR, AL98.1156, June 22, 24, 26, 1939; BR, AL98.1150 (Sept.–Oct. 1938), Sept. 22, 1938, citing *Der Republikaner*, Sept. 22, 1938.

75. For his paper, see BR, AL98.1138 (March–May 1937), May 5, 1937, citing *La France de l'Est*, May 5, 1937, and AL98.1157 (July–Aug. 1939), July 26, 1939, citing *ELZ*, July 26, 1939. For misuse of funds, see BR, AL98.1156 (May–July 1939), June 22, 1939, citing *Le Journal d'Alsace et de Lorraine*, June 22, 1939. For the rally, see BR, AL98.1131 (Dec. 1936), Dec. 20, 1936, citing the press of Dec. 19, 1936.

76. François Bilger, "Reimeringer, Lerch et Strauss, ou comment certains 'historiens' écrivent l'histoire de l'Alsace et des Alsaciens," *Elan: Cahiers des ICS* 24, 5–6 (May–June 1980): 10.

77. Kettenacker, *Nationalsozialistische Volkstumspolitik*, 228; Richard Lieby, "German Population and Resettlement Policy in Lorraine, 1940–1944," *Proceedings of the Annual Meeting of the Western Society for French History* 14 (1987): 293–302.

78. *Affaire Joseph Bilger*, 25; F. Bilger, "A propos d'un polémique: Quelques précisions de Monsieur Fr. Bilger," *Elan: Cahiers des ICS* 24, 7–8 (Aug.–Sept. 1980): 23.

6: THE ALSATION NAZIS

1. Grünewald, *Die Elsaß-Lothringer im Reich*, 57.

2. Kettenacker, *Nationalsozialistische Volkstumspolitik*, 75–92.

3. For money from Germany, see Grünewald, *Die Elsaß-Lothringer im Reich*, 163, 161. For Fasshauer, see Dumser, *Bekenntniße eines waschechten els.-loth. Autonomisten*.

4. Hermann Oncken, *Staatsnation und Kulturnation: Elsaß-Lothringen und die deutsche Kulturgemeinschaft* (Heidelberg, 1922), and *The Historical Rhine Policy of the French* (New York, 1923), 53.

5. BR, AL98.1103, July 18, 1931, citing *Der Stahlhelm*, July 2, 1931.

6. Adolf Hitler, *Mein Kampf* (Munich, 1938), 297; BR, AL98.1109, March 1, 1933, citing *Der Elsäßer Bote*, Feb. 28, 1933.

7. AN, F7.13398, no date, "Roos et le mouvement séparatiste," by Bauer, quoting an article in *Die Volksstimme* dated July 12, 1927 (Roos); AN, F7.13396, Mulhouse, Sept. 24, 1928, Rapport (Ricklin); "Vaterland," *Volkswille*, Oct. 24, 1928 (Landespartei).

8. Hermann Bickler, *Ein besonderes Land: Erinnerungen und Betrachtungen eines Lothringers* (Lindhorst, 1978).

9. Kettenacker, *Nationalsozialistische Volkstumspolitik*, 26.

10. Schall is cited from BR, D286.350, Cabinet du Préfet Bas-Rhin, Strasbourg, Oct. 20, 1928, Rapport; Hermann Bickler, "Was wir wollen" (1933), 6.

11. National Archives, Washington, D.C., Captured German Documents, T-501, reel 186, frames 224–26, "Teilnehmer an dem Berlin-Besuch der Mitgefangen von Dr. Karl Roos"; Anthony D. Smith, "Nationalism, Ethnic Separatism and the Intelligentsia," in *National Separatism*, ed. Colin Williams (Vancouver, 1982), 17–42.

12. BR, D286.350, Cabinet du Préfet Bas-Rhin, Lauterbourg, July 2, Dec. 9, 1929, Rapports; ibid., Strasbourg, Commissaire Spécial à M. le Préfet du Bas-Rhin, Sept. 6, 1930, and Feb. 7, 1931.

13. Bickler, *Ein besonderes Land*, 219, makes this point.

14. "Die Rede des Abg. René Hauss," *Volkswille*, Feb. 13, 1929, a German translation of the original in *Le Journal Officiel*, Feb. 8, 1929; AN, F7.13396, Autonomisme, Strasbourg, July 26, 1928, Note (quotation).

15. AN, F7.13396, Autonomisme, Strasbourg, L'Inspecteur de Police Spéciale (Klein) à M. le Directeur des Services Généraux de Police, Aug. 1, 1928.

16. Baechler, *Le Parti Catholique Alsacien*, 430, citing an article by Abbé Gromer in *Die Heimat*, March 1934. As I mentioned earlier, I prefer to leave the term *Volksfront* untranslated, to avoid confusion with the French Popular Front of 1936.

17. "Landespartei und Fortschrittspartei," *Volkswille*, Nov. 1, 1928; Rothenberger, *Heimat- und Autonomiebewegung*, 170–71; Dreyfus, *La vie politique en Alsace*, 147, 148. The exact composition of the new Strasbourg municipal council was seven representatives from the Landespartei, eleven communists (all of them autonomist), and four autonomists from the UPR, against seven socialists and seven republicans.

18. Rothenberger, *Heimat- und Autonomiebewegung*, 181; *Encyclopédie d'Alsace*, 10:5867, s.v. "Parti Communiste Opposition."

19. Erwin, "Krise der Demokratie," *ELZ*, March 10, 1933.

20. Autonomists cited from Prof. Dr. Guido Bortolotto-Rom, "Faschismus gegen Parlementarismus," *ELZ*, Oct. 31, 1932; Schall cited from AN, F7.13398, Hagenau, Dec. 21, 1931, Rapport.

21. HR, 2J.213, Collection Fernand-J. Heitz, copy of an article by Dr. Didio published in *Die Heimat*, Oct. 10, 1925, 283. Dr. Didio supported the Volksfront as a director of the UPR until March 1933, when he resigned in protest over the continuation of collaboration with pro-Nazi factions. See Baechler, *Le Parti Catholique Alsacien*, 457–58, 723.

22. Erwin, "Krise der Demokratie," *ELZ*, March 10, 1933 (quotation); Nolte, *Three Faces of Fascism*, 537–68. Here I am not employing Nolte's philosophical idea of "transcendence," but simply looking at it as a more pedestrian attempt to create a politically harmonious society that sublimated social diversity.

23. "Im IX. Jahre faschistischer Zeitrechnung," *ELZ*, Nov. 5, 1930.

24. "Geld vom Ausland," *Volkswille*, May 18, 1929; Paul Schall, "Hitler

und die Nationalsozialisten," *ELZ,* Sept. 17, 1930 (emphasis in the original).

25. BR, AL98.1087, *ELZ* (July 1933), Strasbourg, Contrôleur Général (A. Mallet) à M. le Ministre de l'Intérieur.

26. "Dr. Roos in Straßburg," *Volkswille,* Nov. 14, 1928.

27. *Der Komplott-prozeß von Besançon,* 17.

28. AN, F7.13398, "Autonomisme Alsacien 1929–1931," Strasbourg, June 25, 1929, Rapport, and June 26, 1929, Rapport.

29. Dreyfus, *La vie politique en Alsace,* 155–56; National Archives, Washington, D.C., MID, RG165, 2657-C-252.1, "G.2 report on French senatorial elections" (quotations).

30. AN, AL98.1099, "Compte-rendu de la semaine du 18 au 25 octobre," 1929, p. 2.

31. AN, F7.13398, "Autonomisme Alsacien 1929–1931," Strasbourg, Commissaire Spécial à M. le Préfet du Bas-Rhin, Dec. 6, 1930.

32. BR, D286.350, Cabinet du Préfet Bas-Rhin, Strasbourg, Commissaire Spécial à M. le Préfet du Bas-Rhin, April 5, Dec. 6, 1930. Paul Schall also expressed his astonishment at the paucity of attendance (ibid., Dec. 5, 1931).

33. Ibid., Jan. 5, Feb. 8, 1929, describe some heated monthly meetings of the Landespartei. Ibid., March 20, 1929 (quotation), and Feb. 7, 1931.

34. Robert Redslob, "Avons-nous encore une patrie?" *Le Temps,* May 21, 1929.

35. AN, F7.13396, Autonomisme, Strasbourg, Directeur des Services Généraux de Police d'Alsace et de Lorraine à M. le Ministre de l'Intérieur, Sept. 3, 1928; Baechler, *Le Parti Catholique Alsacien,* 410; "Zu den bischöflichen Schreiben," *Volkswille,* Sept. 26, 1928.

36. BR, D286.348, Cabinet du Préfet Bas-Rhin, folder "Questions d'Alsace et de Lorraine, 2e volume commencé le 1 jan. 1925," Strasbourg, Préfet du Bas-Rhin à M. le Président du Conseil, April 16, 1929, and BR, D286.348, Cabinet du Préfet Bas-Rhin, Strasbourg, Préfet du Bas-Rhin à M. le Président du Conseil, Nov. 14, 1928

37. AN, F7.13399, "Alsace 1932–1933, Autonomisme Alsacien, Notes d'ensemble—rapports," Strasbourg, Oct. 12, 1933, "Note sur la Jungmannschaft" (the term was *vieux bonzes*).

38. Ibid., Nov. 16, 1933, "Note sur le Landespartei dans son action de propagande et de réorganisation."

39. For biographical information on Bickler see Fédération des Sociétés d'Histoire et d'Archéologie d'Alsace, *Nouveau dictionnaire de biographie alsacienne* (Strasbourg, 1982–), 216–17; National Archives, Washington, D.C., T-501, reel 186, 85070, frame 305, citing the *Straßburger Neueste Nachrichten,* June 21, 1941; and Bankwitz, *Alsatian Autonomist Leaders.*

40. Bankwitz, *Alsatian Autonomist Leaders,* 90–93.

41. *ELZ,* Jan. 10, 1931.

42. BR, AL98.1103, July 27, 1931, citing *ELZ,* July 25, 1931, and AL98.1104, Nov. 23, 1931, citing *ELZ,* Nov. 20, 1931 (quotation).

43. Hermann Bickler, *Widerstand: Zehn Jahre Volkstumskampf der Elsaß-Lothringischen Jungmannschaft* (Strasbourg, 1943), 22; *La Dépêche de Strasbourg,* Jan. 25, 1931.

44. Bickler, *Widerstand,* 18, *Ein besonderes Land,* 234, and "Was wir wollen" (c. 1933), 5.

45. Bickler, *Ein besonderes Land,* 256.

46. Bickler, *Widerstand,* 16.

47. National Archives, Washington, D.C., T-501, reel 186, 85070, frame 254, Chef der Zivilverwaltung, Straßburg, to Martin Bormann, Jan. 7, 1941.

48. AN, F7.13399, "Alsace 1932–1933, Autonomisme Alsacien, Notes d'ensembles—rapports," Strasbourg, Oct. 12, 1933, "Note sur la Jungmannschaft" (quotation); BR, AL98.1122, Aug. 12, 1935, citing *La Dépêche de Strasbourg,* Aug. 11, 1935.

49. Anon., *Elsaß-Lothringische Jungmannschaft,* no date, c. May 1932.

50. "Neger in den Dörfen," *Frei Volk,* Dec. 3, 1938.

51. BR, AL98.1088, Strasbourg, Henri Weil à M. Chautemps, Vice-Président du Conseil, Sept. 19, 1938, contains a copy of *Frei Volk,* Sept. 17, 1938; *Frei Volk,* Nov. 6, 1937; "Der Antisemitismus allein tut es nicht," *Frei Volk,* Nov. 5, 1938; "Politik und Sport," *Frei Volk,* July 3, 1937.

52. AN, F7.13399, "Alsace 1932–1933, Autonomisme Alsacien, Notes d'ensemble—rapports," Strasbourg, Oct. 12, 1933, "Note sur la Jungmannschaft," and July 17, 1933, "Note sur la Jungmannschaft."

53. AN, F7.13399, Strasbourg, Commissaire Spécial à M. le Préfet du Bas-Rhin, Jan. 11, 1932.

54. Rothenberger, *Heimat- und Autonomiebewegung,* 219–20, citing an undated note from the Préfet du Bas-Rhin files.

55. Hermann Bickler, "Zur gegenwärtigen Lage in Elsaß-Lothringen," *Straßburger Monatshefte* 2, 7 (July 1938): 345–50.

56. BR, AL98.1085, Presse, "Organisation de la presse état des principaux journaux, hebdomadaires et périodiques mensuels paraissant en ALSACE et en LORRAINE, avec leur nuance politique et leur tirage," no date, c. 1937.

57. Fritz Spieser, "Brief an einen Menschenrechtler," *Straßburger Monatshefte* 3, 4 (April 1939): 182–91.

58. Bankwitz, *Alsatian Autonomist Leaders,* 58.

59. AN, F7.13399, Strasbourg, Commissaire Spécial à M. le Préfet du Bas-Rhin, Jan. 11, 1932 (quotation).

60. BR, D286.345, Cabinet du Préfet, Strasbourg, March 7, 1936, "Note no. 37 sur la Jungmannschaft," by Becker.

61. AN, F7.13399, "Alsace 1932–1933, Autonomisme Alsacien, Notes d'ensemble—rapports," Strasbourg, July 17, 1933, "Note sur le Bund der Elsäßischen Wanderfreunde."

62. *ELZ,* Sept. 16–17, 1933 (quotation). For background on Dahlet, see *Die Neue Biographie,* in Fédération des Sociétés d'Histoire et d'Archéologie d'Alsace, *Nouveau dictionnaire de biographie alsacienne,* pp. 568–70; AN, F7.13398, Saverne, Commissaire Spécial à M. le Sous-Préfet de Saverne, April 15, 1930.

63. AN, F7.13399, "Alsace 1932–1933, Autonomisme Alsacien, Notes d'ensemble—rapports," Strasbourg, Oct. 12, 1933, "Note sur la Jungmannschaft."

64. BR, AL98.1116 (Dec. 1934), citing *Le Journal d'Alsace et de Lorraine,* Dec. 6, 1934.

65. Baechler, *Le Parti Catholique Alsacien,* 458–60. The government attempted to allow interior French families in Alsace the right to refuse religious instruction in the schools. Ibid., 461–62, citing *Die Heimat,* June 1934, 168.

66. BR, AL102.109, Presse (Sûreté), Colmar, Feb. 28, 1936, "Etat des journaux lus dans le secteur du commissariat Spécial de Colmar" (quotation); Dreyfus,

La vie politique en Alsace, 250; BR, AL98.1131, Dec. 1, 1936, citing *ELZ,* Nov. 30, 1936.

67. BR, AL98.1155, April 4, 1939, citing *Les Dernières Nouvelles de Strasbourg,* April 3, 1939.

68. Ernst, *Rechenschaftsbericht eines Elsäßers;* Kettenacker, *Nationalsozialistische Volkstumspolitik,* 76–92; and Bankwitz, *Alsatian Autonomist Leaders.*

69. National Archives, Washington, D.C., T-580, roll 86.

70. BR, AL98.1138, March 17, 1937, citing *La République,* March 17, 1937; BR, AL98.1146, Jan. 24, 1938, citing *La Dépêche de Strasbourg,* Jan. 23, 1938 (quotation).

71. BR, AL98.1148, May 3, 1938, citing *Les Dernières Nouvelles de Strasbourg,* May 1, 1938 (quotation); Oscar de Férenzy, "Après les juifs, les Catholiques?" *La Voix d'Alsace et de Lorraine,* June 17, 1933 ; Férenzy, "Judaisme et Hitlérisme," *La Voix d'Alsace et de Lorraine,* Oct. 26, 1935.

72. BR, AL98.1155, March 2, 1939, citing *Frei Volk,* Feb. 25, 1939; *Frei Volk,* Feb. 18, 1939. Alphonse Irjud, "La germanisation des noms en Alsace entre 1940 et 1944," *Revue d'Alsace* 113 (1987): 239–61.

73. BR, AL102.109, Presse (Sûreté), Strasbourg, Contrôleur Général à M. le Préfet du Bas Rhin, Jan. 10, 1938, Publication figures for the month of December 1937. Compare this figure with the PSF's *Le Flambeau de l'Est,* which had a circulation of 16,000.

74. BR, AL102.109, Presse (Sûreté), Strasbourg, March 7, 1936, "Rapport de la presse" (*ELZ* figures); ibid., Strasbourg, Contrôleur Général à M. le Préfet du Bas-Rhin, Sept. 11, 1937 (*Frei Volk* figures), and Nov. 10, 1937 (*Straßburger Monatshefte* figures); Dreyfus, *La vie politique en Alsace,* 250, 318 (Alsatian Nazis).

75. BR, AL98.1156, May 16, 1939, citing *La Dépêche de Strasbourg,* May 14, 1939; Paul Schall, *Karl Roos und der Kampf des heimattreuen Elsaß* (Colmar, 1941), 56; Baron, *Mit Karl Roos.*

76. For Roos, see National Archives, Washington, D.C., T-501, reel 186, 85070, frames 318–33. For Speiser, see Kettenacker, *Nationalsozialistische Volkstumspolitik,* 110, citing Friedrich Hünenburg (Dr. Spieser), *Tausende Brücken: Eine biographische Erzählung aus dem Schicksal eines Landes,* ed. Agnes Gräfin Dohna (1952), 952.

77. National Archives, Washington, D.C., Captured German Documents, T-501, reel 186, frame 336, *Straßburger Neueste Nachrichten,* Aug. 3, 1941.

78. Ibid., reel 186, frame 224, "Teilnehmer an dem Berlin-Besuch der Mitgefangen von Dr. Karl Roos."

79. Ernst, *Rechenschaftsbericht eines Elsäßers,* 258.

7: THE NEW FRENCH FASCISTS

1. The circulation of the AF's Alsatian paper, *La Province d'Alsace,* remained fairly consistent and is perhaps the best guide to the extent of the AF's activism. BR, AL102.109, Presse (Sûreté), Strasbourg, April 11, 1933, "Rapport de la presse" (3,000 copies); ibid., Oct. 22, 1934, "Rapport de la presse" (2,500 copies); ibid., Jan. 14, 1936, "Rapport de la presse" (2,000–2,300 copies); BR, AL98.1085, Presse, Organisation de la Presse, "Liste des principaux correspondants et rédac-

teurs à Paris de la presse alsacienne et lorraine," no date, late 1930s (3,000 copies).

2. BR, AL98.1108 (Jan.–Feb. 1933), Jan. 20, 1933, citing *Der Elsäßer,* Jan. 19, 1933 (quotation); BR, AL98.1156 (May, June, July 1939), June 6, 1939, citing *La Province d'Alsace,* June 3, 1939, advertising an open-air rally.

3. AN, F7.13233 (JP), Saverne, Commissaire Spécial à M. le Sous-Préfet de Saverne, Oct. 20, 1925; AN, F7.13235 (JP), Colmar, Feb. 20, 1936, Rapport "Objets: Manifestations communistes et socialistes lors d'une conférence organisée par les Jeunesses Patriotes de Colmar le 19 feb. 1932"; BR, AL102.90, Sûreté Générale, Elections, Colmar, Commissaire Spécial à M. le Commissaire Divisionnaire à Strasbourg, Feb. 27, 1936.

4. "Frankreich den Franzosen!" *Der Steuerzahler,* Dec. 21, 1933 (quotation); BR, AL102.109, Presse (Sûreté), Strasbourg, Commissaire Divisionnaire de Police Spéciale à M. le Préfet du Bas-Rhin, Oct. 22, 1934, "Rapport de la presse"; *Le Combat,* Jan. 1935, Nov. 1935.

5. Pierre Milza, *Fascisme français: Passé et présent* (Paris, 1987), 123, 125.

6. Marcel Eschbach, "Es lebe die nationale Revolution," *Der Steuerzahler,* Nov. 16, 1933 (quotations). The same themes are frequently repeated, see "Der nationale Staat," *Le Combat,* Jan. 25, 1934.

7. "Wir klagen an . . . !" *Le Combat,* Feb. 17–24, 1934 (quotation). See the same issue for the Steuerzahler-Milize.

8. Marcel Eschbach, "Frankreich den Franzosen!" *Der Steuerzahler,* Dec. 21, 1933. This was a motto on most issues of *Le Combat.* Marcel Eschbach, "Die Verjudung Frankreichs," *Le Combat,* Aug. 1934.

9. "Judenknechtschaft!!" *Le Combat,* Oct. 1934.

10. "Jüdischer Faszismus genannt 'Francisme,'" *Le Combat,* Aug. 1934; "Francisme, der Francisme von Bucard ist doch jüdisch," *Le Combat,* April 1935.

11. See Alain Déniel, *Bucard et le francisme* (Paris, 1979), 45; Marcel Bucard, "Anti-Sémites? Non! Anti Métèques? Oui!" *Le Franciste,* June 1935; "Manifest der franztistischen Partei," *Le Franciste,* March 1936; and *Les tyrans de la IIIe,* 68.

12. *Le Combat,* Aug. 1934.

13. "Edouard Drumont: Der französische antisemitische Kämpfer," *Le Combat,* April 1935; Michel Winock, *Edouard Drumont et Cie: Antisémitisme et fascisme en France* (Paris, 1982), 36.

14. BR, AL98.1087, Valot Akten-Presse, *Le Combat* (1934–Oct. 1936), Strasbourg, Commissaire Divisionnaire à M. le Directeur Général de la Sûreté Nationale, Sept. 4, 1934; ibid., Strasbourg, Commissaire Divisionnaire à M. le Préfet du Bas-Rhin, Oct. 18, 1934 (quotation); ibid., Strasbourg, Commissaire Divisionnaire de Police Spéciale à M. le Préfet du Bas-Rhin, July 31, 1935, no. 4812.

15. Ibid., Strasbourg, Confidentiel, Commissaire Spécial à M. le Préfet du Bas-Rhin, Nov. 18, 1935, no. 6978.

16. BR, AL102.109, Presse (Sûreté), Strasbourg, Jan. 10, 1934, "Rapport de la presse"; BR, AL98.1087, Valot Akten-Presse, *Le Combat* (1934–Oct. 1936), Strasbourg, Commissaire Divisionnaire à M. le Préfet du Bas-Rhin, Oct. 25, 1934.

17. BR, AL102.109, Presse (Sûreté), Strasbourg, Commissaire Divisionnaire de Police Spéciale à M. le Préfet du Bas-Rhin, Oct. 22, 1934, "Rapport de la presse"; ibid., Jan. 1936, "Rapport de la presse."

18. BR, AL98.1087, Valot Akten-Presse, *Le Combat* (1934–Oct. 1936), Strasbourg, Commissaire Divisionnaire à M. le Directeur-Général de la Sûreté Nationale, Sept. 4, 1934.

19. Ibid., Strasbourg, Commissaire Divisionnaire Général de la Sûreté Nationale, Sept. 4, 1934; ibid., Colmar, Préfet du Haut-Rhin à M. le Sous-Secrétaire d'Etat à la Présidence du Conseil, Nov. 20, 1935.

20. Ibid., Strasbourg, Préfet du Bas-Rhin à M. le Sous-Secrétaire d'Etat à la Présidence du Conseil, Nov. 27, 1935 (quotation), Président du Conseil à M. le Ministre de l'Intérieur, July 29, 1936, Préfet du Bas-Rhin à M. le Ministre de l'Intérieur, Sept. 5, 1935, and Commissaire Divisionnaire à M. le Préfet du Bas-Rhin, July 4, 1936, no. 5736.

21. Ibid., Strasbourg, Commissaire Divisionnaire à M. le Préfet du Bas-Rhin, Oct. 18, 1934. The group's leaders claimed one hundred members; Jewish observers thought there were eighty-four activists; the police thought the number was even lower, around thirty (ibid., Strasbourg, Préfet du Bas-Rhin à M. le Ministre de l'Intérieur, Sept. 5, 1934). For Eschbach's mother, see ibid., Strasbourg, Commissaire Divisionnaire de Police Spéciale à M. le Préfet du Bas-Rhin, July 22, 1936, no. 6101.

22. Ibid., Strasbourg, Commissaire Divisionnaire à M. le Préfet du Bas-Rhin, Aug. 30, Oct. 25, 1934; and Commissaire Spécial à M. le Préfet du Bas-Rhin, Confidentiel, Nov. 18, 1935, no. 6978; "Hitlerpropaganda u. antisemitisches Gekeif im Elsaß," Le Combat, May 1935.

23. The Solidarité Française sometimes called itself the Solidarité Française pour la Réforme de l'Etat, which may be the source of the Alsatian name. See "Wir wollen die republikanische Staatsreform!" Die Staatsreform, Sept. 30, 1933.

24. "Unser Programm einer republikanischen Staatsreform," Die Staatsreform, Oct. 21, 1933.

25. "Manifeste," Die Staatsreform, Oct. 21, 1933.

26. "Jeunes générations, venez à nous!" Die Staatsreform, Nov. 4, 1933.

27. AN, F7.13238, Solidarité Française, folder "Mouvement 'La Solidarité Française': Notes et presse sur activité 2eme semestre 1933—1ere semestre 1934," Paris, July 27, 1933.

28. Ibid., Paris, Oct. 24, 1933 (quotation), and July 27, 1933.

29. BR, AL102.109, Presse (Sûreté), Strasbourg, Commissaire Divisionnaire de Police Spéciale à M. le Préfet du Bas-Rhin, June 9, 1934, "Rapport de la presse"; Reimeringer, "Un mouvement paysan extrémiste," 125; AN, F7.13235 (JP), Erstein, Commissaire Spécial adjoint à M. le Sous-Préfet de l'Arrondissement Erstein, Jan. 31, 1928. Le National Populaire d'Alsace, March 1936, lists a G. Pflimlin as the president of the Phalange Universitaire d'Alsace. I suspect that this is a typographical error and that this is actually Pierre Pflimlin.

30. AN, F7.13239, Solidarité Française, folder "Mouvement 'La Solidarité Française': Notes et presse s/ activité année 1934 (2e semestre)," Strasbourg, Commissaire Divisionnaire à M. le Préfet du Bas-Rhin, Sept. 13, 1934. AN, F7.13234 (JP), Strasbourg, May 23, 1927, Rapport, describes Schmidt-Le-Roi as a "délégué des Jeunesses Patriotes pour la région de Strasbourg."

31. BR, AL98.1111 (Oct.–Dec. 1933), Nov. 4, 1933, citing Freie Presse, Nov. 2, 1933.

32. Michael Loughlin, "The Political Transformation of Gustave Hervé, Part 1, 1871–1906" (Indiana University, 1986). Keep in mind that Marcel Bucard had been a contributor to La Victoire during the 1920s.

33. BR, AL102.109, Presse (Sûreté), Strasbourg, Commissaire Divisionnaire de Police Spéciale à M. le Préfet du Bas-Rhin, Jan. 22, 1935, "Rapport de la

presse" (quotation), and Sept. 25, 1935, "Rapport de la presse."

34. AN, F7.13238, Solidarité Française, folder "Mouvement 'La Solidarité Française': Notes et presse sur l'activité 2e semestre 1933–1ere semestre 1934," Mulhouse, Commissaire Spécial à M. le Contrôleur Générale chargé des affaires d'Alsace et de Lorraine à Strasbourg, March 22, 1934; Hurstel, "Du pluralisme au monolithisme," Oct. 19, 1987.

35. Milza, *Fascisme français*, 146.

36. "Die Neue Front: Gründungsversammlung in Mülhausen," *Die Staatsreform,* Nov. 4, 1933.

37. "Ein ernstes Wort," *Die Staatsreform,* Sept. 30, 1933; *Die Staatsreform,* Oct. 21, 1933, p. 3.

38. "Ein ernstes Wort," *Die Staatsreform,* Sept. 30, 1933.

39. The last issue of *Die Staatsreform* to be filed at the Bibliothèque Universitaire, Section des Alsatiques, was that of June 1934. BR, AL102.109, Presse (Sûreté), Strasbourg, Commissaire Divisionnaire de Police Spéciale à M. le Préfet du Bas-Rhin, Oct. 22, 1934, "Rapport de la presse"; AN, F7.13239, Solidarité Française, folder "Mouvement 'La Solidarité Française': Notes et Presse s/ activité année 1934 (2e semestre)," no date, Ministère de l'Intérieur, chart on the departmental strength of the Solidarité Française (probably late 1934).

40. AN, F7.13239, Solidarité Française, folder "Mouvement 'La Solidarité Française': Notes et presse s/ activité année 1934 (2e semestre)," Strasbourg, Commissaire Divisionnaire à M. le Préfet du Bas-Rhin, Sept. 13, 1934.

41. *Le Franciste,* June 1935; Déniel, *Bucard et le francisme,* 60–61; "Der Francisme im Elsass," *Le Franciste,* June 1935 (quotation).

42. Déniel, *Bucard et le francisme,* 62–63.

43. Ibid., 15, 67, 276.

44. Marcel Bucard, "Francismus und Autonomismus," *Le Franciste,* Sept. 1935; see also Michael Ledeen, *Universal Fascism: The Theory and Practice of the Fascist International, 1928–1936* (New York, 1972), 113.

45. For Doriot, see "Wird Doriot Frankreich von der Sowjetgefahr retten?" *Le Franciste,* June 1936. For the socialists, see BR, AL98.1121 (June–July 1935), July 30, 1935, citing *Freie Presse,* July 30, 1935. For Bucard and the autonomist party, see *Le Franciste,* Sept. 1935.

46. BR, AL98.1122 (Aug.–Sept. 1935), Aug. 1, 1935, citing *Der Republikaner,* July 31, 1935, and Aug. 12, 1935, citing a long letter by Bucard that was published in a number of local papers; Marcel Bucard, "Francismus und Autonomismus," *Le Franciste,* Sept. 1935.

47. Emile Gillmann, "P.R.F Schafft's!" *Le Fanal,* March–April 1937; BR, AL98.1147 (March–April 1938), April 9, 1938, citing *Freie Presse,* April 8, 1938 (quotation).

48. D'Appollonia, *L'extrême-droite en France,* 203; Philippe Bernard and Henri Dubief, *The Decline of the Third Republic, 1914–1938* (New York, 1985), 211; and Déniel, *Bucard et le francisme,* 33, 60–61.

49. National Archives, Captured German War Documents, T-580, roll 86, frame 418, Collection of letters to and from Dr. Herbert Scholz; BR, AL98.1283, Fonds Valot, Prefectural Reports, folder "Rapports du Préfet du Bas-Rhin, année 1938, He 27," Metz, Sept. 5, 1934.

50. Déniel, *Bucard et le francisme,* 102; *Le Franciste,* July 1, 1937; BR, AL102.90, Wissembourg, Commissaire Spécial à M. le Commissaire Divisionnaire

de Police Spéciale à Strasbourg, March 14, 1936. For de La Rocque, see "Die Croix de Feu: Versammlung im Straßburger Sängerhaus," *Le Franciste,* March 1936. *Le Franciste,* Dec. 1935, calls the Croix de Feu a "shadow puppet."

51. BR, AL102.90, Sûreté Générale, Elections, Strasbourg, Commissaire Divisionnaire de Police Spéciale à M. le Préfet du Bas-Rhin Cabinet, May 1935; BR, AL102.109, Presse (Sûreté), Strasbourg, Jan. 14, 1936, "Rapport de la presse."

52. *Le Franciste,* Jan. 1936, Dec. 1936, Jan. 1937, Feb. 1937; "Arbeitssuchende Franzisten," *Le Franciste,* Sept. 1, 1937.

53. Cf. Childers, *The Nazi Voter,* 265–66.

54. "Der Francisme im Elsaß," *Le Franciste,* June 1935. For donors' comments, see *Le Franciste,* July 1, Sept. 1, Nov. 1, 1937.

55. Déniel, *Bucard et le francisme,* 25, 59; "Der Francisme im Elsaß," *Le Franciste,* June 1935 (quotation).

56. Bucard, *Les tyrans de la IIIe,* 61–62 (quotation); Marcel Bucard, "Manifest der franzistischen Partei," *Le Franciste,* March 1936 (quotation); "Korporative Syndikate Französische Arbeiter!" *Le Franciste,* Jan. 1937.

57. "Was ist franzistischer Korporatismus?" and J. Goepfer, "Struktur der korporativen Organisation," *Le Franciste,* Oct. 1, 1937.

58. Bucard, *Les tyrans de la IIIe,* 66; "Der Francisme u. die Elsass-Lothringische Frage," *Le Franciste,* Nov. 1935 (quotation).

59. "Wir wollen," *Le Franciste,* April 1936, lists these issues as "special for Alsace-Lorraine" (quotation); "Autonomie, Nein! Regionalismus, Ja!" *Le Franciste,* Aug. 1935.

60. BR, AL102.90, Sûreté Générale, Elections, Strasbourg, Commissaire Divisionnaire à M. le Préfet du Bas-Rhin, April 5, 1935.

61. Ibid.

62. Ibid (quotation); BR, D286.345, Cabinet du Préfet, Strasbourg, Commissaire de Police du 5e Arrondissement à M. le Commissaire Central, April 20, 1936.

63. BR, D414.215, Elections (various), Wissembourg, Commissaire Spécial à M. le Sous-Préfet de Wissembourg, Feb. 12, 1936; BR, D286.344, Cabinet du Préfet, folder "Candidats par circonscription 1935–1936," Wissembourg, Sous-Préfet de l'Arrondissement de Wissembourg à M. le Préfet du Bas-Rhin, Feb. 14, 1936, and Strasbourg, Commissaire Divisionnaire de Police Spéciale à M. le Préfet du Bas-Rhin, March 3, 1936.

64. BR, AL102.109, Presse (Sûreté), Strasbourg, Oct. 22, 1934 (?), Commissaire Divisionnaire de Police Spéciale à M. le Préfet du Bas-Rhin, "Rapport de la presse."

65. Luchont, "Ouvriers, paysans, soldats!" *Le Fanal,* Feb.–March 1937 (first two quotations); Luchont, "Vive la 4e République," *Le Fanal,* April–May 1937 (third quotation); "Programm des P.R.F." and "Eine monatliche Altersrente für die Bedürftigen," *Le Fanal,* Feb.–March 1937; "Unsere Schule," and "Die Steuerreform," *Le Fanal,* March–April 1937.

66. E. Schmitt, "Blutsauger [bloodsuckers] und Arbeitslosigkeit," *Le Fanal,* March–April 1937; "Programm des P.R.F." *Le Fanal,* Feb.–March 1937 (fourth quotation).

67. Doriot and the PPF have received more attention from historians than any other French fascists. See Brunet, *Jacques Doriot;* Wolf, *Die Doriot-Bewegung;* and Jankowski, *Communism and Collaboration.*

68. BR, AL98.1130 (Nov. 1936), Nov. 17, 1936, citing *Der Elsäßer,* Nov.

14, 1936; BR, AL98.1137 (Jan.–Feb. 1937), Jan. 26, 1936, citing *La Province d'Alsace*, Jan. 23, 1937.

69. *L'Action Française*, June 7, 1938; BR, AL98.1138 (March–May 1937), March 23, 1937, citing *ELZ*, March 22, 1937 (quotation).

70. Brunet, *Jacques Doriot*, 235; BR, AL98.1093, *La Voix du Parti Populaire Français*, Strasbourg, Contrôleur Général à M. le Préfet du Bas-Rhin, March 18, 1937; BR, AL102.109, Presse (Sûreté), Strasbourg, Contrôleur Général à M. le Préfet du Bas-Rhin, Nov. 10, 1937.

71. BR, AL98.1093, *La Voix du Parti Populaire Français*, Strasbourg, Contrôleur Général à M. le Préfet du Bas-Rhin, March 18, 1937 ("indiscipline"); Jaques Doriot, *La France avec nous!* (Paris, 1937), 119.

72. BR, AL98.1093, *La Voix du Parti Populaire Français*, Strasbourg, Contrôleur Général à M. le Préfet du Bas-Rhin, March 18, 1937.

73. BR, D286.345, Strasbourg, Commissaire de Police du 5e Arrondissement à M. le Commissaire Central, April 20, 1936; BR, AL102.90, Sûreté Générale, Elections, Strasbourg, Commissaire de Police du 5e Arrondissement à M. le Commissaire Central, April 20, 1936; BR, D286.345, Strasbourg, April 25, 1936, Rapport (quotation); BR, AL98.1131 (Nov.–Dec. 1936), Dec. 20, 22, 1936.

74. BR, D391.6, folder 53, Erstein, Commissaire Spécial à M. le Contrôleur Général des Services Police d'Alsace et de Lorraine à Strasbourg, March 10, 1937; ibid., Sélestat, April 26, 1937, "Rapport de l'adjudant Romand, commandant la brigade, sur une réunion politique ayant lieu à Sélestat"; Baechler, *Le Parti Catholique Alsacien*, 548, 631.

75. H. Stuart Hughes, *The Obstructed Path: French Social Thought in the Years of Desperation, 1930–1960* (New York: Harper Torchbooks, 1968), 126.

76. BR, AL98.1150 (Sept.–Oct. 1938), Oct. 25, 1938, citing *La République*, Oct. 25, 1938 (one observer); BR, AL98.1155 (March–April 1939), April 27, 1939, citing *Freie Presse*, April 27, 1939; BR, AL98.1156 (May, June, July 1939), May 2, 1939, citing *La République*, May 1, 1939. That the government opposed Legrand can be seen in D399.1, Sous-Préfecture de Strasbourg-Campagne, folder 4, Strasbourg, Préfet du Bas-Rhin à M. le Sous-Préfet de Strasbourg-Campagne, April 26, 1938.

77. BR, AL98.1151 (Nov.–Dec. 1938), Dec. 19, 1938, citing *La République*, Dec. 18–19, 1938; BR, D391.6, Sous-Préfecture de Sélestat (ancien V-Z-2), folder 51, Villé, May 30, 1939; AL98.1156 (May, June, July 1939), June 27, 1939, citing *La République*, June 27, 1939; BR, AL98.1154 (Jan.–Feb. 1939), Feb. 20, 1939, citing *La Dépêche de Strasbourg*, Feb. 19, 1939 (Pellepoix).

78. BR, AL98.1156 (May, June, July 1939), June 28, 1939, citing *Le Défi*, June 25, 1939.

79. Ibid., May 15, 1939, citing *ELZ*, May 15, 1939; ibid., May 11, 1939, citing *ELZ*, May 11, 1939.

80. Ibid., May 15, 1939, citing *La République*, May 14, 1939, and *ELZ*, May 15, 1939; ibid., May 17, 31, June 6, 1939. There is some question as to whether the assassination orders were actually issued. The source of information subsequently denied that the Faisceau had ordered Legrand's death (ibid., June 9, 1939, citing *Die Neue Zeitung*, June 9, 1939).

81. Milza, *Fascisme français*, 159.

82. BR, D286.345, Cabinet du Préfet, Strasbourg, Commissaire de Police du 5e Arrondissement à M. le Commissaire Central, April 20, 1936, citing the Naso leader, Luchont.

8: MASS FASCISM

1. BR, D286.345, Strasbourg, Commissaire de Police du 5e Arrondissement à M. le Commissaire Central, April 20, 1936.

2. As will become obvious, I use the term *Croix de Feu/PSF* because the movement itself changed in 1936 from an extraparliamentary movement (the Croix de Feu) to a party (the PSF). The two movements were the same, the PSF merely extending the activity of the veterans' organization, thus allowing the league to survive the Popular Front's ban on paramilitary groups.

3. René Rémond, *The Right Wing in France: From 1815 to de Gaulle* (Philadelphia, 1969), 287, 293. This view is shared by Burrin, *La dérive fasciste*, 25, cited in William Irvine, "Fascism in France and the Strange Case of the Croix de Feu," *Journal of Modern History* 63 (June 1991): 271–95 (272).

4. Jean Plumyène and Raymond Lasierra, *Les fascismes français, 1923–1963* (Paris, 1963); d'Appollonia, *L'extrême-droite en France*, 171–77; Zeev Sternhell, "Strands of French Fascism," in Stein Ugelvik Larsen et al., *Who Were the Fascists? Social Roots of European Fascism* (Bergen, 1980), 496; Irvine, "Fascism in France," 294; Robert Soucy, "French Fascism and the Croix de Feu: A Dissenting Interpretation," *Journal of Contemporary History* 26 (Jan. 1991): 159–88; Soucy, *French Fascism: The Second Wave.*

5. Milza, *Fascisme français*, 133. This position is also reflected in Rémond, *Right Wing in France*, 281; Eugen Weber, "France," in Rogger and Weber, *The European Right*, 107; Machefer, *Ligues et fascismes en France*, 32.

6. John Rothney, *Bonapartism after Sedan* (Ithaca, 1969), 295, 296; Stuart Campbell, *The Second Empire Revisited: A Study in French Historiography* (New Brunswick, 1978), 26.

7. Thomas Childers, "The Social Language of Politics in Germany: The Sociology of Political Discourse in the Weimar Republic," *American Historical Review* 95, 2 (April 1990): 331–58.

8. Plumyène and Lasierra, *Les fascismes français*, 8. See also G. Warner, "France," in S. J. Woolf, ed., *Fascism in Europe* (New York, 1981), 308.

9. Snowden, *Fascist Revolution in Tuscany*, 208; Childers, *The Nazi Voter*; Irvine, "Fascism in France," 279; and Hamilton, *Who Voted for Hitler?*

10. Friedrich and Brzezinski, *Totalitarian Dictatorship and Autocracy*; Sternhell, *Neither Left nor Right*; Zeev Sternhell, *La droite révolutionnaire, 1885–1914: Les origines françaises du fascisme* (Paris, 1978); Zeev Sternhell, "Sur le fascisme et sa variante française," *Le Débat* 32 (Nov. 1984): 28–51; Zeev Sternhell, "The Anti-Materialist Revision of Marxism as an Aspect of the Rise of Fascist Ideology," *Journal of Contemporary History* 22, 3 (July 1987): 379–400.

11. Mühlberger, *Hitler's Followers*; Koshar, *Splintered Classes*; Childers, *The Nazi Voter*, 265–66.

12. Soucy, *French Fascism: The First Wave*, xiv–xv; Robert Wohl, "French Fascism, Both Right and Left: Reflections on the Sternhell Controversy," *Journal of Modern History* 63 (March 1991): 91–98.

13. Soucy, "French Fascism and the Croix de Feu," 169.

14. De La Rocque cited from "In Saarburg und Hagenau," *Le Flambeau de l'Est*, Sept. 18, 1937; Rémond, *Right Wing in France*, 291.

15. For Munz, see *Le Flambeau de l'Est*, Oct. 31, 1936; Claude Mislin, *Les Croix de Feu et le Parti Social Français en Alsace, 1930–1939* (Strasbourg, 1981–1982), 25.

16. See James M. Diehl, *Paramilitary Politics in Weimar Germany* (Bloomington, 1977); Rédier, *Comrades in Courage;* Drieu La Rochelle, *Gilles* (Paris, 1939), and *The Comedy of Charleroi and Other Stories* (Cambridge, Mass., 1973).

17. "Richtlinien vom Lt.-Colonel de La Rocque," *Le Flambeau de l'Est,* Sept. 12, 1936.

18. *Le Flambeau de l'Est,* Sept. 12, 1936.

19. "Korporatismus u. Faszismus," *Le Franciste,* Jan. 1937.

20. *Le Flambeau de l'Est,* Sept. 12, 1936; de La Rocque cited from "Der Nationalkongress des PPF in Magic City in Paris am 18. 19. und 20. Dec. 1936," *Le Flambeau de l'Est,* Dec. 24, 1936.

21. Rémond, *Right Wing in France,* 287.

22. Irvine, "Fascism in France," 281–82.

23. Soucy, "French Fascism and the Croix de Feu," 159; AN, F7.13241, folder "Croix de Feu," Paris, July 3, 1935. At least one estimate claimed that the Croix de Feu had three hundred thousand members in July 1935 (National Archives, Washington, D.C., MID, RG165, 2657-C-296.1).

24. "Der PSF und die Katholiken," *Le Flambeau de l'Est,* April 23, 1938.

25. Mislin, *Les Croix de Feu,* 42, 4–5 (first year). For 1937, Philippe Machefer, "L'Union des Droites, le PSF et le Front de la Liberté, 1936–1937," *Revue d'Histoire Moderne et Contemporaine* 17 (Jan.–March 1970): 113; Soucy, "French Fascism and the Croix de Feu," 160; Irvine, "Fascism in France," 280.

26. *Le Flambeau de l'Est,* July 10, 1937; Philippe Rudaux, *Les Croix de Feu et le PSF* (Paris, 1967), 253; *Le Flambeau de l'Est,* July 27, 1938.

27. BR, D286.344, Cabinet du Préfet, "Elections législatives, 1924–1936," Strasbourg, Préfet du Bas-Rhin à M. le Ministre de l'Interieur, Jan. 25, 1936; Mislin, *Les Croix de Feu,* 3.

28. *Le Flambeau de l'Est,* Sept. 12, 1936; BR, AL102.90, Sûreté Générale, Elections, Commissaire de Police à M. le Commissaire Divisionnaire de Police Spéciale, April 25, 1936.

29. *Le Flambeau de l'Est,* Oct. 3, 1936 (quotation); BR, AL98.1126, Compte-rendu, citing *Les Dernières Nouvelles de Strasbourg,* March 2, 1936 (quotation); BR, AL98.1126, Compte-rendu, March–April 1936.

30. BR, AL102.90, Sûreté Générale, Elections, Mulhouse, Commissaire Spécial, Chef de Service à M. le Commissaire Divisionnaire de Police Spéciale à Strasbourg, March 6, 1936; ibid., Colmar, Commissaire Spécial à M. le Commissaire Divisionnaire à Strasbourg, Feb. 27, 1936 (quotation).

31. Ibid., Wissembourg, Commissaire Spécial à M. le Commissaire Divisionnaire de Police Spéciale à Strasbourg, March 1936. Machefer, *Ligues et fascismes en France,* 93, reproduces a map of the Croix de Feu sections in June 1936 taken from Weng Ting-Lung, "L'historique et la doctrine du Parti Social Français" (Thèse de droit, Nice, 1970).

32. BR, D286.344, Cabinet du Préfet, folder "Elections législatives," Croix de Feu flyer "Elections législatives 1936"; BR, D286.344, folder "Elections législatives," Strasbourg, Commissaire Divisionnaire à M. le Préfet du Bas-Rhin, April 25, 1936 (list of candidates); BR, D414.215, Elections, Wissembourg, folder "Elections législatives 1936," brochure entitled "Elections législatives de 1936: Manifeste de Croix de Feu," 15 pages.

33. BR, D286.345, Cabinet du Préfet, Strasbourg, Commissaire divisionnaire à M. le Préfet du Bas-Rhin, April 26, 1936; BR, AL98.1126, Compte-rendu, citing *Les Dernières Nouvelles de Strasbourg,* March 2, 1936 (quotation).

34. Philippe Bourdrel, *La Cagoule: Trente ans de complots* (Paris, 1970); BR, D391.6, Sous-Préfecture de Sélestat, folder 53, Erstein, Commissaire Spécial à M. le Commissaire Divisionnaire de Police Spéciale à Strasbourg, Feb. 1, 1937.

35. BR, AL102.109, Presse (Sûreté), Strasbourg, Commissaire Divisionnaire de Police Spéciale à M. le Préfet du Bas-Rhin, Dec. 10, 1936, "Rapport de la presse" (5,000); BR, AL98.1085, Presse, Organisation de la Presse, date unknown, c. 1938, "Liste des principaux correspondants et rédacteurs, à Paris, de la presse alsacienne et lorraine"; BR, AL102.109, Presse (Sûreté), Strasbourg, Contrôleur Général à M. le Préfet du Bas-Rhin, Jan. 11, 1938, citing publication figures for December 1937 (16,000); BR, AL102.109, Presse (Sûreté), Strasbourg, Contrôleur Général à M. le Préfet du Bas-Rhin, Sept. 11, 1937 (20,000)—this was shortly before the cantonal elections.

36. BR, AL98.1085, Presse, Organisation de la Presse, date unknown, c. 1938, "Liste des principaux correspondants et rédacteurs à Paris de la presse alsacienne et lorraine." The *Travailleur Syndicaliste* printed twenty-four thousand copies per week. Soucy, "French Fascism and the Croix de Feu," 160 (natural trends).

37. Mislin, *Les Croix de Feu*, 22 (Lapoutroie and Saales); BR, D403.55, Strasbourg-Campagne, "Résultats: Canton de Schiltigheim, dépêches télégraphiques, élections cantonales 1937"; Mislin, *Les Croix de Feu*, 25.

38. BR, D391.6, Sous-Préfecture de Sélestat, folder 53, Erstein, Commissaire Spécial à M. le Commissaire Divisionnaire à Strasbourg, Nov. 13 1936; BR, AL98.1146 (Jan.–Feb. 1938), Feb. 9, 1938, citing *ELZ*, Feb. 8, 1938, and *La République*, Feb. 11, 1938; *Le Flambeau de l'Est*, June 10, 1939; Mislin, *Les Croix de Feu*, 9.

39. "Die neue Ordnung im Staate," *Le Flambeau de l'Est*, June 5, 1937 (Sonderausgabe), quotation. PSF figures from *Le Flambeau de l'Est*, July 10, 1937, p. 4. White-collar employees consisted of office employees and low-level bureaucrats. Professionals included those with technical or professional training; doctors, lawyers, teachers, and engineers constituted the bulk of this group. Philippe Machefer, "Le Parti Social Français et la petite entreprise," *Bulletin—Centre d'Histoire de la France Contemporaine* 8 (1987): 37.

40. Pierre Milza, *Fascisme français*, 138.

41. BR, AL102.90, Colmar, Commissaire Spécial à M. le Commissaire Divisionnaire à Strasbourg, Feb. 27, 1936 (quotation); BR, D286, Cabinet du Préfet, "Elections législatives, 1924–1936," Préfet du Bas-Rhin à M. le Ministre de l'Intérieur (for government employees); Herberich-Marx and Raphael, "'Les Noirs' et 'les Rouges' au village," 93 (farmers).

42. Mislin, *Les Croix de Feu*, 9; Baechler, *Le Parti Catholique Alsacien*, 743–46; BR, AL102.90, Wissembourg, Commissaire Spécial à M. le Commissaire Divisionnaire de Police Spéciale à Strasbourg, March 14, 1936; Déniel, *Bucard et le francisme*, 102.

43. J. H. Mondelange, "Die soziale Seite des Problems der Gemeinwirtschaft," *Le Flambeau de l'Est*, April 17, 1937.

44. "Landwirtschaftliches Programm des PSF," *Le Flambeau de l'Est*, May 8, 1937 (Sonderausgabe); quotation; "Der PSF und die Bauernbewegung," *Le Flambeau de l'Est*, March 14, 1938 (quotation); "Landwirtschaftliches Programm des PSF," *Le Flambeau de l'Est*, May 8, 1937 (Sonderausgabe); BR, D391.6, Sous-Préfecture de Sélestat, folder 53, Erstein, Commissaire Spécial à M. le Commissaire

Divisionnaire de Police Spéciale à Strasbourg, Oct. 27, Nov. 17, 1936.

45. BR, AL102.90, Sûreté Générale, Elections, Mulhouse, Commissaire Spécial, Chef de Service à M. le Commissaire Divisionnaire de Police Spéciale à Strasbourg, March 6, 1936; ibid., Colmar, Commissaire Spécial à M. le Commissaire Divisionnaire à Strasbourg, Feb. 27, 1936 (quotation).

46. Mislin, *Les Croix de Feu,* 17; BR, AL102.109, Presse (Sûreté), Strasbourg, Contrôleur Général à M. le Préfet du Bas-Rhin, Sept. 11, 1937; BR, D391.6, Sous-Préfecture de Sélestat, folder 53, Erstein, Commissaire Spécial à M. le Commissaire Divisionnaire de Police Spéciale à Strasbourg, Nov. 20, 1936.

47. BR, AL102.90, Sûreté Générale, Elections, Saint-Louis, Commissaire Spécial de Saint-Louis, March 17, 1936, Rapport "Mouvement Croix de Feu"; BR, D391.6, Sous-Préfecture de Sélestat, folder 53, June 24, 1936, Procès-verbal.

48. BR, AL102.90, Sûreté Générale, Elections, Wissembourg, Commissaire Spécial à M. le Préfet du Bas-Rhin, Cabinet à Strasbourg, Oct. 4, 1937; ibid., Drusenheim, L'Inspecteur de Police Spéciale à M. le Commissaire Spécial Adjoint Hagenau, Oct. 10, 1939; ibid., Sarreguemines, Commissaire Spécial de Sarreguemines à M. le Commissaire Divisionnaire de Police Spéciale, Chef de la Circonscription Règle, à Strasbourg, March 3, 1936; Milza, *Fascisme français,* 138.

49. BR, AL98.1121 (June–July 1935), July 4, 1935, citing *Der Elsäßer Kurier,* July 3, 1935. Mislin, *Les Croix de Feu,* 29–30, cites an article in *Der Elsäßer Kurier,* July 3, 1935, that emphasizes the differences between the UPR and the PSF and stresses the organizational strength of the former. In the rest of France the Radical Party was the greatest barrier to fascist success. The Radical Party, however, was largely nonexistent in Alsace and therefore played no role in the development of local fascism. Zdatny, *The Politics of Survival;* Zdatny, "The Class That Didn't Bark," 138; and Serge Berstein, "Une greffe politique manquée: Le radicalisme alsacien de 1919 à 1939," *Revue d'Histoire Moderne et Contemporaine* 17 (Jan.–March 1970): 78–103.

50. BR, D391.6, Sous-Préfecture de Sélestat (ancien V-Z-2), folder 53, Erstein, Commissaire Spécial à M. le Contrôleur Général des Services de Police d'Alsace et de Lorraine, Feb. 17, 1937; "Die UPR und wir! Eine Stellungnahme," *Le Flambeau de l'Est,* Nov. 21, 1936 (quotation).

51. Goodfellow, "From Germany to France?"

52. BR, AL98.1137 (Jan.–Feb. 1937), Jan. 4, 1937, citing *La Province d'Alsace,* Jan. 2, 1937; BR, D286.347, Cabinet du Préfet Bas-Rhin, Strasbourg, Commissaire Divisionnaire à M. le Préfet du Bas-Rhin, Oct. 9, 1937.

53. BR, AL102.90, Sûreté Générale, Elections, Thionville, Commissaire Spécial à M. le Commissaire Divisionnaire, March 5, 1936. Although this example is from Lorraine, the same pattern held true in Alsace. "Die Croix de Feu: Versammlung im Strassburger Sängerhaus," *Le Franciste,* March 1936 (quotation).

54. Machefer, "L'Union des Droites, le PSF et le Front de la Liberté," 125.

55. BR, AL102.90, Sûreté Générale, Elections, Colmar, Commissaire Spécial à M. le Commissaire Divisionnaire à Strasbourg, Feb. 27, 1936. Such was also the case in Lorraine. See ibid., Thionville, Commissaire Spécial à M. le Commissaire Divisionnaire, March 5, 1936.

56. Irvine, "Fascism in France," 291–92.

57. Colonel de La Rocque, "Anhaltspunkte," *Le Flambeau de l'Est,* Sept. 19, 1936; de La Rocque, "Warnung," *Le Flambeau de l'Est,* April 16, 1923.

58. *Le Flambeau de l'Est,* April 2, 9, 1938; Mislin, *Les Croix de Feu,* 33.

59. BR, AL98.1148 (May–June 1938), citing *La République,* May 5, 1938.
60. BR, AL98.1150 (Sept.–Oct. 1938), Sept. 27, 1938, citing *La Dépêche de Strasbourg,* Sept. 25, 1938 (quotation); BR, D286.344, folder "Elections législatives, 1924–1936," Strasbourg, Préfet du Bas-Rhin à M. le Ministre de l'Intérieur, Jan. 25, 1936.
61. "Das neue Deutschland und wir," *Le Flambeau de l'Est,* April 9, 1938; BR, AL98.1129, Oct. 6, 1936, citing *Freie Presse,* Oct. 5, 1936.
62. BR, D391.6, Sous-Préfecture de Sélestat, folder 53, Erstein, Commissaire Spécial à M. le Commissaire Divisionnaire à Strasbourg, Nov. 23, 1936.
63. BR, D399.1, Sous-Préfecture de Strasbourg-Campagne, Strasbourg, Sept. 5, 1938, Rapport; "Der PSF und die Judenfrage," *Le Flambeau de l'Est,* Oct. 29, 1938.
64. "Vierzehn Tage im Dritten Reich," *Le Flambeau de l'Est,* Sept. 10, 1936; Bernard Lafeuille, "Die religiöse Krise im Deutschland," *Le Flambeau de l'Est,* May 21, 1938; "Lügen der Wolfsangel," *Le Flambeau de l'Est,* Nov. 7, 1936.
65. National Archives, OSS, RG226, OB 115804, "Tätigkeits- und Leistungsbericht des Personalamtes beim Chef der Zivilverwaltung für das Elsaß für die Zeit vom 1.7.1940 bis 1.6.1941."
66. Marc Lucius, "L'Alsace après la crise de septembre," *Nouveaux Cahiers* 2, 35 (Dec. 1, 1938): 8–11; Bernard Lafeuille, "Die internationale Krisis und das Elsass," *Le Flambeau de l'Est,* Nov. 19, 1938.
67. For an example see "Wir sind loyale Republikäner," *Le Flambeau de l'Est,* Sept. 25, 1937; or Stanislas Devans, *Le petit journal,* Jan. 7, 1938, cited in Machefer, *Ligues et fascismes en France,* 56.

9: THE WAR AND BEYOND

1. National Archives, Washington, D.C., OSS, RG226, OB 127949, Alsace 1939–1940, Notes on evacuation and return of inhabitants and household and industrial goods. Bopp, *L'Alsace sous l'occupation allemande,* 191 (quotation).
2. Lucius, "L'Alsace après la crise de septembre," 8–11.
3. Heinz Boberach, ed., *Meldungen aus dem Reich, 1938–1945: Die geheimen Lageberichte des Sicherheitsdienstes der SS* (Herrsching, 1984), 4:1313.
4. Irjud, "La germanisation des noms en Alsace entre 1940 et 1944"; Kettenacker, *Nationalsozialistische Volkstumspolitik,* 165. Although Alsatians with French names were required to germanize their names, *Reichsdeutsch* of Huguenot parentage did not have to change theirs.
5. Kettenacker, *Nationalsozialistische Volkstumspolitik,* 172.
6. Bankwitz, *Alsatian Autonomist Leaders,* 67, 70; Baron, *Mit Karl Roos.*
7. Johnpeter Horst Grill, *The Nazi Movement in Baden, 1920–1945* (Chapel Hill, 1983). For an extended discussion of Robert Wagner, see ibid., and also Kettenacker, *Nationalsozialistische Volkstumspolitik,* 59–75. Schall, *Elsaß gestern, heute und morgen?* 58.
8. National Archives, Captured War Documents, T-175, roll 260, "Meldungen aus dem Reich," frame 133, Oct. 17, 1940; frame 137, Oct. 31, 1940; frame 143, Nov. 21, 1940 (all of these reports cite the Alsatians as "irregular and uncertain").
9. J. S. Conway, *The Nazi Persecution of the Churches, 1933–1945* (Lon-

don, 1968), 256. For deportation, see Robert Aron, *The Vichy Regime, 1940–1944* (Boston, 1958), 227; Bankwitz, *Alsatian Autonomist Leaders,* 77; Bopp, *L'Alsace sous l'occupation,* 36; M. Mullet, *Etude-statistique de la déportation dans le Bas-Rhin, 1940–1945* (Strasbourg, 1971); Richard A. Leiby, "German Population and Resettlement Policy in Lorraine, 1940–1944," *Proceedings of the Annual Meeting of the Western Society for French History* 14 (1987): 293–302.

10. National Archives, T-175, roll 260, "Meldungen aus dem Reich," frame 160, Feb. 6, 1941; Bopp, *L'Alsace sous l'occupation allemande,* 70; National Archives, OSS, RG226, OB 57262, Jan. 23, 1944, "Economic Conditions in Germany" (quotation).

11. Bibliothèque Nationale et Universitaire de Strasbourg, Section des Alsatiques, M270.010, Armoire 3, "Klare Front: Wortlaut der Rede des Gauleiters und Chef der Zivilverwaltung im Elsaß, Robert Wagner, zum zweiten Jahrestag der Rückkehr des Elsaß, gehalten in Colmar am 21. Juni 1942." Hermann Bickler made the same argument at a Strasbourg speech, in *Die Ehre des Elsaß.*

12. Bibliothèque Nationale et Universitaire de Strasbourg, Section des Alsatiques, M270.010, Armoire 3, no date, "Jedermann weiß."

13. National Archives, T-81, roll 705, OB 000212, *Verordnungsblatt, Gau Baden-Elsaß,* Jan. 2, 1942; Bopp, *L'Alsace sous l'occupation,* 36.

14. Boberach, *Meldungen aus dem Reich,* no. 213 (Aug. 21, 1981), 8:2676–77; Marie-Joseph Bopp, "L'enrôlement de force des Alsaciens dans la Wehrmacht et la SS," *Revue d'Histoire de la Deuxième Guerre Mondiale* 5, 20 (Oct. 1955): 40.

15. Bankwitz, *Alsatian Autonomist Leaders,* 76; National Archives, OSS, RG226, OB 30027, March 10, 1943, Source "Z"; Marie-Joseph Bopp, "L'opinion publique en Alsace occupée: Un témoignage nazi en 1943," *Revue d'Alsace* 96 (1957): 155–59.

16. National Archives, OSS, RG226, OB 34530, "Resettlement of Alsatians," Memo to American Legation, Bern, from Julius C. Jensen, American Vice Consul, Basel, Switzerland, Nov. 27, 1942; ibid., OB 2785, France, "The Situation in Alsace," March 5, 1943.

17. Georges Mouret, *Oradour: Le crime—le procès* (Paris, 1958); Robin Mackness, *Oradour: Massacre and Aftermath* (London, 1988). Fourteen of the sixty-five defendants tried for war crimes in 1953 were Alsatian. Only one of the Alsatians had volunteered for the SS. When the courts convicted all fourteen, Alsace protested vigorously that the convicted draftees were victims of circumstance and could have been any of the thousands of conscripts from Alsace. The case of Oradour demonstrated the fundamental difference of the wartime experience in France and Alsace. The former were victims forced to submit to external authority, whereas the latter had to become German and Nazi and participate against their will in the war effort.

18. Pierre Zind, *Brève histoire de l'Alsace* (Paris, 1977), 171; Robert Aron, *France Reborn: The History of the Liberation* (New York, 1964), 240.

19. HR, Collection Fernand-J. Heitz, 2J.213.62, Poligny, Heitz to Galzant, Nov. 10, 1942.

20. Heitz, *A mort (souvenirs);* National Archives, OSS, RG226, OB 115804, "Tätigkeits- und Leistungsbericht des Personalamtes beim Chef der Zivilverwaltung für das Elsaß für die Zeit vom 1.7.1940 bis 1.6.1941" (quotation).

21. National Archives, OSS, RG226, OB 37557, Lisbon source, June 22,

1943; National Archives, Captured War Documents, T-175, roll 260, "Meldungen aus Dem Reich," frame 1178, April 10, 1941.

22. Bopp, *L'Alsace sous l'occupation,* 32, 108. Bilger's wife wrote in the SS magazine *Der Stürmer,* "My husband was an admirer of Hitler well before the war; the Green Shirts live the Nazi ideal." Reimeringer, "Un mouvement paysan extrémiste," 117.

23. National Archives, OSS, RG226, OB 126739, Pamphlet received May 7, 1945, article entitled "L'Alsace-Lorraine sous la botte allemande de 1940 à 1944." Dr. Ernst made this statement on January 30, 1941.

24. Fédération des Sociétés d'Histoire et d'Archéologie d'Alsace, *Nouveau dictionnaire de biographie alsacienne,* 224; Bankwitz, *Alsatian Autonomist Leaders,* 83–84.

25. Bankwitz, *Alsatian Autonomist Leaders,* 107–8, explains that there were more guilty verdicts in Alsace, but fewer death sentences. Schall, *Elsaß gestern, heute und morgen?* 123, cites statistics from the Cour de Justice du Bas-Rhin. The number of summary executions was under fifty. Compared to the approximately ten thousand executions (both summary and legal) nationwide, the *épuration* in Alsace was fairly slight. See Jean-Pierre Roux, *The Fourth Republic, 1944–1958* (Cambridge, England: Cambridge University Press, 1987), 29–43.

26. Bankwitz, *Alsatian Autonomist Leaders,* 101–14.

27. Pierre Pflimlin, *Mémoires d'un européen de la Quatrième à la Cinquième République* (Paris, 1991), 15, claims that his "entry into political life" took place at the end of the war, and even when he draws a thumbnail sketch of Alsatian history (p. 264) he skips directly from World War I to World War II. It is as if, for Pflimlin, the interwar period did not exist, either for him personally or for Alsace in general.

28. Perhaps the most recent proponent of the importance of populism to fascism is Roger Griffin, *The Nature of Fascism* (London, 1991).

29. This view is coming under attack from a variety of directions. Its earliest expression was Seymour Martin Lipset, *Political Man: The Social Bases of Politics* (New York, 1963).

30. See Denis Mack Smith, *Mussolini* (New York, 1982).

31. Juan J. Linz, "Some Notes toward a Comparative Study of Fascism: Sociological Historical Perspective," in Laqueur, *Fascism: A Reader's Guide,* 4.

32. Nicos Poulantzas, *Fascism and Dictatorship: The Third International on the Problem of Fascism* (London, 1974).

33. Ledeen, *Universal Fascism,* stands alone in treating this subject. I discount the studies of World War II movements that confuse collaboration with fascism.

34. Ibid.

35. "Wie grüssen die Croix de Feu?" *Le Franciste,* April 15, 1937.

36. Linz, "Some Notes toward a Comparative Study of Fascism," 9.

37. Bucard, *Les tyrans de la IIIe,* 56.

38. Benito Mussolini, *Fascism: Doctrine and Institutions* (New York, 1968), 10.

39. Sternhell, *Neither Right nor Left.*

BIBLIOGRAPHY

ARCHIVES

Archives Nationales (AN)

Police Reports: F7.13014, 13028, 13040, 13194, 13196, 13200, 13205–6, 13208–10, 13212, 13229, 13231–39, 13241, 13245, 13383, 13393–99, 13402, 13625, 13983.

Archives Départementales—Bas-Rhin (BR)

1. Presse: AL98.1083–157, 1279–90.
2. Sûreté: AL102.74, 85–90, 104, 107, 109–10.
3. Intérieur Police: AL121.102, 855, 862, 868.
4. Cabinet du Préfet: D286.344–53, 358.
5. Sous-Préfectures: D307.10; D391.6, 22; D395.1; D399.1; D403.55; D414.213, 215–16.

Archives Départementales—Haut-Rhin (HR)

Collection Fernand-J. Heitz: 2J.213.1, 5, 9, 50, 54, 60, 61, 62; 2J.226.1.

National Archives, Washington, D.C.

1. OSS
   RG226: OB 2785, 22378, 22721, 25475, 27125, 30027, 34528, 34530, 35958, 37557, 40407, 57262, 60536, 61094, 63923, 70082, 74266, 76076, 76413, 90976, 100417, 105189, 113180, 114922, 115804, 116932, 126739, 126780, 127949, 130033–61.
2. Captured German War Documents
   T-81, rolls 69, 99, 120, 124, 705, 719; T-82, roll 21; T-84, roll 257; T-175, rolls 13, 15, 18, 26, 50, 65, 232, 250, 277, 409; T-501, roll 186; T-580, rolls 71, 73, 86.
3. MID
   RG165: 77, 2058-408, 2655-C-191, 2657-C-236.1, 244.1, 252.1, 259.4, 287.1, 290.1, 296.1.

JOURNALS AND NEWSPAPERS

L'Action Française
Alsace Française
Le Combat (Der Kampf)
Le Combat National
La Dépêche de Strasbourg
Les Dernières Nouvelles de Strasbourg (Straßburger Neueste Nachrichtung)
Elan: Cahiers des ICS
'S Elsaß
Der Elsäßer
Der Elsäßer Bote
Der Elsäßer Kurier
Elsäßisches Bauernblatt (EBB)
Der Elsäßische Volksbote
Elsaß-Lothringen Heimatstimmen
Elsaß-Lothringer Zeitung (ELZ)
Elsaß-Lothringisches Bauernblatt (ELBB)
L'Express de Mulhouse
Le Fanal
Le Flambeau de l'Est
La France de l'Est
Le Franciste (German language edition)
Le Franc-Parler d'Alsace
Freie Presse
Frei Volk
Die Heimat
L'Humanité d'Alsace-Lorraine
Jetzt Langt's
La Jeunesse d'Alsace
Le Journal d'Alsace et de Lorraine
Journal de l'Est
Jungmannschaft: Beilage zur ELZ
Mülhauser Tagblatt
Mülhauser Volksblatt
Der Narrenschiff
Le National d'Alsace
Le National Populaire d'Alsace
Das Neue Elsaß
Die Neue Welt
Le Nouveau Journal de Strasbourg
Le Nouveau Siècle
La Nouvelle Voix d'Alsace et de Lorraine
La Province d'Alsace
La Régionaliste
Der Republikaner
La République
La Révolution Fasciste
Die Staatsreform

Der Steuerzahler
Straßburger Monatshefte
Straßburger Neueste Nachrichtung/Regierungsanzieger für das Elsaß (SNN)
Le Syndicaliste National
Le Temps
Unseri Heimat
Völkischer Beobachter
La Voix d'Alsace et de Lorraine
La Voix du Parti Populaire Français
Volk
Die Volksbewegung
Die Volksstimme
Volkswille
Die Wahrheit
Weckruf/L'Alarme
Die Zukunft

BOOKS AND ARTICLES

Abel, Hans Karl, ed. *Kriegsbriefe eines elsäßischen Bauernburschen*. Strasbourg: Hünenburg Verlag, 1941.

Adereth, M. *The French Communist Party: A Critical History (1920–1984), from Comintern to "the Colours of France."* Dover, N.H.: Manchester University Press, 1984.

Affaire Joseph Bilger. 1947.

Algazy, Joseph. *La tentation néo-fasciste en France, 1944–1965*. Paris: Fayard, 1984.

Allardyce, Gilbert. "What Fascism Is Not: Thoughts on the Deflation of a Concept." *American Historical Review* 84, 2 (April 1979): 367–88.

Allen, William Sheridan. *The Nazi Seizure of Power*. Rev. ed. New York: Franklin Watts, 1984.

Die Amnestie für die Colmarer Komplottverurteilten und die Geschichte ihrer jahrelangen Verschleppung. Flugschriften der Elsäßischen Volkspartei—Nr. 6. Colmar: Alsatia Verlag, 1931.

Anderson, Benedict. *Imagined Communities: Reflections on the Origin and Spread of Nationalism*. Rev. ed. New York: Verso, 1991.

Anderson, Malcolm. "Regional Identity and Political Change: The Case of Alsace from the Third to the Fifth Republic." *Political Studies* 20, 1 (1987): 17–30.

Angress, Werner T. *Stillborn Revolution: The Communist Bid for Power in Germany, 1921–1923*. Princeton: Princeton University Press, 1963.

Antoni, Victor. *Grenzlandschicksal-Grenzlandtragik*. Saarbrücken: Verlag Karl Funk, 1957.

Applegate, Celia. *A Nation of Provincials: The German Idea of Heimat*. Berkeley and Los Angeles: University of California Press, 1990.

Appollonia, Ariane Chebel d'. *L'extrême-droite en France: De Maurras à Le Pen*. Brussels: Editions Complexe, 1988.

Arendt, Hannah. *Origins of Totalitarianism*. Rev. ed. New York: Harcourt Brace Jovanovich, 1973.

———. *Eichmann in Jerusalem: A Report on the Banality of Evil*. New York: Viking, 1965.

Arnoult, P., et al. *La France sous l'occupation*. Paris: Presses Universitaires de France, 1959.

Aron, Robert. *France Reborn: The History of the Liberation*. New York, 1964.

———. *The Vichy Regime, 1940–1944*. Boston: Beacon Press, 1958.

Arzalier, Francis. *Les Perdants: La dérive fasciste des mouvements autonomistes et indépendantistes au XXe siècle*. Paris: Editions La Découverte, 1990.

Augé-Laribé, Michel, *La politique agricole de la France de 1880 à 1940*. Paris: Presses Universitaires de France, 1950.

Azéma, Jean-Pierre. *From Munich to the Liberation, 1938–1944*. New York: Cambridge University Press, 1984.

Azéma, Jean-Pierre, and Michel Winock. *La Troisième République, 1870–1940*. Paris: Calmann-Lévy, 1976.

Baas, Emile. *Situation de l'Alsace*. Colmar: Alsatia, 1973.

Baas, Geneviève. *Le malaise alsacien, développement et communauté*. Strasbourg: Imprimé par Développement et Communauté Alsagraphie, 1972.

Baechler, Christian. "L'Alsace contemporaine de 1870 à 1945: Un bilan des recherches depuis 1968." *Revue d'Alsace* 107, 585 (1981): 169–88.

———. *Les Alsaciens et le Grand Tournant de 1918*. Strasbourg, 1972.

———. *Le Parti Catholique Alsacien, 1890–1939: Du Reichsland à la République Jacobine*. Paris: Editions Ophrys, 1982.

Baldwin, Peter. "Social Interpretations of Nazism: Renewing a Tradition." *Journal of Contemporary History* 25, 1 (Jan. 1990): 5–38.

Bankwitz, Philip. *Alsatian Autonomist Leaders, 1919–1947*. Lawrence, Kans.: Regents Press of Kansas, 1978.

Baron, Heinrich. *Mit Karl Roos dem Blutzeugen des deutschen Elsaß: Die letzten Tage in der Todeszelle*. Strasbourg: Verlag der Straßburger Monatshefte, 1940.

Barrès, Maurice. *Colette Baudoche: The Story of a Young Girl of Metz*. Translated by Frances Wilson Huard. New York: George H. Doran, 1918.

Baudot, Marcel. *L'opinion publique sous l'occupation*. Paris: Presses Universitaires de France, 1960.

Baumann, Charles. *Zwischen Rhine und Vogesen: Hinter den Kulißen der Politik— gefährliche Spione*. Strasbourg-Neudorf: Verlag Charles Baumann, 1928.

Becker-Christensen, Henrik. *Dansk Mindretalspolitik i Nordslesvig: Udformingen af den danske politik over for det tyske mindretal, 1918–1920*. Åbenrå: Institut for Grænseregionsforskning, 1984.

Bellanger, Claude, Jacques Godechot, Pierre Guiral, and Fernand Terrou. *Histoire générale de la presse française*. 4 vols. Paris: Presses Universitaires de France, 1969–1975.

Berger, Suzanne. *Peasants against Politics: Rural Organization in Brittany, 1911–1967*. Cambridge, Mass.: Harvard University Press, 1972.

Bergeron, Francis, and Philippe Vilgier. *Les Droites dans la rue: Nationaux et nationalistes sous la Troisième République*. Grez-en-Bouère: DMM, 1985.

Berghahn, Volker R. *Der Stahlhelm: Bund der Frontsoldaten, 1918–1935*. Düsseldorf: Droste Verlag, 1966.

Bernard, Philippe, and Henri Dubief. *The Decline of the Third Republic, 1914–1938*. New York: Cambridge University Press, 1985.

Berstein, Serge. *La France des années 30*. Paris: Armand Colin, 1988.

———. "Une greffe politique manquée: Le radicalisme alsacien de 1919 à 1939." *Revue d'Histoire Moderne et Contemporaine* 17 (Jan.–March 1970): 78–103.

———. *Le 6 février 1934*. Paris: Editions Gallimard/Julliard, 1975.

Bickler, Hermann. *Aus den Jahren der Entscheidung: Brief eines elsäßischen Kämpfers*. Edited by Christian Hallier. Frankfurt, 1941.

———. *Ein besonderes Land: Erinnerungen und Betrachtungen eines Lothringers*. Lindhorst: Askania Verlag, 1978.

———. "Was wir wollen." 1933.

———. *Widerstand: Zehn Jahre Volkstumskampf der Elsaß-Lothringischen Jungmannschaft*. Strasbourg: Hünenburg Verlag, 1943.

Bieber, Peter. *Die Geschichte des Elsaß*. Strasbourg: Hünenburg Verlag, 1941.

Blackbourn, David. *Class, Religion and Local Politics in Wilhelmine Germany: The Center Party in Württemberg before 1914*. New Haven: Yale University Press, 1980.

Blackbourn, David, and Geoff Eley. *The Peculiarities of German History: Bourgeois Society and Politics in Nineteenth-Century Germany*. New York: Oxford University Press, 1984.

Blinkhorn, Martin, ed. *Fascists and Conservatives: The Radical Right and the Establishment in Twentieth-Century Europe*. London: Unwin Hyman, 1990.

Boberach, Heinz, ed. *Berichte des SD und der Gestapo über Kirchen und Kirchenvolk in Deutschland, 1934–1944*. Mainz: Matthias Grünewald Verlag, 1971.

———. *Meldungen aus dem Reich, 1938–1945: Die geheimen Lageberichte des Sicherheitsdienstes der SS*. 17 vols. Herrsching: Pawlak Verlag, 1984.

Böhnke, Wilfred. *Die NSDAP im Ruhrgebiet, 1920–1933*. Bonn–Bad Godesberg: Verlag Neue Gesellschaft, 1974.

Bopp, Marie-Joseph. *L'Alsace sous l'occupation allemande, 1940–1945*. Le Puy: Editions Xavier Mappus, 1945.

———. "Les Alsaciens et la colonisation de l'Algérie." In *L'Alsace contemporaine: Etudes politiques, économiques, sociales,* compiled by Société Savante d'Alsace et des Régions de l'Est. Strasbourg and Paris: F.-X. Le Roux, 1950.

———. "L'enrôlement de force des Alsaciens dans la Wehrmacht et la SS." *Revue d'Histoire de la Deuxième Guerre Mondiale* 5, 20 (Oct. 1955): 33–42.

———. "L'opinion publique en Alsace occupée: Un témoignage nazi en 1943." *Revue d'Alsace* 96 (1957): 155–59.

Bourderon, Roger. "Le régime de Vichy, était-il fasciste? Essai d'approche de la question." *Revue d'Histoire de la Deuxième Guerre Mondiale* 91 (July 1973): 23–45.

Bourdrel, Philippe. *La Cagoule: Trente ans de complots*. Paris: Editions Albin Michel, 1970.

Bowen, Ralph H. *German Theories of the Corporative State with Special Reference to the Period 1870–1919*. New York: Whittlesey House, 1947.

Bramwell, Anna. *Blood and Soil: Richard Walther Darré and Hitler's "Green Party."* Buckinghamshire: The Kensal Press, 1985.

Braudel, Fernand. *The Identity of France*. 2 vols. New York: Harper and Row, 1988, 1990.

Braun, André. *L'ouvrier alsacien et l'expérience du Front Populaire*. Paris: Librairie du Recueil Sirey, 1938.

Brose, Eric Dorn. "Generic Fascism Revisited: Attitudes toward Technology in

Germany and Italy, 1919–1945." *German Studies Review* 10, 2 (May 1987): 273–97.

Broszat, Martin. *The Hitler State*. New York: Longman, 1981.

Bruhat, Jean. "Le Parti Communiste Français face à l'hitlérisme de 1933 à 1936." In *La France et l'Allemagne, 1932–1936*, compiled by Henri Michel. Paris: Edition du Centre National de la Recherche Scientifique, 1980.

Brunet, Jean-Paul. *Jacques Doriot: Du communisme au fascisme*. Paris: Balland, 1986.

Brustein, William. *The Social Origins of Political Regionalism: France, 1849–1981*. Berkeley and Los Angeles: University of California Press, 1988.

Bucard, Marcel. *La légende de Marcq*. Paris: J. Dumoulin, 1925.

———. *Les tyrans de la IIIe*. Paris: Editions du Coq de France, 1937.

Burrin, Philippe. *La dérive fasciste: Doriot, Déat, Bergery, 1933–1945*. Paris: Seuil, 1986.

———. "La France dans le champ magnétique des fascismes." *Le Débat* 32 (Nov. 1984): 52–72.

———. *France under the Germans: Collaboration and Compromise*. New York: New Press, 1997.

Büttner, Ursula, ed. *Das Unrechtsregime: Internationale Forschung über den Nationalsozialismus*. 2 vol. Hamburg: Christians, 1986.

Byrnes, Robert F. *Antisemitism in Modern France*. New York: Howard Fertig, 1969.

Cammett, John M. "Communist Theories of Fascism, 1920–1935." *Science and Society* 31, 2 (1967): 149–63.

Campbell, Stuart. *The Second Empire Revisited: A Study in French Historiography*. New Brunswick, N.J.: Rutgers University Press, 1978.

Cardoza, Anthony L. *Agrarian Elites and Italian Fascism: The Province of Bologna, 1901–1926*. Princeton: Princeton University Press, 1982.

Caron, Vicki. *Between France and Germany: The Jews of Alsace-Lorraine, 1871–1918*. Stanford: Stanford University Press, 1988.

———. "Loyalties in Conflict: French Jewry and the Refugee Crisis, 1933–1935." *Leo Baeck Institute Yearbook* 36 (1991): 305–38.

———. "Prelude to Vichy: France and the Jewish Refugees in the Era of Appeasement." *Journal of Contemporary History* 20, 1 (Jan. 1985): 157–77.

———. "The Social and Religious Transformation of Alsace-Lorraine Jewry, 1871–1914." *Leo Baeck Institute Yearbook* 30 (1985): 319–56.

Carsten, F. L. *The Rise of Fascism*. 2d ed. Berkeley and Los Angeles: University of California Press, 1980.

Childers, Thomas. *The Nazi Voter: The Social Foundations of Fascism in Germany, 1919–1933*. Chapel Hill: University of North Carolina Press, 1983.

———. "The Social Language of Politics in Germany: The Sociology of Political Discourse in the Weimar Republic." *American Historical Review* 95, 2 (April 1990): 331–58.

Childers, Thomas, ed. *The Formation of the Nazi Constituency, 1919–1933*. Totowa, N.J.: Barnes and Noble, 1986.

Childers, Thomas, and Jane Caplan, ed. *Reevaluating the Third Reich*. New York: Holmes and Meier, 1993.

Cleary, M. C. *Peasants, Politicians and Producers: The Organisation of Agriculture in France since 1918*. New York: Cambridge University Press, 1989.

Cointet, J.-P. "Marcel Déat et le Parti Unique (été 1940)." *Revue d'Histoire de la Deuxième Guerre Mondiale* 91 (July 1973): 1-16.

Comité Alsacien d'Etudes et d'Informations, ed. *L'Alsace depuis son retour à la France.* 2 vols. and supplement. Strasbourg: Comité Alsacien d'Etudes et d'Informations, 1932, 1933, 1937.

Connor, Walker. "A Nation Is a Nation, Is a State, Is an Ethnic Group, Is a . . ." *Ethnic and Racial Studies* 1, 4 (Oct. 1978): 377–400.

Conway, J. S. *The Nazi Persecution of the Churches, 1933–1945.* London: Weidenfeld and Nicolson, 1968.

Coston, Henry. *Partis, journaux et hommes politiques d'hier et d'aujourd'hui.* Paris: Lectures Françaises, 1960.

Craig, John E. *Scholarship and Nation-Building: The Universities of Strasbourg and Alsatian Society, 1870–1939.* Chicago: University of Chicago Press, 1984.

Dansette, Adrian. *Religious History of Modern France.* 2 vols. London: Nelson, 1961.

Davant, Jean-Louis. *Histoire du peuple basque: Le peuple basque dans l'histoire.* Bayonne: Editions Elkar, 1977.

De Felice, Renzo. *Interpretations of Fascism.* Cambridge, Mass.: Harvard University Press, 1977.

De La Rocque, François. *Service Public.* Paris: Editions Bernard Grasset, 1934.

Déniel, Alain. *Bucard et le francisme.* Paris: Jean Picolec, 1979.

———. *Le mouvement breton, 1919–1945.* Paris: François Maspero, 1976.

Didier, Friedrich, ed. *Handbuch für die Dienststellen des G.B.A. und die interessierten Reichsstellen im Großdeutschen Reich und in den besetzten Gebieten.* Berlin, 1944.

Diehl, James M. *Paramilitary Politics in Weimar Germany.* Bloomington: Indiana University Press, 1977.

Dioudonnat, Pierre-Marie. *Je suis partout, 1930–1944: Les Maurrassiens devant la tentation fasciste.* Paris: La Table Ronde, 1973.

Dobkowski, Michael N., and Isidor Wallimann, eds. *Radical Perspectives on the Rise of Fascism in Germany, 1919–1945.* New York: Monthly Review Press, 1989.

Dollinger, P. *Histoire de l'Alsace.* Toulouse: Privat, 1970.

Dorgères, Henri. *Au temps des fourches.* Paris: Editions France-Empire, 1975.

Doriot, Jacques. *La France avec nous!* Paris: Flammarion, 1937.

———. *La France ne sera pas un pays d'esclaves.* Paris: Les Oeuvres Françaises, 1936.

———. *Je suis un homme du maréchal (notes à leur date).* Paris: Bernard Grasset, 1941.

Doty, C. Stewart. *From Cultural Rebellion to Counterrevolution: The Politics of Maurice Barrès.* Athens: Ohio University Press, 1976.

Douglas, Allen. *From Fascism to Libertarian Communism: Georges Valois against the Third Republic.* Berkeley and Los Angeles: University of California Press, 1992.

———. "Violence and Fascism: The Case of the Faisceau." *Journal of Contemporary History* 19, 4 (Oct. 1984): 689–712.

Dreyfus, François-G. "L'Action Française en Alsace." *Etudes Maurassiennes* 3 (1974): 55–67.

————. "L'Allemagne de Weimar et le problème alsacien (1919–1929)." *Bulletin de la Société d'Histoire Moderne* 14, 15 (1971): 2–13.

————. *Histoire de l'Alsace*. Paris: Hachette, 1979.

————. "Le protestantisme Alsacien." *Archives de Sociologie des Religions* 2, 3 (Jan.–June 1957): 57–71.

————. "Les socialismes en Alsace de 1912 à 1962." *Bulletin de la Faculté des Lettres de Strasbourg* 44, 5 (Feb. 1966): 511–34.

————. *La vie politique en Alsace, 1919–1936*. Paris: Armand Colin, 1969.

Drieu La Rochelle, Pierre. *Avec Doriot*. Paris: Gallimard, 1937.

————. *The Comedy of Charleroi and Other Stories*. Cambridge, Mass.: Rivers Press, 1973.

————. *L'Europe contre les patries*. Paris: Gallimard, 1931.

————. *Gilles*. Paris: Gallimard, 1939.

————. *Le jeune européen*. Paris: Gallimard, 1927.

————. *The Man on Horseback*. Columbia, S.C.: French Literature Publications, 1978.

————. *Socialisme fasciste*. Paris: Gallimard, 1934.

————. *Will o' the Wisp*. London: Calder and Boyars, 1966.

Duhem, Jules. *The Question of Alsace-Lorraine*. New York: Hodder and Stoughton, 1918.

Dülffer, Jost. "Bonapartism, Fascism and National Socialism." *Journal of Contemporary History* 11, 4 (Oct. 1976): 109–28.

Dumser, Jean. *Bekenntniße eines waschechten els.-loth. Autonomisten: Das Hauptquartier der elsäßischen Autonomiebewegung: Berlin–Frankfurt*. Strasbourg: Berger-Levrault, 1929.

Eatwell, Roger. "Towards a New Model of Generic Fascism." *Journal of Theoretical Politics* 4, 2 (April 1992): 161–94.

Eatwell, Roger, and Noel O'Sullivan, eds. *The Nature of the Right: European and American Politics and Political Thought since 1789*. London: Pinter, 1989.

Elbow, Matthew H. *French Corporative Theory, 1789–1948*. New York: Octagon Books, 1966.

Eley, Geoff. "What Produces Fascism: Preindustrial Traditions or a Crisis of the Capitalist State." *Politics and Society* 12, 1 (1983): 53–82.

Ellis, Jack D. *The Physician-Legislators of France: Medicine and Politics in the Early Third Republic, 1870–1914*. New York: Cambridge University Press, 1990.

Encyclopédie de l'Alsace. 12 vols. Strasbourg: Editions Publitotal Strasbourg, 1984.

Ernst, Robert. *Rechenschaftsbericht eines Elsäßers*. Berlin: Verlag Bernard and Gräfe, 1954.

Eude, Pierre. *La chambre de commerce de Strasbourg pendant la guerre, 1939–1944: Souvenirs*. Strasbourg: Imprimerie Alsacienne, 1949.

Evans, Ellen Lovell. *The German Center Party, 1870–1933: A Study in Political Catholicism*. Carbondale and Evansville: Southern Illinois Press, 1981.

Fabre-Luce, Alfred. *Journal de la France, 1939–1944*. Paris: Fayard, 1969.

Faye, Jean Pierre. *Langages totalitaires: Critique de la raison, l'économie narrative*. 2d ed. Paris: Hermann, 1980.

Fédération Agricole d'Alsace et de Lorraine. *Comptes rendus*. Strasbourg: Société d'Edition de la Basse-Alsace, 1923, 1933, 1937.

Fédération Agricole d'Alsace et de Lorraine, ed. *Cinquante ans de Fédération Agricole d'Alsace et de Lorraine, 1905–1950.* Strasbourg: Imprimerie Strasbourgeoise, 1955.

Fédération des Sociétés d'Histoire et d'Archéologie d'Alsace. *Nouveau dictionnaire de biographie alsacienne.* Strasbourg, 1982– .

Feldman, Gerald D. *The Great Disorder: Politics, Economics, and Society in the German Inflation, 1914–1924.* New York: Oxford University Press, 1993.

Férenzy, Oscar de. *La vérité sur l'Alsace.* Paris: Librairie Bloud et Gay, 1930.

Fleury, Alain. *"La Croix" et l'Allemagne, 1930–1940.* Paris: Editions du Cerf, 1986.

La fondation du Parti Communiste Français et la pénétration des idées léninistes en France: Cinquante ans d'action communiste (1920–1970). Paris: Editions Sociales, 1971.

Ford, Caroline. *Creating the Nation in Provincial France: Religion and Political Identity in Brittany.* Princeton: Princeton University Press, 1993.

Ford, Franklin. *Strasbourg in Transition, 1648–1789.* Cambridge, Mass.: Harvard University Press, 1958.

Fourrier, Marcel. *Der Colmarer Komplottprozeß.* Strasbourg: Imprimerie Solidarité, 1928.

France, Ministère de l'Agriculture. *Monographies agricoles départementales.* No. 67, *Bas-Rhin.* Paris: La Documentation Française, 1960.

Friedrich, Karl, and Zbigniew Brzezinski. *Totalitarian Dictatorship and Autocracy.* Cambridge, Mass.: Harvard University Press, 1956.

Fritzsche, Peter. *Rehearsal for Fascism: Populism and Political Mobilization in Weimar Germany.* New York: Oxford University Press, 1990.

Gabriel-Robinet, L. *Dorgères et le Front Paysan.* Paris: Plon, 1937.

Gellner, Ernst. *Nations and Nationalism.* Ithaca: Cornell University Press, 1983.

Gervais, Michel, Marcel Jollivet, and Yves Tavernier. *La fin de la France paysanne de 1914 à nos jours.* Vol. 4 of *Histoire de la France rurale,* compiled by Georges Duby and Armand Wallon. Paris: Seuil, 1976.

Gestermann, André. *Geschichte der elsäßischen Bauern- und Landwirtschaft.* 2 vols. 1936.

Gillouin, René. *De l'Alsace à la Flandre: Le mysticisme linguistique.* Paris: Editions Prométhée, 1930.

Girardet, R. "Notes sur l'esprit d'un fascisme français, 1934–1939." *Revue Française de Science Politique* (1955): 529–46.

Gisevius, Hans Bernd. *To the Bitter End.* Boston: Houghton Mifflin, 1947.

Goguel, François. *Géographie des élections françaises de 1870 à 1951.* Paris: Librairie Armand Colin, 1951.

Golan, Romy. *Modernity and Nostalgia: Art and Politics in France between the Wars.* New Haven: Yale University Press, 1995.

Gooch, R. K. *Regionalism in France.* New York: Century, 1931.

Goodfellow, Samuel. "Fascism in Alsace, 1918–1945." Ph.D. diss., Indiana University, 1991.

———. "From Communism to Nazism: The Transformation of Alsatian Communists." *Journal of Contemporary History* 27 (1992): 231–58.

———. "From Germany to France? Interwar Alsatian National Identity." *French History* 7, 4 (1993): 450–71.

Gordon, Bertram. *Collaborationism in France during the Second World War.* Ithaca: Cornell University Press, 1980.

Die Gottlosenbewegung: Ihr Wesen und ihre Tatigkeit in dem verschiedenen Ländern. Flugschriften der Elsäßischen Volkspartei—Nr. 8. Colmar: Alsatia Verlag, 1931.

Gras, Christian, and Georges Livet, eds. *Régions et régionalisme en France du XVIIIe siècle à nos jours.* Vendôme: Presses Universitaires de France, 1977.

Gras, Solange. "La presse française et l'autonomisme alsacien en 1926." In *Régions et régionalisme en France du XVIIIe siècle à nos jours,* edited by Christian Gras and Georges Livet, 355–59. Vendôme: Presses Universitaires de France, 1977.

Gregor, James A. *Interpretations of Fascism.* Morrison, N.J.: General Learning Press, 1974.

———. *Italian Fascism and Developmental Dictatorship.* Princeton: Princeton University Press, 1979.

Griffin, Roger. *The Nature of Fascism.* London: Pinter Publishers, 1991.

Grill, Johnpeter Horst. "Local and Regional Studies on National Socialism: A Review." *Journal of Contemporary History* 21, 2 (April 1986): 253–94.

———. *The Nazi Movement in Baden, 1920–1945.* Chapel Hill: University of North Carolina Press, 1983.

Gromer, Dr. *Die Elsäßische Jungvolkspartei und die politische Jugendbewegung unsere Tage: Ein Orientierungsversuch.* Flugschriften der Elsäßischen Volkspartei—Nr. 17. Colmar: Alsatia Verlag, 1935.

Groth, Alexander J. "The 'Ism's' in Totalitarianism." *American Political Science Review* 58, 4 (Dec. 1964): 888–901.

Grünewald, Irmgard. *Die Elsaß-Lothringer im Reich, 1918–1933: Ihre Organisationen zwischen Integration und "Kampf um die Seele der Heimat."* Frankfurt am Main: Peter Lang, 1984.

Guchet, Yves. *Georges Valois: L'Action Française—le Faisceau—la République Syndicale.* Paris: Editions Albatros, 1975.

Guerin, Daniel. *Fascism and Big Business.* New York: Pathfinder Press, 1973.

Guernut, Henri. *Le mouvement autonomiste en Alsace.* Paris: Ligue des Droits de l'Homme, 1928.

Hallier, Christian. *Vom Selbstbehauptungskampf des deutschen Volkstums in Elsaß und in Lothringen, 1918–1940.* Buehl-Baden: Verlag Konkordia AG, 1944.

Halls, W. D. *Education, Culture and Politics in Modern France.* New York: Pergammon Press, 1976.

Hamilton, Alastair. *The Appeal of Fascism: A Study of Intellectuals and Fascism, 1919–1945.* New York: Macmillan, 1973.

Hamilton, Richard. *Who Voted for Hitler?* Princeton: Princeton University Press, 1982.

Harp, Stephen L. "Learning to Be German: Primary Schooling in Alsace-Lorraine, 1870–1918." Ph.D. diss., Indiana University, 1993.

———. "War's Eclipse of Primary Education in Alsace-Lorraine, 1914–1918." *The Historian* 57, 3 (spring 1995): 489–502.

Harr, Karl G. *The Genesis and Effect of the Popular Front in France.* Lanham, Md.: University Press of America, 1987.

Hau, Michel. *L'industrialisation de l'Alsace, 1803–1939.* Strasbourg: Associations des Publications près des Universités de Strasbourg, 1987.

Heberle, Rudolf. *Landebevölkerung und Nationalsozialismus: Eine soziologische Untersuchung der politischen Willensbildung in Schleswig-Holstein, 1918–1932.* Stuttgart, 1963.

Heiberg, Marianne. *The Making of the Basque Nation.* New York: Cambridge University Press, 1989.

Heilbronner, Oded. "The Failure That Succeeded: Nazi Party Activity in a Catholic Region in Germany, 1929–1932." *Journal of Contemporary History* 27, 3 (July 1992): 531–49.

Heitz, Robert. *A mort (souvenirs).* Paris: Editions de Minuit, 1946.

———. *Petite histoire de l'autonomisme.* Strasbourg, 1928.

———. "La 'Révolution' strasbourgeoise de novembre 1918." In *L'Alsace contemporaine: Etudes politiques, économiques, sociales,* compiled by Société Savante d'Alsace et des Régions de l'Est. Strasbourg and Paris: F.-X. Le Roux, 1950.

Hélias, Pierre-Jabez. *The Horse of Pride: Life in a Breton Village.* New Haven: Yale University Press, 1978.

Hellman, John. *Emmanuel Mounier and the New Catholic Left, 1930–1950.* Toronto: University of Toronto Press, 1981.

Helsey, Edouard. *Notre Alsace: L'enquête du "Journal" et le Procès de Colmar.* Paris: Albin Michel, 1927.

Herberich-Marx, Geneviève, and Freddy Raphaël. "Les incorporés de force alsaciens, déni, convocation et provocation." *Le Vingtième Siècle* 6 (April–June 1985): 83–102.

———. "'Les Noirs' et 'les Rouges' au village: Mémoires des mineurs-vignerons de Haute-Alsace." *Les Saisons d'Alsace* 92 (June 1986): 83–98.

Herf, Jeffrey. *Reactionary Modernism: Technology, Culture, and Politics in Weimar and the Third Reich.* New York: Cambridge University Press, 1984.

Heumann, Gautier, and Marcel Rosenblatt. "La lutte du Parti Communiste Français contre la réaction impérialiste en Alsace et en Moselle." In *La fondation du Parti Communiste Français et la pénétration des idées léninistes en France.* Paris: Editions Sociales, 1971.

Hiery, Hermann. *Reichstagswahlen im Reichsland: Ein Beitrag zur Landesgeschichte von Elsaß-Lothringen und zur Wahlgeschichte des Deutschen Reiches, 1871–1918.* Düsseldorf: Droste Verlag, 1986.

Himly, François-Jacques, and Françoise Grégoire. *Répertoire numérique des fonds du gouvernement d'Alsace-Lorraine, 1870–1918.* 3 vols. Strasbourg, 1980.

Hirsch, Helmut. *Die Saar in Versailles: Die Saarfrage auf der Friedenskonferenz von 1919.* Bonn: Ludwig Röhrscheid Verlag, 1952.

Hitler, Adolf. *Mein Kampf.* Munich: Zentral Verlag der NSDAP, 1938.

Hobsbawm, E. J. *Nations and Nationalism since 1780: Programme, Myth, Reality.* New York: Cambridge University Press, 1990.

Hochstuhl, Kurt. *Zwischen Frieden und Krieg: Das Elsaß in den Jahren 1938–1940: Ein Beitrag zu den Problem einer Grenzregion in Krisenzeiten.* Frankfurt am Main: Peter Lang, 1984.

Hoffet, Frédéric. *Psychanalyse de l'Alsace.* Colmar: Editions Alsatia, 1973.

Hoffmann, Stanley. "Collaborationism in France during World War II." *Journal of Modern History* 40 (1968): 375–95.

Hoop, Jean-Marie d'. "La main-d'oeuvre française au service de l'Allemagne." *Revue d'Histoire de la Deuxième Guerre Mondiale* 81 (1971): 73–88.

Horkheimer, Max, and Theodor W. Adorno. *Dialectic of Enlightenment.* New York: Herder and Herder, 1972.

Hueber, Charles. *Elsaß-Lothringen in der Kammer.* Strasbourg: Imprimerie Solidarité, 1927.

Hünenburg, Friedrich (Dr. Spieser). *Tausend Brücken: Eine biographische Erzäh-lung aus dem Schicksal eines Landes.* Edited by Agnes Gräfin Dohna. Stuttgart, 1952.

Hurstel, Jean. "Du pluralisme au monolithisme: Brève histoire de la presse alsaci-enne." *Objectif Alsace,* Oct. 19, 1987, and Nov. 19, 1987.

Hyman, Paula. *The Emancipation of the Jews of Alsace: Acculturation and Tradi-tion in the Nineteenth Century.* New Haven: Yale University Press, 1991.

Igersheim, François. *L'Alsace des notables (1870–1914): La bourgeoisie et le peu-ple alsacien.* Strasbourg: BF, 1981.

Irjud, Alphonse. "La germanisation des noms en Alsace entre 1940 et 1944." *Re-vue d'Alsace* 113 (1987): 239–61.

Irvine, William D. *The Boulanger Affair Reconsidered: Royalism, Boulangism, and the Origins of the Radical Right in France.* New York: Oxford University Press, 1989.

———. "Fascism in France and the Strange Case of the Croix de Feu." *Journal of Modern History* 63 (June 1991): 271–95.

———. *French Conservatism in Crisis: The Republican Federation of France in the 1930s.* Baton Rouge: Louisiana State University Press, 1979.

Jäckel, Eberhard. *Frankreich in Hitler's Europe: Die deutsche Frankreichpolitik im 2. Weltkrieg.* Stuttgart: Deutsche Verlags-Anstalt, 1966.

Jacob, Marcel. *Stavisky und sein Hof: Die Sozialisten, die Radikalsozialisten und die Loge im Skandal.* Flugschriften der Elsäßischen Volkspartei. Mulhouse: Al-satia Verlag, 1934.

Jankowski, Paul. *Communism and Collaboration: Simon Sabiani and Politics in Marseille, 1919–1944.* New Haven: Yale University Press, 1989.

Jenkins, Brian. "Debates and Controversies: Robert Soucy and the 'Second Wave' of French Fascism." *Modern and Contemporary France* 2 (1996): 193–208.

Joes, Anthony James. *Fascism in the Contemporary World: Ideology, Evolution, Resurgence.* Boulder, Colo.: Westview Press, 1978.

Juillard, Etienne. *La vie rurale dans la plaine de Basse-Alsace: Essai de géographie sociale.* Strasbourg: Editions F.-X Le Roux, 1953.

Juillard, Etienne, and Philippe Kessler. "Catholiques et protestants dans les cam-pagnes alsaciennes." *Annales Economies—Société—Civilisations* 7, 1 (Jan.–March 1952): 49–54.

Kasten, Frederick H. "Unethical Nazi Medicine in Annexed Alsace-Lorraine: The Strange Case of Nazi Anatomist Professor Dr. August Hirt." In *Historians and Archivists: Essays in Modern German History and Archival Policy,* edited by George O. Kent, 173–208. Fairfax, Va.: George Mason University Press, 1991.

Kater, Michael H. "The Burden of the Past: Problems of a Modern Historiography of Physicians and Medicine in Nazi Germany." *German Studies Review* 10, 1 (Feb. 1987), 40–41.

———. "Generationskonflikt als Entwicklungsfaktor in der NS-Bewegung vor 1933." *Geschichte und Gesellschaft* 11, 2 (1985): 217–43.

———. "Hitler's Early Doctors: Nazi Physicians in Predepression Germany." *Jour-nal of Modern History* 59, 1 (March 1987): 25–52.

Kedourie, Elie. *Nationalism.* New York: Praeger, 1961.

Kedward, H. R. *Resistance in Vichy France.* New York: Oxford University Press, 1978.

Kelikian, Alice. *Town and Country under Fascism: The Transformation of Brescia,*

1915–1926. Oxford, England: Clarendon Press, 1986.

Kemp, Tom. *The French Economy, 1913–1939: The History of a Decline.* New York: St. Martin's Press, 1972.

Kent, George O. *A Catalogue of Files and Microfilms of the German Foreign Ministry Archives, 1920–1945.* Stanford: Stanford University Press, 1962.

Kettenacker, Lothar. *Nationalsozialistische Volkstumspolitik im Elsaß.* Stuttgart: Deutsche Verlags-Anstalt, 1973.

Keylor, William R. *Jacques Bainville and the Renaissance of Royalist History in Twentieth-Century France.* Baton Rouge: Louisiana State University Press, 1979.

Kitchen, Martin. *The Coming of Austrian Fascism.* London: Croom Helm, 1980.

Klein, Paul. *L'Evolution contemporaine des banques alsaciennes: Histoire d'un essai de régionalisme bancaire.* Paris: Librairie Générale de Droit et de Jurisprudence, 1931.

Klein, Peter. *Separatisten an Rhein und Ruhr: Die konterrevolutionäre separatistische Bewegung der deutschen Bourgeoisie in der Rheinprovinz und in Westfalen November 1918 bis Juli 1919.* East Berlin: Rütten and Löning, 1961.

Klein, Pierre, ed. *L'Alsace.* Paris: Editions d'Organisation, 1981.

Kleinschmager, Richard. *L'Economie alsacienne en question.* Colmar: Editions Alsatia, 1974.

Klemperer, Klemens von. "On Austrofascism." *Central European History* 11, 2 (Sept. 1978): 313–17.

Kluke, Paul. "Nationalsozialistische Europapolitik." *Vierteljahrshefte für Zeitgeschichte* 3 (1955): 240–75.

Koehl, Robert L. *RKFDV: German Resettlement and Population Policy, 1939–1945.* Cambridge: Harvard University Press, 1957.

Köhler, Henning. *Autonomiebewegung oder Separatismus: Die Politik der "Kölnischen Volkszeitung," 1918/1919.* Berlin: Colloquium Verlag, 1974.

Der Komplott-prozeß von Besançon vom 10. Juni bis 22. Juni 1929: Gesammelte Verhandlungsberichte. Colmar: Alsatia Verlag, 1929.

Der Komplott-prozeß von Colmar vom 1. bis 24. Mai 1928: Gesammelte Verhandlungsberichte. Colmar: Alsatia Verlag, 1928.

Koos, Cheryl. "Engendering Reaction: The Politics of Pronatalism and the Family in France, 1919–1944." Ph.D. diss., University of Southern California, 1996.

Kornhauser, William. *The Politics of Mass Society.* New York: Free Press of Glencoe, 1959.

Koshar, Rudy. *Social Life, Local Politics, and Nazism: Marburg, 1880–1935.* Chapel Hill: University of North Carolina Press, 1986.

Koshar, Rudy, ed. *Splintered Classes: Politics and the Lower Middle Classes in Interwar Europe.* New York: Holmes and Meier, 1990.

Kriegel, Annie. *Aux origines du communisme français: Histoire du mouvement ouvrier français, 1914–1920.* Paris: Mouton and Co., 1964.

Kühnl, Reinhard. *Deutschland zwischen Demokratie und Faschismus: Zur Problematic der bürgerlichen Gesellschaft seit 1918.* Munich: Carl Hanser Verlag, 1969.

———. *Die nationalsozialistische Linke, 1925–1930.* Meisenheim am Glan: Verlag Anton Hain, 1966.

Kuhlmann, A.-E. *Le problème alsacien.* Paris: Librairie de l'Action Française, 1927.

Kuisel, R. F. *Ernest Mercier, French Technocrat.* Berkeley and Los Angeles: University of California Press, 1967.

Laborie, Pierre. *Résistants, Vichyssois et autres: L'évolution de l'opinion et des comportements dans le Lot de 1939 à 1944.* Paris: Editions de C.N.R.S., 1980.

Laqueur, Walter. *Fascism: Past, Present, Future.* Oxford: Oxford University Press, 1996.

Laqueur, Walter, ed. *Fascism: A Reader's Guide.* Berkeley and Los Angeles: University of California Press, 1976.

Larkin, Maurice. *France since the Popular Front: Government and People, 1936–1986.* Oxford, England: Clarendon Press, 1988.

Larmour, Peter J. *The French Radical Party in the 1930s.* Stanford: Stanford University Press, 1964.

Larsen, Stein Ugelvik, et al., eds. *Who Were the Fascists? Social Roots of European Fascism.* Bergen: Universitetsforlaget, 1980.

Laugel, Anselme. "La situation morale en Alsace." *Revue Politique et Parlementaire* 27, 313 (Dec. 1920): 370–91.

Lavau, Georges. "'Nationalism' and the Rise of the Extreme Right in France." *French Politics and Society* 5, 1–2 (Feb. 1987): 7–17.

Leal, Robert Barry. *Drieu La Rochelle.* Boston: Twayne Press, 1982.

Lebovics, Herman. *True France: The Wars over Cultural Identity, 1900–1945.* Ithaca: Cornell University Press, 1992.

Ledeen, Michael A. *Universal Fascism: The Theory and Practice of the Fascist International, 1928–1936.* New York: Howard Fertig, 1972.

Leiby, Richard A. "German Population and Resettlement Policy in Lorraine, 1940–1944." *Proceedings of the Annual Meeting of the Western Society for French History* 14 (1987): 293–302.

Lejeune, Bernard-Henry. *Avant la défaite de 1940.* Vol. 1 of *Historisme de Jacques Doriot et du Parti Populaire Français.* Amiens: Les Nouveaux Cahiers du CERPES, 1977.

Levey, Jules. "Georges Valois and the Faisceau: The Making and Breaking of a Fascist." *French Historical Studies* 8, 2 (fall 1973): 279–304.

Lévy, Bernard-Henri. *L'idéologie française.* Paris: Bernard Grasset, 1981.

Lévy, Paul. *Histoire linguistique d'Alsace et de Lorraine.* 2 vols. Paris: Société d'Edition, 1929.

Liebknecht, Karl. *Gesammelte Reden und Schriften.* 9 vols. Berlin: Dietz Verlag, 1958–1968.

Linton, Derek S. "Bonapartism, Fascism, and the Collapse of the Weimar Republic." In *Radical Perspectives on the Rise of Fascism in Germany, 1919–1945,* edited by Michael Dobkowski and Isidor Wallimann, 100–127. New York: Monthly Review Press, 1989.

Linz, Juan J. "Political Space and Fascism as a Late-Comer: Conditions Conducive to the Success or Failure of Fascism as a Mass Movement in Inter-War Europe." In *Who Were the Fascists?* edited by Stein Ugelvik Larsen et al., 153–89. Bergen: Universitetsforlaget, 1980.

———. "Some Notes toward a Comparative Study of Fascism in Sociological Historical Perspective." In *Fascism: A Reader's Guide,* edited by Walter Laqueur, 3–124. Berkeley and Los Angeles: University of California Press, 1976.

Lipset, Seymour Martin. *Political Man: The Social Bases of Politics.* New York: Anchor Books, 1963.

Livet, Georges, ed. *Histoire de Colmar.* Toulouse: Editions Privat, 1983.

———. *Histoire de Strasbourg des origines à nos jours.* 4 vols. Strasbourg: Editions des Dernières Nouvelles de Strasbourg, 1980.

Loewenberg, Peter. "The Psychohistorical Origins of the Nazi Youth Cohort." *American Historical Review* 76 (Dec. 1971): 1473–76.

Lorson, Pierre. *Pax Alsatia: Charles Ruch, évêque de Strasbourg.* Strasbourg and Paris: Le Roux, 1949.

Lorwin, Val. *The French Labor Movement.* Cambridge, Mass.: Harvard University Press, 1954.

Loughlin, Michael. "The Political Transformation of Gustave Hervé, Part 1, 1871–1906." Ph.D. diss., Indiana University, 1986.

Loustaunau-Lacau, Georges. *Mémoires d'un français rebelle, 1914–1948.* Geneva: Editions de Crémille, 1972.

Lucius, Marc. "L'Alsace après la crise de septembre." *Nouveaux Cahiers* 2, 35 (Dec. 1, 1938): 8–11.

Luebbert, Gregory M. *Liberalism, Fascism, or Social Democracy: Social Classes and the Political Origins of Regimes in Interwar Europe.* New York: Oxford University Press, 1991.

Luks, Leonid. "Bolschewismus, Faschismus, Nationalsozialismus: Verwandte Gegner?" *Geschichte und Gesellschaft* 14, 1 (1988): 96–115.

Machefer, Philippe. *Ligues et fascismes en France (1919–1939).* Vendôme: Presses Universitaires de France, 1974.

———. "Le Parti Social Français et la petite entreprise." *Bulletin—Centre d'Histoire de la France Contemporaine* 8 (1987): 35–45.

———. "L'Union des Droites, le PSF et le Front de la Liberté, 1936–1937." *Revue d'Histoire Moderne et Contemporaine* 17 (Jan.–March 1970): 112–26.

Mackness, Robin. *Oradour: Massacre and Aftermath.* London: Bloomsbury, 1988.

Mack Smith, Denis. *Mussolini.* New York: Alfred A. Knopf, 1982.

Maier, Charles. *Recasting Bourgeois Society: Stabilization in France, Germany, and Italy in the Decade after World War I.* Princeton: Princeton University Press, 1975.

Malaparte, Curzio. *Technique du coup d'état.* Paris: Editions Bernard Grasset, 1931.

Mannheim, Karl. *Ideology and Utopia.* New York: Harcourt Brace Jovanovich, 1936.

Manoilesco, Mihail. *Le siècle du corporatisme: Doctrine du corporatisme intégral et pur.* Paris: Librairie Félix Alcan, 1934.

Marcus, John T. *French Socialism in the Crisis Years, 1933–1936: Fascism and the French Left.* New York: Praeger, 1958.

Maugué, Pierre. *Le particularisme alsacien, 1918–1967.* Paris: Presses d'Europe, 1970.

Maurras, Charles. *Mes idées politiques.* Arthème: Fayard, 1937.

Mayer, Hans. *Ein Deutscher auf Widerruf: Erinnerungen.* Vol. 1. Frankfurt am Main: Suhrkampf, 1982.

Mayer, Norbert. *Ungewisses Frankreich: Frankreichs Presse zum deutsch-französischen Problem seit 1933.* Munich: Verlag H. Hugendubel, 1936.

Mayeur, Jean-Marie. *Autonomie et politique en Alsace: La constitution de 1911.* Paris, 1970.

———. "Une mémoire-frontière: L'Alsace." In *Les lieux de mémoire,* edited by Pierre Nora. Vol. 2 of *La Nation,* 63–95. Paris: Gallimard, 1986.

Mazgaj, Paul. *The Action Française and Revolutionary Syndicalism.* Chapel Hill: University of North Carolina Press, 1979.

McDonald, Maryon. *"We Are Not French!" Language, Culture, and Identity in Brittany.* London: Routledge, 1989.

Médard, Frère. "La crise des années 1930–1939 en Alsace et la montée du fascisme." *Elan* 24, 7–8 (Aug.–Sept. 1980): 8–13.

Mendras, Henri. *The Vanishing Peasant: Innovation and Change in French Agriculture.* Cambridge, Mass.: MIT Press, 1970.

Menes, Bonnie. "My Father Spoke French: Nationalism in Alsace, 1871–1914, and the Birth and Transfer of Ideals of Separateness." Ph.D. diss., Harvard University, 1982.

Merckling, Charles. *Grenzland-Teufel: Ein politisch-satirischer Zeitroman.* Strasbourg: Hauss and Fils, 1929.

Metzger, Chantal. "Relations entre autonomistes lorrains et alsaciens de 1919 à 1932." In *Actes du 103e congrès national des sociétés savantes, Nancy-Metz 1978: Section d'histoire moderne et contemporaine,* edited by the Ministère des Universités, Comité des Travaux Historiques et Scientifiques, vol. 2. Paris: Bibliothèque Nationale, 1979.

Mey, Eugène. *Le drame de l'Alsace.* Paris: Berger-Levrault, 1949.

Micaud, Charles A. *The French Right and Nazi Germany, 1933–1939: A Study of Public Opinion.* New York: Octagon Books, 1964.

Michel, Henri, comp. *La France et l'Allemagne, 1932–1936: Communications présentées au Colloque franco-allemand tenu à Paris du 10 au 12 mars 1977.* Paris: Editions du Centre National de la Recherche Scientifique, 1980.

Milfull, John, ed. *The Attractions of Fascism: Social Psychology and Aesthetics of the "Triumph of the Right."* New York: Berg, 1990.

Millerand, Alexandre. *Le retour de l'Alsace-Lorraine à la France.* Paris: Bibliothèque-Charpentier, 1923.

Milward, Alan. *The New Order and the French Economy.* Oxford: Clarendon Press, 1970.

Milza, Pierre. *Fascisme français: Passé et présent.* Paris: Flammarion, 1987.

Mislin, Claude. *Les Croix de Feu et le Parti Social Français en Alsace, 1930–1939.* Mémoire soutenu pour l'obtention du diplôme de l'Institut d'Etudes Politiques, Strasbourg, 1981–1982.

Moes-Heinz, Iris. "L'évolution industrielle de Mulhouse et de sa région de 1900 à nos jours." *Revue d'Alsace* 106 (1980): 101–12.

Morrison, Jack G. "The Intransigents: Alsace-Lorrainers against the Annexation, 1900–1914." Ph.D. diss., University of Iowa, 1970.

Mosse, George L. *The Crisis of German Ideology: Intellectual Origins of the Third Reich.* New York: Schocken, 1981.

———. "Fascism and the French Revolution." *Journal of Contemporary History* 24, 1 (Jan. 1989): 5–26.

———. "The French Right and the Working Classes: Les Jaunes." *Journal of Contemporary History* 7, 3–4 (July–Oct. 1972): 185–208.

———. *Masses and Man: Nationalist and Fascist Perceptions of Reality.* New York: Howard Fertig, 1980.

Moulin, Annie. *Peasantry and Society in France since 1789.* New York: Cambridge University Press, 1991.

Mourer, Jean-Pierre. *Heraus aus der Sackgasse! Warum elsäßische Arbeiter- und*

Bauernpartei? Strasbourg: Solidarité, 1935.

Mouret, Georges. *Oradour: Le crime—le procès.* Paris: Librairie Plon, 1958.

Mühlberger, Detlef. *Hitler's Followers: Studies in the Sociology of the Nazi Movement.* New York: Routledge, 1991.

Mühlberger, Detlef, ed. *The Social Basis of European Fascist Movements.* New York: Croom Helm, 1987.

Müller, Klaus-Juergen. "French Fascism and Modernization." *Journal of Contemporary History* 11, 4 (Oct. 1976): 75–107.

Mullet, M. *Etude-statistique de la déportation dans le Bas-Rhin, 1940–1945.* Strasbourg, 1971.

Mussolini, Benito. *Fascism: Doctrine and Institutions.* New York: Howard Fertig, 1968.

———. *My Autobiography.* London: Hutchinson, 1939.

Noakes, Jeremy. *The Nazi Party in Lower Saxony, 1921–1933.* New York: Oxford University Press, 1971.

Nolte, Ernst. *Three Faces of Fascism: Action Française, Italian Fascism, National Socialism.* New York: Mentor, 1969.

Novick, Peter. *The Resistance versus Vichy: The Purge of Collaborators in Liberated France.* London: Chatto and Windus, 1968.

Oberkirch, Alfred. *Le problème politique allemand.* Paris: Editions Lajeunesse, 1945.

Ohdake, Yukihiko. "La structure des exploitations agricoles de villages alsaciens (1660–1942)." *Geographical Review of Japan* 47 (1974): 426–43.

Olsson, Lars. "La politique culturelle de la France à l'égard de ses minorités linguistiques." *Moderna Språk* 74, 3 (1980): 237–54.

Oncken, Hermann. *The Historical Rhine Policy of the French.* New York: B. W. Huebsch, 1923.

———. *Staatsnation und Kulturnation: Elsaß-Lothringen und die deutsche Kulturgemeinschaft.* Heidelberg: Verlag Willy Ehrig, 1922.

Ory, Pascal. "Le dorgérisme: Institution et discours d'une colère paysanne, 1929–1939." *Revue d'Histoire Moderne et Contemporaine* 22 (April–June 1975): 168–87.

Osgood, Samuel M. *French Royalism under the Third and Fourth Republics.* The Hague: Martinus Nijhoff, 1960.

Parti Communiste Français, Comité Central. *Histoire du Parti Communiste (manuel).* Paris: Editions Sociales, 1964.

Passmore, Kevin. "Boy Scouting Got Grown-Up? Paramilitarism in the Croix de Feu and the Parti Social Français." *French Historical Studies* 19, 2 (fall 1995): 527–57.

———. "The French Third Republic: Stalemate Society or Cradle of Fascism?" *French History* 7, 4 (Dec. 1993): 417–49.

Paxton, Robert O. *Vichy France: Old Guard and New Order, 1940–1944.* New York: Knopf, 1972.

Payne, Stanley. *Fascism: Comparison and Definition.* Madison: University of Wisconsin Press, 1980.

Pchibich, Liliane. "La marche sur Rome à travers les journaux alsaciens de langue française." Mémoire 3e Année, Institut d'Etudes Politiques, June 1973.

Pelissier, Patrice, "Diversité du communisme bas-rhinois de l'entre-deux-guerres." *Revue d'Alsace* 110 (1984): 169–82.

Peukert, Detlev J. K. *Inside Nazi Germany: Conformity, Opposition, and Racism in Everyday Life*. New Haven: Yale University Press, 1987.

———. *The Weimar Republic: The Crisis of Classical Modernity*. New York: Hill and Wang, 1989.

Pflimlin, Pierre. *Mémoires d'un européen de la Quatrième à la Cinquième République*. Paris: Fayard, 1991.

Pflimlin, Pierre, and René Uhrich. *L'Alsace, destin et volonté*. Paris: Calmann-Lévy, 1963.

Philipps, Eugène. *Schicksal Elsaß: Krise einer Kultur und einer Sprache*. Karlsruhe: Verlag C. F. Muller, 1980.

Plumyène, Jean, and Raymond Lasierra. *Les fascismes français, 1923–1963*. Paris: Editions du Seuil, 1963.

Poidevin, Raymond, and Jacques Bariéty. *Les relations franco-allemandes, 1815–1975*. Paris: Armand Colin, 1977.

Poulantzas, Nicos. *Fascism and Dictatorship: The Third International on the Problem of Fascism*. London: NLB, 1974.

Proctor, Robert. *Racial Hygiene: Medicine under the Nazis*. Cambridge, Mass.: Harvard University Press, 1988.

Prost, Antoine. *Les anciens combattants et la société française, 1914–1939*. 3 vols. Paris: Presses de la Fondation Nationale des Sciences Politiques, 1977.

Pujo, Maurice. *Problèmes d'Alsace et de Lorraine*. Paris: Editions de l'Action Française, 1920.

Raphael, Freddy. "Une rencontre manquée: Les relations entre les juifs d'Alsace et leurs coreligionnaires d'Europe orientale, 1870–1939." *Saisons d'Alsace* 20, 55–56 (1975): 207–28.

Raphael, Freddy, and Robert Weyl, eds. *Juifs en Alsace: Culture, société, histoire*. Toulouse: Privat, 1977.

Rapp, F. *L'histoire de l'Alsace*. Colmar: Mars et Mercure, 1976.

Rebatet, Lucien. *Les mémoires d'un fasciste*. 2 vols. Pauvert, 1976.

Rédier, Antoine. *Comrades in Courage*. New York: Doubleday, Page, 1918.

Redslob, Robert. "Avons-nous encore une patrie?" *Le Temps,* 3 parts, May 20–22, 1929.

———. *Entre la France et l'Allemagne: Souvenirs d'un alsacien*. Paris: Plon, 1933.

———. *The Problem of Nationalities*. London: Eastern Press, 1931.

Reece, Jack E. *The Bretons against France: Ethnic Minority Nationalism in Twentieth-Century Brittany*. Chapel Hill: University of North Carolina Press, 1977.

Reimer, Klaus. *Rheinlandfrage und Rheinlandbewegung (1918–1933): Ein Beitrag zur Geschichte der regionalistischen Bestrebungen in Deutschland*. Frankfurt am Main: Peter Lang, 1979.

Reimeringer, Bernard. "Un communisme régionaliste? Le communisme alsacien." In *Régions et régionalisme en France du XVIIIe siècle à nos jours,* edited by Christian Gras and Georges Livet, 362–92. Vendôme: Presses Universitaires de France, 1977.

———. "Un mouvement paysan extrémiste des années trente: Le Bauernbund." *Revue d'Alsace* 106 (1980): 113–34.

Reinach-Hirtzbach, Hesso de. *La tragique destinée de l'Alsace*. Paris: Sorlot, 1938.

Rémond, René. *Les catholiques, le communisme et les crises, 1929–1939*. Paris: A. Colin, 1960.

———. *Les Droites en France*. Paris: Editions Aubier Montaigne, 1982.

———. *The Right Wing in France: From 1815 to de Gaulle.* 2d ed. Philadelphia: University of Pennsylvania Press, 1969.

Renan, Ernest. *Oeuvres complètes d'Ernest Renan.* Vol. 1. Paris: Calmann-Lévy, 1947.

Reuss, R. *Histoire d'Alsace.* Paris: Boivin et Cie, 1934.

Rich, Norman. *Hitler's War Aims: Ideology, the Nazi State and the Course of Expansion.* 2 vols. New York: Norton, 1973.

Richez, Jean-Claude. "La révolution de novembre 1918 en Alsace dans les petites villes et les campagnes." *Revue d'Alsace* 107 (1981): 153–68.

Riehl, Wilhelm Heinrich. *Die Naturgeschichte des deutschen Volkes.* 3 vols. Leipzig: Philipp Reclam, n.d.

Rigoulot, Pierre. *Des français au goulag, 1917–1984.* Paris: Fayard, 1984.

Rinckenberger, W. *L'Alsace: Rempart français sur le Rhin.* Paris: La Jeune Parque, 1946.

Robein, Paul. *Conditions économiques et sociales du baillage du Kochersberg.* Guénange: Imprimerie des Orphelins-Apprentis, 1920.

Roberts, David. *The Syndicalist Tradition and Italian Fascism.* Chapel Hill: University of North Carolina Press, 1979.

Rogger, Hans, and Eugen Weber, eds. *The European Right: A Historical Profile.* Berkeley and Los Angeles: University of California Press, 1965.

Rossé, Joseph, Marcel Stürmel, A. Bleicher, F. Dieber, and J. Keppi, eds. *Das Elsaß von 1870 bis 1932.* 4 vols. Colmar: Alsatia Verlag, 1932.

Roth, François. *Les Lorrains entre la France et l'Allemagne: Itinéraires d'annexés.* Nancy: Editions Serpenoise, 1981.

Roth, Jack. *The Cult of Violence: Sorel and the Sorelians.* Berkeley and Los Angeles: University of California Press, 1980.

Rothenberger, Karl-Heinz. *Die elsaß-lothringische Heimat- und Autonomiebewegung zwischen den beiden Weltkriegen.* Frankfurt am Main: Peter Lang, 1975.

Rothney, John. *Bonapartism after Sedan.* Ithaca, N.Y.: Cornell University Press, 1969.

Rousso, Henry. *The Vichy Syndrome: History and Memory in France since 1944.* Cambridge, Mass.: Harvard University Press, 1991.

Roux, Georges. *Divorce de l'Alsace?* Paris: Gallimard, 1929.

Rudaux, Philippe. *Les Croix de Feu et le PSF.* Paris: Editions France-Empire, 1967.

Rutkoff, Peter M. "The Ligue des Patriotes: The Nature of the Radical Right and the Dreyfus Affair." *French Historical Studies* 8 (1974): 585–603.

Sauer, Wolfgang. "National Socialism: Totalitarianism or Fascism?" *American Historical Review* 73, 2 (Dec. 1967): 404–22.

Schaeffer, Eugène. *L'Alsace et la Lorraine, 1940–1945: Leur occupation en droit et en fait.* Paris: R. Pichon and R. Durand-Auzias, 1953.

Schaeffer, Patrick J. *L'Alsace et l'Allemagne de 1945 à 1949.* Metz: Centre de Recherches Relations Internationales de l'Université de Metz, 1976.

Schall, Paul. *Elsaß gestern, heute und morgen?* Filderstadt-Bernhausen: Erwin von Steinbach Stiftung, 1976.

———. *Karl Roos und der Kampf des heimattreuen Elsaß.* Colmar: Verlag Alsatia, 1941.

———. *Warum Autonomie.* Strasbourg: Neuer Elsäßer Verlag, 1935.

Schmitter, Philippe, and Gerhard Lehmbruck, eds. *Trends toward Corporatist Intermediation.* Beverly Hills: Sage, 1979.

Schoenbaum, David. *Zabern 1913: Consensus Politics in Imperial Germany.* Boston: George Allen and Unwin, 1982.

Schor, Ralph. *L'opinion française et les étrangers, 1919–1939.* Paris: Publication de la Sorbonne, 1985.

Schram, Stuart R. *Protestantism and Politics in France.* Alençon: Imprimerie Corbière and Jugain, 1954.

Schüddekopf, Otto-Ernst. *Fascism: Revolution of Our Time.* New York: Praeger, 1973.

Schwab, Roland. *De la cellule rurale à la région l'Alsace, 1825–1960.* Strasbourg: Roland Schwab, 1980.

Sérant, Paul. *Les dissidents de l'Action Française.* Paris: Copernic, 1978.

Seton-Watson, H. "Fascism, Right and Left." *Journal of Contemporary History* 1, 1 (1966).

Shapiro, David, ed. *The Right in France, 1890–1919.* Carbondale: Southern Illinois University Press, 1962.

Sichelschmidt, Hans. *Die grenzländische Bedeutung des Protestantismus im Elsaß.* Frankfurt am Main: Verlag Moritz Diesterweg, 1939.

Sigrist, Francis. *Le problème de l'Anschluß et la presse alsacienne de langue allemande, 1934–1938.* Mémoire de Maîtrise, Université de Strasbourg, 1970.

Silverman, Dan P. *Reluctant Union: Alsace-Lorraine and Imperial Germany, 1871–1918.* University Park, Pa.: Pennsylvania State University Press, 1972.

Sittler, L. *L'Alsace, terre d'histoire.* Colmar: Editions Alsatia, 1972.

Smelser, Ronald M. *The Sudeten Problem, 1933–1938: Volkstumspolitik and the Formulation of Nazi Foreign Policy.* Middletown, Conn.: Wesleyen University Press, 1975.

Smith, Anthony D. *Theories of Nationalism.* 2d ed. New York: Holmes and Meier, 1983.

Snowden, Frank M. *The Fascist Revolution in Tuscany, 1919–1922.* New York: Cambridge University Press, 1989.

Société Savante d'Alsace et des Régions de l'Est, comp. *L'Alsace contemporaine: Etudes politiques, économiques, sociales.* Strasbourg and Paris: Editions F.-X. Le Roux, 1950.

———. *La bourgeoisie alsacienne: Etudes d'histoire sociale.* Strasbourg and Paris: Editions F.-X. Le Roux, 1954.

Soucy, Robert. "Centrist Fascism: The Jeunesses Patriotes." *Journal of Contemporary History* 16, 2 (April 1980): 349–68.

———. *Fascism in France: The Case of Maurice Barrès.* Berkeley and Los Angeles: University of California Press, 1972.

———. *Fascist Intellectual: Drieu La Rochelle.* Berkeley and Los Angeles: University of California Press, 1979.

———. *French Fascism: The First Wave, 1924–1933.* New Haven: Yale University Press, 1986.

———. *French Fascism: The Second Wave, 1933–1939.* New Haven: Yale University Press, 1995.

———. "French Fascism and the Croix de Feu: A Dissenting Interpretation." *Journal of Contemporary History* 26 (Jan. 1991): 159–88.

———. "French Fascism as Class Conciliation and Moral Regeneration." *Societas—Review of Social History* 1 (1971).

———. "The Nature of Fascism in France." *Journal of Contemporary History* (1966).

Starcky, Georges. *L'Alsacien*. Paris: Editions France-Empire, 1983.

Statistique Générale de la France, Office Régional de Statistique d'Alsace et de Lorraine. *Annuaire statistique (Bas-Rhin, Haut-Rhin, Moselle)*. Vol. 1. Strasbourg: Imprimerie Alsacienne, 1932.

Statistisches Reichsamt. *Statistisches Jahrbuch für das deutsche Reich*. Berlin: Verlag der Reimar Hobbing, 1933–1942.

Stern, Frit. *The Politics of Cultural Despair: A Study in the Rise of Germanic Ideology*. Berkeley and Los Angeles: University of California Press, 1961.

Sternhell, Zeev. "The Anti-Materialist Revision of Marxism as an Aspect of the Rise of Fascist Ideology." *Journal of Contemporary History* 22, 3 (July 1987): 379–400.

———. *La droite révolutionnaire, 1885–1914: Les origines françaises du fascisme*. Paris: Editions du Seuil, 1978.

———. *Neither Right nor Left: Fascist Ideologies in France*. Berkeley and Los Angeles: University of California Press, 1986.

———. "Sur le fascisme et sa variante française." *Le Débat* 32 (Nov. 1984): 28–51.

Strauss, Léon. "La crise de Munich en Alsace (septembre 1938)." *Revue d'Alsace* 105 (1979): 173–88.

———. "Review of Déniel (Alain), 'Bucard et le Francisme.'" *Revue d'Alsace* 107, 585 (1981): 292–93.

Streicher, Jean-Claude. *Histoire des Alsaciens*. Paris: Editions F. Nathan, 1979.

———. *Impossible Alsace: Histoire des idées autonomistes*. Paris: Editions Entente, 1982.

Strohl, Henri. *Le protestantisme en Alsace*. Strasbourg: Oberlin, 1950.

Struss, Gilbert. *Die APNA: Wie sie kam, was sie will*. Colmar: Editions Alsatia, 1931.

Stürmel, Marcel. *Die Autonomie Elsaß-Lothringens auf Grund der Verfassung von 1911*. Flugschriften der Elsäßischen Volkspartei—Nr. 7. Colmar: Alsatia Verlag, 1931.

———. *Das Elsaß und die deutsche Widerstandsbewegung in der Sicht eines ehemaligen Abgeordneten der Elsäßischen Volkspartei*. Karlsruhe: Kommissionsverlag G. Braune, 1980.

———. *Landwirtschaftliche Organisation und die Elsäßiche Volkspartei: Die "Grüne Front" in Elsaß-Lothringen*. Flugschriften der Elsäßischen Volkspartei—Nr. 3. Colmar: Alsatia Verlag, 1931.

Stürmel, Marcel, ed. *Muttersprache und katholische Kirchenpraxis: Im Auftrage von Freunden der heimischen Sprache*. Vol. 2 of *Im Kampf um die Muttersprache in Elsaß-Lothringen*. Colmar: Alsatia Verlag, 1935.

Sugar, Peter F. *Native Fascism*. Santa Barbara, Calif.: ABC-Clio Press, 1971.

Sutton, Michael. *Nationalism, Positivism, and Catholicism: The Politics of Charles Maurras and French Catholics*. New York: Cambridge University Press, 1982.

Sweets, John F. *Choices in Vichy France: The French under Nazi Occupation*. New York: Oxford University Press, 1986.

———. "Hold That Pendulum! Redefining Fascism, Collaborationism and Resistance in France." *French Historical Studies* 15, 4 (fall 1988): 731–58.

———. *The Politics of Resistance in France, 1940–1944*. DeKalb: Northern Illinois University Press, 1976.

Taittinger, Pierre. *". . . et Paris ne fut pas détruit."* Reims: Nouvelles Editions Latines, 1956.

Tannenbaum, Edward R. *The Action Française: Die-Hard Reactionaries in Twentieth-Century France.* New York: John Wiley, 1962.

Theweleit, Klaus. *Männerphantasien.* 2 vols. Hamburg: Rowohlt, 1987.

Thorez, Maurice. *Les Communistes et le Front Populaire: Discours prononcé à la session du Comité Central du Parti Communiste Français des 1 et 2 novembre 1934.* Paris: Imprimerie Ouvrière du Centre-Bourges, 1934.

———. *La France du Front populaire et sa mission dans le monde: Rapport et discours de clôture.* Paris: Editions du Comité Populaire de Propagande, 1938.

———. *France Today and the People's Front.* New York: International Publishers, n.d.

———. *Oeuvres de Maurice Thorez.* 23 vols. Paris: Editions Sociales, 1950–1965.

Ting-Lung, Weng. "L'historique et la doctrine du Parti Social Français." Thèse de droit, Nice, 1970.

Tjaden, K. H. *Struktur und Funktion der "KPD-Opposition" (KPO): Eine organisationssoziologische Untersuchung zur "Rechts"-Opposition im deutschen Kommunismus zur Zeit der Weimarer Republik.* Meisenheim am Glan: Verlag Anton Hain, 1964.

Tucker, William R. *The Fascist Ego: A Political Biography of Robert Brassillach.* Berkeley and Los Angeles: University of California Press, 1975.

UPRNA (Elsäßische Volkspartei). Flugschriften der Elsäßischen Volkspartei. Series of pamphlets. Colmar: Alsatia Verlag, 1930–1935.

Valois, Georges. *Contre le mensonge et la calomnie: Les campagnes de l'Action Française, mes réponses, mes accusations.* Paris: Nouvelle Librairie Nationale, 1926.

———. *Le fascisme.* Paris: Nouvelle Librairie Nationale, 1927.

———. *L'homme contre l'argent: Souvenirs de dix ans, 1918–1928.* Paris: Librairie Valois, 1928.

Vinen, Richard. *France, 1934–1970.* New York: St. Martin's Press, 1996.

Wagner, Richard. *La vie politique à Mulhouse de 1870 à nos jours.* Mulhouse: L'Alsace Imprimerie Commerciale SA, 1976.

Wahl, Alfred. *L'Option et l'émigration des alsaciens-lorrains, 1871–1872.* Paris: Editions Ophrys, 1974.

———. "Patrimoine, confession et pouvoir dans les campagnes d'Alsace, 1850–1940." *Etudes Rurales* 63–64 (July–Dec. 1976): 235–45.

Waldman, Loren K. "Confession et comportement dans les campagnes d'Alsace et de Bade (1871–1939), catholiques, protestants et juifs: Démographie, dynamisme économique et social, vie de relations et attitude politique." *Revue d'Alsace* 107 (1981): 245–52.

Weber, Eugen. *Action Française: Royalism and Reaction in Twentieth-Century France.* Stanford: Stanford University Press, 1962.

———. "Fascism(s) and Some Harbingers." *Journal of Modern History* (Dec. 1982): 746–65.

———. *The Hollow Years: France in the 1930s.* New York: Norton, 1994.

———. "Nationalism, Socialism, and National-Socialism in France." *French Historical Studies* 2 (spring 1962): 273–307.

———. *Peasants into Frenchmen: The Modernization of Rural France, 1870–1914.* Stanford: Stanford University Press, 1976.

Weber, Eugen, ed. *Varieties of Fascism*. Princeton: D. Van Nostrand, 1964.

Weber, Hermann. *Die Wandlung des deutschen Kommunismus: Die Stalinisierung der KPD in der Weimarer Republik*. 2 vols. Frankfurt am Main: Europäische Verlagsanstalt, 1969.

Wehler, Hans-Ulrich. *Sozialdemokratie und Nationalstaat: Nationalitätenfragen in Deutschland, 1840–1914*. Göttingen: Vandenhoeck und Ruprecht, 1971.

Weiss, John. *Conservatism in Europe, 1770–1945: Traditionalism, Reaction, and Counter-Revolution*. New York: Harcourt Brace Jovanovich, 1977.

———. *The Fascist Tradition: Radical Right-Wing Extremism in Modern Europe*. New York: Harper and Row, 1967.

Werth, Alexander. *The Twilight of France, 1933–1940*. New York: Howard Fertig, 1966.

White, Dan S. *The Splintered Party: National Liberalism in Hessen and the Reich, 1867–1918*. Cambridge, Mass.: Harvard University Press, 1976.

Wie es zur Spaltung kam? Flugschriften der Elsäßischen Volkspartei—Nr. 1. Colmar: Verlag der Colmarer Parteisekretariats der UPRNA, n.d.

Williams, Colin H., ed. *National Separatism*. Vancouver: University of British Columbia Press, 1982.

Wilson, Stephen. "A View of the Past: Action Française Historiography and Its Socio-Political Function." *Historical Journal* 19, 1 (1976): 135–62.

Winock, Michel. *Edouard Drumont et Cie: Antisémitisme et fascisme en France*. Paris: Seuil, 1982.

Wohl, Robert. *French Communism in the Making*. Stanford: Stanford University Press, 1966.

———. "French Fascism, Both Right and Left: Reflections on the Sternhell Controversy." *Journal of Modern History* 63 (March 1991): 91–98.

Wolf, Dieter. *Die Doriot-Bewegung: Ein Beitrag zur Geschichte des französischen Faschismus*. Stuttgart: Deutsche Verlags-Anstalt, 1967.

Wolf, Georges. *Das Elsäßisches Problem: Grundzüge einer elsäßischen Politik im Zeitalter des Pakts von Locarno*. Leipzig: Generalvertrieb f. Deutschland, L. Fernan, 1926.

———. *Von zweiten zum Dritten Reich: Siebzig Jahre elsäßischer Geschichte, 1871–1941*. Saverne: Zaberner Druckerei, 1941.

Woolf, S. J., ed. *Fascism in Europe*. New York: Methuen, 1981.

———. *The Nature of Fascism*. New York: Vintage Books, 1969.

Wright, Gordon. *Rural Revolution in France: The French Peasantry in the Twentieth Century*. Stanford, Stanford University Press, 1964.

Wylie, Lawrence. *Village in the Vaucluse*. Cambridge, Mass.: Harvard University Press, 1957.

Zdatny, Steven M. "The Class That Didn't Bark: French Artisans in an Age of Fascism." In *Splintered Classes: Politics and the Lower Middle Classes in Interwar Europe*, edited by Rudy Koshar, 121–41. New York: Holmes and Meier, 1990.

———. *The Politics of Survival: Artisans in Twentieth-Century France*. New York: Oxford University Press, 1990.

Zeldin, Theodore. *France, 1848–1945*. 2 vols. Oxford, Oxford University Press, 1973.

Zetkin, Clara, "Der Kampf gegen den Faschismus." In *Theorien über den Faschismus*, edited by Ernst Nolte, 88–117. Berlin: Kiepenheuer, 1967.

Zind, Pierre. *Brève histoire de l'Alsace*. Paris: Editions Albatros, 1977.

———. *Elsaß-Lothringen, Alsace-Lorraine: Une nation interdite, 1870–1940*. Paris: Editions Albatros, 1977.

INDEX

Action Française. *See* AF

L'Action Française, 45

Action Populaire Nationale d'Alsace. *See* APNA

AF (Action Française), 6, 7, 14, 32, 34, 42–52, 63, 99–100, 119, 130, 135; Alsatian party of, 42–52; linguistic issues and, 44–45, 50–51; membership of, 45; social composition of, 46–48; UPR affiliation with, 49

Alsace: Anschluß with Germany, 14; border region role of, 4, 154; education system of, 23; family classification system in, 22; germanization of names in, 150; germanization policy in, 150–51; historical background of, 3–5; identity issues and, 4–5, 15–21, 27, 122, 160; interwar period and, 13–27, 200n. 27; linguistic issues and, 16–17, 23, 44–45, 50–51, 57, 62, 74, 164n. 12; microcosm of Europe in, 9; military service and, 151–52; postwar purges in, 153, 199n. 17, 200n. 25; religion in, 19–20, 48, 51; rural life in, 88–89, 106; social classes in, 18–19, 46–48, 61–62; urbanization of, 22; World War II period and, 149–62

Alsace-Lorraine, 4, 163n. 1

Alsatian Center Party, 18, 29

Alsatian communists, 19, 25, 39; clericalism and, 72; Communist autonomists and, 69–85; Germanophilia of, 72; opposition communists, 70–77

Alsatian folk museum, 16

Alsatian Front, 38

"Alsatian malaise," 6, 13, 106; causes of, 21–27

Alsatian names, 116, 150, 190n. 23

Alsatian Nazi movement, 5, 103–18, 153; as fifth column, 117; membership of, 116–17. *See also specific parties*

Alsatian Progressive Party, 25

Anabaptists, 105, 106

Anschluß, 14; Austrian, 83

Antisemitism, 31, 60–61, 83–84, 112, 120–21, 129, 145–46, 153; as bridge to German-French identity, 122

APNA (Action Populaire Nationale d'Alsace), 30, 33, 114, 123, 124

Arendt, Hannah, 97

Argentina fraternity, 113

Arthuys, Jacques, 56, 58

Association Sully, 48

August Wilhelm of Prussia, 92, 101

Autonomism: arrests of members, 117; clerical, 6, 31, 40–41, 74, 75, 94; communist, 69–85; Germany connections and, 104–5, 152; interwar period and, 13–27; Nazism and, 6–7, 150; press and, 24; radical, 40–41; rallies of, 107; UPR and, 30, 40

Baden, 151

Baechler, Christian, 34

Barrés, Philippe, 56

Bas-Rhin, 20; AF in, 46; communism in, 72; Faisceau in, 62; Landespartei in, 115; PCF in, 79; rural life in, 88–89, 106

Bauernbund. *See* BB

BB (Bauernbund), 7, 19, 86–102, 135, 147, 159; antisemitism and, 91; capitalism and, 91; clerical autonomists and, 94; corporatism and,

90; membership of, 95–96; peasants in, 89, 90, 95, 97; UPR and, 94
Bickler, Hermann, 8, 104–6, 110–17; death sentence, 153
Bilger, Camille, 24
Bilger, Joseph, 7–8, 19, 86–102, 106, 152, 153; fifth column and, 92; French nationalism and, 92; postwar sentence of, 153
Bloody Sunday, 25, 74, 75
Blum, Léon, 31, 38, 91, 141, 145
Bonapartist Party, 136
Bongartz, Albert, 37, 84
Bormann, Martin, 111
Bourgeoisie, 106
Brumath, 72
Bucard, Marcel, 99, 119, 121, 125, 126–28, 133
Bund Erwin von Steinbach, 112–13
Bundschuh Rebellion, 92–93

Cagoule, 141
Calvinism, 106
Camelots du Roi, 32, 33, 47
Capitalism, 91
Cartel de Gauches, 44, 52
Cartel des Gauches, 6, 15, 30
Catholic Union Populaire Républicaine. *See* UPR
Catholicism, 19–20, 24, 51, 106, 150, 152; clerical autonomists and, 31
Cauchois, Edouard, 43
Center (Catholic German Center Party), 17
Chaumont-Guitry, Renauld de, 43
Clerical press, 169n. 30
Codreanu, Corneliu, 98
Colmar, 62; trials, 26, 74–75, 106
Combat, Le, 120–21, 122
Combat movement: membership, 122
Communist autonomists, 69–85, 115; definitions of, 69–70; definition of work of, 82; linguistic issues and, 72; pacifism and, 82; use of term "fascist" by, 82
Comrades in Courage (Rédier), 52
Corporatism, 31, 39–40, 90–91, 124, 132, 138, 147, 157
Coston, Henry, 121

Coty, François, 58, 64, 123, 125
Croix de Feu, 5, 9, 119, 126, 135, 138; auxiliaries of, 139; membership of, 139, 141; parliamentary parties and, 141; veterans organization of, 139
Croix de Feu/PSF, 194n. 2; anticommunism and, 139; beliefs of, 140
Czechoslovakian crisis, 147

Dahlet, Camille, 25, 107, 114
Darré, Walther, 90
Daudet, Léon, 50
Daudet, Philippe, 44
de Man, Hendrik, 70
Déat, Marcel, 70, 137
Degrelle, Léon, 98
Delagrange, Marcel, 61
Denisane, Jacques, 48
Dernières Nouvelles de Strasbourg, Les, 115, 116
d'Halys, Henri, 50
Didio, Charles, 30, 49, 107
Dorgères, Henri, 8, 98, 101
Dorgères's Peasant Front, 90
Doriot, Jacques, 70, 75, 76, 99, 119, 130–34, 137
Drulingen, 72
Drumont, Edouard, 121, 146

EABP (Elsäßische Arbeiter- und Bauernpartei), 78, 79, 83, 152; antisemitism, 83–84; merging with Landespartei, 84
ELP (Elsaß-Lothringische Partei), 110, 115
Elsäßer, 130
Elsäßer Jungland, 93
Elsäßische Arbeiter- und Bauernpartei. *See* EABP
Elsaß-Lothringische Zeitung, 107, 108, 111, 115, 116; pamphlet of, 108
Elsaß-Lothringischen Pressedienst, 104
Ernst, Robert, 84, 92, 104, 113, 115, 118, 153
Erwinia Verlag, 105
Eschbach, Marcel, 120, 121, 122

Faisceau, 6, 56–65; antisemitism, 60–61; funding for, 58; hierarchy

and, 59; linguistic issues, 57; middle class and, 59–60; peasants and, 62; working class and, 59
Faisceau (new), 132
Falloux Law, 24
Fanal, Le, 129
Fascism, 4, 173n. 29; antisemitism and, 31, 60–61, 83–84, 112, 120–21, 129, 145–46, 153; change over time of, 156–57; class and, 155; corporatism and, 31, 39–40, 90–91, 124, 132, 138, 147, 157; cross-pollination between groups of, 125, 158; definitions of, 49, 127–28, 136, 137, 154–55, 160–62; French, 42–65, 119–34, 175n. 69; funding issues and, 133, 167n. 55; homogeneity versus heterogeneity of, 159; Italian, 108, 153–54, 176n. 82; leftist origins and, 69–85, 175n. 69; local context of, 157, 158; national culture and, 159–60; national identity and, 27; plurality of types in Alsace of, 5, 159; populism and, 200n. 28; press and, 142, 167n. 55; regional, 86–102, 154; religion and, 33, 48, 157–58; social composition of, 155; women and, 155–56. *See also specific groups and topics*
Fasshauer, Abbé Joseph, 26, 105
Fédération des Contribuables, 120–22
Férenzy, Oscar de, 116
Flambeau de l'Est, Le, 139, 142, 147
Force Nouvelle, 123, 124
France: Alsatian identity and, 16; "Alsatian malaise" and, 13–27; anticlerical laws in, 20; economy of, 109; family classification system imposed by, 22; "interior" of, 43–44; regionalism and, 110; Third Republic of, 13, 42, 52, 64
Francistes, 7, 119, 125–28, 135, 152; donations to, 126–27; membership of, 126–27; regionalism and, 128; social composition of, 126–27; ties between PSF and, 126
Frei Volk, 115, 116
Freie Presse, 28, 125

Freie Zeitung, 107
French communism, 70–77
French fascism. *See* Fascism; *specific groups*
French Revolution, 59
Frey, Charles, 114
Front de la Jeunesse, 132
Front Paysan, 98

German fascism. *See* Nazism, Third Reich
German Rhenish movement, 163n. 4
German Socialist Party. *See* SPD
Germany: Alsatian identity and, 15; Alsatian refugees in, 104; ethnic Germans versus Reich Germans, 150; federal system of, 17; *Volkstum* and, 16
Gestermann, André, 89
Gillman, Emile, 126, 131
Gleichschaltung, 112, 150, 151
Graffenstaden, 48
Green Shirts, 40, 94, 98, 152
Grégoire, Armand, 126
Gromer, Georges, 40
Grumbach, Salomon, 91
Guebweiler, 117

Haegy, Abbé, 19, 24, 26, 30, 35–36, 109
Hanot, Maurice, 139
"Hans in Schnokeloch," 13
Hauss, René, 26, 37, 93, 106
Haut-Rhin, 20; AF in, 46; BB in, 95–96; Calvinists in, 106; communism in, 72; conscription in, 152; Faisceau in, 56, 62; PCF in, 79; rural life in, 89
Heck, René, 130
Heil, Charles-Philippe, 114
Heimatbewegung, 64, 104
Heimatbund, 24–25, 64
Heimutbund manifesto, 34
Heitz, Fernand, 36, 38, 51
Heitz, Robert, 152
Herriot, Edouard, 15, 23–24, 30, 42
Hervé, Gustave, 123, 125
Hirtzel, August Friedrich, 80
Historiography, 172n. 14; 176n. 82
Hitler, Adolph: aggressive intents of,

149; leadership of, 159; trial for treason of, 109
Hitler Youth, 111, 151
Hoffet, Frédéric, 16
Hueber, Charles [Karl], 7, 19, 21, 69–85, 114, 137; funding for newspaper of, 76; separatism and, 71

Internationale Vereinigung Kommunistische Opposition. *See* IVKO
Irvine, William, 136
IVKO (Internationale Vereinigung Kommunistische Opposition), 77, 78, 83

Jaeger, Jules, 53
Jaurés, Jean, 71
Jeunesses de l'UPR, 39–40
Jeunesses Patriotes. *See* JP
Joffre, General, 21
JP (Jeunesses Patriotes), 7, 98–99, 119, 145, 183n. 67
Jungmannschaft, 110–11
Jungmannschaft, 8, 104, 110–17, 152; antisemitism and, 112; bourgeoisie and, 106; Landespartei and, 113; race and, 112; SS and, 115

Kinder, Küche, Kirche (Rédier), 55
Koessler, Alfred, 76
Kommunistische Partei Deutschland. *See* KPD
Kommunistische Partei Deutschland Opposition. *See* KPDO
Kommunistischen Partei-Opposition. *See* KPO
KPD (Kommunistische Partei Deutschland), 73
KPDO (Kommunistische Partei Deutschland Opposition), 79
KPO (Kommunistischen Partei-Opposition), 7, 77, 78, 79; nazification of, 81

La Rochelle, Drieu, 138
La Rocque, François de, 127, 136, 138, 139, 141, 148
Landespartei, 7, 8, 25, 34, 93, 100, 103, 108, 152; bourgeoisie and, 106; comeback of 1936, 114–15;

Jungmannschaft and, 113; merging with EABP, 84
Lang, Rudolf, 117
Lasierra, Raymond, 137
Laugel, Anselme, 54
Le Pen, Jean-Marie, 153
Légion, The, 32, 52–56; membership of, 54–55; merging with Faisceau and, 52
Legrand, Jean-Charles, 132, 193n. 80
Lévy, Bernard-Henri, 87
Lévy, Paul, 16
L'Humanité, 76, 79
Libre Parole, 121
Liebknecht, Karl, 17, 71
Ligue Millerand, 53
Lorenz, Werner, 92
Luchont (pseudonym), 129
Lutherans, 19, 72, 105
Luxemburg, Rosa, 71

Marty, J. M., 54
Marxism, 69, 70
Maurras, Charles, 45, 99, 130
Mayer, Hans, 81
Mein Kampf (Hitler), 105
Mercier, Ernst, 127
Millerand, Alexandre, 23
Modern state, 59–60
Molsheim, 117
Mourer, Jean-Pierre, 19, 76, 77, 78, 81, 84–85, 93, 107; death sentence, 153
Mulhouse, 56, 62, 124
Munich crisis, 149, 150
Munz, Charles, 138
Mussolini, Benito, 33, 159

Nasos (National Socialistes), 7, 126, 128–29, 135; antisemitism and, 129; banks and, 128–29; social composition, 129
National d'Alsace, Le, 44–45, 51
National Front, 107
National Socialistes. *See* Nasos
Nationale Sozialistische Deutsche Arbeiter Partei. *See* NSDAP
Nationale-Socialistes, 8
Nazism, 8; in Alsace, 78–85, 103–18,

149; antisemitism and, 112, 116; beefsteak, 69, 78–85; "blood and soil," 89; from the left, 69–85; legitimizing, 28–41; newspaper circulation, 116; religion versus secularism, 33, 105–6, 116, 152; Third Reich, 89, 149–53. *See also* Antisemitism; Fascism; *specific groups and topics*
Neue Front, 123
Neue Welt, Die, 76, 80, 82, 115
Nouveau Siécle, Le, 56, 57; industrialist support for, 58
NSDAP (Nationale Sozialistische Deutsche Arbeiter Partei), 4, 33

Oberkirch, Alfred, 32, 49
Oncken, Hermann, 105

Pan-Germanism, 35
Parti Communiste Français. *See* PCF
Parti Fédéraliste d'Alsace-Lorraine, 21
Parti Populaire Français. *See* PPF
Parti Réaliste Français. *See* PRF
Parti Régionaliste Alsacien, 114
Parti Social Français. *See* PSF
PCF (Parti Communiste Français), 25, 69–73, 77, 79
Peasants, 62, 82–83, 89, 90, 95, 97, 143
Peirotes, Jacques, 75
Pellepoix, Darquier de, 132, 146
Pfister, Aloise, 53
Pfleger, Joseph, 32, 49, 54, 108
Pflimlin, Pierre, 100, 123, 124, 153
Pinck, Emile, 24
Plateau, Marius, 44
Plumyène, Jean, 137
Poincaré, Henri, 42, 64, 65
Popular Front, 30, 38, 73, 81, 82, 119, 131, 141
PPF (Parti Populaire Français), 8, 99, 119, 130–34, 135; linkage between ex-communists and industrialists, 130; PSF and, 145
PRF (Parti Réaliste Français), 126, 128–29
Province d'Alsace, La, 52, 188n. 1
PSF (Parti Social Français), 5, 32, 135–48, 152; agricultural policy

of, 143; antisemitism and, 145–46; Banapartist interpretation of, 136; corporatism and, 147; elections and, 142; fascism and, 137; lack of working class support in, 137; membership of, 140, 142; Nazism and, 147; PPF and, 145; social composition of, 142–43, 144; social policy of, 143; UPR and, 144–45, 197n. 49. *See also* Croix de Feu/PSF
Pujo, Maurice, 44

Quiri, Alfred, 81

Radical Party, 136, 197n. 49
Radical-Republican Party, 25
Radical-Socialist Party, 25
Rédier, Antoine, 52, 55, 138
Redslob, Robert, 109
Regionalism, 13–14, 50, 86–102, 128, 154, 176n. 82
Rémond, René, 136, 138
Renaud, Jean, 123, 124
Ricklin, Eugène, 25, 26, 37, 105, 106
Riegel, Camille, 123
Rochelle, Drieu la, 39
Roos, Karl, 3, 17, 26, 104, 106, 108, 117, 150
Rossé, Joseph, 8, 17, 19, 22, 26, 28, 35, 36–37, 94, 106, 111, 152, 153
Rothenberger, Karl-Heinz, 16
Royalism, 52, 152
Ruch, Bishop, 34, 36, 51, 109

Saverne, 48
Schall, Paul, 24, 26, 75, 106, 107, 117; death sentence, 153
Schiffmacher, Edmond, 60, 61, 64
Schiltigheim, 72
Schmidt-Le-Roi, Pierre, 30, 32, 54, 123, 124
Scholze, Herbert, 126
Schreckler, Georges, 76
Section Française de L'Internationale Ouvriére. *See* SFIO
Separatism, 13, 14
SFIO (Section Française de L'Internationale Ouvriére), 71, 76

Solidarité Française, 119, 122–24, 190n. 23
Soucy, Robert, 58, 136
Spanish Civil War, 131, 139
SPD (German Socialist Party), 17, 18
Spieser, Friedrich, 113, 117, 153
SS (Schutzstaffeln), 8, 115
Staatsreform, 7, 124, 191n. 39
Staatsreform, Die, 122, 124
Sternhell, Zeev, 57, 137
Steuerzahler, Der, 120
Steuerzahler movement, 120–21
Stimme der Parti Populaire Français, Die, 130, 131
Stoskopf, Gustave, 16
Strasbourg, 22, 48, 53, 56, 79, 107, 108, 149, 185n. 17
Strasbourg Cathedral, 149, 152
Straßburger Monatshefte, 113, 116
Streicher, Julius, 121, 122, 146
Stürmel, Marcel, 8, 26, 35, 37–38, 106, 152, 153
Stürmer, Der, 121, 122, 146

Tardieu, André, 125
Thorez, Maurice, 73, 74, 81
Transcendence, 185n. 22
Treaty of Versailles, 21, 108
Trois-Epis, resolution of, 117

UPR (Catholic Union Populaire Républicaine), 5, 28–41, 94, 152, 197n. 49; AF affiliation with, 49; antisemitism and, 31; APNA and, 114; autonomism and, 30, 38–39; clericalism in, 19, 30, 38; conservatism in, 28–29; fascism in, 28–29; pro-Nazi faction of, 35; PSF and, 144–45, 197n. 49; regional autonomy and, 34; right versus left in, 29; violence and, 33; Volksfront and, 114; youth group of, 39–40

VAF (Volksständischen Arbeiterfront), 91, 94
Valois, Georges, 56–65, 132
Valot, Marcel, 43
Valot, Paul, 110
Victoire Dimanche, La, 123
Voix d'Alsace et de Lorraine, La, 116
Volk, 31, 35, 74, 82, 85, 100, 112
Volksfront, 39, 80–81, 107, 114
Volksgemeinschaft, 107
Volksständischen Arbeiterfront. *See* VAF
Volkswille, 107

Wackes, 35
Wagner, Robert Gauleiter, 111, 117, 150
Walter, Michel, 32, 75, 76
Weber, Eugen, 50
Wetterlé, Abbé, 16
Weydmann, Joseph, 53, 123
Wilhelm II, 13
Wilson's Fourteen Points, 21
Wolf, Georges, 25

Youth groups, 39–40, 111, 151, 159

Zabern Affair, 35
Zukunft, Die, 167n. 55
Zukunft Movement, 44, 51